# THE DU PONTS

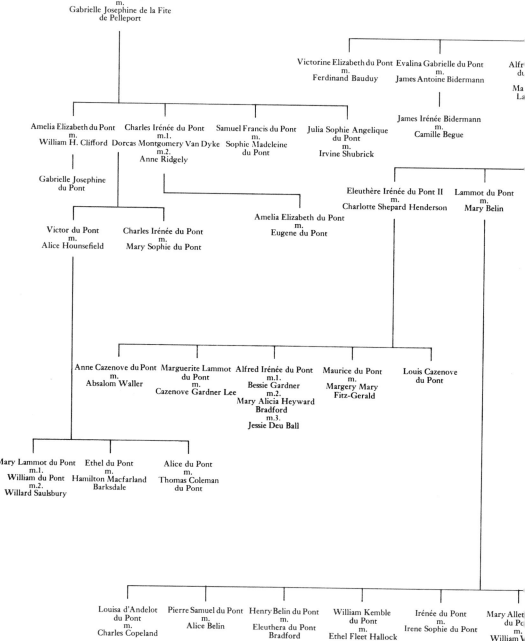

Pierre Samuel Dupont de Ne
m.
Nicole Charlotte Marie Le
le Dée de Rencourt

Victor Marie Dupont
m.
Gabrielle Josephine de la Fite
de Pelleport

Victorine Elizabeth du Pont
m.
Ferdinand Bauduy

Evalina Gabrielle du Pont
m.
James Antoine Bidermann

Alfr
du

Ma
La

Amelia Elizabeth du Pont
m.
William H. Clifford

Charles Irénée du Pont
m.1.
Dorcas Montgomery Van Dyke
m.2.
Anne Ridgely

Samuel Francis du Pont
m.
Sophie Madeleine
du Pont

Julia Sophie Angelique
du Pont
m.
Irvine Shubrick

James Irénée Bidermann
m.
Camille Begue

Gabrielle Josephine
du Pont

Eleuthère Irénée du Pont II
m.
Charlotte Shepard Henderson

Lammot du Pont
m.
Mary Belin

Victor du Pont
m.
Alice Hounsefield

Charles Irénée du Pont
m.
Mary Sophie du Pont

Amelia Elizabeth du Pont
m.
Eugene du Pont

Anne Cazenove du Pont
m.
Absalom Waller

Marguerite Lammot
du Pont
m.
Cazenove Gardner Lee

Alfred Irénée du Pont
m.1.
Bessie Gardner
m.2.
Mary Alicia Heyward
Bradford
m.3.
Jessie Deu Ball

Maurice du Pont
m.
Margery Mary
Fitz-Gerald

Louis Cazenove
du Pont

Mary Lammot du Pont
m.1.
William du Pont
m.2.
Willard Saulsbury

Ethel du Pont
m.
Hamilton Macfarland
Barksdale

Alice du Pont
m.
Thomas Coleman
du Pont

Louisa d'Andelot
du Pont
m.
Charles Copeland

Pierre Samuel du Pont
m.
Alice Belin

Henry Belin du Pont
m.
Eleuthera du Pont
Bradford

William Kemble
du Pont
m.
Ethel Fleet Hallock

Irénée du Pont
m.
Irene Sophie du Pont

Mary Allet
du Po
m.
William W
Lair

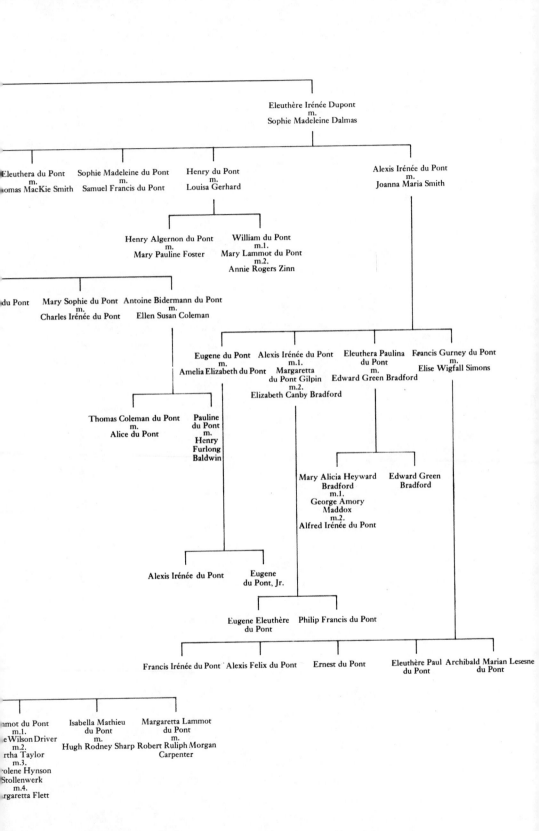

Eleuthère Irénée Dupont
m.
Sophie Madeleine Dalmas

Eleuthera du Pont
m.
Thomas MacKie Smith

Sophie Madeleine du Pont
m.
Samuel Francis du Pont

Henry du Pont
m.
Louisa Gerhard

Alexis Irénée du Pont
m.
Joanna Maria Smith

Henry Algernon du Pont
m.
Mary Pauline Foster

William du Pont
m.1.
Mary Lammot du Pont
m.2.
Annie Rogers Zinn

du Pont

Mary Sophie du Pont
m.
Charles Irénée du Pont

Antoine Bidermann du Pont
m.
Ellen Susan Coleman

Eugene du Pont
m.
Amelia Elizabeth du Pont

Alexis Irénée du Pont
m.1.
Margaretta
du Pont Gilpin
m.2.
Elizabeth Canby Bradford

Eleuthera Paulina
du Pont
m.
Edward Green Bradford

Francis Gurney du Pont
m.
Elise Wigfall Simons

Thomas Coleman du Pont
m.
Alice du Pont

Pauline
du Pont
m.
Henry
Furlong
Baldwin

Mary Alicia Heyward
Bradford
m.1.
George Amory
Maddox
m.2.
Alfred Irénée du Pont

Edward Green
Bradford

Alexis Irénée du Pont

Eugene
du Pont, Jr.

Eugene Eleuthère
du Pont

Philip Francis du Pont

Francis Irénée du Pont

Alexis Felix du Pont

Ernest du Pont

Eleuthère Paul
du Pont

Archibald Marian Lesesne
du Pont

mmot du Pont
m.1.
e Wilson Driver
m.2.
rtha Taylor
m.3.
rolene Hynson
Stollenwerk
m.4.
rgaretta Flett

Isabella Mathieu
du Pont
m.
Hugh Rodney Sharp

Margaretta Lammot
du Pont
m.
Robert Ruliph Morgan
Carpenter

# THE DU PONTS

## *Portrait of a Dynasty*

MARC DUKE

SATURDAY REVIEW PRESS

E. P. DUTTON & CO., INC.

New York

*Library of Congress Cataloging in Publication Data*

Duke, Marc.
  The du Ponts.

  1. Du Pont family. I. Title.
CS71.D935 1976        338'.092'2 [B]        75–40068

920

*To Linda Duke,*
*my companion in life.*

# Contents

*There is little less trouble
in governing a family
than a whole kingdom.*

—MONTAIGNE

*The family is more sacred
than the state.*

—POPE PIUS XI

*Part One*

# EYE FOR WAR,
# EYE FOR PEACE

P IERRE DUPONT cared deeply for his mother.

"I so loved this admirable woman," he recalled in his memoirs, "that every time I felt myself in love I sought out the points of resemblance between her and the beauty who, at the time, had become dear to me . . . it pleased me to imagine that it was my mother I was loving. Alas!"

Pierre was the second child conceived by Samuel Dupont, a Parisian watchmaker, and Anne Alexandrine de Montchanin, his wife. The first had died within days of its birth. Anne feared that the life swelling inside her womb might perish quickly too. She begged Samuel to let her nurse the child at her own breasts, rather than send it off to a country woman to be weaned. Samuel refused: no respectable wife of a master tradesman suckled her own young. Anne must deliver the baby and return to painting delicate scenes on the faces of the timepieces her husband crafted.

On December 14, 1739, after three days in labor, Anne gave birth to a son, named Pierre Samuel after her oldest brother and her husband, kissed it tenderly, and offered its hungry lips to the waiting farmer's wife. Samuel had not completely ignored his wife's pleading; the infant's nurse lived only an hour's carriage ride from Paris. If she wished, Anne might visit her newborn son on Sunday afternoons.

Anne Alexandrine de Montchanin came to the cluster of watchmakers' shops in Paris's Rue de Richelieu after a pleasant childhood spent as companion to the daughter of a wealthy uncle and aunt. Her own parents, of noble lineage but impoverished, had sent their youngest child to relatives gladly; only with their help might she hope to receive an education commensurate with her titled birth.

But when Anne reached her seventeenth birthday the aunt and uncle decided that their daughter no longer needed a playmate. Anne was offered a choice: assume the position of housekeeper on their country estate or leave. She chose to take up life in a back room above the Paris watchmaking shop of her brothers, Pierre and Alexandre.

Anne began painting watchfaces by the fading evening light that filtered through the shop's front window. From her workbench she looked across the narrow Rue de Richelieu directly into the *horlogerie* of Samuel Dupont. Each day at dusk Samuel locked the door to his shop, placed lighted candles in its windows, and practiced his one passion, fencing. Anne's first glimpse of her future husband was a darting shadow thrusting and parrying against a white wall.

Soon Samuel's fencing sword began to rust. Late customers and friends learned to seek him out in the drawing room above the workshop of his competitors across the Rue de Richelieu. Anne did not lack for suitors; her birth into the nobility, her obvious refinement, and, not least, her lithe figure and fair skin caused many hearts along the street of watchmakers to stir. But Anne spurned them all except the man whose shop faced that of her brothers. Samuel, she believed, possessed a degree of dignity unusual among Frenchmen not born into the upper class. He was tall, slender, and handsome, with thick dark hair and a long, bulbous nose reminiscent of King Louis XIV's own famed protuberance. He stood remarkably erect for one who bent each day over a workbench. He was quiet, fastidious, and sober. He fenced well, a skill usually reserved for the nobility. Above all, he was, like Anne, a Protestant.

Within a few months Samuel and Anne married. She moved her possessions across the Rue de Richelieu, placed herself at a workbench near the window of her new husband's shop, and learned that the dignity she had admired in Samuel was little more than the stubbornness of ignorance.

Samuel Dupont could neither read nor write. He had learned, with difficulty, to do the simple sums his business required. As a young man he had come to Paris from the provincial city of Rouen, where for five generations the Duponts had been farmers and tradesmen. Rouen had for centuries been a center of religious foment. Joan of Arc had burned in the city's square for her heresy; Catherine de Medici had laid siege to the city's high walls for a year to rid her empire of the infidel Protestants living within. French kings regularly sent raiding parties of soldiers, accompanied by Catholic priests, into Rouen, to coax the citizens into joining the true church, under pain of death by hanging or burning. The ancestors of Samuel Dupont, like many other devout Protestants, swore faithfulness to the Catholic tenets and continued to practice the teachings of John Calvin in private. Samuel could name many relatives whose lives had ended at the stake and whose children had been kidnapped during the night and sold into captivity at convents run by zealous Catholic priests. Only when he learned that the Montchanin family had for many generations been Protestants did he decide that Anne would make a suitable wife.

Religious persecution had, unfortunately, taught Samuel little. He wished not to see the Protestant church accepted in France, but to find a way to live happily under the Catholic oppression. A number of his friends had been dragged off to Paris prisons for their religious views. All, Samuel believed, had a single fault in common: they sought to educate themselves beyond their stations in life. Had they applied their energies to their work alone, they would never have brought the wrath of the government down upon themselves. Knowledge, Samuel believed, encouraged the mind to wander, the body to seek pleasures outside the fruits of hard labor. And so, since making watches did not require that he know the alphabet, Samuel had never learned to read.

Anne thought otherwise. After Pierre's country nurse nearly killed the infant by feeding him only watered-down flour, Samuel agreed to bring his son home to live. Anne resolved to give him an education befitting the son of a woman nobly born and raised.

Pierre, recovering from rickets, played at Anne's feet while she painted watchfaces. She amused him with stories of valiant men who had conquered physical shortcomings greater than his, and through courage and devotion to a gallant cause become the champions of mankind. In her idle hours Anne taught Pierre to read. By his third birthday he had far surpassed his father's meager ability to scrawl a few numbers. Anne continued to fill his head with tales of heroes and great warriors. Pierre's health remained delicate. He limped, and always would, and his legs were permanently bowed. He fell and broke the cartilage in his nose, which robbed him of the single physical characteristic he had inherited from Samuel. His growth lagged; he would never reach his father's height. He walked awkwardly and could not run at all. But while his body stagnated, his mind, under Anne's prodding, stretched and grew agile. Her son, Anne discovered, possessed a remarkable degree of intelligence. She began to conceive of it as a pathway out of the drudgery of her life and the tedium of her marriage.

Samuel Dupont had an easily ignited temper. Anne feared his rage nearly as much as she loathed his distrust of education. After her husband's outbursts, she would gather Pierre in her arms, flee to a quiet room in the apartment above the workshop, and weep with the child over their lot in life. Soon Samuel became, for his son, the opposite of all Anne taught him to admire and respect in men.

Samuel agreed to Pierre's education on one condition: his son must not be taught to write poetry. Versifying far exceeded what a watchmaker's son might ever find useful in life. After nearly eight years of argument with her husband Anne made the concession readily.

A Dupont family friend had migrated from Rouen to open a private school in Paris, Anne discovered. She enrolled Pierre in the classes of schoolmaster Viard without difficulty. Struggling to establish himself and his school, Viard agreed to the prohibition against poetry. He soon found that he had struck a good bargain: his new student was a prodigy. Anything Viard set before Pierre, the boy could memorize; anything the schoolmaster explained, Pierre could understand.

Viard took Pierre from the classroom and tutored him individually. The lame boy's schoolmates became jealous, forcing him into numerous fights. Osborne, an English boy attending the school, taught Pierre to box; the other students learned to fear his small fists. They salved their envy by beating Pierre in schoolyard games that required physical agility beyond their rival's. The games were played for stakes of apples brought to class as luncheon desserts; in short order Pierre stood one hundred fifty apples in debt.

Schoolmaster Viard cared little for Pierre's recess fortunes: only his protégé's mind interested the teacher. Education, like all other institutions in Bourbon France, was monopolized by a nobility and clergy that closely guarded their privileges. Enormous class barriers kept men like Viard from achieving prominence—and attracting students from wealthy families. Rarely, a teacher from the lower classes captured the attention and imagination of the Parisian elite. Viard saw his opportunity in Pierre Dupont's unique mental abilities.

The schoolmaster decided upon a public display of the boy's intellect. He drilled Pierre in the *Institutes* of Justinian, Restaut's French grammar, Latin syntax, rhetoric, and the epistolary style. He announced that a student of his, a mere child of twelve, would answer questions on these and other subjects publicly, as well as present dissertations on French prose and orally translate excerpts from the most difficult Latin texts.

Four hundred people, including Samuel and Anne, turned out for the exhibition of Pierre's learning and wit. The watchmaker's son triumphed; after the performance he was carried on a chair to where his parents stood weeping with pride. Pierre felt that, for once, his father loved him, and that he had conquered Samuel's prejudice against education. That evening Pierre's classmates gathered by torchlight at the Dupont home in the Rue de Richelieu to announce the cancellation of his schoolyard debt. The next morning Pierre brought his fellow students pastries and fresh cider, purchased with money Samuel gave him. He basked in the glow of public acclaim; he had tasted the sweet rewards of the orator's life, and an appetite for them had awakened within him. It would never be fully sated.

Viard arranged another display of Pierre's talents; he could not resist courting the prestige his prodigy might bring him. A hall was hired; printed invitations went to the intellectual elite of Paris, to the local administrators of government, to the faculty members of the Royal College and University of Paris. Viard pounded knowledge into Pierre's willing mind. Pierre's first exhibition had overwhelmed his classmates and friends; his second, Viard planned, would dazzle all Paris.

Pierre studied diligently and dreamed of genius and renown. His confidence and hopes soared. But on the eve of the demonstration the rector of the University of Paris forbade Viard to show off his student's acumen: the protégé of a private teacher, a child who had never taken classes at any recognized college, tutored by a provincial upstart without degrees from any reputable institute of higher learning, simply must not be permitted to capture the public limelight. The exhibition was cancelled. So, too, was Pierre's education under the schoolmaster Viard.

Samuel had seen enough. Powerful forces were being brought to bear on his son. Notoriety had already come his way, precisely what Samuel feared most. The time had arrived, Samuel told his son, for Pierre to take his place beside his father at the watchmaker's bench. Anne became distraught; Pierre felt his hopes dashed in his father's narrowmindedness. Together, mother and son plotted. Anne convinced Samuel that no Protestant child became apprenticed to a trade before taking his first communion in the church. She had pierced the single chink in Samuel's armor: he could not abide raising a child outside the dictates of his religion. He agreed that Pierre must undergo formal training in Protestant theology.

Anne was not satisfied. Outside Samuel's hearing she announced that Pierre would use his intellectual gifts to become a Protestant minister, a dangerous endeavor in Catholic France. Prominent members of the Protestant faith were consulted; they directed Anne to the best teachers in Paris. Paul Bosc d'Antic, a graduate of the theological seminary in Lausanne, Switzerland, agreed to tutor Pierre. Daily they pored over texts in philosophy, physics, metaphysics, the principles of debate, Tacitus, Horace, and Cicero—and a small amount of Protestant theology. Samuel quickly grew suspicious of the range of subjects Pierre needed to master before being declared fit to pass his first communion. Anne explained that, since their son was a special pupil, he required an unusual course of study. It had been undertaken upon the advice of the Dutch ambassador to France: did Samuel wish to dispute so eminent an opinion? Samuel did not.

After eighteen months Pierre's first communion could no longer be delayed. Samuel demanded that his son begin learning the trade that would occupy his working life. Anne reasoned with her husband that if Pierre was to become a watchmaker he must at least rise to the top of his craft. No prominent *horloger* survived without a knowledge of mathematics. Samuel was forced to agree; he recalled that his own teacher, Julien LeRoy, had studied mathematical theory. Pierre's apprenticeship would be put off long enough to give him a solid grounding in the principles of algebra and geometry.

Anne had achieved her last victory: no excuses remained to keep Pierre from bending over the workbench at Samuel's side. Her lame child, still frail, with his enlarged joints and crooked nose, whose head she had filled with romantic visions of mythical warriors, would spend his life constructing timepieces in a tiny shop on a narrow Paris street. Anne resigned herself to her son's fate. Pierre, steeped in the profound writings of Horace and Tacitus, hungry for adventure and public acclaim, did not.

Samuel Dupont's sister, Marie, had married a ship's captain named Oulson. In a storm off the coast of Labrador, Oulson's ship was wrecked; the captain died soon after from exposure. Samuel offered to take his sister's daughter, Marianne, into the Dupont household. Pierre was not drawn to his cousin. Marianne was neither pretty nor intelligent. But when she was struck down with smallpox Pierre decided to nurse the girl day and night, as befitted a future warrior and hero; he had decided to become one of the valiant men his mother so deeply revered.

He had found the study of mathematics dull, but not so repulsive as a life spent making watches. Algebra and geometry, he reasoned, might be useful in a military career. Although young men were prohibited from becoming officers in the king's army without proof of four quarters of nobility—evidence that all their grandparents had noble blood flowing in their veins—and Pierre could display only the Montchanin coat of arms, it was possible to rise through the ranks by becoming an engineer, assuming a position of command on the battlefield, and earning a commission. Pierre bought books on strategy, tactics, and artillery manufacture. He slept on the floor to harden his body for the rigors of war. When Marianne became ill he resolved to test his courage.

Soon Pierre contracted the disease. Doctors were called in; they could do little. Marianne Oulson's case had been slight and she a healthy girl. Pierre's frail body succumbed more easily to the ravages of the pox. Marianne would recover, the doctors said. Pierre would not.

Anne nursed Pierre in vain. Within days, the doctors, unable to find a pulse, pronounced him dead. Anne prepared her son for burial and, as was the custom, called in a peasant woman to sit with Pierre through the night before his funeral. Just before dawn the woman screamed. Anne and Samuel found her cringing in a corner of Pierre's room. The dead child had stirred and moaned, she said: he was alive!

Anne brought Pierre gently back to health, remaining at his bedside day and night. No longer could he be recognized as the son of a handsome man and beautiful woman; deep pockmarks surrounded his disfigured nose, reached across his cheeks and down his neck. His eyes, too, had been affected. One had become extremely farsighted, the other severely nearsighted. Pierre reacted to his impaired sight as a boon to his talents.

"I call my left eye, which sees far, my eye for war," he wrote in his memoirs. "And my right eye, which is useful for fine work, my eye for science and peace. I have therefore to thank nature and accident for having given me two eyes covering the full range of vision while other men have only one eye in two volumes."

Pierre's flirtation with death ended his mathematical training. Samuel seized the moment to bring his son into the proper atmosphere for the child of a watchmaker: a watchmaker's shop. Mornings, Samuel announced, Pierre would devote to mastering his trade. Afternoons, if Pierre wished, he might study geometry at home. In the evenings father and son would fence, to strengthen Pierre's body and give him grace.

Pierre despised the regimen and turned to Anne for support. But Pierre's illness had broken Anne's will to do battle with Samuel; she admonished her son to respect his father's wishes and apply himself to learning the *horloger*'s trade.

Life in the Dupont household settled into a routine Samuel found acceptable. Business was good. Anne hired a cook and maid and returned to painting scenes on watchfaces. Together, father, mother, and son constructed timepieces. Samuel found great pleasure in his wife's final submission to his desires and his son's start on the road to what he believed would bring the boy true happiness. He and Anne drew closer than they had been since before Pierre's birth. Their satisfaction with life extended to the conjugal bed. Anne became pregnant.

She had last given birth ten years earlier, to a daughter Samuel sent off to Switzerland to be raised; beyond the borders of France a child was safe from the king's kidnappers. Anne's new child, a girl also, was ill from birth and died within weeks. Days later she discovered that she was once again carrying a life inside her womb. This, the fifth child she had borne, came easily, but was sickly too, and survived only a few days. Anne could not bear the loss of two children in less than a year; she never rose from her bed after the last baby's birth, and Pierre began a deathwatch at her side.

In six weeks, on July 21, 1756, Anne Alexandrine de Montchanin Dupont, aged thirty-six years, died, holding in one hand the fingers of the husband she had fought with through nearly two decades of marriage, and in the other those of the son she had fought for. Her last words, whispered as life slipped from within her, encompassed her repentance and despair. "Try to make each other happy," she said.

*2*

PIERRE DUPONT enjoyed the forty-mile hike from Paris south
and east to the village of Nemours. Outside the teeming dirty city he
could forget the anguish and failures of his life since his mother's
death. Long ago he had left the Rue de Richelieu, humiliated and
deeply hurt, rejected by his father, excised even from Samuel's will.

Father and son had fought bitterly almost since the moment of Anne
Dupont's death. Pierre openly refused to accept the destiny Samuel had
chosen for him; Samuel banished his son to an attic storage room, to
meditate and repent his ways. Pierre climbed through a window and
down an outside wall, to the waiting pleasures of Paris at night. He
joined a crowd of itinerant writers and actors, composed poetry, and
learned the inspirations a woman's flesh could arouse. Samuel discovered
his son's transgressions, and for the first time in Pierre's memory, beat
him, drawing more of a response than he had anticipated: Pierre attempted suicide with a rusty knife he found among the stored belongings in the attic. Marianne Oulson, since Anne's death the doyen of the
Dupont household, surprised Pierre as he prepared to plunge the knife
into his heart. Samuel, despairing of ever changing his son, threw him
into the streets of Paris, penniless and without hope of employment.
Pierre survived on the charity of friends.

Hunger and homelessness nurtured remorse in Pierre's heart. He
apprenticed himself to a watchmaker, learned to pound silver into
watchcases, and presented himself at the Dupont *horlogerie* each Sunday, where Samuel, as he ate dinner, ridiculed his son. Late each night
Pierre slaved at his workbench to create a monument to his father, to
discharge his debt to the man he hated and free himself from the guilt he
carried. On a cold January day in 1763, Pierre appeared at the Dupont
workshop bearing an exquisite timepiece he had crafted. On its edge he
had engraved the words *Dupont Filius Composuit, Fecit, Dedicavit
Patrio Suo:* Dupont the son designed, made, and dedicates this to his
father. They were mocking words Pierre knew his father could neither

read nor understand. Silently he placed the watch in his father's hands and shut the door of the Dupont home behind him, never to return. Decades later, when Pierre walked freely down the corridors of Versailles, a confidant of princes and kings, Samuel died in Paris, a short carriage ride away. Pierre chose not to attend his father's funeral.

Pierre called the timepiece his "talisman of liberty." He had no profession, no trade save the hated work of making watches, and no money. He appealed to acquaintances for introductions to wealthy Parisians who had sons or daughters in need of tutoring. But people of wealth—which meant people of noble birth—would not consider hiring a wastrel and rake turned out by his father, who had had no formal education beyond the age of thirteen. Forever hungry, invariably in debt, Pierre found solace only in his freedom and his country walks to the home of Monsieur and Madame Dore in Nemours, family friends who looked kindly on Pierre's predicament.

Monsieur Dore was rarely at home; Madame Dore treated Pierre as she might a son. Pierre considered his benefactress pretentious and superficial. Still, he called her Maman, as did a young cousin who lived with the Dores, Nicole Charlotte Marie Louise le Dée de Rencourt, an eighteen-year-old woman whose name was a good deal more noble than her family. Marie's father, a minor collector of taxes, had inherited and could pass on no fortune. Madame Dore, childless herself, had agreed to take on the task of properly placing Marie in French society.

Madame Dore pressed Marie and Pierre upon each other. Pierre squired Marie through the verdant Nemours countryside; Marie listened wide-eyed to Pierre's tales of Paris life, his throbbing desires for greatness, his poetry. He recounted for Marie the duel he had fought, earning a deep scar in his chest, over a woman's honor. He described the horrors of studying medicine, which he had briefly done. He revealed the plans he and a friend, Berneron de Pradt, had laid for the conquest of Corsica, and how, as a benevolent king, he, Pierre Dupont, would rule wisely and well. Beneath the willow trees of the Dore estate Pierre poured the dreams and hopes he had hidden since his childhood into Marie's willing ears. Marie, gentle and modest and, Pierre believed, intelligent, soothed his tormented conscience and fell in love.

Pierre had not failed to notice Marie's beauty, her waterfall of black hair, her "figure of a nymph and soft black eyes." Madame Dore urged the young couple to embrace each other as brother and sister, but Pierre refused even a sibling closeness. He cherished, in his mind and heart, fantasies of conquest and glory and rule; he wanted no ties, least of all those of romance or love.

One afternoon in the drawing room of the Dore home, Pierre's Maman announced that a husband had been chosen for Marie. She would wed the local collector of taxes, Monsieur Desnaudiers, a stolid fifty-five-year-old widower who was known to have treated his dead wife none too well. But Monsieur Desnaudiers offered Marie security, and, at eighteen, she was nearly past her most marriageable years.

Pierre protested loudly: how could Madame Dore think of marrying so lovely a young flower to a seedy tax collector with a reputation for wife beating? Marie would remain unhappy her entire life; she would be tempted from the path of virtue to the sin of adultery. What Madame Dore proposed amounted to a cruel fate.

Madame Dore shrugged off Pierre's objections. She had no choice: Desnaudiers offered stability, money, a comfortable home. Noble birth aside, Marie had no dowry, no lands, no social position. Who else could be found to marry the girl? Madame Dore asked.

Pierre found the answer on his lips: himself. If Madame Dore would give him two years to make his fortune he would marry Marie.

Maman hesitated—but not too long—and consented. That morning Marie had wept in Pierre's arms over her destiny. Now she cried on the shoulder of her fiancé. Toasts were drunk to the newly betrothed; Pierre slipped into the reverie of a young man suddenly in love. Friends arrived, slapped his back jovially, congratulated him on Marie's beauty. Pierre slept that night drunk with pleasure and romance.

At dawn his reverie fled. He did not really love Marie; he neither could support her nor had hopes of making his fortune. He and Berneron de Pradt had plotted for six months their invasion of Corsica, to free the island people from the oppression of dictatorship. Even if he had died fighting for Corsica's liberation, Pierre knew, a place in history would have been his. Now, and forever, he must struggle simply to support a wife—and that might mean returning to the hated watchmaker's bench. Anne had bequeathed him the principles of chivalry and valor as a guide for his life; to serve them he must sacrifice power, fortune, and glory. But he had given his word, and he resolved to keep it.

The Duc de Choiseul, noble to the very tips of the smallest twigs on his family tree, presided as first minister of Louis XV's kingdom over weekly public audiences at the palace of Versailles. Here the lowest commoner could approach the king's chief adviser. One day a pock-marked, limping, unfashionably dressed young man appeared with a memorandum and petitioned the duc to read it. His words, Pierre Dupont said, concerned grave matters of national importance, foremost among them the rejuvenation of France's economy.

Choiseul thanked the young man and decided to forward the paper unread to his minister of finance. Pierre summoned the most eloquent phrases at his command; he flattered and charmed the duc into promising to read the memorandum himself. Choiseul dismissed Pierre with a wave of his scented handkerchief, ordering him to return the following week.

Since promising to wed Marie le Dée, Pierre had struggled to escape his poverty, not by constructing timepieces, but by bringing himself to the attention of France's ruling class. Berneron de Pradt had been understanding when Pierre announced that they must dissolve their plan to conquer Corsica; love must prevail over glory. Still, Pierre believed himself to be a military genius. France was then embroiled in the Seven Years' War with England. Between the nations stood the natural rock fortress of Gibraltar, in British hands. If only France could wrest it from her enemy, Pierre reasoned, the war would be won.

Pierre studied Gibraltar furiously, the size and appointments of its fort, the sieges laid upon it since Roman times. In exacting detail he constructed a plan that would—in his estimation—allow King Louis's soldiers to scale the island's ramparts, and he prepared to present this plan at Versailles. He tore his work to shreds when England and France signed a peace treaty days before Choiseul's next public audience.

Pierre's military genius became worthless specie. But peace had not ended France's ills. Extravagant kings and senseless wars had emptied its coffers. An idle, pampered noble class taxed and overtaxed the nation's masses. The fields and groves and vineyards yielded huge crops, yet millions lived in poverty. Pierre decided to create a plan that would remedy France's ills. Alone, in his sparse Paris room, he wrote another memorandum to the Duc de Choiseul, and he became a thinker of dangerously radical proportions for eighteenth-century France.

"The earth and waters are the only sources of wealth," Pierre wrote. From nature flows all prosperity and all that makes a nation wealthy. Therefore, the proprietors of the land, the farmers and their helpers, must have liberty, happiness, and immunity from oppression by all other classes of people; only then will they do their job properly. He recommended, in the pages of his memorandum, suppression of the many taxes on the peasantry, freedom of commerce, and recruitment, rather than drafting, of soldiers for the royal army. He sought in precise ways to upset the class hierarchy that allowed a few thousand Frenchmen to live luxuriously while millions starved.

Pierre's thoughts impressed the Duc de Choiseul. He granted the young man a singular honor, the right to visit him at any time without an appointment. Pierre wrote an ode extolling the duc for ending the military draft, as he felt the minister surely would upon his recommendation. Fortunately, the poem never reached the duc; Choiseul had no intention of following Pierre's proposals.

Pierre visited Choiseul regularly. Always, he was received graciously and encouraged to continue his work. The duc seemed interested in the watchmaker's son, but offered him no position or money. Soon Pierre realized that the king's first minister intended to do little for him.

He appealed to friends for help. The Abbé de Voisenon, a minor Parisian writer and priest, met and liked Pierre. Voisenon knew Choiseul socially. He called on the duc in Pierre's behalf, drawing attention to the remarkable parallels between Pierre and Jean-Jacques Rousseau: both were watchmakers' sons; both had romantic temperaments; both possessed unusual character and brains.

Choiseul was unmoved. Rousseau had captured the imagination of the French people with his novels *Émile* and *Julie ou la Nouvelle Héloïse*. His immortal *Social Contract* had made him a god to the masses and a dangerous revolutionary to the ruling class. Choiseul could do little to stop Rousseau from gripping the people's minds, but he had no intention of creating another literary giant by accepting Voisenon's comparison. He dismissed the priest with a promise to do something for Dupont. He never fulfilled his pledge.

In May, 1763, Roussel de La Tour, a prominent nobleman and counselor to the Parliament of Paris, published a pamphlet, titled *La Richesse de l'Etat*, which said more about France's poverty than her wealth. La Tour proposed a daring change in government: replace the current tax system with a single levy based on the income of the taxpayer. The nation would be divided into classes of taxpayers; their contributions would provide a continuing source of revenue to the state.

La Tour's ideas captured the minds of most Parisians who could read,

Pierre Dupont among them. Pierre agreed with La Tour's concept of the single tax but believed the lawyer had badly overestimated the income it would produce. Working feverishly, he wrote a thirty-two-page rebuttal to La Tour. A bookseller, Moreau, bought Pierre's manuscript for two *louis*, which he never paid, and published it. The pamphlet carried no signature, to avoid the wrath of the king's censors; Pierre had neither La Tour's title nor position to keep him from being thrown into the Bastille for his radical views.

La Tour had created a sensation with his pamphlet; Pierre rode its tide. Another author answered Pierre's answer to La Tour, and Pierre decided to reply to that, too. The literary battle, such as it was, was joined, but Pierre earned as much from his second pamphlet as he had from the first. Poverty chased close at his heels. Still he called upon Choiseul, and still he drew comfort from his growing friendship with the Abbé de Voisenon. He was no closer to making his fortune than he had been on the day he promised to make Marie his wife, but he had chosen his profession: the watchmaker's son would become a writer.

Charles-Blaise Meliand, royal *intendant* of the district of Soissons, exerted the combined influence of governor, magistrate, and political ward heeler over the area he administered in the name of the king. On a visit to Paris, he met Pierre Dupont at the home of his distant cousin, the Abbé de Voisenon. Voisenon urged Meliand to hire Pierre as an assistant. Meliand, just then, needed a bright young man interested in agriculture to compile reports on conditions in Soissons. He offered Dupont a job and membership in the Royal Society of Agriculture of Soissons.

Pierre accepted immediately. Writing reports for Meliand, he could familiarize himself with the intricacies of government. In the Society membership rested his first opportunity to escape anonymity. Meliand gave his new assistant two books to read, *Theory of Taxation* and *The Friend of Man*, both by the Marquis de Mirabeau. Pierre devoured them; in clear, explicit language, they set forth thoughts that conformed to his own about the importance of agriculture to the regeneration of ailing France.

The Marquis de Mirabeau was one of the few noblemen who had not been magnetized to Versailles and the dissipation of the French elite. *The Friend of Man* had made him wildly popular with the common Frenchman unable to resist its lively style laced with lessons on how to live. Mirabeau's own luxurious life-style, on vast lands at Bignon, in Nemours, could be forgiven; so, too, could his curious habit of keeping both a mistress and a wife in residence behind the gates of his estate. But after becoming a friend to the common soul, Mirabeau became an enemy to the government with his book on taxation, a violent attack on the nation's tax structure using inaccurate facts dreamed up in the marquis's head. The Duc de Choiseul ordered Mirabeau's arrest and imprisonment in the Bastille. He was set free after a few days—the people loved him too much for the minister to keep him in jail long—but he found himself banished to his country estate and ordered to cease writing against the king's policies.

Pierre impulsively dashed off a letter to the marquis after reading his books. Mirabeau answered warmly; he had read Pierre's two pamphlets and liked them. He encouraged the young writer to study two articles in Denis Diderot's encyclopedia, entitled *Fermiers* and *Grains*. The marquis discreetly failed to mention that the anonymous author of both was Dr. François Quesnay, personal physician to Madame de Pompadour, Louis XV's royal concubine.

François Quesnay loathed political influence. He refused titles for himself and would not seek favors from the king's mistress for his family or friends. He took no part in the intrigues of the court, seemingly content to minister to Madame de Pompadour's medical needs. Twice Louis offered him the position of physician to the king; twice Quesnay turned his monarch down.

His single passion outside the practice of medicine was the new science of political economy, which to Quesnay meant agriculture. He had no desire to milk cows or prod a mule, but he owned a large farm that his son ran. He walked quietly through the corridors of Versailles, possessed of huge power through his relationship with the king's consort; never was he known to exercise it. But under the very noses of the king and his ministers François Quesnay led a group of titled Frenchmen, the Marquis de Mirabeau among them, who disagreed violently with the way France was governed. In time, when he had constructed a new system for the government of France, the doctor believed he could, through Madame de Pompadour, change the face of the nation.

Mirabeau did not bring Pierre Dupont to François Quesnay's attention; his exile to Bignon had ended his regular meetings with the doctor. Nor did he intend to jeopardize Quesnay's position by revealing his identity to the fledgling writer. But Quesnay thirsted for new material on agriculture; he found his own way to Pierre's pamphlets. He mentioned them to Bertin, the controller general of finance, and a member of his group. Bertin vaguely remembered that a friend, Intendant Meliand, had once introduced him to a young assistant, a rather ugly youth with a pockmarked face and crooked nose, whose ideas resembled those in the pamphlets. Quesnay decided to seek out the young writer.

Pierre accepted the messenger's salute in astonishment—and fear. The servant wore the royal livery of the king. Pierre had returned from an afternoon walk to find him standing outside the door to his shabby room. The messenger had made no mistake; the envelope he carried bore the name Pierre Samuel Dupont, assistant to Charles-Blaise Meliand.

Pierre watched the servant disappear and opened the envelope. It bore a summons for him to Versailles, to the presence of Dr. François Quesnay, physician to Madame de Pompadour. Perhaps, he reasoned, his pamphlets had offended the court. He considered fleeing Paris, but friends urged him to remain and answer the summons; if the court knew his name he could not hide from its long tentacles.

At the appointed hour Pierre appeared nervously before the doctor. Quesnay quizzed him on the grain trade, taxation, and agricultural economy. They discussed the principles Pierre had espoused in his pamphlets. Quesnay revealed his authorship of the encyclopedia articles, told Pierre of the group of men he led, and invited him to make his home at Versailles. He would be given a private apartment in the palace and enough money to buy clothing suitable to his new environment. Together they would construct a system of government and inaugurate a new era in the history of France.

Quesnay recognized in Pierre the potential of a great disciple for his teachings. Pierre found in the doctor the wise and patient father Samuel had failed to be. Each morning, in Quesnay's Versailles office, they worked on the intricacies of a new method for the administration of the nation. The physician attended his patient in the afternoons, and Pierre worked alone in Quesnay's apartment. Quesnay assigned his protégé a long essay on France's grain trade. Pierre rarely left the palace, forsaking the Paris nightlife he had learned to love in his poverty. His years of bohemian wanderlust, and his constant hunger, ended. The physician to the royal whore of King Louis XV taught Pierre to fill his stomach and discipline his mind.

Madame de Pompadour received her physician's young protégé in her elegant private apartment at the summer palace, Fountainbleu. She called him "our young agriculturist," spoke of Dr. Quesnay's glowing praise, and of the important plans she and her doctor were making for his future, including the creation of a special committee, with Pierre Dupont at its head, to study agricultural conditions throughout France.

Quesnay had arranged the meeting after he read Pierre's essay on the grain trade. It had pleased him enormously, and an interview with the king's mistress fit well into his plan to convert her to his way of thinking. Quesnay urged Pierre to dedicate his first book to Madame de Pompadour; what better way to assure her patronage toward him and at the same time promote the work among the people of France?

Exhilarated, Pierre burst into Madame Dore's drawing room with the news. A year had passed since his promise to marry Marie; this was the first evidence he could bring to her guardian that he was making his way in the world. Madame Dore was impressed; a connection with the king's mistress could be of priceless social value to her, as well as insuring Marie's happiness. Pierre returned to Versailles to begin revising his manuscript. He paid a visit to Mirabeau at Bignon. The marquis told him of Quesnay's words to him soon after the doctor and Pierre met.

"Let us encourage this young man," Quesnay had said. "As he will be talking long after we are dead."

Soon Pierre's book was ready for the presses, awaiting only his final corrections on long sheets of printer's proofs. Quesnay arranged another audience with his patient, who was ill and required his attention around the clock.

"The doctor has not neglected to tell you how in spite of my bad health we have been thinking of you," Madame de Pompadour said to Pierre. "We have been preparing a great career for your talents."

Quesnay found no cause for great concern in his patient's illness. She had long suffered from minor ailments, but none had ever threatened her life. After Pierre's audience with her, however, Madame de Pompadour's condition worsened. Quesnay's only serious rival, the Duc de Choiseul, who had long coveted the doctor's influence with the king's mistress, saw an opportunity to discredit him; the minister insisted that another physician be called in. He chose one with much less talent and experience than Quesnay.

Madame de Pompadour died, probably of pneumonia, under the new doctor's care. Choiseul had outmaneuvered Quesnay; the physician who had allowed his mistress to become ill in the first place was blamed for her death. Without Madame de Pompadour's patronage Quesnay soon lost all influence at court.

Pierre's book, bearing a dedication to the dead mistress of the king, was on the presses. Quesnay and Mirabeau urged him to remove the few lines of praise for the dead courtesan; rumors floated through Versailles that Choiseul intended to imprison all those who had been intimate with the king's last mistress—or execute them.

Pierre knew that his recently bright future might now plunge into devastating darkness. Madame Dore informed him that his engagement to Marie was broken; Marie's father concurred. He forbade Pierre ever to see his daughter again.

But the months of living at Versailles, the exposure to court intrigue, and the belief Quesnay had given him in his talents and his cause had hardened Pierre. He recalled his mother's teaching that a man of genius, character, and substance must also have honor if he would achieve greatness. Pierre refused to stop the presses from printing his dedication to Madame de Pompadour. Instead, he added a line to its end.

"Woe to the man," he wrote, "who would fear to fling a flower on the tomb of one to whom he had offered incense."

*3*

MARIE LE DÉE embroidered ruffles for her forbidden lover's sleeves in a room overlooking the garden of her father's Paris house. She worked by lamplight, far past sundown, stopping now and then to peer down a hallway toward her father's bedroom, waiting for the sliver of light beneath his doorway to disappear.

When she was certain Papa le Dée had retired for the night, Marie turned her own oil lamp down low and placed it on the sill of her window. By the dim light she read one of her lover's letters until, growing sleepy, she undressed and lay still upon her bed, struggling to stay awake, listening intently for the soft pinging of a few dried peas thrown against a windowpane.

When the sound came she hastened to the garden, embraced Pierre, wept at their dilemma, kissed him tenderly, and slipped back into the house. Pierre stumbled through the hedges and wandered in the midnight darkness to his rented city room.

Monsieur le Dée and Madame Dore had broken Marie and Pierre's betrothal, but not their will. After a few weeks of moonlight encounters the lovers grew bold. Marie's elderly deaf aunt, Madame Benevault, discreetly accepted Pierre's visits while her niece happened to be sitting in her drawing room. Once or twice, when the risk of discovery was not great, Pierre and Marie chanced a few moments together in the dining room of the le Dée house. Letters passed between them frequently, carried by a midwife, Madame Saulnier, to Berget, the le Dée gardener, transferred to the hands of the le Dée governess and brought tucked in the folds of her dress to Marie's bedroom. Destitute as usual, Pierre paid for the servants' silence with cash pressed into his hand by Marie's kindly aunt.

Soon the desires of the flesh overcame both Marie and Pierre. A few francs and a bottle of wine bought a private afternoon in Berget's unlocked and unattended cottage. The midwife Saulnier's home chanced, too, to be vacant on occasion. Monsieur le Dée, preoccupied with collecting taxes, assumed that his daughter had broken off all contact with the former protégé of Madame de Pompadour. He never discovered Marie's disobedience.

The editors of the *Gazette du Commerce*, a successful Parisian magazine designed to inform the public of the government's policies, found their columns filled with arguments for and against the controversial teachings of the *économistes*, as François Quesnay's friends had taken to calling themselves. The *Gazette* survived on the whims of the king's censors; controversy of any sort threatened its existence. Its proprietors decided to remove the burden of opinion from the magazine by printing a supplement, to be called the *Journal of Agriculture, Commerce, and Finance*.

They offered editorship of the *Journal* to Pierre Dupont, the *économistes'* youngest spokesman, with a salary attached that would allow him to propose marriage to Marie le Dée. Anne-Robert-Jacques Turgot, the *intendant* of Limoges and a baron, put forth Pierre's name for the position. Turgot sympathized with the principles of the *économistes* and liked Dupont; he believed Pierre had a fine administrative mind and a bright future.

Pierre thanked Turgot profusely and hungrily took the job. Already he was a year overdue in his promise to wed Marie. Over the winter of 1764, after François Quesnay's downfall, Pierre had done little but live off the doctor's charity—Choiseul's dreaded revenge had failed to materialize—and attend the theater. The stage triumph of the season, Pierre Belloy's *Siege of Calais*, became his favorite. When the text of the play was printed, Pierre bought a copy and decided it was badly written. He devised five hundred eighty corrections to the script and sent them to the playwright. Word of Belloy's anger at Pierre's gall reached him; he was genuinely surprised that the author did not agree with his criticisms.

Pierre fell easily into the gay Parisian nightlife, stumbling drunkenly from party to party after the curtain fell at the theater or opera. Marie understood; she advised him on what clothes to wear, turned his collars when they frayed, and encouraged him to continue making contacts in Parisian society. But Pierre's conscience soon overcame his enjoyment of the theater and cultured conversation in ladies' drawing rooms. At one of their garden trysts Marie was shocked to see that Pierre had cut off all the hair on one side of his head. She was pleased as well; her lover's strange haircut meant that he had forsaken the pleasures of the night for hard work during the day.

Pierre prepared to ask Monsieur le Dée for his daughter's hand in marriage. Now that he had a steady job editing the *Journal* and an income sufficient to support a wife, he would bare his secret courtship of Marie to her father. A date for the nuptials would be chosen at once.

Papa le Dée disagreed. The le Dées were, and had always been, devout Catholics. He had learned that Pierre Dupont subscribed to the Protestant faith. No daughter of his would ever marry one of those impious usurpers of the true faith.

Marie resigned herself to never marrying Pierre. Poverty might be overcome; Pierre's tendency to dream of royal favor could be excused; her noble family tree would even bend to embrace the common bush from which he sprang. But religion was too deep a chasm to cross. She wrote Pierre a tragic letter of farewell, pledged him eternal and undying love, and advised him to accept their lot.

Pierre refused to be discouraged. He wrote Papa le Dée a long letter denying that he had ever seen a Protestant and assured him that Marie's soul would not be consigned to hell if she married him. Conveniently, Pierre forgot his tortured and executed ancestors of Rouen, his kidnapped cousins, his own parents' fear of persecution. He had given his solemn word to marry Marie. And he had fallen in love with her.

Marie took heart at Pierre's display of nerve. She pleaded daily with her father, as Pierre continued to write, convinced that his words and her tears would soothe Monsieur le Dée's worried religious conscience. One evening Marie gingerly told her father that Pierre wished to call on him in person: would he object? No, Papa le Dée said, he would not; let the young man come and ask for her hand. Would he consent? Marie asked in a whisper. Yes, he would offer no further objections; Pierre obviously felt no allegiance to the outlawed faith. Marie fell on her father's neck, streaming tears of joy.

Pierre called on Monsieur le Dée. The betrothal was made formal—almost. Now Samuel Dupont, whose approval was required by law, chose to object to Marie's religious heritage. And, after his own marriage to a woman of high birth, he feared that Pierre's choice might lead him even farther from the path of righteous living than he had already strayed. Pierre appealed to his uncle, Pierre de Montchanin, to intercede with Samuel. After weeks of battle, Pierre's namesake won the watchmaker over.

On January 28, 1766, two days after the wedding contract was signed, both parents—grudgingly—consenting, Pierre Dupont and Nicole Charlotte Marie Louise le Dée de Rencourt were united in holy matrimony in the Catholic church of Saint Sulpice in Paris.

Pierre and Marie engaged rooms in an ordinary Paris hotel, the Saint Martin. Marie, twenty-four, gentle and at the same time spirited, removed from her husband the drudgery of household chores. Pierre devoted his full energies to editing the new *Journal of Agriculture, Commerce, and Finance*.

The owners of the *Journal* had intended it to serve as a conduit to the people for the king's views on agricultural matters. Pierre worked diligently to turn its emphasis into support for the doctrines of François Quesnay. When letters attacking Quesnay's ideas were published Pierre added comments designed to destroy the arguments of the opposition. He devoted large spaces to articles by Quesnay, Mirabeau, and himself. The *Journal*'s circulation increased steadily; so too did its owners' anger with their editor.

Pierre's employers admonished him against allowing his own views to dominate the *Journal*'s pages; they forbade him to publish his own work. Pierre adopted pseudonyms. He convinced François Quesnay to write letters mildly critical of his own ideas and printed them over more false signatures. The *Journal*'s owners were neither amused nor fooled. They awaited an opportunity to free themselves of Pierre's services. When the Parliament of Brittany failed to register a tax ordered by the king, Pierre was ordered to castigate the provincial assembly in the *Journal*. He refused and was immediately dismissed: the *Journal* would not be turned into a vehicle for the propaganda of François Quesnay and his followers.

In his few months editing the *Journal* Pierre had become the sole public voice for a system of economics fathered by no less a luminary than Madame de Pompadour's former private physician. Even after Quesnay's fall from power the doctor held regular meetings of the *économistes* in his Versailles apartment, which Choiseul had graciously allowed him to keep. Pierre attended always, the favored disciple now of a school of thought endorsed by many powerful French noblemen.

Foreign visitors to Paris often fell into Quesnay's orb, among them the young tutor to the Duke of Buccleuch, a British subject named Adam Smith. From Quesnay and Mirabeau, the doctor's heir apparent, and Pierre Dupont, Smith started to cull the ideas he eventually distilled into the *Wealth of Nations*.

Another Englishman, destined to become the most lionized personality of the age, and its most brilliant revolutionary, found Quesnay's thoughts engaging. The gentleman visited Paris briefly in 1766, called on the doctor, and expressed a desire to meet the young writer who carried the *économistes'* principles to the people with such daring and candor. Pierre was too busy to see the visitor; he seemed, in fact, not to have known until Benjamin Franklin left Paris that the inventor wished to make his acquaintance. A decade was to pass before they finally met.

But Franklin had made the *économistes* his friends. A few months after his visit to Versailles he received a copy of Pierre's latest published work, accompanied by a personal letter. The book fared less than well. It contained many of Quesnay's articles, with an introduction by Dupont. Turgot, Meliand, and even Mirabeau found Pierre's writing disappointing. But the unemployed editor had posed a thought that captured Benjamin Franklin's imagination: the fortunes of a nation, Pierre wrote, could be shaped into a science of human interaction.

Franklin answered Pierre's letter, embracing the young writer with all the charm at his command. He had, he wrote, read the book "with great pleasure, and received from it a great deal of Instruction. There is such a Freedom from local and national Prejudices and Partialities, so much Benevolence to Mankind in general, so much Goodness mixt with the Wisdom, in the Principles of your new Philosophy, that I am perfectly charmed with them."

Benjamin Franklin, Adam Smith, and Voltaire, the exiled Sage of Ferney, with whom Pierre had begun to correspond, knew that times of great turmoil loomed on the horizon. When the human order changed, by revolution if necessary, new methods would have to be found for governing nations. François Quesnay's principles held one possibility, but the doctor was aging rapidly, even, it was said, slipping into senility. Pierre Dupont seemed to be Quesnay's best young disciple and so held the interest of men with subtle intellects and great vision.

Yet Pierre found little time for Smith or Franklin or even Voltaire. Married less than a year, he was unemployed. Turgot and Meliand, to help him along, asked that he write reports on their districts, offering what funds they could, which amounted to little more than Pierre needed to cover the expense of hiring clerks who would compile statistics for him. Quesnay, who was indeed growing senile and spending much of his time constructing strange mathematical systems by which he hoped to discover the secrets of the universe, could not help him. Mirabeau quietly relieved Quesnay of the leadership of the *économistes* and began holding weekly meetings in his Paris townhouse. Pierre rarely attended, for his mind was consumed with finding a way to support the coming addition to his family: Marie had become pregnant.

On October 1, 1767, Marie gave birth to a son. Pierre asked Mirabeau to stand as his firstborn's godfather. The marquis agreed, and the child was named Victor Marie Dupont, taking Mirabeau's given name as his own. Victor was a healthy, active baby. To his mother's comfort, for religious reasons, and his father's, for political ones, he was baptized a Catholic. Pierre dreamed still of rising to the summit of power through the morass of intrigue at Versailles; being a Catholic in good standing was among the first requisites.

Catholicism fit, too, with the new job Pierre had found. The Abbé Baudeau, a priest, had started a monthly magazine of church-inspired gossip called the *Éphémérides du Citoyen*. Mirabeau converted Baudeau to physiocracy, as the *économistes* called their system of thought. When the priest was offered a lucrative position abroad he approached Pierre with a proposal to take over the *Éphémérides*. If Dupont would edit the magazine for six months at a small salary, Baudeau would then sign over its ownership. Pierre's friends cautioned him against the arrangement; they knew his affinity for strong words and defiance of the king in print. Pierre shrugged off their objections: he must find a way to feed his wife and son. He accepted Baudeau's proposition.

Pierre made a short pilgrimage to visit Voltaire in Switzerland. He, Marie, and Victor journeyed out of Paris for a short holiday. They found an apartment convenient to the office of the *Éphémérides* in the Rue de Faubourg St. Jacques, with a small garden Pierre could plant and Victor might use as a playground. They held a quiet celebration in their new lodgings on the eve of Pierre's first day at the magazine. The toasts they drank were premature, and the garden more important as a provider of food than a yard: the *Éphémérides du Citoyen* was destined to fail from its start.

# 4

PIERRE EDITED the *Éphémérides* through four tumultuous years. Baudeau had promised him four hundred paid subscribers; less than one-fourth that number actually turned up. The columns of the magazine spouted a continuous stream of political heresy, much of it from Pierre's pen. Each month he was summoned before the king's censors to justify the articles he printed; in time, the censors threatened to ban the *Éphémérides*, and would have, but Pierre's good fortune held: five arbiters of public opinion fell from power before finding enough excuses to silence him.

Income from the magazine's subscribers barely paid Pierre's printing bills and left nothing for his salary. He could not pay writers and so took upon himself the enormous task of creating all the words he printed. In November, 1772, the *Éphémérides* lagged seven months behind schedule. Pierre's debts had mounted to fifteen thousand francs, a sum he could never hope to raise. The newest royal censor stamped him irresponsible and with a swirl of his pen left Pierre once more unemployed, this time deeply in debt. His creditors, sympathetic to the principles of physiocracy, agreed to wait for payment. Pierre was saved from debtor's prison, to the chagrin of the king's censor.

He could not so easily put off other obligations. Marie had borne another son in the spring of 1772, a healthy male child. Pierre asked Jacques Turgot to stand as the boy's godfather. Turgot, one of the few who did not desert Pierre in the face of royal disfavor, agreed and suggested that the child be named Eleuthère Irénée, "in honor of liberty and peace." Pierre hesitated; it was an unusual name. He wished nothing to stand in his son's way, and he needed no more notoriety for himself. But the honor of naming a newborn infant went to its godfather, and Pierre liked and respected the baron. He acquiesced; the founder of the world's largest manufacturer of gunpowder and explosives was baptized "in honor of liberty and peace."

Pierre could barely feed the woman he had married and the children he had fathered. Marie had taken over the planting of vegetables in the garden outside their apartment. For months the Dupont family survived on freshly picked tomatoes, lettuce, cucumbers, and grapes. Pierre soon realized that he had lost more than a job and meager income with the demise of the *Éphémérides:* his political influence, voice, and popularity, had died as well.

Prince Adam Czartoryski, brother of the king of Poland, scoured Europe for tutors worthy of educating his royally bred son. The prince encountered Pierre Dupont's name whenever he asked the advice of the Continent's more enlightened thinkers. Czartoryski himself had read much of Pierre's work and agreed with most of his ideas. He decided to raise his son according to the principles of physiocracy.

The prince offered Pierre ten thousand francs a year, apartments in his palace for the Dupont family, travel expenses from Paris to Warsaw, and a title, Honorary Councillor of the King and Republic of Poland. After ten years of service Pierre would receive a cash bonus of one hundred thousand francs, an estimable fortune.

Czartoryski's terms flattered Pierre; he could remember when not one of Paris's noble families would risk hiring him to teach its sons. But a singular honor had just come his way. The Margrave of Baden, supreme ruler of a small kingdom in the Black Forest, had named Pierre his representative to the king of France. Louis XV had balked briefly; Frenchmen did not often serve as emissaries from a foreign monarch to their own. The margrave intervened personally, and Louis approved the appointment. On July 1, 1774, Pierre was due to become an ambassador to his own king.

The Polish prince waved Pierre's objections aside and sweetened his offer. He would have his brother name Pierre Secretary of the High Council of National Education and Director of the Academy in Warsaw. He would mortgage a piece of property he owned in Holland and pay Pierre one-third of his bonus in advance.

Pierre's eyebrows lifted at Czartoryski's new terms. Acceptance meant an end to his frustrations at earning money; his influence in French intellectual circles would stop, too. The bonus would allow him to fulfill a dream and buy a country estate in Nemours; he and Marie and their sons would, however, be in far-off Warsaw, unable to enjoy their land. He might control the education of an entire nation's youth; unfortunately, they would be Polish children, not French. The Duponts would reside in a princely castle, attended by liveried servants, fawned on by lesser mortals; the palace would not be Versailles. Prince Adam's proposition amounted to a decade of luxurious exile, Pierre realized.

Yet exile might be what he needed most. The wrath of the king's censors had kept him unemployed and poor for nearly two years. He had made enemies in high places. Wherever in France he attempted to preach his doctrine of the rule of nature, he encountered hostility and scorn. Perhaps he would never flourish under the iron rule of the Bourbon kings. Pierre wrote Prince Czartoryski that he would accept his newest offer, told Marie to pack their belongings, and prepared to desert his homeland.

Louis XVI, heir to the Bourbon throne, the Bourbon nose, the Bourbon obesity, and the ultimate destiny of the Bourbon dynasty, was not yet twenty when he donned the crimson robe of rule, clutched the scepter of Charlemagne in his hands, and knelt to be anointed from the vial of Clovis.

Louis was neither intelligent nor attractive. Mounds of bluish flesh cascaded down his neck and limbs and his eyes seemed to disappear into his corpulent face. His marriage to Marie Antoinette and his death under the blade of the guillotine elevated his brief life to legend and settled upon his memory forever the mark of a ruthless, plotting, and cruel dictator.

In reality, Louis ruled more benevolently than any other Bourbon king. Often he visited Parisian hospitals in disguise and when conditions in them repulsed him ordered immediate changes. He believed that the peasants of France deserved a greater share of the nation's wealth and set in motion drastic, at least to the entrenched nobility, measures to end their virtual serfdom. He studied the prisons of Paris and, long before the masses stormed it, planned to have the infamous Bastille torn down.

His flaws, and they were great, were dullness and stupidity. Notably weak-willed for a king, Louis allowed anyone with influence to ply his way through the antechambers of French power. Marie Antoinette, whom he married to unite France with her birthplace, Austria, loathed her master's company and had little trouble ridding herself of his annoying presence. Each night, while courtiers danced with their queen, Marie set the clocks of Versailles forward an hour and Louis simply retired an hour early to the royal bed. On July 14, 1789, when Paris's enraged citizens attacked the Bastille, Louis described the day's events in his diary in a single word: "nothing," as he did each day the weather prevented him from going hunting.

In May, 1774, when Louis ascended the throne, Pierre Dupont had not yet left Paris for Warsaw. He knew that the new king brought with him to Versailles an open mind toward choosing the ministers who would run his kingdom. He dallied as long as he dared en route to Poland, taking a month to make a week's journey over summer-hardened roads. Baron Jacques Turgot had been brought into Louis's cabinet; Pierre hoped his old friend would find a place for him at Versailles. But Turgot wrote to Pierre that he might as well settle himself in Warsaw; no position worthy of bringing him back to France had materialized.

Then Louis elevated Turgot to the office of controller general of finance, charged with rejuvenating France's tottering economy. The baron wanted Pierre at his side. Louis was cooperative; with a swirl of the royal pen he named Pierre inspector general of commerce for the French nation and ordered him to Paris to assume the pressing responsibilities of his job. Pierre lingered a few weeks in Warsaw, enjoying the limelight of a lame-duck tutor turned confidant of the king of France. Aboard his carriage to Paris he wrote a long letter to François Quesnay, his patron and first teacher, spilling onto the paper all the frustration and insecurity of his years of poverty and the exhilaration he felt at constructing a new France at Jacques Turgot's side. Pierre addressed himself to a dead man; Quesnay, senile and lonely, perished two days before Pierre took up his pen.

In twenty months of office Jacques Turgot and Pierre Dupont extorted from Louis XVI greater reforms than France had seen in a thousand years. Together they ended internal tariffs and restrictions on the grain trade, abolished the craftsmen's guilds, stopped the hated forced labor on public roads, granted royal funds to inventors of new farming and manufacturing methods, established public-work projects, and installed a fair property tax that applied even to the nobility. Pierre came to know and revere the pliable Louis as a dog knows its master: it is his master, murderer and saint alike. He learned that rulers can be ruled and manipulated; he came to respect his monarch's desire for change. Never, even when all France turned away from Louis XVI, did Pierre desert him or, even after his downfall, Jacques Turgot.

Turgot had proclaimed that the reign of women was over in France.

He slashed the expenditures of the king's household, to the point where Marie Antoinette ruled over a staff of only fifteen thousand, an unheard-of paucity of servants for a French queen. He demanded a reduction of Marie's budget; no longer would she be able to buy diamonds or dole out lifetime pensions to flattering—and useless—courtiers. Marie fumed. She demanded that her husband throw Turgot in prison. Louis, admiring the changes Turgot had wrought and the discomfort he inflicted upon Marie, refused. Marie set about to ruin the controller general of her finances.

She and a few faithful courtiers conjured a set of letters, purportedly to and from Turgot, that contained treasonous remarks about the king and open references to his famous sexual impotence. Mysteriously, the letters surfaced beside Louis's bed one morning. Pierre noted an indecent amount of joy at court when Louis asked for Jacques Turgot's resignation.

Dupont's work with Turgot forced him into retirement. He had used the advance from Prince Czartoryski to put a down payment on a country estate in Nemours, not far from the Marquis de Mirabeau's château at Bignon. Louis decided to be lenient with Pierre; he had, after all, been forced to relinquish a lucrative post abroad to serve his king. He would be allowed to retain the eight-thousand-franc salary that made up his sole income. But he was to remove himself from Versailles to his country home, Bois-des-Fosses, to await the pleasure of his monarch. Louis's command amounted to exile less than fifty miles from Paris. And it deprived Pierre of the idea-rich society he had enjoyed since coming to Versailles.

As Jacques Turgot's assistant Pierre had been welcomed into the innermost circles of France's intellectual elite. He had befriended a young scientist, Antoine Lavoisier. Noble, wealthy, and dedicated to the infant science of chemistry, Lavoisier still respected those who sought to change France's social order. He did not neglect human relationships, as many brilliant scientists have. The discoverer of oxygen enjoyed the company of children and spent much time with Pierre's sons, Victor and, as he liked to be called, Irénée.

Once, when Irénée was fourteen, Lavoisier noticed the boy growing plants on a windowsill in his father's home. On his next visit Antoine brought an envelope of white powder to his friend's son and sprinkled it on the plants. The green shoots miraculously grew into mature plants in days rather than weeks. Lavoisier had introduced the lad to one of his discoveries, nitrogen used as a fertilizer. Four years later, when the scientist headed the French Powder Commission during the revolution, he gave Irénée Dupont a job as an assistant bookkeeper. Irénée learned then that this same white powder, nitrate of soda, could be used as a basic ingredient in gunpowder.

In the countryside of Nemours, Pierre awoke each morning to the aroma of fertilized fields rather than the scent of perfumed and powdered wigs. He listened to the cock's crow rather than the gentle strains of Couperin and Rameau played upon harpsichords by court musicians. Instead of the frilled cravats of courtiers, the dank and austere corridors of Versailles, and the delicate elegance of mansion drawing rooms, he saw the coarse shirts of peasants, the small rooms of his manor house, and the crude, if tasteful, furnishings selected by his wife.

Marie had greeted the chore of running Bois-des-Fosses with ambition and optimism. She was content to stay outside Paris with her sons, their tutors, a small domestic staff, and the people of Nemours, while Pierre pondered matters of state at Versailles. She had assumed the posture of genteel countrywoman with ease; in weeks she had become the lady of open and noble grace the local peasants often approached with problems, questions, and requests.

Marie acted in amateur theatricals, cultivated the land, dined two or three times a week with the Mirabeaus, and raised her sons. Victor and Irénée roamed the woods and fields, roughhoused with the peasant children, and spent sweaty hours with private tutors learning the classical facts of life as their father had studied them. Their Papa, they knew, was a man of some importance, but he was away much of the time. They looked to their mother for daily guidance.

Marie Dupont struggled alone to make the estate pay for itself. Pierre returned from Versailles after Turgot's dismissal to find Bois-des-Fosses a hive of activity that pleased his most discerning physiocratic eye. Marie had raised calves, chickens, and ducks, and cultivated wheat and oats and large vineyards of healthy grapes that were crushed, fermented, and sold as wine. Bois-des-Fosses produced enough food to supply the family and an excess that Marie sold at market to pay the debts Pierre had amassed in his various failures. Pierre even approved of the tutor Marie had hired for the boys, Philippe Nicholas Harmand.

The master of Bois-des-Fosses found that he had little to do on his estate. He could retire to his study, which Marie had furnished to his taste, and write, or to the small island in one of the property's streams, where Marie set up an office for him in the summer heat. Still in his mid-thirties, Pierre Dupont discovered awaiting him in Nemours all the pleasantries of life as a country squire, and he hated them: he had not come so far to end up with so little.

*5*

KING LOUIS XVI replaced Jacques Turgot with a Swiss financier rumored to be the wealthiest man in Europe. Jacques Necker had amassed millions through ruthless international trading in gold and currency. He seemed, to Louis, the perfect choice for a man who must rescue France from the brink of bankruptcy. Within weeks after Necker arrived at Versailles every reform Turgot and Pierre Dupont had instituted was reversed. Necker earned the confidence and trust of Marie Antoinette. The king found his wife much easier to live with and praised Necker for his brilliant work.

But Jacques Necker had no idea of how to run a nation. He searched the French bureaucracy for someone capable of keeping the country's economy alive. He discovered, much to his displeasure, that only Pierre Dupont, living in exile at Bois-des-Fosses, was qualified to administer the nation's department of finance.

Necker hated Pierre. For years, in his magazines, Pierre had attacked Necker's monopoly over the European trade with the Indies. Pierre distrusted Necker, but when the king's order to return to Versailles arrived in Nemours, the gentleman farmer leaped at the chance to resume his public service.

Marie Dupont rented a large flat in Paris's fashionable Cul-de-Sac de la Corderie, with eight rooms and separate servants' quarters. She indulged in dresses of silk and taffeta, a few fringed with squirrel. She traveled the city in a lacquered carriage, drawn by four horses with three liveried attendants astride. She purchased elegant furniture and brocaded draperies to fill the new Dupont apartment. Marie's shrewd management of Bois-des-Fosses had erased her husband's debts; she planned to spend four or five months each year in Paris and at Versailles, to be near Pierre and take advantage of the social status his new position brought.

Pierre worked diligently at Jacques Necker's side but allied himself with France's foreign minister, the Comte de Vergennes, who resented, as did many Frenchmen, Necker's Swiss birth. Vergennes coaxed Louis into granting Pierre a patent of nobility. Pierre designed a coat of arms for himself, a shield with one perpendicular column on a field of scarlet, surmounted by a helmet, visor raised. Beneath the shield ran the new Dupont family motto, *Rectitudine Sto*, Be Upright. Pierre quickly became fond of swearing by the uprightness of his column.

The Dupont coat of arms adorned the carriage Marie had purchased. Each morning when he was not at Versailles Pierre rode in the carriage to Bellechase, the Passy house of a young priest, Charles-Maurice de Périgord. The eldest son of a count and heir to one of France's most ancient family trees, the priest had been crippled at the age of four by a fall, condemned forever to drag one leg along as he walked. Parisian wits snickered that each generation of the Périgord family, now in its seventh century, produced at least one clubfoot. Before his twentieth birthday Charles-Maurice earned the nickname "talons." Benjamin Constant, one of the many lovers Germaine Necker de Staël, Jacques Necker's daughter, took during her lifetime, believed the priest's character had been fashioned after his feet. He had good reason to hate Périgord; Constant inherited Germaine's favors from the priest. In later years Napoleon Bonaparte entrusted his empire's foreign policy to Charles-Maurice, whose elegance and aloofness became legendary. Privately, Napoleon referred to the priest as "shit in a silk stocking"; publicly, he called him by his favorite name, Talleyrand.

Pierre considered himself one of Talleyrand's closest friends. Talleyrand cultivated Pierre's esteem, used him as a pawn during the French Revolution, and rescued his son's foundering gunpowder business from bankruptcy in 1807 with a large loan.

The cream of Parisian intellectuals joined Pierre at Bellechase each day, and at Antoine Lavoisier's house each night. Lavoisier demonstrated his latest experiments, served fine wines at his table, and encouraged open discussion of ways to improve France. Nearly all Lavoisier's guests were monarchists, dedicated to keeping the Bourbon dynasty in power, at least in name; yet many were excited by news of the revolution in Britain's American colonies, brought to Lavoisier's drawing room by the Marquis de Lafayette, freshly returned from his heroic—and overblown—campaign beside the rebels. Lafayette's stories were confirmed by the aging inventor Pierre introduced to Lavoisier's circle of friends, Benjamin Franklin.

The fledgling United States had sent Benjamin Franklin to Paris as its first foreign ambassador. At Lavoisier's dinner parties Franklin sat silent much of the time, smiling wisely, running his wrinkled hands through the gray wisps of hair that trailed from his head. Pierre and his friends interpreted the ambassador's simple style of dress as faithfulness to the spartan principles of the new American nation; no one guessed that he had no funds to use for buying new clothes. They attributed his quiet manner to his obvious wisdom; they never guessed that his French was, at best, as poor as his purse.

Pierre and Franklin saw each other often. Franklin had been charged with convincing Louis XVI that the United States should be favored with French foreign trade. Pierre oversaw the administration of the nation's foreign commerce. Franklin and Marie Dupont had in common a fascination for the newest rage, hot-air ballooning. The ambassador escorted Marie to a spring balloon demonstration in Paris a few days before she was due to leave the city for Nemours, where she would oversee the seasonal planting.

Marie wrote to Pierre in late summer that she had attended another hot-air ascent. She felt slightly ill, she told her husband, perhaps from the changing seasons. Pierre found no cause for alarm; it was not uncommon for his wife to be affected by the weather. Four days later Nicole Charlotte Marie Louise le Dee de Rencourt Dupont lay buried beneath freshly turned earth in the graveyard of the parish church in Chevannes, a town near Bois-des-Fosses. The doctors told Pierre his wife had died of a lung congestion contracted during her outing to watch the balloon ascent.

Pierre prepared to turn Bois-des-Fosses over to a tenant farmer. He instructed Victor and Irénée to pack their belongings; they would return with him to Paris. Not since Victor's birth, seventeen years earlier, had Pierre been called upon to serve as a full-time parent. He decided to take the boys' tutor, Philippe Harmand, with him to the city to continue his sons' education and watch over them while he worked at Versailles and maintained his social status. Pierre did not intend to allow Marie's death to interfere with the life he had built for himself.

Pierre sat in his favorite armchair in the parlor at Bois-des-Fosses, his hat on his head, his sword girded about his waist. A marble bust of Marie Dupont on a pedestal at Pierre's left cast shadows in the candlelit room. To his right, on a lower chair, rested another sword and the hat of a young man. On the floor at Pierre's feet lay a small pillow.

From the doorway of the room Victor Dupont called out, "My father, I bring my brother to receive your blessing and his first arms."

Victor led Irénée into the parlor, to the front of Pierre's armchair. The younger boy bowed his head.

"My son," Pierre said, "I had hoped that your mother's presence would honor the ceremony in which I endow you with your rank. I no longer have a wife, you have no mother. But we have here her likeness, and perhaps from Heaven she looks down on us and is glad to see whatever we do that is worthy and good."

Pierre stood up on the platform that elevated his chair.

"You must understand," he continued, "I have told you that no privilege exists that is not inseparably bound to a duty. The nation confides the privilege of bearing arms to such families as she deems most distinguished by education, by the virtues that are supposed to be hereditary, by a finer honor, by a stricter honesty, by an unconquerable desire to use all one's strength and to sacrifice even one's life for the general welfare."

Pierre sat down and motioned to Irénée to kneel before him.

"Promise to God your master, to mankind your brothers, to the French your compatriots, to the memory of your mother, to me, that you will never give way to anger and still less to hatred . . . promise at the same time that you will not allow yourself to be cowed by any danger when you are called upon to defend your country, or your wife, or your children, or your brother, or yourself, or any other human being who, in danger not deserved by his own wrong-doing, has need of your help."

Irénée gave his solemn word. Pierre took the sword from the lower chair, reached down, and fastened it around his son's waist. He admonished his younger son against engaging in duels, lest he kill in cold blood, but urged him never to fear to fight in the cause of righteousness. He ordered Irénée to learn the art of fencing, so that he might never cower before those stronger than he.

Pierre stood once again, drew his sword, and struck Irénée on the left shoulder with it.

"The blow I am giving you, my son," he said, "is to teach you that you must bear any blow when it is honorable and right. Rise and embrace me."

Father and son held each other briefly. Pierre placed Irénée's hat upon his head and called Victor forward.

"Draw your swords, my children," he said. "Salute and embrace each other. Promise each other to be always firmly united, to comfort each other in every sorrow, to help each other in all efforts, to stand by each other in all difficulty and danger. . . . Love each other always."

"We promise it, my father," Victor and Irénée said in unison. "We promise it to you and to the memory and portrait of our mother."

The ceremony ended; Irénée Dupont was thirteen years old. Within a day the Dupont men left Bois-des-Fosses for Paris in the carriage emblazoned with the family's coat of arms. Victor and Irénée soothed their grief in the pact they had made to each other a day earlier. Pierre comforted himself by clutching the one thousand thirty-five letters Marie had written to him during their marriage.

*6*

W HAT BROUGHT Thomas Jefferson, the Apostle of Democracy, and Pierre Dupont, the Apostle of Physiocracy, together was the soil.

"Cultivators of the earth are the most valuable citizens," Jefferson wrote to John Jay from France. "They are . . . the most independent, the most virtuous, and they are tied to their country, and wedded to its liberty, by the most lasting bonds."

Pierre shared Jefferson's view, but not because he sought to protect the dignity of man. Dupont saw the land as the way to wealth; Jefferson perceived it as insurance for liberty.

In the years between the American and French revolutions, the Virginian and the Frenchman became unlikely friends. Jefferson looked upon titles with disgust; Pierre coveted them. Jefferson believed every man should have a vote; Dupont wished to enfranchise only landowners. Jefferson, while President, refused to divulge his birthdate to reporters, believing that public celebration of a chief executive's first day on earth did not coincide with the principles of democracy; Pierre ritualized even giving a sword to his son.

The Virginian had come to Versailles to replace Benjamin Franklin as ambassador from the United States. Franklin, old, ill, and frail, was weary of the plots and intrigues of the French court. He had become a legend to the French people. Jacques Turgot wrote that the inventor "ravaged the lightning from the skies and the sword from tyrants." Parisian women plotted to spend a few moments in his parlor—and bedroom. Louis XVI's ministers feared the wily ambassador's ability to manipulate them and respected his towering intelligence and wit.

When Thomas Jefferson called upon the Comte de Vergennes to present his credentials, Vergennes assessed his spare, bony frame, his backwoods manners, and his simple, ill-fitting clothes, and sighed with relief: France would be rid of the United States' annoying pleas for money at last. Vergennes decided to disgrace Jefferson in the eyes of the court immediately. He asked the Virginian if he had come to take Franklin's place. Jefferson's backwoods manner evaporated. In impeccable French he answered that no man alive could replace the inventor; he had come to Versailles only to succeed him. Vergennes scowled; Jefferson's reputation was made.

Benjamin Franklin had emptied the French treasury to help the thirteen colonies win their independence. Congress charged Jefferson with scraping the vaults to keep the new nation afloat. Vergennes knew this and knew that the United States might hold the key to frustrating England's goals of conquest on the high seas.

But the comte also realized that the American states were more united in name than reality, that Spain and France laid claim to huge chunks of the western continent, that land speculators were already counting bags of gold from get-rich-quick schemes, that the government of the United States was unworkable, that only the magnetism of George Washington, serving as President, held the states together. Jefferson asked for a share of France's foreign trade. Vergennes considered the request, decided that the United States would not receive his nation's largesse, and, in true French style, appointed a committee to study the situation.

He assigned Pierre Dupont to the American Committee. Pierre was France's expert on foreign commerce and, since he owed both his position and his title to Vergennes, could be controlled. The Marquis de Lafayette joined Pierre; Lafayette would give the appearance that France was seriously trying to help the United States. Pierre and Jefferson plodded through the centuries of treaties and cross-treaties that enveloped France in a tangled web of commerce with other European nations. Pierre soon realized that no small cry would be raised if France broke her treaties to deal with a band of rebels who had usurped Britain's sovereign power. When Vergennes's opposition to the United States became obvious—Pierre discovered a loophole in France's treaties that the minister immediately plugged—Jefferson suggested they spend less time reading musty documents and discuss their common personal problems. Aside from their love for the soil, both the Frenchman and the Virginian had recently lost their wives to illness, and both had young children to raise.

Thomas Jefferson's daughters, one with him in Europe, the other soon to arrive accompanied by the Virginian's mulatto lover, Sally Hemings, had, like Pierre's sons, only their father to guide them through the difficult years.

But Jefferson's offspring were female; he needed only to raise them with proper manners and find them suitable husbands. They would live out their lives in a nation already beyond the horrors of revolution, where their father was a hero destined to become President. Pierre's sons would soon be caught up in France's most difficult times, the children of a member of the despised nobility.

Jefferson perceived in France the seeds of revolution. Had he wished to, he might have taught the French liberal faction a good deal about the art of shaking off a monarch's rule. But the United States needed France's money, and so Jefferson refrained from political involvement. Pierre still cherished the hope of reforming France under Bourbon rule. Louis XVI, interpreting his work on the American Committee as a mark of loyalty to the crown, elevated Pierre to the position of counselor of state and raised his salary to thirty thousand francs. The Dupont family lived comfortably amid a France spiraling into revolution. Pierre seemed unaware of the undercurrents that would turn the Seine into a river of blood. He sought professions for his sons suitable to their newly titled heritage. But neither Victor nor Irénée seemed suited for anything.

Victor—tall, handsome, elegantly turned out in velvet coats and silver boot buckles—walked, talked, and spent like a nobleman's son. Nearing twenty, he had already failed as an undersecretary in Pierre's office, preferring to gamble and carouse rather than work. Out of desperation Pierre begged Vergennes to attach Victor to the French mission to the United States; he could not support his son's extravagances. Vergennes agreed to make Victor an unpaid and untitled aide to France's ambassador to America. Jefferson wrote letters of introduction for Pierre's elder son to prominent men in the United States. Pierre stuffed a note to Ben Franklin in Victor's pocket as he was about to leave Paris, entrusting his firstborn to the inventor's care.

Irénée Dupont was a different sort of child, studious, sober, awkward in social situations. At fourteen, out of admiration for Antoine Lavoisier, he wrote an essay on the manufacture of gunpowder. Pierre acknowledged the effort without praise; he knew little of the science and considered any manufacturing process far beneath the study of agricultural economics. But he fixed upon Irénée's studious bent and, as was his right since becoming a nobleman, enrolled his younger son in the Collège Royal in Paris. Pierre had mistaken interest for dedication. Irénée lasted less than one unremarkable year at the college.

Antoine Lavoisier had been appointed head of the French Powder Commission shortly before Victor left for the United States. Irénée was too young to be helped by Vergennes or Jefferson, so Pierre asked Lavoisier to give his second son a job. Since Marie Dupont's death Lavoisier and his wife had treated Pierre's children as their own. The chemist offered to make Irénée an assistant bookkeeper in his office; even in the case of a close friend Lavoisier would allow only hard work and proven value to rule his choices for responsible positions in the national gunpowder administration.

Irénée began at the age of fifteen to learn how a gunpowder business functioned. In his spare hours he sat quietly watching chemists under Lavoisier's direction as they experimented to improve the powder-making process. Lavoisier noticed Irénée's interest in the deadly black substance; soon the bookkeeper was allowed to perform experiments on his own after the day's columns of figures had been added. Within a few months Eleuthère Irénée Dupont had learned the rudiments of gunpowder manufacture.

Victor and Irénée wrote to each other often across the Atlantic Ocean. Victor filled his pages with requests for more and better clothes, descriptions of his exploits among the American women with their amazingly relaxed morality, and tales of the toasts drunk even to an unpaid attaché to the French embassy. Irénée wrote back telling of a strange and wondrous parade he had witnessed.

Deaths are often followed by funeral processions. Irénée watched the grandest cortege of all time take place years before life slipped from its subject, the Bourbon dynasty. Perched high on a balcony above the town of Versailles, he viewed the opening of the Estates General of France.

It was a sunny morning in May, Irénée wrote to his brother. The windows lining Versailles's streets filled early with noble ladies who paid absurd prices for the only seats in town. In stunning regalia, the king and queen, the archbishops and cardinals, the clergy and nobility marched down the street. Behind them, humbled in simple black dress by the order of the king, came the representatives of the Third Estate. Irénée could pick out his father among the delegates, walking not far from the Marquis de Mirabeau's son.

Irénée's heart jumped with pride in his father. Since the king had ordered the nation's representative body convoked—for the first time in two centuries—to solve France's financial blight, Pierre had been an influential and respected man. Nemours, with ease, elected him its delegate to the Estates General; he had been chosen to write the list of grievances from the district and would present it to the gathered delegates.

Irénée's letters carried no political commentary. He did not see that, beneath their simple black gowns, the delegates from the Third Estate represented not the common people of France but the wealthy and conservative bourgeoisie. Among the delegates there were, it was true, serious reformers, many of them friends and supporters of Pierre Dupont. Nor did Irénée envisage the anarchy and chaos that would halt his education in the manufacture of gunpowder.

When the Third Estate demanded vote by head, not order, so that the common people would have at least equal representation with the nobility and clergy in the Estates General, Pierre cast his ballot in favor of the motion. The First and Second Estates of course refused. An impasse was reached and the orderly procession Irénée had watched dissolved into a morass of spite, jealousy, and confusion.

Pitched battles began over who would certify the credentials of the various delegates. The Third Estate wanted to pass not only on its own members, but on the noblemen and priests as well. Delegate Dupont de Nemours—he added the last two words to avoid confusion with other Duponts who sat in the ranks of the Third Estate—found his name on the list of delegates assigned to negotiate with the clergy and nobility. His primary duty would be to report to the Third Estate on the negotiators' progress.

After days of intense discussions Pierre rose to say that nothing had been accomplished. He attempted to blunt his colleagues' wrath by adding that the royal family had removed itself to Marly to grieve over the death of one of Louis's children. The delegates were in no mood for excuses; they decided to call the roll of all the representatives in all three estates. Those that answered would be considered present. Those who did not would be marked absent. A motion was made to proceed with the business of the Estates General: the rejuvenation of France. Pierre joined in the unanimous approval.

Dupont de Nemours was assigned to a committee to consider the credentials of the delegates. He found that the representatives from Brittany demanded that no law passed by the Estates General be considered valid until the Breton Parliament also approved it. Dupont judged the demand unacceptable; he believed that only centralized authority would bring France back from the brink of economic chaos. He attacked the Breton mandate fiercely on the floor of the Estates. Accusations flew at him: his opponents claimed his objections were a guise to serve the aristocratic interests of the nobility, of which he was a part.

Pierre's confidence was shaken. After the session ended he hastened to the Café Amaury on the Avenue de Saint-Cloud, where the Brittany delegates congregated, to plead his views. In minutes he was jeered into silence and out of the café. A few months later the faces he had confronted in the Avenue de Saint-Cloud reappeared as the charter members of a bloodthirsty group called the Jacobins. High on their list of expendable Frenchmen was the balding delegate from Nemours.

Louis XVI was out riding to the hounds on the day the Estates General reconstituted itself as the National Assembly of France. The Abbé Sieyès, a renegade priest and author of the pamphlet that asked, "What is the Third Estate? Nothing. What does it aspire to be? Everything!" had congratulated Pierre Dupont in the pamphlet's second edition as a man dedicated to bringing orderly reforms to the French government. When the priest thundered from his delegate's seat that the Estates General must turn itself into a truly legislative body, Pierre roared his assent.

A friend of Pierre's, the astronomer Bailly, was nominated as the Assembly's first president, in addition to his new post as mayor of Paris. Pierre stood behind Bailly's election. Jacques Necker, who had been dismissed by Louis and then recalled as a last resort in the nation's financial struggle, trembled: the bourgeoisie of the Third Estate were threatening the very sovereignty of the king.

Necker sought out Louis on his hunting trip and pleaded that the monarch control the Estates General before it became impossible to overrule. Louis decided to call a royal session of the delegates, at which he would speak, for June 22, 1789. On the twentieth the representatives arrived at the delegates' hall for their usual day's work to find the doors locked and royal guards barring the way inside. Placards posted on the building proclaimed the meeting place closed while preparations for the king's appearance were being made.

Enraged, the delegates gathered on the steps. If force could be used to bar them from inside their meeting room, then force might be used to make them disband. As a body, they charged to a nearby tennis court, convoked a session of the National Assembly, and drew up a pact not to disband until France had a formal constitution guaranteeing the rights of man. In his turn, Pierre Dupont de Nemours signed the Tennis Court Oath.

Pierre set his final solution to France's ills before the National Assembly: seize all church property and income, he said, then sell some of the land and retire the national debt.

A gasp arose from the clergy, then a cataclysmic response. How dare a country bumpkin tamper with the property of the keepers of the Lord's flocks? Let the state sink into poverty: God's kingdom must prevail!

Up from his hard bench rose the lame priest, Talleyrand, to muster all his force behind Pierre's bold proposal. He, a member of the clergy, saw the need to nationalize church lands, and he would suffer along with his holy brethren. Listen to delegate Dupont, he urged, for he is not a radical, but, rather, a reasonable man, an open supporter of the monarchy, a member of the leading group of royalists, the Society of 1789, who all—Lafayette and Sieyès included—support Pierre's idea.

A single speech even by Talleyrand would not have spurred the delegates into confiscating the church's wealth. He had lobbied secretly for weeks among the most powerful representatives. He could, at any time, have brought the matter before the Assembly, at the risk of losing support from many quarters. A pawn had been needed. Pierre had made dozens of monotonous speeches to the delegates that often contained strange ideas which were generally disregarded. Talleyrand had brought the idea of confiscating church property to Pierre's attention in a casual conversation. Soon afterward it reached the rostrum of the Assembly. Within ten days the church's property had become the state's and, purposely or not, Pierre had in some measure avenged the Protestant Duponts who had been tortured and persecuted for their religious beliefs.

Pierre's popularity increased. He believed in, and preached, constitutional monarchy as the ultimate government for France. He and his fellow monarchists held a strong hand, at least for the time being; nearly all the delegates feared that removing the king would make the uneducated masses of peasants uncontrollable. If the bourgeoisie could retain control of the government the people's historic allegiance to the king would make them pliable. Pierre's political beliefs did little damage to his reputation. Except by the clergy, he was considered a moderate, and his moderation provoked no one in power.

The National Assembly elected Pierre its president in August, 1790, a post held only for fifteen days to keep any one man from gaining too much power. The delegates had rewarded his work on eleven important committees, if not his droning voice at the podium. Pierre believed, along with most of the other members of the National Assembly, that a new France would be created out of the old without either violence or bloodshed.

Thomas Jefferson watched the people of Paris attack the Bastille. He witnessed the destruction of public order and law that heralds the crumbling of a social system; he saw starvation and disease creep among the masses. He packed his belongings and left France: Benjamin Franklin's successor had failed in his mission. He grasped Pierre Dupont's hand warmly on his last day in Paris and promised that they would remain close friends.

From across the Atlantic, Jefferson wrote Pierre of the difficulties in the new United States. There were enormous problems in feeding the people, establishing trade, and stabilizing the government. But, he added, they were the troubles of youth, sure to disappear when the nation matured. Pierre could imagine a new world, free from centuries of treaties and alliances and monarchic dynasties so entwined that even the loyalties of his own king now had to be questioned.

Pierre had followed his principles in the National Assembly, and days after he relinquished the Assembly's presidency he had fallen from popularity by opposing the issuance of paper money to replace gold. He damned the *assignats* from the podium as inflationary and destructive of the nation's already weak economy. Outside the Assembly's meeting hall a crowd of angry Parisians attempted to drown him in the Seine; only a passing squad of police saved his life. Thomas Jefferson's new nation across the sea became steadily more attractive.

The ship *Missouri* brought Pierre more news of America. Late in 1789, the National Assembly recalled France's ambassador to the United States. His entourage, including Victor Dupont, returned with him. Victor recounted to his father and brother the wonders of the New World, and his exploits in it. He had partaken of the rich American life, growing fat and content outside Paris's constricting social customs. He had become friendly with many of the nation's leading thinkers and politicians; he had become intimate with Alexander Hamilton, drunk toasts at George Washington's inauguration, paid homage at Benjamin Franklin's bedside. He had traveled the backwoods of New York State, lived briefly among hardy pioneers, acquired their habit of speaking their minds without fear of a king's police. He had drunk the sweet new wine of liberty.

Back in France, Victor took to strutting about Paris, ready to join any quarrel that happened by, even political arguments between soldiers and civilians. He kept his sword about his waist; he drew it readily. Soon the son of the moderate delegate from Nemours became widely known as *Victor l'intrépide:* Victor the Fearless.

Pierre recognized the danger immediately. If his elder son were ever to reach his twenty-third birthday alive, he must be silenced. New York society had sharpened Victor's tongue; it might just be the barb to drive Pierre himself out of the political arena and into serious trouble with the people of Paris. Pierre lectured and warned Victor; Victor refused to heed his father's advice. Pierre banished Victor to Bois-des-Fosses, to look after the estate and stay out of trouble. If his son wished to shout his views in public, a village square was much more appropriate than the center of Paris.

But Victor had become too popular for Pierre to keep him isolated. The people of Nemours elected him to a provincial assembly where, due to a rule that all delegates be at least twenty-five years old, Victor was refused his seat. The peasants of Nemours did not desert their newest hero; Victor was appointed the district's representative to the Fête of the Federation in Paris, a celebration marking the first anniversary of the fall of the Bastille.

Pierre refused to have his son walking freely about the city. He appealed to Lafayette, newly named commander of the National Guard: would his compatriot find Victor a place among his subordinates? Since Victor had already been commissioned a lieutenant in the militia, Lafayette named him an aide-de-camp. Victor Marie du Pont de Nemours— he reveled in splitting the syllables of his last name and adding the aristocratic de Nemours to it—took to shouting his views at the side of France's most revered military hero.

In a very few weeks Lafayette decided that Victor's boldness was less than helpful in the impossible task of keeping order in revolutionary France. When the National Assembly appointed a new minister to the United States Pierre and Lafayette found Victor a place in the ambassador's retinue. Victor protested that he had been promised the next vacant secretaryship to Germany; the opening might come up in only two or three months. But Pierre felt that even so short a delay might endanger his son's life, and perhaps his own. Within days Victor was out of France, aboard a ship bound for Philadelphia. With his other son bent over account books at Lavoisier's side, Pierre felt, mistakenly, that he could draw his political breath more easily now.

Powerful Jacobins, urged on by their ruthless leader, Robespierre, twice took the floor of the radical club's meetings to denounce Dupont de Nemours for his reactionary ideals and faithfulness to the king—which meant, of course, fickleness to the people. Each time, Pierre appeared to answer the charges; his words were met first by silence, then angry jeers.

Pierre's physiocratic ideals sat him on a political fence. True to the doctrines of François Quesnay, Pierre advocated renunciation of feudal rights and privileges. But he also demanded that the monarchy be kept intact and in power. For the first he was praised; for the second, damned.

The monarchists were losing power; the common people believed that the Assembly was in league with the nobility to deprive them of their security, rights, and food: why else would Lafayette's National Guardsmen ride, swords flashing, into the angry crowds surging through Paris? Robespierre reigned in Paris. His powerful radical faction grew daily in number; its members had taken to wearing blood red bonnets as symbols of their political feelings.

As the summer of 1791 ended the red hats could be seen everywhere in Paris. Pierre found little support for his views, even among old colleagues like Lafayette, Talleyrand, Bailly, and Sieyès: each had his own head to protect. The National Assembly's avowed purpose, to create a constitution for France, neared reality. By September the document was finished. On the first day of the month Pierre stood before the Assembly with a motion.

"Now that the constitution is finished," he said, "I ask that it can in no way be changed." The delegates roared their approval.

Louis XVI reluctantly signed the document into law and secretly informed the other European monarchs that he had done so only to save his family's lives. The constitution called for election of a new representative body for the nation, a Legislative Assembly; the National

Assembly prepared to disband. Exhausted by two years of intrigues and unrest, the delegates heard last-minute motions from the floor. One came from Robespierre, his ashen complexion even more pale than usual: to insure that no one involved in writing the constitution benefited from it politically, he said, let us resolve that no delegate here be allowed to stand for election to the Legislative Assembly. The proposal seemed truly patriotic, since Robespierre himself would fall under its provisions. The motion was easily passed.

Pierre blanched at Robespierre's words: his political career was now surely ended. The tired men of the Assembly did not realize that Robespierre and his Jacobins could now dictate from Paris. Many of the delegates, in fact, seemed relieved that their years as representatives were over; they cared little that the Legislative Assembly would be composed of inexperienced amateurs Robespierre might bend to his will without difficulty. But Pierre did not find the courage to debate the Jacobin's proposal. The National Assembly passed Robespierre's motion and adjourned.

Pierre trudged wearily from the Assembly's meeting hall. He had quit his government jobs and renounced the income from them as a gesture of his support for economy in government. He was devoid of political influence, left behind by the onrush of the revolution and Robespierre's wily maneuvering. He was, once again, unemployed and nearly destitute. Pierre limped slowly through the garbage-cluttered, winding streets of Paris. By the time he reached his apartment, in the Avenue de Saint-Cloud, a new resolve had formed in his mind. He would spend the remainder of his life plying the trade Benjamin Franklin had followed at the start of his: as a printer and publisher of books. He might be neither influential nor famous, but he would at least escape the wrath of Robespierre. Like thousands of other unfortunate Frenchmen, Pierre failed to hear the sound of hammers constructing the guillotine.

# 7

F ALL CAME EARLY to Paris in 1792. By the first day of August
  dead leaves were piled against the marble walls of the Tuileries, the
Parisian residence of Louis XVI. Since their abortive attempt to flee
France a month earlier, Louis and Marie Antoinette had found the
Tuileries more prison than palace.

Late on the morning of August 10, a small procession passed through
the tall doors of the Tuileries, led by Louis himself. The king, queen,
their daughter, and a son destined never to ascend the throne of Charlemagne huddled against the palace walls and began the short walk to the
Manège, a converted riding school where the Legislative Assembly held
its meetings. On the other side of the Tuileries, a battle raged between
eight hundred Swiss Guardsmen, Louis's last remaining loyal army unit,
and thousands of French National Guardsmen from Marseilles and
Brest.

Angry mobs of citizens threatened to make Louis's walk to the
Manège a funeral march; the people had gathered through the previous
night and early morning to await the victory of the National Guardsmen, ransack the Tuileries for Marie Antoinette's legendary jewels, and
murder the king and queen. Louis spied a familiar face in the crowd. A
short, spindly man in his forties, adept with a sword despite a marked
limp and advancing gout, pushed his way through the crowd.

"Ah, Monsier Dupont," Louis said. "One always finds you where one
has need of you."

With a band of fifteen ragged men, Pierre Samuel Dupont de
Nemours, counselor of state, former president of the National Assem-
bly, of late a printer by trade, had come to save his king. Since April,
Pierre had drilled his small band of fighters, loyal monarchists all,
grandly named by him the Chasseurs and Grenadiers of the Army of
Paris, for a single mission: to protect the lives of the royal family.

The Grenadiers arrayed themselves around Louis. Amid a flurry of
bullets and blades the king made his way to the Manège, threw himself

on the mercy of the Assembly, and surrendered the oldest throne in Europe. Pierre gathered what remained of his band of fighters, including his younger son, Eleuthère Irénée, and marched them quietly down the narrow streets leading away from the Tuileries, as though they were a band of National Guard irregulars. He and Irénée bade the other Grenadiers a hasty farewell in the Rue Neuve des Petits Champs and melted into the crowds; no time could be spared to mourn their seven dead comrades. Pierre was a well-known figure in Paris and had very likely been recognized defending Louis and his family. With the monarch out of the way, the radically controlled Assembly, dominated by Robespierre's Jacobins, would hunt down the enemies of the revolution.

Maximilien de Robespierre, in the name of Revolutionary Virtue, dispatched men on a house-to-house search for Pierre Dupont. Irénée heard of the Jacobin's orders and persuaded his father to seek a hiding place safer than the family printing establishment, where since the adjournment of the National Assembly father and son had labored.

Pierre appealed to his royalist friends; none would risk harboring a most hunted fugitive of the revolution. He considered fleeing to Bois-des-Fosses but realized that Robespierre would not be satisfied with his exile. Philippe Harmand, Victor and Irénée's former tutor, now supervisor of the Dupont printshop, offered to ask a friend, Jerome Lalande, to hide Pierre in the dome of the Paris astronomical observatory, which Lalande ran.

Lalande agreed. In the barren dome of the observatory Pierre slept on the floor, ate dry bits of bread smuggled to him in the pockets of Harmand's coat, and listened to his employee relate news of the revolution—none of it, from Pierre's viewpoint, very good.

Three days after the battle at the Tuileries the royal family, stripped of titles and power, was imprisoned in the Temple, a medieval tower surrounded by a ditch and built of unscalable walls. Four days later the Assembly yielded to public and Jacobin pressure and set up a special court to try the "criminals" who had defended the king on August 10. Within a week three had been condemned to death; before the end of the month Paris's nine jails held twenty-six hundred prisoners. Revolutionary justice had begun.

On August 20, General Lafayette, having failed to inspire the troops under his command to march on Paris and resurrect the monarchy, stepped across the French border into Austrian exile. With him went a young military architect named Bureaux de Pusy.

Three days after Lafayette's defection the Prussian army under the Duke of Brunswick culminated an eleven-day march by capturing, with little resistance, the French city of Longwy. Seven days later the commandant of French troops at Verdun placed a gun to his forehead and blew out his brains. Verdun fell; foreign troops were less than one hundred miles from the locked gates of Paris. Philippe Harmand received orders to report to his National Guard unit, and Pierre's meager supply of food stopped.

The people of Paris rioted in fear of Prussian conquest. In the confusion the city's gates were left open. News of the disorders reached Pierre in his hideout. Weak from hunger and inactivity, Pierre decided to flee Paris or die in the streets trying. He descended through the deserted observatory, walked slowly and safely past the tall gates of the city, and trudged the ten miles from Paris to the village where Philippe Harmand maintained a small cottage.

During his youth Pierre had studied medicine for a few weeks. Now he played the country doctor, an eyeshade pulled low over his face, treating the minor ills of the peasants who lived near Harmand's cottage. In the long solitary evenings he wrote a memoir, in the form of a letter to his children, of how a watchmaker's penniless son migrated to the most inner chambers of national power and the confidence of kings. Soon, he believed, Robespierre's henchmen would discover his hiding place and disguise, and he would ride the tumbril to the guillotine. He prepared himself for death, resigned to his fate, but, thanks to Philippe Harmand, not sad.

In his last visit to Pierre at the observatory Harmand had brought a bit of good news to the fugitive. A year earlier Irénée—over his father's objections—had married a woman of common birth, Sophie Madeleine Dalmas. On the last day of August, Sophie had given birth to a healthy girl, named, out of a desperate need for hope amid the chaos of the revolution, Victorine Elizabeth. Should the justice of the revolution descend upon him, Pierre knew at least that the Dupont blood would continue.

The Committee of General Security, run by Robespierre, issued an order for the arrest of Pierre Dupont on July 13, 1793. Pierre had eluded capture for nearly a year. He had decided that Bois-des-Fosses would be as safe as Harmand's cottage, and he had developed an over-whelming desire to see his granddaughter.

Unknown to Pierre, spies had followed him from Harmand's house to Nemours. They reported to Paris that Citizen Dupont treated the local people's illnesses and spent much time in meditation and writing; his political activities were nil.

On a stormy summer night a company of soldiers burst into Bois-des-Fosses, dragged Pierre from his bed, and shackled him in a carriage for the ride to Paris. Pierre's daughter-in-law, Sophie, begged the soldiers to allow her to accompany him; he was ill and aged, she said. The soldiers refused. In an open wagon Sophie drove through the rain to Paris to tell Irénée, working in the printing house, of his father's imprisonment.

Pierre outlined the plan to his fellow prisoners: they would adopt the ancient order of battle. Since, in all, twelve of them occupied the same cellblock, they would form a wedge: one man in front, two behind him, three behind them, four in the rear. The other two inmates, chosen as the strongest, would guard the flanks.

The alarm bell had sounded hours earlier and rumors flared, first that Robespierre had been put in chains, then that he had regained the upper hand. But information came slowly to the men imprisoned at La Force, and it was rarely reliable. Still, Robespierre's downfall might signal an attack by the mobs on the prison; Pierre judged that they must have a plan for their defense, even if they would be armed only with pocket-knives and table legs. He asked his fellow inmates to join in a rehearsal of his plan. They refused; all knew, however, that if an attack came, they would follow Citizen Dupont's orders.

Pierre had found prison life bearable. On the day he was seized he wrote to Sophie asking that she send him a bed, four towels and two washcloths, writing paper, a straw armchair, a small hairbrush, and a box to hold his belongings. Pierre set up classes in political economics for his fellow prisoners. He talked with the men at length, inquring into their health, their families, the state of their personal affairs. He strolled with them in the little prison courtyard every afternoon. Sophie, staying in Paris even though Victorine Elizabeth remained at Bois-des-Fosses, came each day to the prison gates disguised as a peasant woman, bearing fresh food for her father-in-law.

Pierre had been in prison a week when Robespierre fell from power: for once, the rumors that reached La Force were true. He said goodbye to all of the eleven other inmates in the days that followed. Robespierre's followers made no haste to release him; they feared that his time in prison had already turned him into a living political martyr. Irénée petitioned and bribed numerous officials. A month later the prison's turnkey called the name of Citizen Dupont, and Pierre walked into freedom. For the moment, the revolution had ceased to covet the physiocrat's head.

Gabrielle Josephine de La Fite de Pelleporte, daughter of a marquis and brother to three counts who had fled France at the start of the revolution, thought that Victor du Pont was the most handsome man she had ever seen. Victor returned home from the United States in 1793 and, at the height of the Reign of Terror, needed to prove his loyalty to the revolution. He applied for a position on the police force in Chevannes; at the end of August he was named a gendarme.

Victor believed that a policeman's uniform looked well on him. Gabrielle, whom he met at a party in Nemours, thought it disgusting: she hated the revolution and all it stood for. It had cost her family its fortune, lands, and titles. She could no longer practice the religion of her ancestors and her now dead king; Catholicism had been outlawed.

Gaby, as Victor called her, although she preferred her second given name, Josephine, fell in love with the elder Dupont son despite his uniform. Pierre was pleased when Victor announced that he intended to marry the noblewoman. Gabrielle was not. She loved Victor but could not bear being wed to anyone who wore the uniform of the revolution. And she would never submit to marriage by civil ceremony; she could conjure no worse sin than entering wedlock without Catholic rites.

Victor, by dyeing his skin green with spinach juice, convinced the revolutionary committee in Chevannes that they ought to issue him a medical discharge from the police force. He searched Nemours for a priest who would perform the ceremony; discovery meant death for them all under the guillotine's blade. The Abbé—supposedly the *former* Abbé—of Branles agreed to marry Victor and Gabrielle after Victor vowed that the ceremony would be carried out in the strictest secrecy: not even Gabrielle would know that it was to take place.

A well-concealed room at Bois-des-Fosses was chosen. Inside, Pierre, a distant cousin called to serve as witness, and the priest waited. Victor fetched Gaby from the parlor, where she and her sister had been watching visitors play backgammon. Gabrielle pleaded with Victor to call her sister in to the ceremony. Victor said no: it was marriage now and in this way, or never. Gabrielle felt that she was taking the most important step in her life under "circumstances so precipitate, so incomprehensible to myself, that I could scarcely believe it."

The marriage remained secret for three weeks. Gaby continued to live with her sister, a former nun, at a retreat for ex-Catholics. Victor remained at Bois-des-Fosses. When the proper documents had been obtained the couple presented themselves in Chevannes for a civil ceremony under the laws of the revolution. Gabrielle noted, with disdain, that their union was solemnized by a former carpenter.

Pierre strode from La Force directly to his printing plant, housed in a former convent where kidnapped Protestant children had, before the revolution, been taught the principles of Catholic life. Irénée and Sophie welcomed him jubilantly; Pierre removed his coat and set about planning a new magazine that he would edit and publish.

He had many debts to pay. Bois-des-Fosses had been mortgaged, to Antoine Lavoisier, for enough money to buy the printing presses and paper and type and ink Pierre had needed to begin his publishing enterprise. The guillotine had claimed Lavoisier's head and, on the same day, that of his wife's father. Madame Lavoisier had turned recluse since her husband's and father's deaths. She was, in the years following Robespierre's downfall and the end of the Reign of Terror, the most eligible widow in Paris: rich, educated, cultured, and heir to Lavoisier's reputation.

Pierre grew tired of paying off the mortgage on Bois-des-Fosses. His new magazine, *L'Historien*, sold well and, as a survivor of Robespierre's regime, he became a celebrated, and respected, fount of administrative knowledge. The new and prestigious Institute of France elected him to its morality and politics section. Each week Pierre met with other scholars in the great hall of the Paris observatory, one hundred feet beneath where he had hidden from the revolution's vengeance. The people of Nemours chose him as their delegate to the Council of Ancients, the upper house of France's new legislature.

Pierre's sons were both happily married. Sophie had given birth to another daughter, Evalina Gabrielle. Josephine became pregnant early in 1795. Pierre began to dislike being without a wife almost as much as he loathed owing Madame Lavoisier money. He decided to remedy both situations at once: he asked his friend's widow to marry him. Madame

Lavoisier spurned Pierre and left for Switzerland to escape his daily calls at her home, first arguing with him over back payments on the mortgage she held. Pierre winced under her insult but was overcome by the urge to find a wife.

"I wish I could forget her," he wrote to Irénée soon after Madame Lavoisier left France. "But her husband, who was my friend, entrusted her to my care when he was about to die. . . . Sometimes I think I will end it all by writing to Citizeness Poivre, getting her to come here, and marrying her. But that is a very radical step to take."

Pierre took it. Madame Françoise Robin Poivre was the widow of another old friend of Pierre's, Pierre Poivre, former governor of Ile-de-France, a French colony. Citizeness Poivre accepted Pierre's proposal at once and rode from her country house to Paris to be wed. She brought with her an excellent pension and a beautiful daughter, named Ile-de-France, who was married to Bureaux de Pusy, Lafayette's fellow prisoner in Austria. All of chic Paris applauded the marriage of one of its leading publishers and public servants. Pierre paused to celebrate only briefly; his new wife's inheritance was not sufficient to pay off the mortgage on Bois-des-Fosses.

On September 4, 1797, three members of the French Directory, which ran the government in cabinet style, bolted under Napoleon Bonaparte's influence and overthrew the ruling moderate faction. Days earlier Pierre had ended his term as president of the Council of Ancients. Napoleon's radical directors wanted desperately to dispose of Pierre and his conservative supporters. Napoleon ordered that they suppress L'Historien, which frequently took issue with the wisdom of pursuing the wars that gave Bonaparte his power. Pierre and Irénée, working quietly in their printing house, were arrested and carried off to La Force.

That same day Pierre's name headed the list of prisoners destined for passage aboard ship to French Guiana, the penal colony that would earn fame as Devil's Island. Napoleon Bonaparte had chosen Citizen Dupont as the first casualty in his bid to become Emperor of France.

Word of Pierre's arrest and planned deportation spread quickly to his friends. On the floor of the Council of Five Hundred, the Council of Ancients' larger sister, Jean-Marie Chénier, one of the Council's most powerful members, deplored the arrest of Pierre Dupont: he was an old man, nearing eighty, Chénier said, exaggerating by more than twenty years, and an outstanding supporter of the French Republic. To deport Pierre, Chénier added, would be an act worthy of the Reign of Terror, but not of civilized France. Germaine Necker de Staël, pressed by her newest lover, Talleyrand, hurried about Paris entreating friends and former bedmates to use their influence in Pierre's behalf. Late on the night of Pierre's imprisonment, Napoleon's Directors decided that Citizen Dupont and his son did not, in truth, belong among the steerage passengers destined for Devil's Island.

Just after dawn Pierre and Irénée heard a key turn in the lock of their cell at La Force and were surprised and pleased to find themselves set free—until they reached the Dupont printing house. During the night, on orders from Bonaparte, a gang of men had broken into the office, scattered papers and type, and smashed the presses. Memories of the Reign of Terror echoed in Pierre's mind. A few days later, pleading ill health, he resigned from the Council of Ancients.

Irénée Dupont had spent eight years running the family printing business. He was willing to rebuild the presses and start anew, but Papa Dupont felt the political climate in Paris too close for himself and his children: they needed cleaner air to breathe, he decided, the air of the United States.

Pierre sent Irénée to see Robert Fulton, then experimenting with submarines in the Seine, who was an old correspondent of Pierre's. Fulton was encouraging: good farmland could be bought for as little as ten francs an acre in Virginia, where ownership of a single piece of property made one a citizen. A sizable farm's products could be sold easily in the markets of Philadelphia and Baltimore. Irénée returned to his father convinced they could succeed as planters in America.

Pierre's imagination soared; he would organize a huge company, Dupont and Sons, to take over a large tract of Virginia land. He would reign as feudal baron over millions of acres. When the venture became profitable enough he would ask for separate status from Virginia, and the Dupont family would own a kingdom.

Irénée printed and sent out advertising circulars. Pierre journeyed to Holland and Switzerland to raise money. He needed, he believed, four million francs to make his plan work. But Swiss and Dutch bankers found no reason to sink cash into Pierre's company. After eighteen months, Pierre discovered that he was 3,800,000 francs short of his goal.

Since the end of the Terror, Victor du Pont had found his diplomatic talents valued by the rulers of the new France. He and Gabrielle had been posted to the United States, first to Philadelphia, then to Charleston, South Carolina. They had encountered yellow fever and, worse for Victor's career, the growing anti-French sentiments of the Americans. Victor brought his family back to France in 1799, after four disappointing years as charge d'affaires in Charleston, to find himself deeply embroiled in his father's plans. Pierre had named Victor one of the new company's principal partners, praising his son's diplomatic expertise and his contacts in American commercial and business circles. Victor attempted to convince Pierre that his plan would not work. He argued that land prices were skyrocketing in the United States, that the government looked askance at any foreign plan to establish a business in the country, that the newly passed Alien Act, a piece of legislation created by President John Adams, made obtaining citizenship difficult and deportation, at the whim of the government, a possibility.

Pierre was in no mood to be discouraged; he told Victor not to worry. He was raising the needed capital and lobbying to have all three Dupont men named *savants voyageur*—traveling scholars—by the Institute of France. Irénée had been studying botany at the National Gardens to justify the Institute appointment. A prestigious mission for a respected intellectual establishment would cover all their political tracks, making them immune to attack by the American government and allowing them to return to France if necessary. And, of course, Pierre expected help from his old friend Thomas Jefferson: his American Plan, as Pierre called it, would surely succeed. Victor resigned himself to following his father and brother back across the Atlantic Ocean.

Pierre charged Victor with finding a vessel to carry the Dupont family across the sea. Victor secured passage aboard the *American Eagle*, a commercial schooner wasting away in a French port, held there by order of Napoleon. He used his influence with the diplomatic corps to free the ship; in return, the captain agreed to transport the Dupont entourage, its baggage—including two pianos—and its hopes, for a modest sum.

The *American Eagle* was not a very seaworthy ship. After two years in port barnacles encrusted its hull. The captain was able to find only a cargo of salt to transport on his return across the Atlantic; the schooner's torn sails and leaking hull encouraged no one to provide him with better freight for its hold. But the captain did not wish to linger making repairs; he had seen enough of French hospitality.

On October 2, 1799, the *American Eagle* set sail for North America. The winds were not favorable; the captain proved himself a poor navigator. Seldom was the ship on course. Twice, British ships bound for Europe came upon the *Eagle* and gave her captain provisions and bearings. More often than not, the flag of distress flew from a mast to attract help.

Passage by sailing ship across the Atlantic usually required less than thirty days. After two months at sea, fighting broke out between the crew and the *Eagle*'s passengers. With his sword drawn Pierre defended his party of eighteen: Victor, Gabrielle, and their two children; Irénée, Sophie, and their three offspring; Pierre's step-daughter, Ile-de-France Pusy and her infant child, born only days before the ship's departure; Charles Dalmas, Sophie's brother; three nurses; and two male servants.

Pierre struggled to keep the family's spirits high. By day he played with the children, wrote poetry, and plotted the success of his new company with his sons. At night he stood armed guard over the family's belongings. Victor and Irénée did their best to hide their fears of being lost or shipwrecked from the women and children, with little success. The food from the British ships ran out, and the Duponts resorted to eating a soup of boiled rats to keep from starving.

After ninety-three days at sea the *American Eagle* docked in Newport, Rhode Island, far from its destination of New York Bay. The hungry passengers ran to the nearest house, which they found warmly lit but empty; its occupants were at church, but a fulsome dinner awaited their return, warming over a roaring fire. Pierre led his band of emigrants inside, seated them at the dinner table, and instructed the servants to dish out the food. After eating his fill Pierre found himself guilty of a crime and fined himself one coin of gold, which he left at the head of the table. He hurried his family away from the house to search for the nearest inn.

Pierre had paid a high price for one meal, but he had robbed the house's owners of more than a dinner: the calendar read January 1, 1800. The Dupont family had stolen a celebration.

*Part Two*

# THIS PEACEFUL FRIEND
# OF LIBERTY

## 8

MADAME FRANÇOISE ROBIN DUPONT sailed for the United States two weeks before Pierre led the main party of Dupont emigrants aboard the *American Eagle*. Her crossing had been uneventful and swift. In New York City letters to Pierre from George Washington and Thomas Jefferson awaited her. Washington, retired at Mount Vernon, greeted Pierre on behalf of all the citizens of the United States. Jefferson, now the Vice President, welcomed his old diplomatic comrade warmly. Unaware of Pierre's plight at sea, Jefferson expressed relief that his friend's ordeal in France had ended and that he had landed safely on American soil.

Françoise did not despair over her husband's life when the *American Eagle* lagged weeks behind its scheduled arrival. Pierre had survived the wrath of the revolution; a bad sea voyage would not end his life. Calmly, she selected a home for the Dupont family and business in the New World. Pierre had envisioned an elegant Manhattan townhouse as a suitable base for his scheme to colonize a part of Virginia. Françoise found the bricks of New York City dearly expensive; a townhouse would devour most of the funds Pierre had wangled from European investors. She chose, instead, a ramshackle wooden farmhouse on the coast of New Jersey, west and south of New York.

After their stolen feast and a night in a roadside inn, the Dupont band of immigrants set out for New York City. The January winds were harsh; nine days later Pierre embraced Françoise in her New York hotel and read the letters from Washington and Jefferson. Aboard the *American Eagle* he had planned the streets and buildings, homes and schools, farms and factories that would distinguish his wilderness estate. He had chosen a name: Pontiania. It would commemorate the first ruler of the world's only physiocratic state.

Jefferson warned Pierre in his letter that land speculation could be dangerous. Many, the Vice President wrote, had plunked down hard cash and been fleeced; many more would be before the land fever ended. The Virginian omitted more serious barriers to Pierre's plan. President John Adams, in a rage against everything and everyone French, had actually signed an arrest order for the senior Dupont, should he ever be found on American soil. The warrant had expired before Pierre landed in Rhode Island, but the sentiment had not. The people of the United States feared that the nightmare of Europe's past might become America's future. Stringent laws had been enacted to prevent foreign ownership of land and, except in Virginia, citizenship was difficult to acquire.

Pierre decided to heed Jefferson's warning. He informed Victor and Irénée that the plan to build Pontiania would be abandoned. In its place the family would establish a great house of commerce. They would, first, settle themselves in their new home in New Jersey and then construct a scheme that would make them invaluable international agents to the governments of the world.

Twenty acres of fertile land, promising mounds of vegetables each summer, surrounded the house Madame Dupont had purchased. Streams on the property glimmered with fish; deer and other game wandered through nearby forests. Pierre assessed the house and land and pronounced it fit for his family. He named it Good Stay; here the Duponts would set their roots and flourish.

Good Stay thrust upward from a windswept beak of land on the edge of the New Jersey peninsula. From his bedroom window Pierre could see richly-laden schooners tacking up New York Bay, their masts flying the colors of the United States, their cargoes bound for frontier settlements up the Hudson River. The bay reminded Pierre of the Seine where it broadened at Rouen before reaching into the sea, but here, unlike in France, government agents would not pound on his door at midnight, to drag his family off to prison or exile on a remote tropical island. Pierre exuded confidence: the very air seemed filled with liberty and opportunity.

He outlined to Victor and Irénée his ideas for their new venture. An international house of commerce, designed to deal with foreign governments, must first have the backing of its own. He dispatched Victor to New York to see Alexander Hamilton. Hamilton had introduced Victor to American society when the elder Dupont son first came to the United States as an unpaid attaché of the French diplomatic mission. As John Adams's Secretary of the Treasury, Hamilton could help counter the

President's dislike of the Duponts' French blood. Victor offered Hamilton a retainer and the Secretary of the Treasury became the Dupont family's first lawyer in the United States. Victor hurried home with the news; Pierre was jubilant.

Hamilton advised that at least one of the Duponts become an American citizen. Pierre instructed Victor to journey to Virginia, buy a small house, and petition the state's legislature for citizenship. Victor hesitated. His wife, Gabrielle, had given birth to an infant girl shortly before the family left France. The child had died. After the horrors of the sea voyage Gaby had slipped into a deep depression. Pierre urged Victor not to worry about his wife; she would be well cared for by Françoise and Irénée's wife, Sophie. Victor prepared to ride a carriage to Virginia.

Pierre announced that he himself would undertake the most important task before them: securing the backing of the United States government. He would visit the American heads of state in Philadelphia. He would remind John Adams of his fervor for liberty and tell him that his youngest grandchild, Irénée's firstborn son, brought into the world while the Duponts still lived in France, had been named Alfred Victor Philadelphe in honor of his adopted homeland's capital city. Pierre believed that his long association with Thomas Jefferson would convince the government to conduct its foreign trade through his new house of commerce, and that John Adams would be unable to ignore Pierre's many contacts throughout Europe.

Adams received Pierre coldly, tossed aside his compliments and pleadings, and asked if Madame Dupont's son-in-law, Bureaux de Pusey, might be interested in designing fortifications for New York City. Otherwise, the United States government had no business to do with the Duponts. Pierre found himself dismissed quickly. His hopes dashed, he boarded a carriage back to Good Stay, hardly able to believe that his years of learning to wangle patronage from noblemen and kings at Versailles had had little effect on John Adams.

Victor returned from Alexandria, Virginia, a landowner and citizen. He noticed that Pierre had become depressed and had lapsed into dreaming once again of Pontiania. Gabrielle, although her spirits had improved, clearly hated living in the country. Over the years of Victor's diplomatic career she had grown accustomed to the luxuries of city life. She had no desire to grow vegetables or hunt game.

Victor suggested to his father and brother that part of the family move from New Jersey to Manhattan. After only a few weeks' living in Good Stay the family was accumulating servants and even slaves. The crowded conditions had already grown irksome. At best, the land surrounding the house might produce a few bushels of wheat to be sold at market in the city. Irénée, Victor proposed, could be left in New Jersey to run Good Stay; he would be of little use in a house of commerce, where the diplomatic talents of Pierre and Victor would spell the difference between failure and success. Irénée offered no objections. Pierre pronounced the matter decided. They would acquire a home in New York's business district and issue a prospectus announcing the formation of Du Pont Father, Sons, and Company, international house of commerce (the syllables of the family name looked far more impressive separated).

Irénée was pleased to be staying behind in New Jersey. He did not mind that the new company's prospectus contained pages of praise about his father and brother and only a single line adding that the younger du Pont son would, too, be available to serve the house's clients. Near Good Stay, Irénée had found gardens run by Frenchmen that shipped American plants to Paris. In the workless weeks after Pierre and Victor left, Irénée's boyhood love for the flowers and trees of Bois-des-Fosses was rekindled. He hired Dutch farmers to till the land around Good Stay and indulged in long walks through the countryside, gathering specimens of the wonderful American flora.

Evenings he gave to entertaining the many French emigrants who called to pay tribute to Pierre and his family. They seemed not to mind that Pierre and Victor were absent; if Irénée appeared endlessly sober and melancholy, Sophie was gracious, and the conversation was less likely to center around Pierre's philosophical platitudes or Victor's empty banter.

Settled French-Americans came to Good Stay, too. One, Colonel Louis de Toussard, had fought beside Lafayette in the American Revolution. When Lafayette returned to France, de Toussard decided to stay behind. He liked the United States and had left a part of himself—an arm—on an American battlefield. Toussard was an avid hunter. He told Irénée of a gunpowder mill in Pennsylvania owned by William Lane and Stephen Decatur. Their product, he said, was inferior to French powder in strength and accuracy. Often it misfired when damp. Lane and Decatur's mill was, for the moment, the only working gunpowder factory in the nation. Toussard invited Irénée to join him in a visit to the Pennsylvania mill.

Irénée was astounded at what he saw. Lane and Decatur made black powder using methods France had abandoned a century earlier. Yet the Pennsylvanians charged nearly as much for it as French powder, brought across the Atlantic, sold for. If this was the best powder Americans could produce, he, even with his rusty knowledge of the manufacturing process, could do infinitely better.

Irénée returned to Good Stay brimming with enthusiasm. He could not, he knew, rely on his father's courtly arts of intrigue and innuendo to support the du Pont family. Pierre's heart and mind, no less than those of the unfortunate Frenchmen who had ridden the tumbril to the guillotine, lay severed on different sides of revolution's sharp blade. His father had not come to America to turn boulders out of fields, and Victor, for all his desire to open a house of commerce, still hoped that France would find a place for him in its diplomatic ranks. Only he and Sophie, amid the survivors of a civilization, had learned to carve out a living—he in the family printshop; she, since the age of seventeen, running Bois-des-Fosses.

Irénée approached Pierre with a plan for a gunpowder factory of his own. Pierre scoffed at the idea. He intended to make millions trading with governments; no such fortune would rise from a gunpowder mill. It was not fit work for a du Pont, with all the dirt and complaining workers. Pierre's physiocratic ideals saw the soil as man's proper domain, or at least dealing in the products of the land. And a gunpowder mill would be useless to the grand dream he still cherished of building Pontiania.

But Pierre believed his quiet son would never be of use to Du Pont Father, Sons, and Company. He was preparing a number of proposals for Victor to take to France, plans that would make the family wealthy beyond any of their wildest fantasies. If Irénée wished it, he would add the idea for a gunpowder mill to his list of proposals, but only at its end. Irénée might accompany his brother to Paris to seek backing for his factory: none of the family funds could be spared to finance his enterprise.

Scarcely a year after the *American Eagle* deposited them in Rhode Island, Victor and Irénée boarded the *Benjamin Franklin*, bound from New York to Le Havre. Sealed in their luggage were eight proposals from Pierre to his friends and backers in Paris. Seven were grandiose schemes for reaping mountains of gold from international trade, shipping, and banking. The eighth suggested that a modest gunpowder mill be constructed on the site Irénée du Pont had chosen along the banks of a stream in the tiny, isolated state of Delaware.

Napoleon Bonaparte walked slowly through the grand hall of the Hotel Gallifet, bowing from side to side, on occasion granting a word or two to a favored subject. Guards clad in gold army uniforms, two-foot-high white feathers adorning their caps, walked before and behind him. Talleyrand, his lameness exaggerated by rheumatism and age, shuffled along near the first consul, making an introduction here, soothing a slighted citizen there.

The Hotel Gallifet, in Paris's fashionable Rue de Bac, housed Talleyrand's ministry of foreign affairs. Twelve hundred guests had assembled to honor Napoleon, at Talleyrand's invitation. Carriages began arriving at nine in the evening; not until well past dawn did the Parisian elite stop coming. Homage to Bonaparte was not governed by the hours on the clock.

The first consul noticed two men standing together, one tall, slender, almost young, the other older, portly, with a shock of brown hair that belied his age. Talleyrand dropped away with a bow: he did not need to introduce Napoleon to General Lafayette. Bonaparte asked about the health of the general's son, a soldier, who had been wounded recently in Italy. They chatted about the French army's many successful campaigns and in a few moments the first consul moved on to receive the adulation of other guests. He had not spoken to Lafayette's companion, Victor du Pont.

Victor and Irénée had arrived in Paris four days prior to Talleyrand's celebration. Everywhere, Victor found himself welcome: the du Pont name, a surviving relic of the old France, was social magic. Victor dined and danced each night until dawn, or gambled, a habit he had picked up in New York, with the rulers of French government and commerce. By day he called upon the wealthy and powerful, showing to each Pierre's elaborate proposals. Pierre wanted France to turn all the business of its island colonies to him. He would supply the French navy, provide lumber for the rebuilding of ships, sell sugar from Guadeloupe and French Guiana, and outfit Napoleon's forces for an attack on Santo Domingo. The du Pont house of commerce would market French goods in the United States, run a string of packet boats across the Atlantic, and,

Pierre suggested, handle a loan to the United States government that would ease France's trade debt to the Americans. Pierre counted his commissions for the work in tens of millions of francs each year.

The ministers and bankers listened politely to Pierre's seven proposals, urged Victor to convince his father that France would welcome the former counselor of state if he wished to return, and invited Victor to a dinner or ball. As to business for Pierre's New York firm—that was out of the question. Napoleon had returned from the disaster of his Egyptian campaign in triumph, overthrown the Directory, and seized absolute power. Tribute poured in from Europe's trembling monarchs. Talleyrand's clever treaties installed puppet governments that dared not even whisper unless Paris pulled a string. For the first time since the revolution, Victor was told again and again, France believed in herself. Why should Napoleon trade when he could conquer? Why should bankers send money abroad when the first consul had opened wide the markets of Europe? Least of all did they wish to do business with an émigré philosopher, a remnant of the old regime who had abandoned France and demanded enormous sums as the price of doing business with the house of du Pont.

Soon Victor ran out of ministers and financiers to call upon. Paris had stunned him, with its dirty streets, ragged crowds, gangs of roaming criminals, and women parading about in bare-breasted gowns. He found himself longing for New York, with its air of cleanliness and optimism. Before he boarded the *Benjamin Franklin* in New York, Gabrielle had told him that she believed his mission was folly, a desperate clutching for business that would never be made available to the du Ponts. Victor began to agree. Even when Madame Germaine Necker de Staël, at Talleyrand's fête for Napoleon, fawned over him and introduced him to her friends as Victor the Superb, he found Parisian society as empty and difficult as dealing with Parisian bankers.

Jacques Bidermann, Pierre's largest investor, urged Victor to cross the Pyrenees into Spain: business might be better there. Talleyrand offered to provide him with a passport across the border if he would accompany the minister's former secretary as far as Bayonne. Talleyrand's man was retired now, but he would meet Lucien Bonaparte in Spain—nothing important, really, just some dreary discussion with Napoleon's brother about the Spanish colonies in North America. In April, 1801, Victor boarded a carriage for Bayonne. His traveling companion, under the guise of guiding a prominent American businessman across the Pyrenees, carried with him Napoleon Bonaparte's demand that Spain secretly cede to France its land in North America—an area equal to the original thirteen states, from which the first consul could launch an invasion of the American nation.

Irénée said goodbye to his brother in Paris. He had not accompanied Victor on his nightly forays into Parisian society, nor had he called upon businessmen during the day. Irénée had spent the months since their arrival in France at Essonnes, the national gunpowder factory a short distance from Paris, reviving old friendships and studying the newest techniques the French used to manufacture black powder.

The French government had disagreed with Pierre's assessment of his son's plan to open a gunpowder mill in the United States. Irénée had taken his proposal to Talleyrand. The foreign minister trusted Pierre's younger son; he was a man of solid character and uncomplicated purpose. Talleyrand knew that a gunpowder mill on American soil, backed by the French treasury, would sharply undermine England's trade with the United States. And he saw clearly Napoleon's bottomless greed for world power. Talleyrand had constructed the language of Bonaparte's demand that the Spanish turn over the Louisiana Territory to France. If Napoleon ever ordered an invasion of the United States, Irénée du Pont's gunpowder mill would be invaluable.

Talleyrand opened the heavily-guarded doors of Essonnes's laboratory to Irénée: the French chemists would reveal to him even their most secret new processes. Irénée needed machinery that only the French could make. Talleyrand ordered it built to his specifications. He needed men to work the mills when they were established. If they were willing to leave France, Talleyrand said, the government would be pleased to let a few of its experienced powdermakers go. And Irénée needed money, at least twelve thousand dollars, to buy machinery and land. Talleyrand guided him to open French pocketbooks.

Irénée repaid the minister's kindness with seeds from American trees and plants for his gardens. Talleyrand introduced the young powdermaker into his own circle of friends. When Josephine Bonaparte heard that Irénée had been giving away American seeds she asked him for a few to plant in her own garden. Irénée regretted that he had already given away the seeds he had brought with him but promised to send her a large assortment as soon as he returned to the United States. Josephine assured Irénée of the French government's patronage for his new enterprise.

Talleyrand suggested that Irénée spend a few days shopping for gifts to take back to his family; he himself would see that all the business preparations went well. Irénée booked passage aboard the *Franklin*, due to leave Le Havre on May 1, 1801. The minister assured him that his new company's articles of incorporation, being printed on government presses, would be ready in time for his sailing. The articles would name Irénée director of the gunpowder concern, at a salary of eighteen hundred dollars a year, give him sole right to run the business as he saw fit, and allow him to sell shares to anyone he chose: the French government would not demand ownership, even in part, as a return for its generosity.

And, as Irénée had requested, the articles of incorporation would give his gunpowder factory a name: E. I. du Pont de Nemours and Company. Neither Pierre nor Victor would be mentioned. Talleyrand agreed that the gunpowder mills should rise or fall on Irénée du Pont's strength and ability alone.

During the summer and fall of 1801, Victor learned from Talleyrand's former secretary, D'Autremont, that his visit to Lucien Bonaparte in Spain was no casual stopover on a pleasure trip: he had informed Lucien that Napoleon wanted Louisiana. D'Autremont told Victor that the first consul planned an extraordinary expedition to Santo Domingo, thirty-five thousand men under his brother-in-law, General Leclerc, with orders to decimate the rebellious slaves. From Haiti, Leclerc could easily invade the American mainland, if France owned Louisiana. The United States would be trapped in a ring of foreign domain: Canada, the Floridas, and the Louisiana Territory, each controlled by a different government. Talleyrand would then carve up America as he had Europe.

Victor left France for the United States late in November. He had been separated from his wife and family for nearly thirteen months. Yet after three days in New York he hurried Gabrielle aboard a coach that galloped day and night for Washington. On the road he explained to Gaby that he had come upon information in Europe which would make Du Pont Father, Sons, and Company a giant success. If the French government would allow him to outfit Leclerc's expedition, even a small percentage of what the ships and men would need in provisions and cargo would amount to millions of francs. He revealed his reason for asking Gabrielle to pack her finest gowns for their stay in the capital: they would be dining with the President. But first, he would consummate his arrangement with the French consul general in Washington, Louis Pichon.

Louis Pichon was one of the few Frenchmen who knew of Napoleon's plan to recapture Santo Domingo. Victor had known the diplomat when both were junior members of the French delegation to the United States. He revealed to the consul general the depth of his knowledge of Napoleon's scheme to take North America. Pichon said he would be glad to do business with Victor, when the time came to outfit Leclerc's forces—but not with Victor's father.

While Victor and Irénée visited France, Pierre had called upon Pichon in Washington. He had demanded the consul general's help in his attempts to draw patronage from the United States government. Pierre had treated him like a child, Pichon complained to Victor, ordering him about on a valet's errands and scolding him like a servant. No, France would not deal with Pierre du Pont, but if Victor were willing to leave the family business and start one of his own the entire Santo Domingo trade would be his. Victor replied that he would be happy to ease his father into retirement. Pichon added that he would be most appreciative if Victor saw fit to return a portion of his commissions to the man who had directed the Santo Domingo trade his way. Victor smiled: how else was business done? They shook hands on their agreement, and Victor hurried off to pick up Gabrielle on his way to the White House.

He had much to tell the President; many of Jefferson's French acquaintances sent their regards and best wishes on his election to the nation's highest office. Life had changed in Paris since the rise of Bonaparte, Victor said: Jefferson would not recognize the city if he saw it now. The President pushed aside Victor's views of French society; he needed desperately to know the state of French diplomacy. Rufus King, his ambassador in England, had managed to secure a copy of France's secret treaty with Spain. Few were in Victor's position to know what Bonaparte and Talleyrand truly intended: was the Treaty of San Ildefonso real, or just another of Talleyrand's clever ploys?

Jefferson felt certain that he could count on Victor to relate all he had learned in Paris and Madrid. Pierre had visited the President to press for his support of Irénée's new gunpowder mill. It would be acceptable—even correct—for Jefferson to place the weight of his office behind the powder mill, and the other du Pont family enterprises, if he could count on the unquestionable loyalty of the du Ponts to the United States.

Victor made his decision instantly. Since he had arranged with Pichon only to supply Leclerc's forces as far as Santo Domingo, he could still proclaim his loyalty to the United States and tell Jefferson all he knew. He and Gabrielle dined at the White House on five consecutive nights. Soon after they boarded a coach back to New York an astonished nation heard Thomas Jefferson speak publicly about an alliance with England, his avowed enemy, against France, his dearest friend, should Napoleon Bonaparte even whisper plans to land French soldiers on American soil.

Madame Françoise du Pont ran weeping from her husband's bedroom, a lace handkerchief pressed to her eyes. Pierre murmured that she needed only a moment to compose herself, but his voice carried little conviction. The others gathered around his desk—Victor, Irénée, Sophie, and Gabrielle—knew the truth: the grand dreams of Pierre du Pont de Nemours were near an end. Their money, more than two hundred thousand francs, had dwindled to almost nothing. Du Pont Father, Sons, and Company, since opening its office at 91 Liberty Street in New York, had done precisely no business. The family faced ruin.

Irénée, as usual in family councils, said nothing. Sophie and Gabrielle deferred to their father-in-law's wisdom as always. Victor, too, rarely spoke except to agree with Pierre. Now, however, he was on his feet, his voice decisive, his manner far from the bored detachment he typically affected. Only one course remained for the family, he said. They must separate, Irénée to build his gunpowder mill, Pierre to go whatever way he wished. He, Victor, would stay in New York and, under a new business name, Victor du Pont de Nemours and Company, bear the entire burden of the older firm's losses, both in money and reputation. He would even undertake to answer the outrage that was certain to come from Pierre's European investors.

Victor's offer carried with it a single proviso: his father was in no way to interfere in the new company. Pierre agreed at once. Exclusion from Victor's new firm carried a bitter sting, but his son's offer of a way out of his embarrassment soothed it. Pierre thanked Victor privately for so generously considering his reputation in France. Victor did not tell him that he had sacrificed Pierre on the altar of money at the demand of the French government.

# 9

I RÉNÉE DU PONT struggled against the reins of his horses, fighting to keep the careening wagon on the rutted, summer-hardened roads. Sophie sat quietly beside him, her throat parched from the billowing July dust, her face streaked with perspiration. Victorine, ten, Evalina, six, and Alfred, four, dangled their feet over the wagon's rear edge, separated from their parents by mounds of luggage and household goods.

They had endured the heat since leaving Good Stay four days earlier. Irénée had guided the wagon steadily southward through the flatlands of New Jersey and the lush hills of Pennsylvania, past Philadelphia and finally into the state of Delaware. There they met the Brandywine Creek, rushing past Chadds Ford where Washington fought the British and Lafayette stopped a muzzleload of Redcoat shot. The waters of the Brandywine twisted across the land at the bottom of a deep gorge, shaded by tall birch and willow trees, breaking into swirls of white foam over huge gray boulders.

Irénée pulled the horses to a halt beside a broad span of water. The land sloped gently, hiding the Brandywine's insistent current. Across the Creek, the shoreline arched upward in a cliff; a blanket of trees climbed to its crest and fell nearly to the water's edge. But where Irénée had stopped a plateau stretched back from the Brandywine before the hills began. He pointed to a long abandoned cabin. For now, he told Sophie, its crude walls and crumbling roof would shelter their family.

Legally, Irénée did not own the land; Delaware law prevented aliens from buying property. Alexander Hamilton had appealed to the state's legislature for a special exemption allowing Irénée to purchase the ninety-five-acre tract, but anti-French sentiment outweighed Hamilton's prestige. Peter Bauduy, one of Irénée's investors, found a friend willing to put the land in his name. Bauduy, a brother of one of Victor's New York acquaintances, had poured thousands of dollars into the powder company and used his credit to prod Delaware banks into lending Irénée cash. He had been a wealthy plantation owner in Santo Domingo before the slave rebellion. With many other Haitian Frenchmen he had fled to

America and settled near the Brandywine. Bauduy's capital and the swift Brandywine had convinced Irénée to build his gunpowder mill in Delaware, on land he had paid for but did not own.

He had chosen the land well. The children could play along the Brandywine, swimming in it where the current eased, climbing the hills amid thousands of trees and tall grass. Close to the Creek the air was damp throughout the year and poisonous snakes slipped in and out of the water. But a few hundred feet away, where Irénée planned to build his house, the air was clear and dry and the sun drenched a higher shelf of ground, wide enough for gardens and lawns, carriage houses and barns.

Sophie settled the children into their rough home. Men arrived from Philadelphia and Wilmington, four miles east, to begin the building. Irénée worked among the carpenters and stonemasons, explaining in his halting English the plans he had drawn. Small buildings were to line the water's very edge, each with three thick walls of Brandywine stone, a flimsy roof sloping toward the water, an even lighter wooden wall facing the Creek. The mixing, stamping, graining, and storage of gunpowder would all take place in different buildings. Should an explosion occur, the force would blow out the light roof and the Creek wall, over the water, away from the powdermakers' homes and other mills. Even the French factory at Essonnes had no such precautions; Irénée intended the du Pont gunpowder mill to be the safest in the world.

Far up the hill, a giant piazza would cantilever off the back of Irénée and Sophie's house, with narrow pillars reaching two stories to the roof, shading the terrace in summer and protecting it from the winter winds and snow. Irénée could stand at the piazza railing and shout orders to his workers through a bullhorn, or sit at his desk just inside the house and gaze down on the powder yards and past them to the Brandywine.

Water from the Creek, diverted to a half-dozen wooden wheels in races near the mills, would power Irénée's machinery and feed the roots of the willow trees that his ovens would eventually burn into charcoal. Pipes would channel water to springhouses for the workers and Sophie's basement kitchen. Poured over the charcoal, sulfur, and saltpeter—gunpowder's three ingredients—clear Creek water would lessen the chance of stray sparks starting a fire. If fire did break out the powdermen and their wives would fill buckets of water at the Brandywine's edge to pour on the roofs of the mills. Even the damp air held a margin of safety.

Irénée's house would open on a grassy plain. Entering through large double doors, visitors would walk down a long hall and turn into the parlor. Beyond it, near Irénée's office, a library would hold his thousands of books. Sophie could decorate a large bedroom on the main floor, with an alcove for any children born on the Brandywine. Victorine, Evalina, and Alfred would have rooms up on the second floor, reached by an oval staircase. Irénée could plant trees and flowers in a large meadow a few yards from his front door.

Through the summer and fall of 1802, workers laid stone and fashioned wood into walls and roofs. Irénée worried over the slow pace of the construction; his machinery had arrived from France only to remain stacked in crates on Wilmington's wharves. Winter struck early, adding cold to the dampness that seeped into the cabin near the water. Sophie and the children fell ill. Irénée grew lonely and morose in the dreary winter cold. He began to question his decision to build on the Brandywine.

Victor had moved permanently from Good Stay to the New York house on Liberty Street shortly after Irénée left for the Brandywine. Gabrielle was pregnant again, hoping for a son. Gabrielle's pregnancies had always been difficult; Irénée was glad his brother and sister-in-law had moved to the city, where they might consult eminent doctors, but he missed Victor's company. Gabrielle wrote that her elegant husband was starting to grow fat. Business must be good, Irénée thought, yet he wished deeply that Victor would forsake his dreams of international trade and settle with him on the Brandywine.

Charles Dalmas, Sophie's younger brother, arrived on the Brandywine by boat, bringing with him most of his sister's furniture, her piano, and Irénée's twin hunting dogs. Irénée welcomed Charles's company and tried to shrug off his depression with leisurely hunting trips along the Creek. He knew it would be at least spring before Sophie's piano could sit in the parlor of the new director's house, and months beyond that when the waterwheels first turned his machinery to make gunpowder. In his spare moments, wandering through the woods, Irénée dreamed of leaving the United States to become a botanist in the French administration of forestry.

In spring the director's house was finally ready for Sophie to decorate, its stucco rooms awaiting the rolls of wallpaper she had ordered from Paris. Two hundred fruit tree seedlings arrived from the French National Gardens, courtesy of Josephine Bonaparte, along with sixteen grapevines, dozens of bushes, and boxes of flower seeds. In a year or two the soil of the Brandywine might yield a vintage like the wine that had flowed from the grapes at Bois-des-Fosses.

The powder mills neared readiness; even the workers' quarters were under way. In July, Irénée wrote to President Thomas Jefferson that E. I. du Pont de Nemours and Company was eager to receive government orders for refining saltpeter; the complete powdermaking process would have to wait another few months. Jefferson ordered Henry Dearborn, his Secretary of War, to send Irénée a trial batch of saltpeter. He wrote to the Brandywine that he would be pleased to reciprocate the du Ponts' kindnesses to his administration.

Pierre, in a steady stream of letters, had implored Jefferson to use his influence on behalf of his son's new enterprise. He told the President that Irénée intended his lethal product to be used solely in maintaining peace.

"This peaceful friend of liberty," Pierre wrote to Jefferson, "although he manufactures gunpowder, hopes that it will not be used for war but for those deeds which prevent war, those functions to which our military and our youth justly devote themselves—that is, to the business of the country, to hunting, to the opening of mountains and canals, to all public works."

Irénée thought differently. England and France were again at each other's throats; the Treaty of Amiens, just twenty months old, had collapsed. An undeclared war was being fought on land and at sea. Irénée sent word to Pierre that the mills were nearly completed and that he would soon manufacture the first grains of du Pont black powder. Pierre urged him to name the powder yards Eleutherian Mills, so that the world would know that he stood for peace. Irénée bowed to his father's wishes, although he knew well where the success of his mills rested.

"The condition of war that exists in Europe is very promising for my enterprise," he wrote to Pierre. "I will do all I can to profit by it."

Pierre drew the parcel of letters from within his coat and placed it on the small writing desk before him. He and Françoise had engaged a stateroom aboard the ship *Virginia*, bound from New York to Le Havre, because of the desk set against one wall within it: here Pierre could pass the voyage writing. But Pierre had forgotten his valise of papers on Liberty Street. Only the packet he studied now remained, thankfully, having been committed to a deep pocket for safekeeping.

A large outer envelope was addressed to Chancellor Robert R. Livingston, American minister to France, and bore the diplomatic seal of the United States. The seal had been applied over the flap of the envelope, but the flap had been left open and the writer, President Thomas Jefferson, had enclosed dissolving wax wafers for Pierre to use in fixing the seal after he read the envelope's contents.

Pierre had written Jefferson of his planned return to Paris, entrusting to his friend the care of his sons and their families. The President had urged him to delay his departure and visit Washington for important discussions.

"I believe," Jefferson wrote, "that the destinies of great countries depend on it, such is the crisis now existing."

Pierre declined the President's invitation. His French investors were clamoring for an explanation of his turning what little remained of their money over to Victor. And Madame Germaine de Staël had written that the Emperor Napoleon needed but to see Pierre on French soil: he would appoint him to the Senate immediately.

The rebuff did not rankle Jefferson. He dispatched a messenger to the Liberty Street house at once, bearing the unsealed diplomatic envelope and a letter to Pierre.

"I wish you to be possessed of the subject," the President wrote, "because you may be able to impress on the government of France the inevitable consequences of their taking possession of Louisiana . . . this measure will cost France, and perhaps not long hence, a war which will annihilate her on the ocean."

Pierre read Jefferson's communiqué to Livingston aboard ship and brooded over the President's words. He agreed with Jefferson that Louisiana represented "the embryo of a tornado which will burst on the countries on both sides of the Atlantic and involve in its effects their highest destinies." But his friend's words nearly declared war. Pierre could not believe that France's boldest ally in America would abandon her to stand by England. Yet Jefferson had written to Livingston that the United States would solve the problem of having no navy by relying on Britain's warships. At least the President's war fever had not turned to delirium; he had asked Pierre to intercede with the French government, with his old friend Talleyrand if necessary, to make the position of the United States known.

In thirty-two days the *Virginia* docked at Le Havre; soon Pierre was bustling between Talleyrand's suite in the Hotel Gallifet and the offices of the Consul Lebrun, Bonaparte's third in command, and François de Barbé-Marbois, director of the treasury. Barbé-Marbois embraced Pierre as an old companion in arms. Both had served Louis XVI; Barbé-Marbois had fought beside Pierre on the fateful August 10, when Louis surrendered his throne. Both had felt the sting of the revolution's hatred for monarchists, but Barbé-Marbois had decided to remain in France under Napoleon. Even after two years on Devil's Island—he had been deported on the same ship that was to have carried Pierre—Bonaparte had found his talents useful in the new republic.

Barbé-Marbois knew nothing of Napoleon's plans for Louisiana and dared not reveal, even to Pierre in private, that his ruler had gained the territory back from Spain. The Consul Lebrun complained that Bonaparte kept him equally in the dark: the Emperor revealed his schemes for conquest to no one except, perhaps, Talleyrand. Lebrun regretted that President Jefferson's warnings were wasted on his unprivileged ears.

Talleyrand's ears were another matter. The foreign minister had already convinced Napoleon to tread gently on America's toes: brandishing his weapons could lead to a disastrous sea fight with England and the loss of France's rich island colonies. Bonaparte, quite uncharacteristically, had agreed.

Talleyrand listened to Pierre recite Jefferson's angry warning but did not respond. Publicly, France claimed that Spain still owned Louisiana; Spanish troops did indeed occupy the territory. The minister knew of Napoleon's plan to invade North America and hated it. England, he believed, would never agree peacefully to carve up a continent she had almost completely controlled less than three decades earlier. Pierre could not be trusted with either Bonaparte's plans or Talleyrand's own thoughts: within hours, word of the invasion plan would be en route to Washington, and Jefferson would convince Congress to declare war.

Still, Talleyrand realized, Pierre might be useful. An audience with Napoleon was arranged. Bonaparte talked pleasantly with Pierre for a long while. Pierre's friends thought it a good sign; soon Louis XVI's former defender would be beckoned to the inner corridors of Napoleon's regime. In the meantime, Talleyrand urged Pierre to report anything new he happened to hear about Thomas Jefferson's attitude toward France.

Pierre busied himself settling into an apartment on the Rue Montholon and calling upon the investors in his Compagnie d'Amérique. He touted Irénée's powder mills and Victor's New York commission house and proudly displayed the card Josephine Bonaparte had given him, allowing him the honor of admission to the Tuileries at any time without an appointment.

Pierre wrote to Jefferson that war between France and the United States would be ruinous for both. He had another idea: why not offer to *buy* Louisiana? Certainly the cost, whatever Napoleon demanded, would be less than the ravages of war, and no American lives would be lost. Pierre added that he would, of course, be pleased to act as intermediary between the two nations.

Jefferson bristled at Pierre's suggestion: to purchase territory on North America would be an admission that other nations had a right to occupy it. He had always interpreted the Constitution as prohibiting the President from bartering with foreign nations for land, and he knew that buying Louisiana would open the door to increased federal power over the states. Jefferson had gained the White House by opposing national usurpation of the states' rights. The President saw clearly his dilemma: if Talleyrand or Napoleon had prompted Pierre's suggestion, he stood between abandoning his principles on one hand and war on the other.

Pierre sent a continuous stream of letters to Washington. He had constructed a simple treaty calling for the payment of six million dollars for Louisiana and retaining for France the right of deposit at New Orleans and free navigation of the Mississippi River. The terms would, Pierre told Jefferson, satisfy both the United States and France. The President answered that he had neither the right nor the desire to purchase Louisiana. By diplomatic pouch Jefferson urged Ambassador Livingston to assure the French government that Pierre spoke only for himself, not the United States.

Thomas Jefferson had, however, made the most important decision of his presidency: to avoid war he would act on Pierre's suggestion. He ordered his Secretary of State, James Madison, to instruct Livingston that his entire energy was to be directed toward negotiating with Talleyrand for Louisiana. Jefferson knew that the ambassador could not be trusted with the intricacies of bartering with Talleyrand; a consummate diplomat, who held the confidence of Congress as well as the President's, was needed. He selected James Monroe, on the surface an odd choice. Monroe's last diplomatic mission, to France, had ended in his formal expulsion from the country. But Monroe was riding a crest of public popularity in the United States, and Napoleon would know that his negotiating sword was double-edged: the press had reported often that James Monroe did not wince at the thought of war over Louisiana.

Jefferson wrote Pierre that Monroe would soon arrive in Paris to take the Louisiana question out of Robert Livingston's hands. He asked that Pierre inform Talleyrand and Napoleon—in private—not to lend great weight to Livingston's words. The President again denied to Pierre that the United States would ever purchase the Louisiana Territory. Jefferson realized that Livingston and du Pont would carry contradictory versions of his intentions to Talleyrand: he had decided that it was France's turn to sweat, even though his spies reported that Napoleon had an enormous fleet ready to sail from a European port, awaiting only Bonaparte's order to weigh anchor for New Orleans.

Pierre passed Jefferson's message along to Talleyrand. The minister was amused by Jefferson's diplomatic antics and unimpressed by Monroe's coming: Napoleon had already decided to risk war. But Bonaparte feared the United States more than his foreign minister knew. Leclerc's expedition to Santo Domingo, at first victorious, had run into difficulty. Yellow fever was decimating the French troops; thousands who might have joined the invasion force died each day. Bonaparte summoned Talleyrand and Barbé-Marbois to his office. He was aware, he told his ministers, that France could never hope to defeat both the United States and England in a sea battle. Why fight over Louisiana, Napoleon reasoned, when it was Europe he really wanted, and his armies could overrun England at any time? He had decided to let Jefferson have Louisiana —for a price—if it would keep the Americans away from England's side.

Talleyrand exploded: there were methods other than either war or sale. How did Napoleon plan to recapture Canada, his objective since the French Revolution ended, without a foothold on the Mississippi? Bonaparte raised his hand for silence. He had decided: that was enough.

That evening at a party Talleyrand casually asked Livingston what the United States would pay for the whole of Louisiana. Livingston was dumbfounded: here, finally, was proof that France did indeed wish to barter for the territory. Now his President would learn to listen to his ambassador rather than a lame old French philosopher named du Pont. Livingston, pitifully in the dark about Jefferson's plans, had no idea that Pierre had been the first to suggest buying Louisiana.

James Monroe arrived in Paris early the next day. Barbé-Marbois— appointed by Bonaparte to negotiate the sale since, unlike Talleyrand, he was not in the habit of taking huge bribes for his services—approached him within hours. Would Monroe's government like to buy the whole of Louisiana? Barbé-Marbois asked. France just happened to own it by treaty and Napoleon might be willing to sell—if the Americans acted quickly.

Monroe paled. Jefferson had instructed him to bargain only for New Orleans and the Floridas, which, oddly enough, were not included in Spain's treaty with France. The President, without Congress's approval, had authorized Monroe to offer ten million dollars for the city and countryside. Monroe knew well that the United States government could not hope to raise even that amount, much less what Bonaparte was likely to demand for the entire territory: all the money in circulation in the nation did not add up to ten millions. Napoleon knew the financial condition of the United States; where did he expect Monroe to raise such sums?

Monroe had his answer the following day. A British banker called on him at the American embassy. His firm, the banker said, was willing to put its resources at the diplomat's disposal for the current negotiations. To what extent? Monroe asked. To the extent of ten million dollars, the banker answered.

Somehow the British, and probably the French as well, had learned precisely what Jefferson said to Monroe in Washington. The most obvious leak in security would be Pierre du Pont, but Monroe was certain the President had not mentioned the figure to him. Monroe himself had spoken of it only to embassy employees. He ordered an investigation. Jefferson, it seemed, had been correct not to trust Livingston. The ambassador had hired, as his personal secretary, one of Great Britain's top spies.

Fortunately, not even Livingston knew that Monroe had been instructed to barter only for New Orleans and the Floridas. He decided to negotiate for the whole of Louisiana, and leave to the President the problem of squaring the deal with Congress. In two weeks the conditions were set: for fifteen million dollars Napoleon would surrender the entire Louisiana Territory. In return, as Pierre had suggested, France would retain her right of deposit at New Orleans and freedom to sail the Mississippi.

After the treaty was signed Monroe cheerfully revealed the true nature of his mission to Pierre. None of the men who bartered over the Louisiana Territory—not Jefferson, Monroe, Livingston, Napoleon,

Talleyrand, or du Pont—ever saw it. Louisiana's boundaries were unknown; Bonaparte never discovered that he had given away nine hundred thousand square miles of land for about four cents an acre. Jefferson did not live long enough to find out that the land he had sacrificed his lifelong political principles for, a vast area bounded by Canada, Texas, the Mississippi, and the Rocky Mountains, held better soil and more natural resources than the rest of the civilized world combined. Pierre did not then, or ever in his lifetime, understand that his suggestion to avoid war had doubled the size of the United States.

But Thomas Jefferson had an inkling of the importance of the Louisiana Territory. Rarely did the President praise anyone personally; he believed man merely fulfilled his responsibilities to other men by admirably performing the act of governing nations. When Monroe returned to Washington, Jefferson wrote to Pierre that his work on Louisiana would provide as yet unimaginable benefits to millions of descendants of those people now alive in the United States. His government, the President added, would be pleased to avail itself of the services the du Pont family offered both in Europe and the Americas. Two months later, near the end of 1804, Jefferson sent word to Irénée in Delaware: he had ordered the army and navy of the United States to purchase the gunpowder they needed exclusively from the new Eleutherian Mills on the banks of the Brandywine Creek.

Nearly one million francs passed through Victor du Pont's business in the year after Pierre returned to Paris. The money kept both Victor's and Pierre's families alive, for, despite Napoleon's warm welcome, the bankers and financiers of Paris had laughed at Pierre's pretensions to commercial prowess. Victor began to regret the day he had agreed to Pierre's plan for a return to France; his father would have been far less damaging to Victor's business affairs safely out of the way at Good Stay.

For a time, all went well. Victor knew many important New Yorkers from his diplomatic days; they gladly extended their influence on his behalf. He had even hired a secretary and bookkeeper, Raphael Duplanty, to keep the threads of his complex business web in order. But Victor knew he was building an empire of paper. He had started with a net worth of precisely forty-five dollars less than zero. He relied on Duplanty to keep the paper rolling; otherwise, his empire might at any moment crumble.

Louis Pichon's promise of the Santo Domingo trade materialized, but Pichon began demanding larger and larger kickbacks. When Leclerc's expedition fell to yellow fever, Napoleon Bonaparte accused Pichon of padding payment drafts for supplies, as he had, and ordered the treasury not to pay the bills Pichon endorsed. Pierre wrote to Victor from Paris that the millions in unpaid drafts they held were worthless. Irénée, on the Brandywine, expected Victor to send him six thousand dollars, payment for his shares of stock in the powder mills. Victor penned a note of regret to his brother: he had not even one hundred dollars to pay on the stock.

Victor's wife, Gabrielle, railed at him for accepting responsibility for Pierre's debts. Victor angrily reminded Gabrielle that he owed his father much more than money and that he could never allow so swift a business demise to taint Pierre's reputation. Gabrielle was pregnant once again; she nagged at Victor that their children would suffer for their grandfather's mistakes. Amelia, their daughter, and Charles, their son, depended on Victor's success for their futures; without the money to pay for schooling they might even grow up illiterate. Victor promised his wife that the children would not bear the burden of his own or Pierre's failures.

Victor searched for a way to gain special attention from Napoleon to his Santo Domingo drafts. Lucien Bonaparte, Napoleon's youngest brother, had jumped ship in New York, tired of the sailor's life. Lucien courted and married a local debutante, Elizabeth Patterson, and promptly ran out of money. Victor agreed to loan Lucien whatever he needed. Lucien wished to live in a style that befitted the brother of the ruler of the French Empire. Soon Victor was providing the newlywed with eight thousand dollars a month.

Lucien tired of New York society and boarded a ship bound for Le Havre. Napoleon stopped the ship before it reached France, ordered his brother to Paris, and sent his wife back to America. He shrugged off Victor's demands for payment of Lucien's debts; he had not sanctioned his brother's marriage and did not intend to pay for his frivolous behavior. Victor learned that Elizabeth Patterson had returned to her parents' home in Baltimore. He did not attempt to collect from her the one hundred forty thousand dollars Lucien Bonaparte had borrowed from him.

Even Raphael Duplanty's astute bookkeeping could not help him now. The Liberty Street office had to be closed, the house sold. A smaller home, in a less fashionable section of Manhattan, would have to do. Victor stopped meeting the deadlines on his notes to New York banks and sold off his business assets until only a few twenty-five-pound bags of black gunpowder Irénée had sent him on consignment remained. These he had no way to sell or pay his brother for. Irénée, dangerously in debt on the Brandywine, could offer no help. Pierre survived in Paris on his salary from a minor government post and his wife's small pension. Victor's New York friends no longer saw any point to persuading his creditors not to press their claims.

Victor decided to follow the one course that might keep him from debtor's prison: bankruptcy. The courts ordered him to stay in the city until they finished deliberating his case. Victor realized that Gabrielle, still nursing their youngest child, Samuel Francis, and pregnant with another, could never stand the strain. He sent his wife and children to Good Stay to escape witnessing the disaster. On August 26, 1805, Gabrielle sat weeping in the dining room at Good Stay, watching the hands of a clock on the mantelpiece turn toward three, unable even to comfort her husband when the hour struck and Victor du Pont de Nemours and Company ceased to exist.

# 10

IRÉNÉE DU PONT wrote to his father in 1807 that Eleutherian Mills stood on the edge of a disaster worse than Victor's. He was many thousands in debt, he told Pierre, and his customers paid slowly. Government orders rarely came; Thomas Jefferson's promise appeared to be an empty one. The war against the pirates of the Barbary Coast had ended; he had sold only twenty-two thousand pounds of gunpowder to the United States navy. Each American city, it seemed, had a government agent who ordered supplies from whatever firm offered the highest kickback.

Powder mills sprang up everywhere to meet the agents' demands. Crude, ill-run affairs, they lasted only until an explosion killed the workmen and scared the owners into safer businesses. Even after the Eleutherian Mills black powder proved superior to every other brand in tests run by the Secretary of War, army and navy agents refused to purchase it. Irénée believed he was feeling the sting of American prejudice against Frenchmen. If only he were out of debt, he wrote Pierre, how quickly he would set sail for France!

Pierre answered that he would try to find money to save the powder mills. With Victor's business gone and his own Paris firm empty of assets, the powder company held his only chance for wealth. Pierre decided to appeal to Talleyrand. France still had an important reason to support his son's enterprise, he told the minister: war with England always loomed just over the diplomatic horizon. Unless he, Talleyrand, saved them, Eleutherian Mills would go bankrupt.

The foreign minister listened sympathetically and did nothing. Pierre soon learned why: Talleyrand had resigned, exhausted from doing Napoleon's bidding. But a few days later his old friend sent for him. A way might be found, Talleyrand said, for Irénée to secure the money he needed. He had instructed an associate, Menestriere, to look favorably should Pierre apply to him for a loan—say, one hundred thousand francs —to go to Irénée on the Brandywine. Of course, the gold would come from Talleyrand's own purse and, in return, he expected an assignment of Pierre's interest in the mills—as collateral, not with any intent to influence Irénée's management of the company.

Pierre accepted Talleyrand's terms gladly, signed a note for the money, nearly twenty-five thousand dollars, and promptly spent half of it paying his own debts. He wrote Irénée jubilantly of the loan. Of course, he expected his son to assume responsibility for the entire amount: call his share a commission for negotiating with Talleyrand. Irénée had no choice but to take on the obligation. Even one-half the sum Talleyrand had given Pierre meant the difference between life and death for Eleutherian Mills.

Thunderbolts of flame shot up from the powder yards. Dense black smoke obscured the sky over the Brandywine. Injured workmen crawled through falling debris and sparks. Women screamed for their husbands. Irénée shouted to his brother-in-law, Charles Dalmas, from the piazza of the director's house, shielding his eyes against the windowpanes breaking about him. A baby cried inside the house, Irénée's youngest child, Eleuthera, barely two years old. It was August 18, 1807. Irénée and Sophie's daughter was the youngest witness to the first explosion at Eleutherian Mills.

After supper in the director's house Charles Dalmas had gone down into the powder yards to check on a large batch of charcoal he had seen being taken from the ovens just before the powdermakers had quit for the day. Dalmas worried over the charcoal throughout his meal; it was hot from the furnaces that turned willow branches into lumps of black soot and he considered it dangerous. He mentioned it to Irénée and offered to descend the hill himself after supper: his brother-in-law looked too tired to go.

Dalmas answered Irénée's calls through the smoke. He had stopped for a moment to talk with one of the workers before reaching the charcoal house. The blast had thrown him to the ground, but he was uninjured. Irénée hugged his wife's brother; he had been certain the blast had killed him.

Together they ran to the scene of the fire. Black powder had been drying in a building sixty feet long, one of the few structures Irénée had not designed himself. The charcoal had been left under the same roof. Irénée knew that hot charcoal might ignite spontaneously; he hated himself for giving in to Peter Bauduy's complaints about the cost of new buildings for the mills.

Bauduy was a constant source of irritation. He had been a slaveowner in Haiti, and Irénée's ideas about treating his workers well goaded Bauduy into continuous criticism about the way Irénéc ran the business. When the mills turned out the first pounds of gunpowder Bauduy had had cards printed up calling the firm Du Pont, Bauduy, and Company. Irénée had seethed: if the gunpowder factory ever achieved prominence, he told his partner, the name it bore must be his own and no other.

And now Bauduy's nagging and Irénée's carelessness had caused an explosion. No one had been killed, but two buildings were reduced to rubble. Near the Creek, Irénée felt a cool wind blowing on his face. With luck, the wind would dampen the roof of the graining house a few yards from where the charcoal and seven hundred fifty pounds of powder had exploded. Throughout the night bucket brigades poured water over the other mill buildings. One stray spark, Irénée knew, and all he had worked for would float away down the Brandywine.

At dawn the danger was gone. The powder yards were a shambles; days would pass before the mill wheels turned again, weeks until the rubble was cleared, months before every broken window was replaced and new buildings—safer ones—were erected to house the charcoal furnaces and drying powder. Only the time Delaware's long summer gave him to rebuild cheered Irénée. The gentle Brandywine autumn and the twelve thousand dollars he had just deposited in a Philadelphia bank, courtesy of his father's oldest friend, Talleyrand, kept him from abandoning Eleutherian Mills.

Victor du Pont sailed up the Hudson River in December, fighting a hundred miles of bitter cold and freezing winds. At the mouth of the Mohawk River he switched to horseback for the long ride to Angelica, an outpost of a few score hardy settlers, all farmers.

Gabrielle and the children had gone to the Brandywine for the winter. Victor planned to join them at his brother's house, but first, the bitter taste of his bankruptcy a mere four months old, he needed to get away, and to scout the valley of the Genesee River for a place to live. A wealthy New York friend, Phillip Church, owned vast lands near Angelica. He offered to sell Victor a small parcel, to settle and farm, where he might escape the disgrace he felt walking the streets of New York City and begin a new life.

Victor saw the land and liked it. A few months' working in the fields would wear down his large stomach, he reasoned, and set his affairs straight. If other settlers came to the Genesee his land would appreciate;

eventually, even his old business debts might be paid. In his pocket Victor carried the last of Gabrielle's inheritance, three thousand dollars from the sale of a Paris house her father had bequeathed her. He decided to buy five hundred acres from the Church family, rolling land covered with thick forests no man had ever cut, bounded on three sides by the pleasant Genesee River, a few miles outside the town limits of Angelica. Victor returned to New York, signed the deed to his new estate, and reached the Brandywine before the spring of 1806 warmed the winds off the Creek.

Irénée welcomed his brother with a rare smile. Together they walked the hills of the Brandywine, hunted game, and surveyed Irénee's new gardens, growing more lush each spring day. Irénée urged Victor to stay on; the powder business had improved and he would be pleased to set his brother up in business nearby. Gabrielle, pregnant again, felt less afraid of childbirth near her relatives. Sophie loved having Gaby to talk to, and the children enjoyed playing with their cousins. The director's house was quite large; surely it could accommodate both families until Victor established himself and built one of his own. Victor said he would consider his brother's offer.

Gabrielle gave birth to a daughter in June. Victor named her Julia Sophie Angelique. He had decided: it was to be Angelica and the Genesee for his family, a river of his own to rival the Brandywine. Julia still nourished at Gabrielle's breast when Victor took the reins of a wagon and leaned down to wish his brother farewell. Behind him another wagon turned in the dust of his own, carrying a thousand pounds of Eleutherian Mills' best gunpowder, to be sold in the general store Victor planned to open on the outskirts of Angelica. He left Irénée payment for the months in his home: Raphael Duplanty stayed behind to keep the powder company's books of account.

The bookkeeper had just returned from a journey to France, sent by Victor to try to raise money that might save the New York company. Duplanty had been remarkably successful: Talleyrand had offered to buy an interest in Victor's firm for three hundred thousand francs—sixty thousand dollars. But when Duplanty finally reached Victor's New York house with the good news he found a court seal on its doors. Victor had remarked ruefully to Irénée that not even the largess of a Talleyrand could save him.

Winter came early to the upper reaches of New York State. No time remained after Victor and Gabrielle arrived on the Genesee to clear land or build a house. With silver from the sale of much of her furniture and gold she had secretly saved on Liberty Street, Gabrielle bought a small house in Angelica. Victor planned to build a store in the spring on a lot next door, stocking it with gunpowder and the other goods Genesee settlers needed to sustain life.

Victor needed credit to fill his shelves. He asked a Philadelphia businessman, Archibald McCall, to send him tools, grain, and seeds on consignment. McCall, who had joined Peter Bauduy in buying a share of Irénée's powder company stock, refused unless Irénée would sign for the merchandise. Victor appealed to his brother. Irénée agreed to set his name under Victor's. Otherwise, Victor's family might starve; Irénée knew that his brother had no idea of how to clear land or plant crops, much less run a general store.

Even an experienced shopkeeper, Victor soon learned, would have difficulty doing business in Angelica. The settlers of the Genesee grew their own food, fashioned their own tools, spun their own cloth. Animals roamed the valley in such abundance that it was easier to trap than shoot them; except for a few pounds sold to fur traders sent by John Astor, the kegs of Irénée's powder lay covered in the wagon they had come in.

Snow covered the banks of the Genesee for six or seven months a year. Farming was impossible in the frozen ground and the settlers rarely left their log homes: it was simply too cold to ride even the few miles into town for a pipeful of Victor's tobacco. Gabrielle passed the time teaching her oldest daughter, Amelia, to play the piano. Victor taught Charles, now nearly ten years old, reading and arithmetic. Samuel, still a toddler, followed Charles about like a faithful puppy. Julia grew fat and healthy. All four of Gabrielle's children had been born in the United States. At times, listening to the cruel winter winds, Gaby daydreamed of France and longed for the streets of Paris: the backwoods of America were not her idea of a homeland.

All the amenities of life seemed to be slipping away from her family. To satisfy New York creditors everything but their most personal possessions had been sold. The few sticks of furniture they had brought to Angelica went as Victor's embarrassment in relying on Irénée's credit grew. Soon even their last slave, a girl named Charlotte, and her four-week-old daughter were sold to another Angelica settler, an old friend who paid Victor two hundred dollars for his human chattel—much more than they were worth on the open market.

Gabrielle drew the line at selling the family's piano. It had come with them from France aboard the *American Eagle*, and listening to Amelia play it was her mother's sole remaining pleasure. That, too, came to an end. Amelia's music drew buckskinned Indians out of the woods, who would crowd into the house in amazement, scaring Gabrielle into cooking large meals for them to draw attention away from her twelve-year-old daughter.

Victor's worries exceeded even the benefits of his rugged frontier life. Through the four years on the Genesee his stomach grew steadily larger. His eyes sank into puffy flesh; his hands roughened with the hard work he had never before done. Little about him reminded Gabrielle of the dashing army officer she had met at a party in Nemours almost fifteen years earlier. The New York creditors hounded her husband for payment. They rarely spoke of it, but Gabrielle knew that without Irénée's signature her family would go hungry in days.

One afternoon Victor looked up from the counter of his store to see a tall, gaunt, unsmiling man standing before him. It was Irénée! He had ridden the three hundred miles from the Brandywine on horseback. Duplanty was with him, outside tending the horses. He had only one purpose in coming, he told his brother: Victor and Gabrielle must abandon their frontier life and return with him to the Brandywine. Duplanty and Victor would go into business together. Yes, Irénée said, he would supply the money, but it would be much better paying for Victor to begin a fruitful life near him than continuing to lose money while his brother failed in the wilderness.

Over dinner the brothers talked. Victor could do little but agree. He and Gabrielle would come to the Brandywine, but he would first gradually dispose of his goods, thus not alarming his New York creditors, and turn the land over to Irénée, to preserve it in case prices did one day rise. Irénée did not care: he wanted his brother near him, whatever the cost.

Early the next morning Irénée mounted his horse and reached down to clasp his brother's outstretched hand. He would begin designing a home for Victor's brood across the Brandywine from his own. Victor was surprised: Irénée seemed resigned to spending the remainder of his life on American soil. Had he given up his dreams of returning to France? Irénée had even sent their father a power of attorney to sell his share in Bois-des-Fosses. He suspected that a war would soon begin between England and the United States; already British warships engaged American vessels on the seas. The powder business would boom, Irénée be-lieved, and his days of pleading with bankers for more credit and with Pierre for fewer demands for money would end.

Before summer began Victor and Raphael Duplanty loaded two wagons for the journey to Eleutherian Mills. Victor stopped in New York to inform his creditors of his move while his brother's bookkeeper continued on to the Brandywine with Gabrielle and the children. The city's merchants and bankers were less than pleased. Twice they had Victor arrested and held until Irénée arrived with bail money. Victor thanked his brother humbly, blaming himself for the blot he had brought to the family name.

Irénée brushed aside his brother's words: did Victor not remember the oath they had taken as children, kneeling before their father, soon after their mother's death? They were pledged to each other for life: what befell one of them befell the other. They must hurry back to the Brandywine. A huge party was being planned for Irénée's birthday, his thirty-ninth. Sophie needed everyone's help: she was carrying another child. And it might be the last party for a long time to come. Irénée had heard from friends in Washington that the United States Congress was planning to declare war.

Victorine du Pont, Irénée's eldest daughter, inherited her mother's good looks: a long, slender neck curving above high shoulders and high, wide breasts; her mother's clear forehead beneath piles of sleek black hair; her mother's narrow nose and curving lips. From her father came a strong jaw and clear, gray eyes. Like her father, too, Victorine was slender and lanky, her long legs strong from climbing the hills near the Brandywine. She was seventeen when Peter Bauduy's son called on Irénée to ask for his eldest daughter's hand in marriage.

Irénée scowled at young Ferdinand Bauduy: he was after the factory, not his beautiful Tini. He was too young, too inexperienced, the son of too great an antagonist. The Bauduy style, which Ferdinand had inher-ited, was not the du Pont style. Peter Bauduy laughed, talked loudly, gloried in carousing with friends. Irénée had grown more silent with each year on the Brandywine, his business difficulties exaggerating what had always seemed to others a cold, insensitive personality. Perhaps, as she had before, Sophie would convince their daughter to rebuff the young Bauduy for his advances. Other suitors had come and gone; so too would this son of Irénée's bitter enemy.

Sophie smiled at her husband's objections. Victorine was no longer a child; she had passed by almost two years the age Sophie had been when Irénée fought with Pierre to be allowed to marry her. And Ferd Bauduy was no Raphael Duplanty, who had courted Tini for over a year, an older man with few prospects and little in common with their daughter. Young Bauduy had been to college. He was bright, handsome, and he and Victorine had grown up together on the Brandywine. Their differences aside, Irénée and Peter Bauduy were partners. Perhaps, Sophie suggested, it was not too bad a match at that.

Irénée was unconvinced. He had spoken with Peter about his son's intentions. Bauduy had been just as surprised and dismayed as Irénée himself. Both children were special to their fathers, their firstborn. But Victorine adored Ferdinand. Peter thought he might have a remedy to their dilemma. His son had asked to go to France for two years, where he hoped to complete his education. Bauduy would send him if Irénée would agree to put off any engagement. After two years apart, if the children still loved each other, their fathers would give their approval. Irénée told Sophie and Victorine what he had decided. Ferd Bauduy hurried his departure from the Brandywine. He would return, he told Victorine, to marry her. Until then, he would picture her in the garden outside her father's house, sitting among the roses she loved so much, and write to her there.

Irénée told Victor about his daughter's love affair on the long walks the brothers enjoyed in Sand Hole Woods, not far from the director's house. Victor said he could understand Irénée's predicament. His own Amelia had turned sixteen, but she was not the great beauty Tini had grown to be. Still, she played the piano skillfully and had learned household arts her mother never dreamed of trying. She had the du Pont touch with growing things, Irénée's gift really, but she was a plain girl, homely if the truth were told, without even a spark of Victorine's intelligence or wit. Yet, Victor told Irénée, his Amelia had a suitor of her own.

Since coming to the Brandywine Victor had labored building a woolen business across the Creek from his brother's powder mills. American fabric had always been inferior to French and English goods. Irénée had convinced his brother that the country needed a textile factory to turn out fine cloth for fashionable dresses and coats and had given him the money to erect a large weaving mill. Victor thanked Irénée often for giving him an opportunity to start again, and for Louviers, the lovely home his brother had built for him, peering down through the trees of the Brandywine. It was a marvelous house: Irénée had sent the plans to Thomas Jefferson for his approval. The architect of Monticello made a few suggestions but no changes. Gabrielle loved her family's new home. She remarked to Irénée that her gratitude increased as the masons and carpenters added each story to the house. Irénée answered that, if such was the case, he would build her a home reaching all the way to heaven. He thought his sister-in-law might yet learn to love America; he knew that Victor would not soon leave the Brandywine.

But he also realized that his brother knew less about textiles than farming. Victor needed skilled help, hands trained to set looms and eyes practiced in judging the quality of fabric. Both brothers wrote to friends asking if they knew of a master weaver who might be looking for a position running a new woolen mill. On board a ship bound from England to the United States, an acquaintance of Victor's from his diplomatic days met a man leaving his father's textile mill for a life of his own in America. William Clifford was twenty-seven years old and claimed to have spent twenty-two of them at his father's side in a Gloucester woolen factory, learning to fashion fine cloth. Yes, he told Victor's acquaintance, he would be interested in a position on the Brandywine if the pay were high enough.

Victor welcomed Clifford to the east bank of the Brandywine, showing him the new woolen mill with its shiny, unused machinery. The pay would be four dollars a week, he said, and the hours long at first, but Clifford would have a free hand in running the factory, and room and board would be provided in the house of his brother's bookkeeper, Raphael Duplanty. They shook hands when Clifford agreed to start work immediately.

Within weeks the looms were spewing out their first bolts of cloth. In the close quarters of the Brandywine community Bill Clifford spent many evenings with Victor's family. He began taking long walks in the woods with Amelia. To her parents' surprise and delight, the Englishman seemed to be forming a strong attachment to their daughter. Amelia had never before known the attentions of a man. Within months after Clifford arrived she was spending every waking hour daydreaming about him, cutting flowers for his room in Duplanty's house, and bringing him lunch in the woolen mills. Her heavy body, usually clumsy, seemed to float in the light of Bill's attentions. Gabrielle recognized the signs of love in her ugly duckling of a daughter.

Victor announced to Irénée that the Brandywine was about to see its first wedding among the du Ponts. Clifford was more than a good catch for Amelia, he told his brother. Even Thomas Jefferson had complimented him on the quality of his new fabrics. In time, Jefferson wrote from Monticello, the United States would have no need to import cloth from England or even France. Amelia and Bill would be married at Louviers, Victor said, and live there until he could build them a house of their own along the Creek.

On a warm September morning Irénée closed the powder mills and sent his workers across the Brandywine in skiffs to attend the party Victor and Gabrielle were giving for the newlyweds. Irénée, Sophie, and their five children crossed the water in boats loaded with gifts for their cousin and her groom. Irénée rowed carefully; Sophie was pregnant again. The last child had been a girl, Sophie Madeleine, born soon after Victor and Gabrielle moved down from Angelica. He hoped this next child would be a son.

Victor regretted that he could not give Bill and Amelia time for a honeymoon. The War of 1812 had begun, and cloth from the mills was in great demand. New workers were being hired almost daily. Clifford was frantically busy overseeing the weaving, so Victor interviewed the new men himself. One, an Englishman, seemed to remember Bill Clifford's face. He approached Victor a few days later: he had recognized the foreman, he said. His name was not Clifford, but Nathaniel Perkins, and he was certain the man had a wife and children in Gloucester, where the Perkins family owned a textile mill.

Victor confronted his son-in-law with the weaver's accusations: were they true? Clifford admitted they were. Victor thought of Amelia, pregnant now, still deeply in love with her husband and looking forward to the home her father had promised them. Even in winter his daughter hunted through the woods for the last remaining wildflowers she might cut and place on the windowsill of the bedroom Victor and Gabrielle had given the newlyweds. She was timid and soft-spoken, his first daughter, and only her love for Bill Clifford had ever cracked the shell her ugliness had built around her. But the du Pont family would have no bigamist in its midst. Victor decided that his foreman was to leave the country on the next ship bound for Europe. He was not even to say goodbye to Amelia. Gabrielle would care for their daughter, if it mattered to him, and Victor would see to the child.

Six months later Amelia gave birth to a daughter, the first grandchild of a Brandywine du Pont, and named her Gabrielle Josephine. Victor trudged sadly into a Wilmington court to have the infant legitimized: she would carry the name du Pont, not Clifford. Victorine crossed the Brandywine when she could, to help Amelia with the baby and sit with her in the garden while she stared blankly at the flowers she had planned to transplant to her own garden. Victorine shared her cousin's love for the rich soil of the Brandywine and all it produced; Amelia would not risk leaving the safety of the Brandywine's trees and flowers for many years to come. Even her clumsiness had returned. As best she could, Victorine hid her own joy from Amelia and never spoke of the letters Ferdinand Bauduy had written weekly, which she carried everywhere in the bosom of her dress.

Bauduy had left the Brandywine nearly two years earlier. He wrote to Victorine that he would be home in the summer of 1813. Pierre sent his regrets to Irénée from Paris. He had always hoped Victorine would marry Charles Dalmas, her uncle, a union legal in France if not in the United States. He could send his granddaughter no gift of value from Paris: his firm had failed two years earlier, and even the powder company shares now belonged to others. Pierre barely survived by writing political tracts and editing the works of Jacques Turgot. Napoleon no longer knew his name. Nearly all his old colleagues were dead, save for Talleyrand and Lafayette. But he wished Ferdinand and Victorine well in their new life.

Neither Irénée nor Peter Bauduy could any longer object to the match. Ferdinand had proved his devotion. Victorine's eyes had searched in the distance for two years for her errant lover; other men simply did not exist. Sophie had planned the wedding. Now it was Victor's family's turn to cross the Brandywine. Victor hoped the union might in some way stop the constant bickering between his brother and Bauduy. Gabrielle wished Sophie's daughter better luck than her own had found.

It was a November wedding, inside the director's house, away from the bitter winds that at times beset the Brandywine early in winter. Victorine and Ferdinand were radiant, the family laughing for the first time since Bill Clifford left the woolen mills. Even Amelia consented to play her uncle's piano for a few moments. Irénée welcomed young Bauduy into the family; he and Tini must live in his house while they planned and built a home of their own farther down the Brandywine. Irénée and Peter drank toasts to their children and to the peace between them the marriage might bring.

Eleven weeks later Ferdinand Bauduy lay dead.

The Brandywine winter had been too much for his slight constitution. France's mild weather had thinned his blood; he was unable to withstand the icy gusts off the Creek. In the second-floor bedroom Irénée gave to his daughter and her husband Victorine nursed Ferdinand's fevered body. He became delirious; doctors could do nothing. Pneumonia quickly claimed his breath and life. Victorine wandered in the rose garden where she had read her lover's letters from France, searching the empty, thorny vines for something of her husband to keep. Unlike Amelia, she had not even a child in her womb to remind her of Ferdinand. But she shared her cousin's fate: never, in fifty years more of life, would either of them remarry.

Irénée returned to the powder yards after his son-in-law's burial. He had much work to do: the United States was at war, and the President had just ordered a half-million pounds of black gunpowder from Eleutherian Mills.

# 11

I RÉNÉE DU PONT watched the husky teamsters hoist themselves aboard the driving seats of their Conestoga wagons. He admired the courage of the men who hauled hundreds of gunpowder-filled wooden kegs across the wilderness. Even among the workers who mixed and grained tons of black powder on the Brandywine, the drivers commanded a special respect: no one had ever survived an explosion of a powder-filled Conestoga.

Irénée watched the drivers whip their mules and set off from the powder yards. With luck, the wagons would arrive on the shores of Lake Erie in a few days. Commodore Perry, locked in battle with a British fleet, urgently needed Irénée's gunpowder to repel the attack and keep English soldiers from establishing a foothold on land. The western front of the war hinged on how quickly Irénée's wagonmasters could deliver their dangerous cargo to the American troops.

The War of 1812 had gone that way since the beginning. Orders from Washington poured into Eleutherian Mills faster than Irénée could fill them. He had raised new mills down the Brandywine, on a farm he bought for thousands more than it was worth, and called them the Hagley Works. Bauduy had objected, as usual, to the expense. But the government began buying powder in hundred-thousand-pound lots and even with the new mills Irénée could not meet Washington's pleas for black powder.

Irénée had sensed years earlier that war was coming. In 1809 he advised Thomas Jefferson to buy up as much saltpeter as the government could get from India. If England blockaded the Atlantic Coast, Irénée told the President, the precious ingredient would be unobtainable. The United States might lose simply because her factories could not turn out enough gunpowder to wage war. Jefferson stockpiled fifty thousand pounds of Indian saltpeter in government warehouses. It had been expensive—sixteen cents a pound. When Congress declared war Irénée bought all of it at the price the government had paid. His competitors were forced to pay twice as much for inferior saltpeter mined in caves in Kentucky. When government agents asked for price lists and samples from powder mill owners, they found that Du Pont Powder was considerably less costly and more efficient than any other brand.

The war had drawn dangerously close to Eleutherian Mills. British ships blockaded Delaware Bay along with most of the Atlantic Coast. British soldiers burned Washington, marched on Baltimore, and planned an attack on the powder mills. Irénée called for help. The Secretary of War ordered Pennsylvania guardsmen to camp on the factory farm, a few hundred yards from the gate to the mills. Their protection was not sufficient, Irénée complained to Washington. Congress asked the Delaware legislature to authorize the du Pont brothers to enlist their men in the North and South Brandywine Rangers. Powdermakers were issued uniforms and carried rifles while they worked.

The town of Lewes in southern Delaware was shelled. Riders brought urgent requests for kegs of powder to Irénée. The townspeople fought and held: British troops were not going to invade Delaware. A suspicious explosion wrecked part of the mills. The damage was not serious, but Irénée suspected that the blast was caused by strangers seen lurking near the powder yards when it occurred.

Day and night the mills churned, lighted by dangerous kerosene lamps suspended from the ceilings of Irénée's cautiously planned buildings. It was a necessary evil. One night nine men died in an explosion caused by a faulty lamp. Irénée explained to their wives that the deaths were Eleutherian Mills' sacrifice to victory.

Irénée's family worked long hours beside him. Sophie was pregnant with her seventh child; Victorine helped her in the cleaning and running of the workmen's quarters, planning the communal meals cooked every afternoon and evening. Evalina led the powdermakers' wives in sewing bags to hold gunpowder. Alfred, only twelve years old, followed his father around the powder yards, carrying messages and imitating Irénée's long stride and sober expression. Eleuthera was only seven when the war began, Sophie Madeleine just two. Their mother kept them out from under foot.

Napoleon had carefully orchestrated the War of 1812, driving the angers of England and the United States ever higher until only fighting would resolve their differences. Irénée had not needed the war; his mills already produced one-seventh of all the gunpowder manufactured in America. But the war boosted his profits to nearly twenty percent of sales, over forty thousand dollars a year, enough to buy fine furniture for his home, pay Bauduy interest on his investment that, for the time being, quieted his complaints, and send both his own sons and daughters and Victor's to fine schools. He even found money to cover Pierre's continuing extravagances.

In Paris, Pierre wrote coded letters to his sons glorying in the powder company's success. To the powder company shareholders—Jacques Bidermann, Ile-de-France Pusy, Germaine de Staël, and a half-dozen others—Pierre gloated over how rich they would become when Irénée began paying dividends. Since 1800 nothing had come of the money Talleyrand convinced them to give to the du Ponts; now, all together, they clamored for a share of the war profits. Ile-de-France Pusy, widowed recently when her husband died in Napoleon's service, boarded the first available packet boat for the United States. She approached Irénée on the Brandywine and demanded twenty thousand dollars as her portion of the profits, the amount Pierre had assured her was her due. Irénée refused: he had no such sum—even the government's accounts were not yet paid—and he had plowed all the profits back into new and safer mills. He was sorry, but even for his step-sister he could not hope to raise so much cash. Madame Pusy cried that she had been cheated. She and her poor dead husband had placed all their money in Irénée's hands. How was she to support herself and her daughter in America? She angrily wrote Pierre that his son was obviously lining his pockets at her expense.

Peter Bauduy joined the attack, demanding that Irénée step down as director of the company. His partner, Bauduy wrote Pierre, spent outrageous sums on new buildings and machinery. Where, he wanted to know, had the profits gone? Pierre fumed. He would sue his sons, he wrote Irénée. He would empty their pockets and throw them to the wolves. They were thieves, ingrates, unnatural children: he disowned them. Pierre set about destroying Irénée's reputation with the other Paris stockholders.

Jacques Bidermann listened carefully to Pierre's story. France's constant wars had nearly ruined the banker. Once he had been the wealthiest man in Paris; now he had little more than his estate in Switzerland and a few business interests. And he owned more shares in E. I. du Pont de Nemours and Company than Irénée, Bauduy, or anyone else. He told Pierre he would send his son, Antoine, to America to investigate the powder company's affairs.

Antoine found Irénée oddly friendly for a man who might have much to hide. Irénée told Antoine to examine the company books. He would make himself available to answer any questions young Bidermann had. Antoine had none. Not only were the company accounts in order, but he discovered that Peter Bauduy was the only one on the Brandywine who had gained from the mills. For his original investment of about twenty-four thousand dollars Bauduy had been paid nearly one hundred thousand in interest and dividends and his shares were still intact. Irénée had taken precisely none of the profits for himself; even most of his salary remained on the company ledgers to be invested in new buildings and machinery. Disregard Pierre's rantings, Antoine wrote his father: perhaps the old philosopher's seventy-three years were beginning to tell on his mind. He offered a copy of the letter to Peter Bauduy.

Bauduy was stunned: were not Antoine Bidermann's interests his own? How could he side with Irénée, a madman building mill after mill until they stretched out of sight up and down the Brandywine? When the war ended, Bauduy warned, what would the dozen waterwheels that turned all the machinery do? Antoine informed Bauduy that Irénée would be pleased to buy his shares in the company. Would he not rather leave the Brandywine for places where business was conducted differently?

Bauduy's anger collapsed. His pleas to Paris had turned against him. The woolen mill across the Creek, in which he owned a one-third interest, was doing poorly. Even his son, his only son, was dead. Irénée could have the powder company, he told Antoine. He would move on. Secretly, Bauduy had decided to build his own powder mills, steal Irénée's methods and designs for machinery, and lure his partner's workers away. And he planned to file suit against Eleutherian Mills and its director for all they were both worth. Still, he could not quite understand Antoine's siding with the du Ponts.

Irénée could. Antoine was twenty-four, and France was heading toward self-destruction under Bonaparte. Jacques Bidermann did business in the old way, plotting with ministers, supplicating himself to Napoleon, hanging on the whims of the emperor's ministers for every dollar. Antoine wanted his own life. When his father died, nearly a fourth of Eleutherian Mills would be his. War or not, the powder business thrived as America grew. Well before war broke out, Du Pont Powder was being shipped to the Carolinas, Boston, and Ohio. Irénée had proved himself to be more genius than scoundrel: in little more than a decade

Eleutherian Mills had become the largest manufacturer of gunpowder in the United States.

And there was Irénée's second daughter, Evalina, more beautiful than her mother and older sister combined, a young woman of eighteen now, certain someday to inherit her own share of the mills. The day after Peter Bauduy signed his interest in the company over to Irénée, Antoine came to the director's office to begin work at the former partner's old desk. He slept in a bedroom near Irénée and Sophie and ate at the family table, comfortable with the French manners Irénée enforced in his family. After supper he sat near Evalina while she played the piano in the parlor or walked with her in the gardens.

Antoine's appraisal of the way Irénée ran the mills had calmed Pierre. He was an important man once again, head of the welfare system Napoleon had set up to care for the indigent and ill of Paris. Madame Pusy had sailed back to France; she was living with Pierre and her mother, a good deal less outraged at Irénée after Antoine joined the company. Pierre apologized to Irénée and Victor and urged them to return to France. Victor, he felt certain, could find a place in the diplomatic service; Irénée could always manufacture something or other on French soil.

Irénée wrote his father that his life had changed. The Brandywine was his home now. He had given more than a decade to the powder mills, and he was well over sixty thousand dollars in debt; every few weeks he had to appear at the banks to renew his notes. His daughter had lost a husband to the Delaware winter. His wife had borne three children in their house and now she carried another.

All of Victor's children had been born in America, two of them near the Brandywine. He, too, had lost a son-in-law—or at least exiled one—because of what their life in the United States had brought. Victor's oldest son, Charles, attended college in Philadelphia; he was a spirited young man, destined to do well in the United States. And Victor had decided to enter American politics. He and Victor were even captains in the Delaware guard, a useful sideline to powdermaking, Irénée had discovered.

Victor decided to run for the lower house of the Delaware legislature in the election of 1814. The war had ended prejudice against the du Ponts, even if Congress had decided to investigate the role of Eleutherian Mills in the conflict and the profits the company had earned. Irénée was certain he would be absolved of any wrongdoing. But elections were tricky. The South Brandywine Rangers, under Captain Irénée du Pont, assembled in front of the director's house on election day. Irénée marched them to the polls, colors flying. He lectured them about their duty to the country to vote, and to the company to be loyal. Later, legislative investigators took statements from some of the men asserting that Irénée had ordered them to vote for his brother. Others swore that he had said nothing of the kind—implied it, perhaps, but never commanded the men to vote one way or the other. The question remained muddled; the issue was finally dropped when, as a direct result of Victor's election, the United States Congress passed a law prohibiting individuals from forming military organizations, even in time of war. In 1814, soon after President James Madison agreed to sign the Treaty of Ghent, ending the thirty-month war, the North and South Brandywine Rangers disbanded, and Victor called Charles home from college to take charge of the woolen mill. He himself had no time to oversee the weaving of cloth; he must journey to Dover, the capital of the state, to take his elected seat among the lawmakers of Delaware.

Talleyrand summoned Pierre du Pont to him from the ranks of the National Guard. Our time has come, he told Pierre. The allied armies of England, Austria, and Russia have taken Paris. Napoleon will soon be disposed of by the Senate. The empire will fall, Talleyrand assured his old friend. Pierre did not belong marching in the guard like some common citizen. He was seventy-four years old. Talleyrand would find him an important post in the provisional government he planned to install. Soon, he confided, he would restore the Bourbons to their rightful throne. He urged Pierre to join him.

Sergeant of the Guard Pierre du Pont surrendered his sword and uniform when Talleyrand named him secretary general of the provisional regime. Only by the signature of Pierre du Pont would acts of the Senate become law, and only where Talleyrand instructed him to place it would Pierre's name appear.

First came the abdication of Napoleon, Emperor of France. Pierre affixed his name to the document and to the announcement of it that printers spread throughout France. The Emperor, it said above Napoleon's signature and his own, was the only obstacle to peace in Europe. Contemplating this at the palace of Fountainbleu, Napoleon had decided to descend the throne, for the good of France. He would remove himself, read another paper certified by Pierre, to the island of Elba, with a suitable contingent of servants and soldiers. Elba would be the Emperor's domain; a thousand men his legions.

Bonaparte left Paris under guard. Pierre wrote to his sons that the despicable little Corsican, Napoleone Buonaparte, had finally left France to the French. Talleyrand was preparing Paris for the return of the Bourbons. Pierre's beloved Louis XVI would be avenged at last. Irénée need no longer send boxes of seeds for him to use in bribing government officials. The powdermaker's father stood near Talleyrand's right hand, at the very center of power. Soon he would bow to the new king, Louis XVIII.

Louis took the crown and scepter of Charlemagne from Talleyrand's hands and appointed his brother, the Comte D'Artois, to run the government. Talleyrand did not object; he had been offered the foreign ministry once again, and he knew Europe would soon be carved into new states. He relished the prospect of matching wits with Metternich in Austria. Artois could run the government as he wished. The comte did not wish to consult Pierre du Pont: the old philosopher's ideas about a government patterned on that of the United States were dangerously radical, especially for the comte's tastes. Pierre would be released from his arduous duties, as befitted an elder statesman of a former era. Eight days after signing Napoleon's abdication, Pierre walked heavily into the parlor of his new apartment on the Rue de Surenne, where all the powerful French bureaucrats lived, and wondered out loud to Françoise what he would do with the remainder of his life.

The Comte D'Artois appointed a younger man to take Pierre's place in the Paris department of welfare, but Louis XVIII did not entirely forget Pierre's loyalty to him in the face of Napoleon Bonaparte's rule. He presented Pierre with the Décoration du Lis, soon to become the Ordre du Lis, France's highest award for patriotism. Once again, the king assured Pierre, his advice would be welcomed in the highest councils of government. At the same time, Louis instructed his ministers to listen respectfully to Pierre's suggestions, answer politely his long memoranda, and ignore his ideas.

Pierre took to pacing his apartment in frustration. He would leave France, he kept telling his wife. He had written to Talleyrand; he would get his passport back from the foreign minister and join his sons on the Brandywine. Françoise urged him not to go. She had had a bad fall, on the icy winter streets of Paris, and she needed him at her bedside; it would be months before her broken hip healed. Talleyrand agreed. Stay, he wrote Pierre, there is much to do and you will be needed. Spring will bring into bloom a new Europe eager for the services and wisdom of the likes of Pierre du Pont.

Instead, spring brought Napoleon Bonaparte back to France.

Elba had proved to be less of a prison than Talleyrand intended. Word of the French people's hatred for Louis XVIII quickly reached Napoleon, and the former Emperor convinced his thousand-man guard that they could recapture the throne: the good of France demanded that they try. With three shiploads of soldiers Napoleon sailed from Elba, landed safely near Fréjus, and began a triumphal march to Paris to begin his Hundred Day reign. When word came that a contingent of Bonaparte's faithful were hours from Paris under orders to imprison him, Louis XVIII announced his abdication and fled the city. The Comte D'Artois ran with him.

The news reached Pierre immediately. He hurried through the streets to the American consulate, where William Crawford, the United States ambassador, wrote out a passport for one Peter Du Pont, citizen of America, resident of Louisiana, aged more than sixty years, white-haired, blue-eyed, large-nosed, oval-faced, and fair of complexion, on official business for the American legation to the President of the United States, accompanied by his secretary, Maurice Bureaux. The bearer was to be passed without question through the boundaries of France and all other nations on to the soil of the United States.

Pierre pleaded with Françoise to accompany him. He would have her carried to Le Havre on a litter if necessary, then brought to the Brandywine by special chair. They must leave at once: if Napoleon found him, Pierre would be shot as a traitor.

No, Françoise said, she was too weak to go. Pierre should take along someone to help him aboard the ship. She would stay behind. Bonaparte would never dare visit his wrath on her, she was certain. She had a distant relative who might be persuaded to travel to America under a false name as Pierre's secretary; he had numerous large debts he would never be able to pay.

The relative was summoned. Pierre quickly packed his clothes and a sheaf of manuscripts. His traveling companion saddled two horses and awaited Pierre outside the apartment on the Rue de Surenne. They would ride the back roads, Pierre decided, until Napoleon's growing horde of supporters passed them on the way to Paris, then take to the main highway, and finally board the first ship leaving Le Havre.

Pierre assured Françoise that they would soon be together again. He would write from America at once, and by then she would be able to make the journey. He would design a house for them near his son's and he would be welcomed by his old friend Thomas Jefferson. Already the retired President had asked his help in planning a constitution for what were called the Equinoctial Republics in South America. Françoise must not despair: a new world awaited them, where they would build a richer, better life.

Pierre leaned over his wife's bed and kissed her gently on the cheek. She wished him a safe journey and returned his affection sadly. France, she knew, would not again allow Pierre du Pont to set foot on her soil. And she would never forsake Paris for a crude existence on the banks of the Brandywine Creek.

Pierre retired exhausted to his second-floor bedroom in Irénée's house, delighted at what he had seen that morning in the powder yards. Irénée had conducted him through each building in the mills, showing his father where sulfur, charcoal, and saltpeter were dampened, pounded, and mixed, where the raw mixture was pressed into large cakes and the moisture forced out, and where the cakes were sent through sieves to produce different-sized grains of black powder.

The mills, he wrote Françoise in Paris, were like hens that laid golden eggs. All this carved out of an uncultivated wilderness by Irénée's courage alone! Pierre had never dared expect his quiet younger son to have the strength and tenacity to build such an enterprise.

And the children! He had watched the sons and daughters of Victor and Irénée at work and at play: jewels glistening in an untamed land. He had bounced his great-grandchild, Amelia's daughter Gabrielle, on his knee. They were all healthy, handsome children. They called him Bonpapa and listened for hours to his tales of the old France and Napoleon. Victor's sons, Charles and Samuel, were especially bright. Irénée's Alfred loved the powder yards; he would grow into them. Irénée's daughters were all beautiful and talented. But poor Victorine! She seemed to have so little to live for, so few joys. She would become his special friend, his closest confidant on the Brandywine.

Evalina was starry-eyed over Antoine Bidermann: it would be an excellent match, and the marriage would be soon. And still more children would come. Sophie was pregnant again, at forty years of age. It seemed odd that Irénée, already turning gray, so fatigued and worried by the mills, would still be fathering offspring. Sophie had been giving birth since 1792, nearly a quarter-century of childbearing.

Victor had become a politician, Pierre wrote to his wife, in the best tradition of the du Ponts. He gave grand speeches in the Delaware Assembly while Charles ran the woolen mills, indeed, ran them well for a boy of eighteen. But Victor was still fat, and Gabrielle as always begged and plotted to return to France, alone if need be. Nothing could overcome her hatred for America.

Pierre saw greatness in his grandchildren; they would meet his expectations for the men and women named du Pont. For himself, a few years remained, years of contemplation and writing on the banks of the Brandywine, sweet years of love once François joined him. When would she be able to travel?

Soon, Françoise answered.

His plans for their house were ready, Pierre wrote, a small two-story home near Irénée's with a pleasant patio and a garden. Until it was finished, he would move his desk away from his bed in the room Irénée had given him, and place her desk near his so that they might hold hands while he worked at his writing. He had, he supposed, ten years left on earth. They must be spent with the woman he had loved for thirty years, courted for twenty-eight, lived with for twenty. Soon he would journey to Monticello to see his old friend Jefferson. They had been writing to each other, of their philosophies of men and nations, of the future of the world, of the implications of the past. He would ask Jefferson to help place his grandson, Samuel Francis, in the United States navy; the boy yearned for the sea. President Madison, he told Françoise, had been kind enough to offer him the White House as a mailing address, so his letters from Françoise would not be lost crossing the ocean. Write to him there soon, he urged her and come soon: they must die together.

Irénée, he added, was terribly tormented and unhappy because of his troubles with Peter Bauduy. He came to his father often for affection and advice. He had even spoken of abandoning the mills and moving to the Kentucky woods to farm or graze sheep. Banks hounded Irénée, customers refused to pay him, the government patronized others who made inferior powder. And the constant danger of explosions weighed heavily on his son's shoulders.

Throughout the spring, summer, and autumn of 1815 Pierre wrote to Françoise in Paris, letters of love and pleading, finally begging his wife to join him in America. With each answer Françoise delayed. She complained that a sea voyage would damage her weakened leg. She was comfortable in Paris, with her old friends calling daily and her daughter and grandson to care for her. She urged Pierre to beware of the Brandywine's dampness; he must rest and take care of his gout and arthritis. Perhaps he need not arise each dawn with the trumpet calling the men to work in the powder yards. Françoise congratulated Pierre on Evalina's wedding to young Bidermann, joined in his depression over an explosion in the mills that left five women widowed and a dozen children fatherless, relayed her hopes that Irénée would recover from his despair and rebuild the mills quickly.

Pierre became discouraged. His wife might be too lame to travel the seas, but she might, too, not wish to journey to America. He toyed with returning to France. Irénée and Victor convinced him it would be folly: his children, his grandchildren, his great-grandchildren all needed their Bonpapa. The plans for a small house for himself and Françoise gathered dust. Pierre began drawing a small addition to Irénée's home, with just enough room to accommodate a single man.

Daily, through the spring and summer of 1816, Pierre worked at the writing desk where he had hoped to hold hands with his wife. A breeze off the Brandywine cooled the hot summer afternoons. From his window he could see Sophie bringing Irénée his dinner while her husband worked among the powdermen, loading wagons, testing batches of the black granules, or building another mill. Victorine's sorrowful notes rose from the piano in the parlor below, and a baby, another of his descendants, cried to be fed in Irénée's bedroom next door. The Brandywine Creek might not be the Seine, Irénée's house not Versailles, his gardens not the gardens of the Tuileries. But, Pierre knew, he was at last home.

# 12

O N A HOT July night in 1817 a powder yard watchman's shrill whistle snapped Irénée du Pont's mind automatically out of deep sleep into consciousness. He listened in the darkness for the dread boom of the alarm going, signaling fire in the mills. It came, rolling echoes miles up and down the Brandywine.

The household awakened instantly, dressing, running out into the night. Irénée spotted his father on the stairs and urged him to stay inside; the powder workers would handle whatever had happened. Pierre refused: he would fight alongside his son.

A charcoal worker, tired from the long day and summer heat, had emptied one of the furnaces too soon. In barrels and sacks the charcoal had rekindled itself. Within minutes the water pumps ran dry, and powdermen and their wives formed long lines from the Creek to the charcoal house. If the fire spread, they all knew, the gunpowder stored a few yards away would explode.

Charles Dalmas and Antoine Bidermann worked dangerously near the burning building, directing the men. Irénée fought to save the powder magazine and pounding mill. Pierre pushed his way into the bucket brigade, urging the men and women to work faster, passing pail after pail of water with his own hands.

Irénée felt for the wind off the Brandywine. At this time of year it might be dry and would spread the fire quickly. The walls of the charcoal house collapsed, narrowly missing Dalmas. Sparks flew high into the air, but there was no wind, and they fell back onto the ruins. A cry came for more water. Pierre prodded the workers on. His hands bled from the bucket handles; his face was blackened with soot from the clouds of charcoal dust.

The fire was contained. At dawn Irénée sought out his father and helped him up to the director's house. Pierre could barely speak, his voice hoarse from hours of yelling. His nightclothes—he had not stopped to change—were soaked from splashing water and crusted with dirt. His feet were black from standing for hours in inches of tar Bidermann had spilled out of barrels to keep it from igniting.

Sophie led her father-in-law to his bedroom, covered him with heavy quilts, and ran to tell Irénée that she believed Pierre was very ill. Irénée asked her to care for him until he returned: he must inspect the mills, begin clearing the rubble, and thank his men for stopping the blaze.

Gabrielle hurried across the Brandywine. Sophie had sent word that Pierre was desperately ill. A messenger rode for Dover to tell Victor that his father could not rise from his bed: he must hurry home. Doctors sped from Wilmington to treat the old man. Pierre's strength drained quickly; his face, browned by the summer sun, paled within hours. The doctors left: Pierre was dying, they said. The pain must be excruciating—pneumonia, perhaps his heart as well, but for the most part his age. Men of seventy-seven should not spend their nights fighting fires or carrying buckets of water. It would be over soon, they told Irénée. Comfort him; it is all that can be done.

But Pierre refused to die. He had been on the Brandywine only two years. Jefferson awaited him at Monticello; they had important matters to discuss. President James Monroe needed his counsel. Irénée must have his father's advice. And poor Victorine wanted company in the rose garden. He would live to see Evalina and Antoine's first child, their second—their last! Irénée's youngest, Alexis, barely knew his grandfather. Pierre urged Irénée to return to the mills. A little rest and he would be out of bed again: just a few days' rest.

For two weeks Pierre fought, staying conscious while he suffered pain the doctors could not stop. One morning Sophie could not arouse him from his sleep. She listened for his breath; it came, barely, but his eyes would not open. He had slipped into a coma. Irénée ran from the yards to the house. Victor and his son Charles rowed across the Creek from Louviers. Through two days they listened to Pierre's low groans and watched his pale skin turn transparent. Late on the second night Pierre's lungs gave out an eerie wheeze and he died.

In a clearing in Sand Hole Woods, less than five hundred yards from Irénée's house, a grave had been dug. The powder mills were quiet; Irénée had ordered his men to stop work for the day. The family watched silently as shovelfuls of dirt covered Bonpapa Pierre's coffin. No one cried; it was not the du Pont way. Here, Irénée had decided, would be the family burial ground, near the director's house, where he could walk easily from his library or his office to visit with his father.

The beech trees and oaks would shade the clearing forever. The mills were out of sight but within hearing.

Irénée walked to his house, through the hall ablaze with Victorine's roses, and out onto the piazza. Messages had to be sent, to Lafayette and Jefferson, to his father's widow in Paris, to the Institute of France, to the White House in Washington. He looked down on the powder yards, stretching now as far north and south as he could see, to where the charcoal house had stood and the lines of men and women had passed buckets of water to be poured on the fire. Slowly, the oars of a boat dipped into the Creek beyond the mills, carrying Victor back to his home. The current of the Brandywine obliged, slipping past the boat's bow gently, constantly, carrying the skiff slightly downstream but not too far.

Near where Irénée leaned on the piazza railing stood the small wooden rocking horse his workers had fashioned from the first trees cut down along the Brandywine fifteen years earlier. Pierre had loved playing with the children on the piazza, telling them stories as he tipped the rocking horse back and forth. Now his father's flesh would mingle with the soil the Creek fed in a thousand underground springs. No, Irénée reflected, the du Ponts would not soon leave the shores of the Brandywine.

Irénée visited Sand Hole Woods daily, standing alone for hours near his father's fresh grave. Life and work on the Brandywine must go on, he knew: the nation needed his gunpowder. The family had gathered to send Victor's son Samuel Francis off to the navy; soon the boy would become Midshipman du Pont, the first of Pierre's descendants to leave the Brandywine for service in America's armed forces. Pierre would have been pleased that the du Pont men were proudly willing to defend their homeland.

His father had taken great pride in Victor's political career, too. Victor had been elected to the Delaware senate, without the help of the North and South Brandywine Rangers. It looked as though Charles might follow in his father's footsteps; he had the easy wit and open manner politicians needed.

Irénée was glad his sons were more serious about life than their cousins across the Creek. Alfred, his eldest boy, had graduated from Dickinson College in Philadelphia, majoring in chemistry. On vacations Alfred had refused to leave the powder yards, often sleeping in a clearing near the water. As a child he had retrieved the dummy cannonballs Irénée shot through small fieldpieces to test the strength of Du Pont Powder. Now he took to tinkering with the powdermaking process. Irénée saw in Alfred a glimpse of his own youth at Essonnes, working in Lavoisier's laboratory after finishing his bookkeeping for the day.

Henry reminded Irénée of himself, too, but in a different way. The boy was sober, tall, slender, even as silent as his father—and a mere six years old. He would attend school after Victorine finished teaching him the ABC's. Alexis, the baby, seemed much like Alfred, frail and gentle, but inquisitive. If they did not follow their cousin into government service, Irénée thought he could make powdermen of them all. He had taken over Victor's share in the powder mills and would soon need sons to run the yards. Except for a few French stockholders, he and Antoine Bidermann owned the company outright.

Antoine had turned into a marvel of a businessman. His energy never seemed to give out, riding dusty coaches across the country to confer with the company's fifty agents, writing hundreds of letters to customers, fighting competitors in Washington for precious government orders. He and Evalina had moved into Hagley, their own home down the Creek, and she had presented Antoine with a strapping son, James. Irénée had become a grandfather soon after his own father's death. Evalina often came to her father's house to read letters from her sister Eleuthera, who had been sent to Madame Rivardi's, an exclusive Philadelphia girls school. Eleuthera was as beautiful as her sisters.

Victorine had begun to lose the mask of sorrow Ferd Bauduy's death had imprinted over her own lovely smile. She had started teaching school on Sundays, taking the children of the powdermakers into her class, giving them reading and writing skills their parents, mostly Irish immigrants, had never learned. The workers and their families addressed her as "Madame Bauduy." She had devoted her life to the Brandywine.

Victorine was much better off than his brother's daughter Amelia, Irénée believed. Even little Gabrielle Josephine gave her mother no joy. Amelia had turned to Catholicism for solace. Victorine had grown religious, too, but in the face of her lonely life Irénée did not object: at least she had attached herself to the Episcopal church rather than Catholicism. Most of Irénée's workers thought it odd that their boss had no liking for religion; they themselves wished to be square with their maker at any given time. Explosions did not wait for Sunday's sermon to end.

Soon after Pierre died Talleyrand demanded repayment of his ten-year-old loan. Irénée wrote that he could not pay; perhaps his father's old friend would be willing to take his money over a period of ten years. He would try to send it sooner, but he could promise nothing. Most of the powder company's customers bought on long credit and paid long after their credit ran out.

The United States bordered on a major economic crisis. Businesses were failing by the thousand. Banks, it was rumored, had not the gold in their vaults to back up their specie. Irénée often rode to Philadelphia to plead with his bankers for more time to meet his notes. Peter Bauduy had frightened Irénée's creditors with tales of his former partner's mismanagement of the mills and with a lawsuit that dragged on for eight years, aimed at forcing dissolution of the company. Bauduy charged that powder company profits paid off Victor du Pont's debts and that Irénée had had the audacity to invest company funds in two new businesses, a cotton mill and a tannery, just when the nation's commerce ebbed to a new low. He claimed that both were dismal failures which dimmed the powder company shareholders' chances for any return on their investment.

Ile-de-France Pusy joined Bauduy in his suit, first from Paris, then Philadelphia. Irénée coolly fought his former partner and step-sister, winning in the end, but not before he had to call Alfred home from Philadelphia to run the powder yards: he could not both oversee the mills and spend two or three days a week in Philadelphia convincing the banks that Eleutherian Mills remained a good business risk.

Sophie du Pont lay dazed amid the rubble of her bedroom. She had been hit on the side, either by the force of a powder blast or the falling stone that came afterward. She could hear the shouts of men and women from the powder yards. Alexis, her youngest son, stood crying a few feet from her. Rubble from a falling wall had broken around him, covering his black hair with stucco dust. Sophie could not move to answer his screams.

Shock waves rumbled through the ground from the north. Sophie realized the newest mills, the Upper Yard as Irénée called it, must have blown. Irénée had built five new mills in the Upper Yard. The ground shook as though all of them had exploded at once.

In the Upper Yard the powdermen's wives converged on the one building that had gone, the glazing mill where grains of powder were polished and smoothed. As many as a hundred people ran for the same spot. Workers began rolling kegs of power into the Creek to keep them from the fire the explosion had started.

And then it came, a thunderous roar, starting in the hills above the Brandywine, shaking trees and the soil, lifting stone houses high off the ground, tossing bodies through the air. Sophie knew it could only be the grand magazine, hewn from solid rock, deep inside a hill where her husband felt sure neither fire nor blast could reach the stored gunpowder.

In the city of Wilmington panic gripped the people: some great force had shaken the streets, broken windows, torn the brick walls off strong old homes. Women huddled in cellars clutching their children; men ran frantically from their businesses to their homes. Someone yelled earthquake; someone else ran from the shore of the Delaware River screaming that a steamboat had blown up. A farmer from the west, near the mills, galloped down Market Street shouting that the grand magazine had exploded. People surged toward the river in horror; another crowd ran for the powder yards, senselessly propelled by their fascination with destruction. Riders streamed in from every town within miles bearing tales of shattered windows and falling chimneys. Soon a man breathlessly fell off a lathered horse: he had felt the blast in Lancaster, forty-three miles to the northwest.

Charles Dalmas writhed on the ground near the edge of the Brandywine. He had gone to comfort a powderman's wife when the magazine blew. His arm was broken, perhaps a leg as well. He could be of no use to the injured; he simply stared up at the blackened sky.

Across the Creek, Victor watched the scene in horror. A man had been standing next to him when the blast hit: he had been blown to pieces. Victor could see bodyless limbs hanging in the trees above him, carried hundreds of yards in the burning wind that followed the explosion.

Women wandered through the destroyed yards, searching for their husbands and children. Those men left whole hunted for their friends. Smoke, acrid with the odor of sulfur, billowed from every building of the mills, gathered above the Brandywine, and hung there. The usually quiet Creek rolled and crashed in waves along its banks.

Every home along the Brandywine had been turned into a makeshift hospital. Injured men, women, and children, wrapped in torn sheets that served as bandages, lay on pallets in the parlors. Workers began dragging lifeless bodies from the wreckage while a dozen fires still burned, laying the dead side by side as far from the flames as possible. The death count rose to eight, but no higher. Yet many more were missing: twenty men could not be accounted for. Soon the men could no longer hide the truth from the women: what was left of their husbands hung in bits of flesh up and down the Brandywine.

Irénée had been in Philadelphia on one of his frequent money-raising trips when a messenger brought him the news in his hotel room. He galloped up to his house to see empty air where the side wall of his bedroom had stood. Sophie and Charles Dalmas had been carried to beds. The children were unhurt, but Alexis still cried, refusing to be comforted. Irénée ran down into the yards, to the strange scene of a powder blast's aftermath that left some buildings untouched while others, a few feet away, were reduced to pebbles and splinters of wood. Only a black hole remained where the grand magazine had been. The Upper Yard was completely gone. The main mills, the oldest, were useless. Even the Hagley Works, far downstream, had been devastated. A half mile beyond them the workers' small homes, built of solid rock, no longer existed. Irénée could not escape the truth: Eleutherian Mills had ceased to be. It was time for him to talk with the workers and their wives.

No one blamed the disaster on him, they all said. A man had been seen running from the glazing mill just after the first blast. It had been carelessness, they all agreed. Irénée visited with the women, trying to quiet their grief. As always, he said, the company would take care of them. Those whose husbands had died would receive pensions for life, a home for as long as they wanted it, and education for their children. Any orphans would become wards of the du Pont family itself. The Brandywine was their home; they would never want for shelter or food. He would provide decent burials for all who had perished, even coffins and graves and markers for the ones whose bodies could not be pieced back together again.

Irénée sat with the wounded, consoling them, promising that their injuries would not cause them to be fired. This was the Brandywine, he said, not some other factory: all his workers were part of his family, part of his life. They need not worry about the future, just get well. Some, Irénée realized, were dying. He thanked them quietly for their years of loyalty, praised their courage, and assured them that their families would never become paupers, that their sons would forever be welcome to work for him, to carry on their fathers' tradition in the mills.

Haggard after two nights without sleep, Irénée sat down heavily at

Charles Dalmas's bedside. He recounted the toll: thirty-six dead in the blast, at least four more dying, six orphans, a half-dozen women gone. Fully half the mills had been razed, the rest damaged beyond repair. They would need a year to rebuild, at the least, if the money could be borrowed. The powder workers still alive were demoralized; they talked of leaving the Brandywine for a safer home. If they left Irénée could never hope to replace their experience. He shook his head in disbelief: forty of a hundred and forty workers gone in one explosion.

It would be years, if ever, before Sophie walked erect again: her side was almost completely paralyzed. They were leaving the director's house, Irénée told his brother-in-law. The roof might collapse at any moment. Victor had set up beds in the parlor and living room at Louviers. Irénée ordered Dalmas to rest. He had sent word to Antoine Bidermann, away on a business trip, to return at once. Alfred was barely twenty, but he could direct the men while Charles recovered. He himself must ride back to Philadelphia at once, to convince the banks that he needed fifty thousand dollars in cash or all of Eleut' erian Mills would become a graveyard. At least, Irénée remarked wryly, the explosion would quiet the demands for money from France.

# *13*

IRÉNÉE DU PONT rebuilt Eleutherian Mills with money and credit from Philadelphia banks and the loyalty of the powdermakers of the Brandywine. Only two had chosen to leave after the explosion. Many sons of men who had died in the blast grew to adulthood and took their fathers' places in the yards. Irénée did not press them into his service: he did not allow child labor at Eleutherian Mills. The fatherless, and in some cases motherless boys spent happy childhoods playing along the Creek, swimming in summer and sledding down the hills in winter. True to his word, Irénée saw to their physical needs. Victorine, on Sundays, taught them reading and arithmetic and commended their souls to God.

Alfred du Pont took much of the burden of running the powder yards from his father's shoulders. Irénée joined the Whig party and became one of its most important policymakers. He was appointed a director of the Bank of the United States and worked to stabilize the nation's economy. He had reconstructed the powder mills during the worst economic crisis the United States had seen since the revolution; he wanted urgently to prevent another depression.

Sophie took great pride in her husband's political stature and importance among manufacturers. The explosion had crippled her, stopping the daily work she did, cleaning the unmarried workmen's quarters and making the communal evening meal; she relied heavily on Victorine to take over her tasks. Often she spoke to Irénée about returning to France for a long visit, to see Paris and the country house in Nemours where their married life had begun. Irénée wished, too, that they might journey across the Atlantic; he promised that they would one day make the trip. He and his workers had rebuilt the mills in a year. Since then orders for Du Pont gunpowder had rushed in from explorers and trappers and miners and road builders who pushed the boundaries of the United States ever farther westward. In five years black powder production at Eleutherian Mills had doubled and doubled again. Yet Irénée could not plan a visit to France; he still rode to Philadelphia every few days to renew his notes and plead for more credit.

Six years after the explosion of the grand magazine the Marquis de Lafayette decided to visit the burial place of his old companion Pierre du Pont. He had been invited to tour the United States as a guest of the President. For the first time in many years the community on the Brandywine exploded in gaiety. Each of Irénée and Sophie's four daughters ordered long white gloves embossed with Lafayette's picture and two dresses, one for the fête their father and Uncle Victor planned for the marquis, another for the wedding of their cousin Charles.

Victor's eldest son, Charles, was engaged to Dorcas Montgomery Van Dyke, daughter of a United States Senator, one of Pennsylvania's most respected citizens. Lafayette had agreed to extend his stay long enough to attend Charles's wedding. Many celebrities would travel to the Brandywine from Washington for the celebration and wedding, and crowds of local folks would line the roads near Eleutherian Mills to catch a glimpse of the famous marquis.

Irénée wondered at his children and Victor's, marrying so quickly in this country. Victor's little Julia—eighteen already—had chosen Navy Lieutenant Irvine Shubrick as a husband, a solid young man from a fine military family. His own son Alfred had brought a Philadelphia girl, Margaretta Lammot, home to meet Irénée and Sophie. Margaretta was from a French immigrant family Irénée knew well; he and Daniel Lammot had done business together for years. Irénée felt certain Alfred would spend his entire life running Eleutherian Mills; the Lammot girl would make a fine wife for a powderman.

Irénée realized that these marrying du Ponts would want homes of their own. On the road to Hagley, Antoine and Evalina's house, there was room for another. He would call it Nemours and give it to Alfred and Margaretta as a wedding present. And Victor had approached him with a plan for a second home across the Brandywine, farther up the steep hill. Victor wanted Charles and Dorcas to have his own home, Louviers. The young couple had decided to start a tradition: they would plant two evergreen seedlings outside the door to Louviers right after the wedding ceremony. Victor needed Irénée's help to build the new house. His political life-style cost a great deal to sustain, and his gambling debts—he had never broken the old habit—ran rather high. Irénée smiled at his brother and agreed to provide the money for Upper Louviers.

Irénée felt a certain emptiness about the director's house after Lafayette's visit and Charles's and Alfred's weddings. Henry was away at school in Pennsylvania. Alexis would soon follow, if Irénée could tear him away from the powder yards; dressed in blue overalls and heavy boots, the boy looked and acted like a miniature powderman. Eleuthera was off at school, too, although Irénée knew Philadelphia's social life, not the lessons taught at Madame Rivardi's, occupied most of her thoughts. Soon only Victorine and his youngest daughter, Sophie Madeleine, would sit down to supper each night with their mother and father.

Much had changed since the explosion of the grand magazine, both in Irénée's family and in the powder yards. Most of the powder workers had given up smoking their pipes, afraid that a single spark might set off another blast. New safety measures had been instituted: the workers' boots were made especially for them at company expense with wooden plugs instead of nails. No smoking materials—lit or unlit—were allowed through the mill gates. Irénée had assigned men to guard the gates twenty-four hours a day, just in case an irate competitor tried to sabotage his factory. Each morning at dawn the workers left their wives at the high white fence and the guards locked the gates behind them. Irénée could not bear the thought of another explosion like the last, with women running toward their husbands and fathers, only to lose their own lives.

Even with their boss's deep regard for their safety, the workers had developed an almost fatalistic attitude toward their jobs. They spoke of going "across the Creek," of leaving their wives and children well fixed when their time came. Many bought farms outside the mills with the high salaries Irénée paid and rented them out until retirement, or until they went "across the Creek."

Irénée knew each of his men by name. They called him Mister Irénée, his sons Mister Alfred and Master Alexis. Sophie rarely went beyond the director's house and gardens, but when she ventured into the yards the workers gathered around her, helping their Madame Sophie down the steep hill, inquiring about her health. Antoine Bidermann rarely went into the powder yards, either; most of his time was spent in the small company office, writing letters and managing the company's daily finances. The business had grown enormously under Antoine's deft hand. He had quickly hired agents to replace those lost in the nationwide depression. Railroads were being built throughout the East, their roadbeds often blasted with Irénée's best gunpowder. Ships rarely left

Delaware Bay without at least a quarter-load of Du Pont Powder, or kegs stamped with the other names Irénée used to market inferior grades of black powder.

Alfred worked to eliminate these inferior kegs. The powdermen loved and trusted Mister Alfred even more than they revered his father. Alfred never shirked a task and never left the powder yards until the last of the workers had gone for the day. His frail body was not as strong as Irénée's, his courage in the face of danger not as apparent, but the men never questioned Mister Alfred's word on any matter: they said he knew more about powdermaking than even Mister Irénée. And Alfred spoke without a trace of the accent that betrayed his father's birthplace and set him off from the Irish workers.

Alfred set up a little laboratory in one of the Upper Yard buildings. From the remains of gunpowder's three ingredients he had developed new products: a dye called iron liquor and a preservative known as creosote. Even the dust of refined saltpeter was being packaged and sold through Du Pont Company agents. Irénée knew that the sales amounted to very little compared with gunpowder, hardly enough to justify the work involved. But someday in the future Alfred with his test tubes and flasks might discover something really useful in the manufacture of black powder, and so Irénée encouraged his son: gunpowder, after all, was the only product Irénée ever intended E. I. du Pont de Nemours and Company to make.

Victor du Pont died in his Philadelphia hotel room on a cold January day in 1827. He was fifty-nine years old. He had spent the morning with friends, then walked back to the United States Hotel. Within a block of the building he collapsed in the street and was carried to his room. A doctor came, but Victor was already gone, dead of a ruptured cavity in his heart.

Irénée drove a carriage to Philadelphia to claim his brother's body. He had instructed his workers to dig a grave to the right and below Pierre's. As the elder son, Victor would be buried there. When his own time came, Irénée decided, he would rest to his father's left. And so it would proceed from then on, Victor's descendants to Pierre's right, Irénée's to his left.

Charles would take over his father's woolen mills. He ran them already—had for many years. Even Victor's political place would be filled by his elder son. But nothing could replace his brother completely, as foolish as Victor had always been, a spendthrift, a gambler, some said a blowhard. Seventeen years had passed since Irénée rescued Victor from the woods of the Genesee River valley. Victor had been his childhood idol, carefree and robust, traveling the world while Irénée struggled as a bookkeeper and printer. Even when Victor had failed, time after time, and grown bloated on food and his own ego, Irénée had admired and loved him.

Yet they had little in common. Victor, as a young man, had been the pretty du Pont, gay, untroubled. Irénée had always worried about the large red birthmark on his left cheek; his brother had no such physical burdens. Victor had been their father's favorite, Pierre's choice for the diplomat and statesman who would inherit the du Pont mantle. Irénée had seemed dull to his father, a plodding, laboring man who rarely smiled, knew little of how to converse with the giants of government, and cared less. But Irénée had not the capacity to hate or envy or even dislike his brother. He had cherished, in his own silent way, every moment they had spent together.

Now only Sophie remained to lift him from his melancholy over Victor's death. And Sophie was not well. The old injury from the explosion had eased, but something had taken its place. His wife rarely smiled; her legs were often swollen beyond all recognition; her color was not right. Irénée drew closer to Sophie as the spring after Victor's death came and passed. Antoine spent most of his time on the Brandywine; Irénée had little need to look after the daily affairs of the mills. Alfred, at the age of twenty-nine, ran the powder yards as well as Irénée himself ever had. Irénée could afford the luxury of afternoons spent in the garden with his wife, talking of their youth in France; only his rides to Philadelphia to extend his company's credit farther and farther need interrupt his days with Sophie.

With summer Irénée ceased even his short journeys to Philadelphia. Sophie had taken to bed, unable to walk the few yards to the garden. Irénée rarely left her side, talking when she was up to it, thinking and staring through a window out onto the Brandywine while she rested. He slept on a hard chair, never daring to leave the room, writing brief notes to business associates on his lap when Antoine said it must be done, bringing the children into their mother's bedroom when she asked for them. Always, Victorine's roses brightened Sophie's bedside table.

Irénée stayed at his wife's side late into the fall. When the pain became unbearable doctors gave her pills and potions, but little helped except holding her husband's hand. On a late November day, warm for the season, Sophie Madeleine Dalmas du Pont died. After the burial Irénée wandered down into the powder yards and for once the workers did not question their boss's unsmiling face.

Irénée stared at the large portrait of himself. His children had presented it to him on his sixtieth birthday. The light brown, nearly blond hair of his youth was gone; at best, a few wisps of gray trailed across his forehead where a waterfall of curls had been. He could not argue with the painter's ability; Rembrandt Peale had sketched and immortalized most of his family over the years, and he liked the renowned artist's portraits of his daughters. But these sunken eyes, these long folds of skin about the jaw: was this the same man he had seen in a drawing made forty years ago? He recognized the cleft chin and heavy eyebrows, but little else. Time had taken its toll.

So, too, had business. Running the mills had become an enormous task. Even he had never dreamed they would succeed so well. His father's prophecy for the United States had come true: the vigor and resources of the people could be matched only by the wealth of the land. Americans seemed eternally restless, eager to spread out into the wilderness, to pound stakes into earth untouched except by herds of buffalo and unshod Indian ponies. Minds matched bodies in strength in America. Inventions flowed through Congress's patent office by the hundreds each year, and machines became the tools of farmers and miners and trappers. Every step, it seemed, required Du Pont Powder to make it worthwhile. While pioneers pushed back the boundaries of civilization in the West, Congress moved jealously to protect the stake Eastern factories had in the hungry new markets the settlers opened. But there were those who did not enjoy hearing Washington make laws that affected the welfare of the states.

South Carolina was the most fiery of the objectors. When word came from Washington that new tariffs would tax raw materials and textiles at a much higher rate than manufactured goods, the Southerners exploded in anger. South Carolina's legislature proclaimed the "tariff of abominations" illegal in that state and forbade United States customs agents to collect their bounty inside South Carolina's borders. President Andrew Jackson, fuming at the state's lawmakers, reinforced Fort Sumter near Charleston. Word came that the legislators, in a resolution, had proclaimed their right to secede from the Union if Congress passed laws not to their liking. Talk of secession spread like wildfire through South Carolina towns. Jackson damned the Southerners for their insolence: a state could not secede, he said, without breaking up the Union, an act of treason against the Constitution, which he was sworn to uphold and which, if necessary, he would enforce with bullets.

South Carolina prepared for war. They could never fight Jackson's troops, the legislators knew, without munitions. And so a Mr. C. R. Holmes, a private citizen of Charleston, asked the Du Pont Company's New York agent to place an order with Irénée for one hundred twenty thousand pounds of his best black powder which, Holmes said, he would pay for in cash. Irénée's suspicions were aroused. He wrote the agent that, regretfully, he would not fill such an order. He had the powder, and sorely needed the cash, but there was no question in his mind where the cannon, musket, and rifle powder was bound. E. I. du Pont de Nemours and Company would be pleased to provide rifle powder to its Southern friends when they wanted it for peaceful purposes, but cannon and musket fuel: never.

The South Carolina legislature abandoned its plans to secede; the state could not hope to defeat Jackson's troops without Irénée's gunpowder. The President called Irénée to Washington to help set up compromise tariffs that his Northern friends would find acceptable. Irénée disliked Andrew Jackson, especially for his attempts to disband the Bank of the United States, but both men knew that the price of war might be the life of the Union. The Nullifiers of South Carolina, as they liked to be known, and the monopolist manufacturers of the North, as Irénée called them, reached terms. For the time being, the United States avoided civil war.

Sophie Madeleine du Pont, named for her mother, reminded Irénée of his wife. The girl had a quiet kind of beauty his own Sophie had possessed. Her shyness hid a sensitivity and intelligence that matched Victorine's and far surpassed that of the other du Pont girls. For the most part, his children had become adults with their own lives and loves, even in the close quarters of the Brandywine. Victorine, of course, still lived with him, taking her mother's place as mistress of the house and mills. Irénée marveled at her ability to grasp the needs of his household, with its many political and business visitors—hundreds each year—and the requirements of the powdermakers' families.

His sons were hardly boys any longer. Alfred ran the mills, really, while Irénée wrote letters to his agents and helped push his nephew Charles into a race for the Delaware governorship. Henry had graduated from West Point just a year after the South Carolina crisis. His letters described the fighting in the Southwest against the Creek Indians. They were much alike, he and Henry; his son's writing showed the same sober attitude and critical attention to the details of a battle that Irénée's displayed in his descriptions of affairs on the Brandywine. Alexis had been sent to school with his own nephew, Evalina's son James, and now attended the University of Pennsylvania. He, like Alfred, would be a chemist.

Only Eleuthera remained in the house with Victorine and Sophie Madeleine and Irénée. She had turned into a rather wild girl, by Irénée's standards, forever rushing to Philadelphia parties with her old friends from Madame Rivardi's school. She and Sophie Madeleine were close, yet apart, since the younger girl tended to stay at her father's side. Irénée knew the reason: Sophie had fallen in love with her cousin, Sam Francis, and the navy had a way of sending the young lieutenant home on little or no notice.

Samuel's career had progressed well. He had served in the Mediterranean, the Far East, and soon would be elevated to command in Mexican waters. Like Victor's other children, Sam had no ties to the powder mills his uncle owned except through his friendships with Irénée's sons and daughters. When he visited Upper Louviers, Sam spent little time with his mother and Amelia, and his brother Charles's life had taken a different shape than his own. Only with his younger sister, Julia, did Sam feel comfortable. They exchanged stories about navy life, Julia showing him her husband Irvine's letters and listening carefully to Sam's sea tales.

Julia enjoyed crossing the Brandywine to visit Sophie Madeleine and Eleuthera. Often Samuel went along, standing in the bow of their skiff and calling the stroke while a servant rowed. Soon he found himself drawing away from his sister to spend time with his shy cousin Sophie in the woods above the mills.

Irénée did not try to hide his pleasure when Sophie announced that she and Sam Francis were pledged to marry. Since Victor's death the families on either bank of the Brandywine had drawn steadily apart. Irénée's children became more dedicated to the tight community of powdermakers and their kin each year. It had been his father's plan, long ago while he contemplated Pontiania, that du Pont cousins would marry each other, maintaining, as Pierre wrote, a purity of the blood. The Bourbons had consolidated their power and lengthened their reign that way; so too would the rulers of Pontiania.

Samuel's uniform was not a king's robe, but he did look splendid in the navy dress clothes, his hair a light shade of red, his sideburns long in the fashion of the time. Sophie also gleamed in the June sunlight that spread across the meadow outside her father's house, where the families gathered to celebrate the first marriage of du Pont cousins. Irénée gave his daughter away in a simple ceremony and allowed himself to enjoy the first celebration his house had seen since his wife died five years earlier.

Gabrielle, Victor's widow, invited the newlyweds to live at Upper Louviers. Only she and Amelia would be there all of the time, and Julia planned to join her husband when he left on his next tour of duty. They could not move in with Charles and his wife; Dorcas was ill much of the time and needed privacy. Upper Louviers would be much less lonely with Sophie and Sam around, and perhaps a new baby or two to brighten up the house.

Irénée agreed with his sister-in-law. He worried that Sophie and Sam might leave the Brandywine completely. His daughter had talked of traveling with her navy man since before the wedding. Samuel accepted his mother's offer; there were times when a navy wife was better off at home with the family and, he suggested, Eleuthera needed Sophie to advise her on the many love affairs she became involved in among her Philadelphia friends.

Irénée had noticed that Eleuthera paid closer attention to one of her many suitors than most. Long ago men had learned the way to the du Pont daughters' hearts. Rarely did one come to call without bringing pots of plants or exotic seeds, or at least bunches of flowers. Irénée's daughters had inherited his love for growing things; when he looked for one of them he was sure to find her working in the garden. The plants brought by a young Philadelphia doctor, Thomas Smith, received better care than others. As they flowered Eleuthera placed them in the long center hall or on the piazza. Doctor Smith was a likable man in his twenties who seemed drawn to the Brandywine. Irénée was not surprised when Eleuthera asked him to plan a wedding, and he was delighted when she wondered if he might find a bit of land not too far from the mills where she and Tom could build a home and clinic. Irénée enjoyed the wedding, a larger affair than Sophie Madeleine's had been, studded with his daughter's socialite friends and Tom's large family. Alexis, home from college for the summer of 1834, seemed to find the doctor's younger sister, Joanna, intriguing, and monopolized her attention throughout the wedding day. Irénée retired from the party early, excusing himself with a word about having to ride at sunrise for Philadelphia.

The need to cater to his bankers had, if anything, become more insistent since Irénée's wife died. These were inflated times, with paper rather than gold building cities and exploring the West. Irénée knew the bubble would soon burst, but he could not stop enlarging the mills to fill orders or deny old and good customers credit until their own customers paid them. He did not really enjoy Philadelphia, with its bustling population and dirty streets; the city was becoming old already, its streets littered with trash, its buildings turning gray. Irénée preferred his gardens on the Brandywine, where he could slip into thinking in French of the old days in Paris and conjure visions of his youth with Sophie.

But he had come to know Philadelphia, and the city knew him. Merchants respected him as a man of means, a bit odd perhaps, with his old clothes and deep French accent, a sober man not given to joining them for evenings at cards or with the city's frolicsome corps of paid ladies. Irénée spent his evenings alone, reading in his room at the same hotel he had lodged in for thirty-two years, the one Victor had always used and had died in.

On a Thursday night, after two days of haggling with his bankers, Irénée trudged back to the United States Hotel, along the same street his brother had walked nearly six years earlier. Within sight of the hotel he stumbled in pain, as his brother had. People passing in the street carried him to his room, as they had Victor, and a doctor rushed in. The terrible pain in his chest would not subside. At three the following morning the doctor pronounced him dead, like his brother, of a heart attack. What befell one of them, Irénée had told Victor, befell the other.

Word reached the Brandywine quickly. Irénée's sons arranged for their father's body to travel down the Delaware River aboard the steamer *Wilmington* on the day of his death. The people of Wilmington waited silently at the docks for Irénée's body to arrive, then trailed behind his large family as they followed the hearse three miles to the Brandywine. Alfred had ordered the mills shut down when word of his father's death came, telling the workers that their boss had taken his turn to go "across the Creek." With their families the powdermen filed slowly past Irénée's resting place near his father and brother, walked down the hill where the gates of the mills stood locked, and returned to their homes for a day of quiet and rest. At sunrise the trumpet would echo up and down the Brandywine, calling them to the yards. In two months 1834 would be over, and they must work hard to meet Mister Irénée's goal: one million pounds of gunpowder for the year, the most his Eleutherian Mills had ever produced.

# 14

ALFRED DU PONT sat nervously behind his father's old desk in the office near Sand Hole Woods. He had never felt comfortable in the small, airless room; his place was in the powder yards or at the raised bench in his laboratory. But this was a special day. Still, he vowed to rest his elbows on the worn dark wood, as his father had, only long enough to finish writing the new partnership agreement.

Alfred's six brothers and sisters crowded into the office around him. These were the new owners of E. I. du Pont de Nemours and Company, the seven children of Irénée, four women and three men. At thirty-eight Alfred was the oldest male. Henry, who had resigned from the army at his brother's request and come home to work in the business, was nearly fourteen years Alfred's junior. Alexis had just turned twenty-one.

Together with Victorine, Evalina, Eleuthera, and Sophie Madeleine, the brothers had decided to keep their father's name on the company and to run the business precisely as he had. For two years Evalina's husband, Antoine, had dealt with the outside affairs of the mills while Alfred saw to the manufacture of powder. Antoine had trained Henry to manage accounts, write correspondence, and handle bankers and customers. He had nearly felt he was working with Irénée himself; Henry even picked up the nuances of selling powder to foreign governments in a matter of weeks.

Alexis rarely left Alfred's side during the twenty-four months. He had come to know as much as his brother did about the manufacture of black powder. Alexis married Tom Smith's sister Joanna soon after Irénée's death and built a house of his own near the Brandywine. Henry was courting a Philadelphia girl, Louisa Gerhard, a stern young woman with a temperament to match Henry's own. They would occupy Irénée's house, which everyone had taken to calling Eleutherian Mills. Alfred and Margaretta were content with Nemours, on the road between Hagley and the director's house. None of the brothers would ever sleep beyond running distance to the powder yards.

Antoine and Evalina planned to leave the banks of the Brandywine soon. Bidermann had spent twenty years near the powder mills. He longed to get the sour smell of sulfur out of his head. He and Evalina had returned to France for a year, paying off Irénée's old debts and buying up the last outstanding shares in the company. He had given them, plus his own quarter-share in the mills, to Irénée's seven children, his wife included, to split up as they chose, and loaned Alfred fifty-six thousand dollars to get the business on its feet after he left. Evalina had been enchanted with the old Bidermann estate in Switzerland. When Antoine bought Irénée's four-hundred-fifty-acre sheep farm from the company heirs to build a house on, Evalina insisted on calling it Winterthur, after the Swiss mansion her husband had been born in.

The seven signatures under Alfred's writing would solemnize the new ownership of the mills. No shares, except through Sophie's marriage to Sam Francis, would go to Victor's side of the family; even Sophie had agreed with Antoine that only Irénée's children deserved an interest in the company. The seven elected no officers. Theirs would be a simple partnership, with each of the brothers and sisters to draw an equal part of the profits at the end of each year; not even Alfred would receive a salary. What had to be bought for them or their homes, the company would buy. Personally, they would own nothing, not the furniture in their parlors, not the china they ate off, not even a carriage or horse. Should they need transportation, they merely had to inform Henry, and a buggy and driver would be dispatched.

As a final touch to the agreement, a stroke of genius that would keep the company intact for generations and insure that business would be conducted as the partners intended, the shares were allotted to the seven brothers and sisters only for their lifetimes: when they died their children would not inherit their stake in the powder company. Instead, the remaining partners would choose a new partner from among the many younger du Ponts who worked in the mills. No du Pont would ever be poor: the company would see to their needs and desires. But it would pay enormously to stay near the Brandywine, perform as the older partners deemed a du Pont should, and someday ascend the rungs of ownership. And when one became a partner he had no choice but to remain in the family fold. The shares were not salable, not even to a relative. The seven sons and daughters of Irénée demanded at least as much loyalty from each other and their descendants as they did from their workers. Other wealthy families might spoil their sons and daughters and bequeath them huge sums to fritter away. Du Pont money would remain where it belonged: on the Brandywine.

The seven partners knew that decisions would have to be made in the course of business, and Alfred would make them, as the unnamed senior partner, by virtue of being Irénée's oldest son. It was understood that none of the seven would ever question any decision Alfred reached. Henry, as the second son, would write letters for all seven, deal with the company's growing ranks of agents across the nation, and keep financial matters on an even keel. Alexis would be the foreman in the powder yards.

Alfred had no taste for the power his age gave him, or the responsibility. As a boy his delicate health had kept him out of school for months at a time. He had little more energy than his work in the laboratory required, but he had a deep trust in his brothers and sisters. Alexis was left to run the mills as he chose. Henry wrote letters and extended credit, or revoked it, at his own discretion. Victorine ran the workers' quarters, as she had since her mother died, and saw to it that the needs of the Brandywine community were met from the company's bank accounts. When Victor's Gabrielle died, little more than a month after the seven brothers and sisters took over the company, Alfred arranged for her burial next to Victor, but it was Victorine who comforted Amelia and the rest of Aunt Gaby's large brood. When offspring came to Irénée's and Victor's many children, it was Victorine who sent presents and congratulations and saw to it that extra servants were assigned by Henry to the houses of the newborn. She had lived so many years with her father that she understood well the weight of responsibility Alfred felt. It was as though the powder mills were the children Victorine had never borne to Ferdinand Bauduy.

Within weeks after the brothers and sisters signed their partnership agreement the United States entered another depression, the worst since George Washington had been unable to pay or even feed the soldiers of the revolution. Alfred's face became drawn and more pale than usual. When a small explosion—by du Pont standards—took the lives of two workers Alfred could not transfer the duty of consoling the men's families to any of his brothers or sisters. He had feared this more than any other portion of his responsibility. The congenial powdermakers, many of whom had known Mister Alfred since the mills opened thirty-five years earlier, found their new boss unreceptive to their jokes about the dangerous work he had once shared. Alfred had become as sober as

Irénée and even more withdrawn than the founder of Eleutherian Mills had been on the day his wife had died.

Sophie Madeleine rowed across the Brandywine from Upper Louviers whenever a letter from her husband arrived. The partners would gather in the parlor of the director's house to listen as she read aloud Samuel's tales of sea battles and invasions. Captain du Pont commanded a ship in the war between the United States and Mexico. He had landed, on his own initiative, to chase a party of soldiers deep into the finger of land that extended below California, which Mexico claimed as its own.

Alfred did not enjoy stories about men killing men. He listened for other reasons: the powder mills were insanely busy making cannon and rifle fuel for American troops and ships. This was not a war like past wars, when the du Ponts had received only a minor share of the government business. Du Pont powder was the best, and the government knew it had to beat Mexico's forces with superior munitions as well as braver men. Initially, the Secretary of War had written Alfred, he could count on a million-pound order. If the war dragged on the American forces would need millions more.

Henry had been jubilant. The government business would place the company on solid ground for the first time in its history, recoup all the thousands lost in the Panic of 1837, and allow the partners to claim huge profits at the end of each year. Alfred knew his brother's hunger for enormous profits and understood it. But he himself feared the government orders more than welcomed them, and his brother's calculating mind disturbed him even more than the extra work.

With all the strength he could muster Alfred firmly took the reins of the company: Henry was to forward all large orders to him for approval before giving them to Alexis. Alexis was not to change a single part of the methods used in the mills and was not to abandon any of the many safety precautions. Within weeks Alfred's curly brown head of hair had dwindled to a few patches of gray, and his girth nearly doubled as he ate out of nervousness.

Soon, however, his diligence paid off. When an order for two hundred thousand pounds of powder came from a Frenchman in Havana, Alfred rushed to Washington to consult with the Secretary of War. He suspected that the request, backed with cash, came from agents of the Mexican government. The Secretary ushered Alfred into the office of President James K. Polk. Polk and the du Ponts were violent political enemies; he had edged Henry Clay, the same Clay after whom Irénée had named a small town near the Brandywine, out of the presidency by a few thousand votes. The President told Alfred of the danger Mexico presented to United States sovereignty and reminded him of the doctrine his grandfather had first suggested to James Monroe: the American people must expand their nation to its geographical limits. Alfred knew that Pierre had warned both Monroe and Jefferson of the danger Mexico brought to the continent, and that sooner or later the United States would have to grapple with the Spanish settlers to the south. Alfred swore to the President that Mexico would fire no Du Pont Powder from its cannon or rifles and that the company would supply any and every need the United States forces had. He did not bother Polk with tales of the added danger wartime production brought to the men on the Brandywine.

Alexis du Pont enjoyed lingering over breakfast with his children, cooking them eggs and discussing their plans for the day. Even in time of war he refused to sacrifice the luxury. The powdermen knew their work well enough to begin by themselves at dawn. Alfred, who might not have gone to sleep until two or three, awoke automatically at the morning trumpet call and usually arrived in the yards before the first of the workmen. And so Alexis lingered over breakfast.

Halfway through the Mexican War, this habit saved his life.

He intended, one morning, to begin work in the mills of the Upper Yard. A few hundred feet away from the pounding, stamping, and glazing houses he was thrown from his feet high into the air, landing yards away from where he had stood. One building had gone, quickly, in a bright flash of powder and smoke. Debris rained on other parts of the Upper Yard. Instinctively, Alexis felt for the Brandywine wind as his father had taught him to, and it bore bad news. There was no dampness, and a stiff summer breeze came off the Creek: it would be bad this time.

Soon the rumbling came. A rushing force rose above the Brandywine and set off for towns miles away. The trees along the shore bent with the shocks, marking each wave with a loud whoosh and snapping back into eerie silence.

Henry ran for the yards from his office, shoving aside the powder-makers' wives who clamored and cried at the locked gates. Armed guards stopped them from climbing over the high fence. Alfred had been farther down the Creek. He could see the deadly chain reaction of the explosion approach, sending buildings into the air and bodies over the water. He knew that nearly every member of his family old enough to work would be somewhere in the yards: the war production had drawn them all into the mills. Only a miracle would save at least some of them from death.

When the waves of shock passed him Alfred headed upstream toward his brother. Alexis was not hurt, and he had found all the other du Ponts in the yards. They, too, had escaped injury. But at least a dozen men had died, perhaps more. And it had been one of those devastating explosions that left sickening traces of flesh on walls and trees. The powdermen were already fighting the fires. The time had come for Alfred to count the dead and maimed.

Alexis searched for each worker individually—he knew them all—and brought his brother the report: eighteen powder workers had gone across the Creek. Alfred could not bear the destruction; he turned away from the scene. Henry could handle the burial arrangements, pension the widows, see to the children. Victorine would console the families, and Alexis begin the cleaning up and keep the mills running. He had known what this war would bring, with its night work under kerosene lamps to make the ten thousand pounds of powder a day the government demanded. His father had toiled for this shining down of the eyes of Washington, with its sure payment of bills and giant profits. Alfred had worked hard to make the mills safer, inventing new metal kegs to hold powder, new ways of processing ingredients, even new designs for wagons to carry his gunpowder to its destinations. He had feared the sudden spark to the point of using only unshod horses inside the mill gates. He had seen that behind their masks of courage and gallows humor the powdermen revered his concern for their safety. And the result of all his care had been this tragedy. He left Henry and Alexis to their work and trudged home to Margaretta.

Alfred had relied heavily on his wife's gentle support to keep him going with his work. Often he told her that if the family and workers did not lean so heavily on his shoulders, he would give up the senior partnership and spend all his days in the laboratory. Now, he told her, eighteen had perished. He damned the Brandywine and the insane business of making black powder.

Margaretta tried to comfort him. He had done all he could, taken every precaution, worked tirelessly for safety in the yards. The explosion was not his fault. Her words did not help; the devastation had been too great. Alfred trembled and shook uncontrollably. He had roamed the powder yards for thirty years, as a boy at play, at his father's side learning to make powder, and finally as the boss. He would never again be able to face the Brandywine, he told his wife. He had seen too much.

Henry performed his duties soberly, consoling the women who had lost husbands, drawing pensions from the company accounts, taking inventory of the dead men's personal effects. He left Alexis to white-wash the stains of blood and flesh off walls, inspire the men to begin work again, and call masons and carpenters to rebuild the mills. It seemed to the powder workers that the spirit of Mister Irénée lived in his second son. Like his father, Henry had a way of comforting the widows without pitying them, of turning their sorrow into pride that their husbands had died in the mills, working alongside their friends, working for the du Ponts. Henry pushed them to find strength in the greater purpose of what the powdermen did, in the community of life the Brandywine represented, in the security that their husbands' loyalty had earned them the eternal loyalty of the du Ponts. Henry had learned from watching his father that it was the only way to keep the workers on the Brandywine in the face of tragedy.

The company ledgers were proving Henry right, both about war and his paternal attitude toward the powdermen. If the orders kept coming in from Washington, Henry could travel to Philadelphia to retire the last of the company's debts and begin stockpiling thousands of dollars against the possibility that when the war ended so too would the profits. He had always scorned the ways of his cousins across the Creek, but Charles might be useful now, in the Delaware senate, with his second wife, Ann, the daughter of the state's most prominent attorney. Charles could help Henry win a charter to open a bank with war profits if all went well. Henry disliked politics, in general, and politicians, in particu-lar, but they had their uses. He might even bring one or two members of the Senate from Washington to see how marvelously the du Ponts supported the war effort, and at what great sacrifice.

Perhaps the Senators might think him too young a man to reckon with. While he worked to keep his youth well hidden in his correspon-dence, there was little chance that anyone would mistake him for the boss of the mills while Alfred still lived. He decided to grow a beard, the style now since the freshman Congressman from Illinois, Abraham

Lincoln, appeared on the floor of the House of Representatives wearing one. Beards had always been the fashion among powdermen; they found it a useful way to hide the scars from the hundreds of little flashes and explosions that marred nearly all their faces after a year or two in the mills. A beard would make him look older, Henry decided, and cover the cleft in his chin that marked him as his father's son. People must learn to deal with Henry du Pont as himself.

Henry pitied Alfred when the war ended and his brave front gave way to the harried, nervous look he had had on the day of the great explosion. Victorine had pushed him into the yards each morning, invoking the mission his position and birth demanded he perform, calling upon the memories of their father and grandfather. She had borne a greater personal tragedy than Alfred had ever known—he had been there when her husband died—and she managed to go on. He *must*, for the good of the family, the company, even the nation. He need not really work in the yards. Alexis would see to the running of the mills, and Henry would manage the business. Alfred had a half-dozen children of his own, two already working in the yards. He must not embarrass them. Alfred had always looked up to Victorine; his eldest daughter had been named after her. He said he would try.

For a time Victorine's encouragement worked. Alfred thought that after the war ended business would slow down, the danger of explosions ease, the kerosene lamps leave the mills. He might then be able to grasp tight control of the family and company once again. But, as Henry hoped it would, boom followed war, and the inevitable rush to California came. Gold was discovered; miners clamored for Du Pont Powder. Henry established an agency near the Pacific Ocean and another in the coal fields of Pennsylvania, where his family's powder became a primary tool for drawing the precious black ore from the earth. Railroad companies decided to go through rather than around mountains. Only Du Pont blasting powder had the strength and accuracy to tunnel into solid rock. Canals became the surest way to speed supplies and manufactured goods to the mushrooming cities, and blasting soil away proved a hundred times more efficient than digging it up.

In the twelve months following the end of the Mexican fighting Henry sent out bills for a half-million more pounds of gunpowder than he had in the best of the war years. He hired workers daily and set them to turning out gunpowder without the years of training given new men in Irénée's time. The kerosene lamps never came down from inside the mills.

Finally, Alfred was unable to stand the pressure and his nerves gave way. He became skittish around the mills, rare even among the workers, never before seen in a du Pont. He could do little more than wander through the gardens and woods after an hour or two in his laboratory, or play with the grandchildren his sons and daughters were quickly giving him. Alfred's eldest son, Eleuthère Irénée the second, worked alongside Alexis learning to run the mills and brought his father reports on production and anecdotes from the yards, carefully leaving out stories of the frequent accidents. Henry brooded over the damage his brother's condition was doing to the powder workers' confidence. He decided that Alfred must leave the mills.

When Henry went to his brother to ask that he step down from the senior partnership, he found a broken, haggard man, old beyond his fifty-one years, plagued by nightmares of explosions and workers who had died. Alfred wanted only to be released from the awesome burdens he felt. If his brothers and sisters would agree to accept Eleuthère Irénée in his stead he would gladly turn over his share in the company to his son. Henry said the brothers and sisters had already conferred; they would have it no other way. And, as Irénée the first's next oldest son, Henry would assume the role of senior partner.

Henry told Alfred that he had plans to expand, to build new factories away from the Brandywine. It was a time of confidence, a time when the nation needed the du Ponts' powder more than ever before. And, through his new political friends, he had heard that rumblings of discontent were coming from the South on the slavery issue. Alfred remembered that President Jackson had told their father, back in the days of the South Carolina trouble, that slavery would become a problem, perhaps even cause for war between the states. Alfred need not worry, Henry said. The company would stand squarely behind the Union if Civil War came. No one on the Brandywine owned slaves, and no one ever would.

Henry left Alfred to stare from his patio down into the powder yards, called his twin hunting dogs—descendants of Irénée's that followed him everywhere—and walked back to the office near Sand Hole Woods. He wrote out a new partnership agreement and assembled his brothers and sisters to sign it, telling them that Alfred had agreed to step down. From a drawer in his desk he took a shiny new top hat, black to match his coat, that he had kept waiting for the day he would take over leadership of the company and family. Henry was shorter than his brothers, shorter even than one or two of his sisters. In his top hat and thick red beard, the powdermen would see him coming and look up to him, and visitors to the Brandywine would recognize at once which of the du Ponts ruled Eleutherian Mills.

*Part Three*

# THE POSSIBILITY OF
# DISUNION

# 15

L AMMOT DU PONT, son of Alfred, grandson of Eleuthère Irénée,
asked his uncle, Henry the Red, in 1852 for a position at Eleutherian
Mills. Henry welcomed his nephew's ability as a scientist; Lammot had
earned a degree in chemistry at the University of Pennsylvania. The
senior partner put Lammot to work in the tiny laboratory Alfred had
first set up, hoping that his experiments would make Du Pont Powder
better than it already was. In the test tubes and flasks his father had
bought decades earlier Lammot struggled to refine the powdermaking
process. Henry began calling him "our Chemist" in letters to customers
and agents. The suggestions Lammot made to his uncle for better and
safer ways to manufacture black powder were immediately implemented
in the mills.

And as quickly as Henry came to rely upon Lammot's scientific judgment, so too did the Red Fellow come to fear the influence of his
brother's son over the powdermen on the Brandywine. Eleuthère Irénée
the second, Alfred's eldest son, had ascended to the partnership when his
father retired. If Lammot continued to make important contributions to
the success and safety of Eleutherian Mills, Henry would find it difficult
to exclude his nephew from the partnership. Together, the two sons of
Alfred might take from the Red Fellow his absolute power over the
company. Henry decided that Lammot needed experience traveling in
the service of E. I. du Pont de Nemours and Company.

War broke out on the Crimean peninsula of Russia in 1853. For nearly
two years England and a host of allies fought the tsar's troops until the
tide turned against the defenders of Mother Russia. The tsar sent agents
to Henry du Pont to purchase gunpowder badly needed in the Crimea.
Eleutherian Mills had supplied England with powder since the start of
the fighting. Now Henry decided, alone, to sell black powder to both
sides. Washington had assured him that the United States would remain
neutral. The Red Fellow informed London and St. Petersburg that his
gunpowder would be available to any nation with ready cash. England

balked; it was not possible, her emissaries protested, for the Du Pont Company to remain loyal to both parties warring in the Crimea.

Henry's reply was brusque: the du Ponts claimed loyalty to no one but the du Ponts. If England wanted his gunpowder—and how would the British navy continue to bombard the Crimea otherwise?—the peers of the realm had better leave unspoken their objections about his sales to other nations. It was not, Henry believed, a question of loyalty or even morality, but one of profit. As long as the United States supported neither Russia nor England, his mills on the Brandywine would not discriminate against either His Majesty's troops or the soldiers of the tsar. Du Pont gunpowder would send bullets into bodies on both sides— without prejudice.

Russian agents forwarded a massive order for black powder to Eleutherian Mills. Henry hired a ship to take the powder halfway around the world to the Crimea and instructed his nephew Lammot to deliver it personally. Before dawn on an autumn morning in 1854, Lammot hunched low in a dinghy for the short trip from shore to the powder-laden schooner awaiting him in Delaware Bay. Tons of black powder, in kegs marked *Du Pont*, were jammed beneath the ship's decks. A single spark would transform the schooner into a deadly firecracker.

Lammot knew the dangers of his mission. Russia needed the powder to defend Sevastopol. England wanted the military lifeblood of Russia squeezed into the earth of the Crimea, and the port city of Sevastopol was the Crimea's throat. British ships prowled the waters between America and the Black Sea under one order: gunpowder from the Brandywine was not to reach Sevastopol. A heavy cargo craft would be an easy target for the men-of-war, not difficult to outmaneuver and blow from the water with a single cannon blast. Why, Lammot wondered, had Uncle Henry sent him on a mission where he might be killed at sea—or worse, captured by the British and executed?

Lammot's ship weighed anchor and set sail across the Atlantic. Soon the cargo vessel was sighted, and the British gave chase. By sheer luck Lammot's schooner evaded capture, passed near Gibraltar and entered the Mediterranean. Urgent word had reached the British sailors blockading the Crimean peninsula: stop Lammot du Pont. If necessary, kill him to do it. Du Pont gunpowder may have propelled British, and French, bullets, but the life of a du Pont could not be equated with the havoc his family's gunpowder would wreak if it reached the guns of Sevastopol.

Off the Crimean coast two British ships drew alongside Lammot's schooner. He instructed his captain to ignore the warning shots they fired. Broadsides roared across the water; gaping holes appeared in the schooner's side. Lammot awaited the explosion, calmly prepared for death. None came. Maneuvering deftly between boulders along shallow shoals, the schooner struck bottom, only yards from solid ground. Russian soldiers dove into the water, emptied the schooner's holds and ferried the gunpowder ashore. In a few weeks the forces of England and France laid siege to Sevastropol. The ancient fortress's cannon answered with the roar of Du Pont Powder, and more Du Pont Powder echoed back. Through a cruel Russian winter the city held out, then through a spring and summer. For eleven months the defenders of Sevastopol fired the powder from the beached schooner, but the British in the end won, and Mother Russia mourned one hundred two thousand six hundred seventy dead.

On the leisurely journey home from the Crimea Lammot pondered the meaning of Sevastopol and the nagging question of why he had been sent. There had been no money to collect: Uncle Henry would never deliver gunpowder halfway across the earth without first being paid for his efforts. Lammot had done nothing to protect the gunpowder that the ship's captain would not himself have thought of. Henry had his dream: the profits from selling gunpowder to both sides would eventually bring the family business three million dollars in sales, nearly a third of that clear profit.

Certain murmurs from within the family had reached Lammot's ears, rumblings of discontent that in the four years since his father had surrendered the senior partnership to Henry, the Red Fellow, as the powdermen called his uncle, had seized too much power on the Brandywine. Already Henry had demanded, and been given, a slightly larger share in the profits than the other partners. Lammot's salary was only a few dollars above an apprentice powderman's; the boss millwrights and senior powdermakers earned more than a grandson of the company's founder. His brother, Eleuthère Irénée, might be a partner but he had little say in the company's affairs. Henry was not the oldest living male descendant of the family's founder, Pierre Samuel, yet he had taken upon himself the running of the family as well as the company.

Even Henry's own brother, Alexis, dared not give advice to the Red Fellow. The day after Alfred's retirement Henry had examined the company accounts, found Eleutherian Mills nearly a half-million dollars in debt, and ordered the men to begin making inferior gunpowder. Quality, the company reputation, even safety, must be sacrificed: profits, only profits mattered. Still, Lammot wondered, why send him to

Sevastopol? Perhaps the Red Fellow did not want too many relatives mixing into the way he ran Eleutherian Mills. It would be difficult to complain of Henry's constant additions to his own house, his willingness to risk the lives of the powder workers, or his demands for total, silent loyalty, from the other side of the world—or the bottom of the sea.

On the twentieth day of January, 1852, Eleuthera du Pont Smith poisoned her husband, Thomas, to death. They had lived near the Brandywine, happily married, for eighteen years. Doctor Tom, as the powdermen and their families called him, ministered to the medical needs of the workers and the du Ponts. Eleuthera had blossomed into a beautiful and charming woman, liked by the powder workers, popular with her relatives. She mixed little into the affairs of the company, content to let her father, her brother Alfred, and finally her brother Henry see to the business and dole out what funds were due her from the mills' profits.

Smith cared little for the company or family business matters; he loved the practice of medicine, and he healed well when he could and saw his patients through to the end when he could not. When an explosion maimed and killed workers Doctor Tom would attend them, but he did not serve as undertaker. The local barber, an Irishman and Catholic like most of the workers, prepared those who had gone across the Creek for their final rest.

Early in January of 1852 Tom Smith fell ill. It was not serious, a flu, perhaps, with a touch of pneumonia setting in. His wife nursed him, freed from household chores by the Irish girls who worked as servants in her home. The Smith house was not large; it need not be. Perhaps the single disappointment Eleuthera had furnished her husband was her barrenness; the seed that gave her brothers children every year apparently had not passed to her. But to be childless on the Brandywine did not mean to live without the company of children. By 1850 Eleuthera could spread her mothering instincts among twenty nieces and nephews.

In bed, too ill to fetch his own medicine, Tom asked his wife to bring him a bottle from the cabinet in his office, attached to the house. He trusted his wife; the strain of wildness Eleuthera showed in her youth passed quickly after they married. Often she could be found helping her husband with patients. Over the years she had come to know much about the practice of medicine. And so, without bothering to look at the bottle, Thomas Smith drank heavily of wolfbane, a deadly poison. In tiny doses, wolfbane, or monk's hood as it was sometimes called, could be useful in deadening pain. In large doses it was nearly always fatal. Doctor Tom realized what he had taken too late. He could not blame Eleuthera; it had been a mistake. In a few hours he was dead.

Eleuthera spoke to Henry about finding her husband a place in the cemetery in Sand Hole Woods. Henry said yes, there was room. When the barber finished his work the family gathered to pay its final respects to their doctor and relative. Victorine brought flowers she had grown inside Henry's house. Evalina came from Winterthur. Alexis supported his wife, Joanna, Doctor Tom's sister, as she wept. Sophie, invalided from an illness that took her health soon after she and Sam Francis married, did not journey across the Creek from Louviers.

Down the hill from Sand Hole Woods, out of sight, the droning grind of the powder mills continued throughout the simple ceremony. Henry had seen no need to stop making gunpowder during his brother-in-law's funeral: it was, after all, not a du Pont who had died. The women children of Eleuthère Irénée, Henry's sisters, might take comfort in the church; Eleuthera would certainly turn to God now that her husband was dead and spend her time praying alongside Victorine. Henry found solace only in the constant turning of the gunpowder mills.

Eleuthère Irénée de Pont the second, called, as his grandfather had been, Irénée, said a hasty farewell to the two youngest brothers outside the gates of the powder mills. Alfred Victor, named for their father, was barely twenty, Antoine Bidermann a mere eighteen. Irénée had found it difficult to accept their desire to leave the Brandywine, to begin a new life elsewhere, but he and his other brother, Lammot, understood well the frustrations of dealing with Uncle Henry.

Irénée's place in the yards had been the price Henry paid for edging Alfred from the seat of power. Lammot, a brilliant chemist, simply could not be ignored. The two boys were different. Henry would gladly have given them powdermen's jobs, and perhaps, in time, they might have risen to positions of some small responsibility. That one brother was a partner and another the firm's chief—for many years only—chemist, would not matter. Henry had proven, more than once, that men were not indispensable, even men of Lammot's talent and education. And then there was Henry's attitude toward the powder workers themselves.

Not long after Henry took over the senior partnership an explosion wrecked two mills and killed two workers. It had been an accident, the price Eleutherian Mills often paid for long hours and difficult, intense work. Henry had refused to let the matter pass. He conducted an investigation to find out who caused the explosion: otherwise, the workers might blame Henry himself. He found his man, Christopher Cowan, not long after the dead workers, both Catholic Irishmen, were buried in the cemetery at St. Joseph's-on-the-Brandywine, the church Alfred had built for the workers. Cowan was dismissed at once, with Henry laying the blame for the two men's deaths at his feet—publicly. Less than a year later, unable to find work anywhere in the gunpowder industry, the former du Pont employee hanged himself. Henry believed it was punishment well suited to Christopher Cowan's sins.

The men in the yards thought little of swearing oaths against the senior partner. To his face he was always Mister Henry. When his back was turned "Boss Henry" would do, or worse. Irénée, working alongside his Uncle Alexis, heard and disregarded what the powdermen said: better to let them curse under their breath and continue working hard and well than to become careless in the mills.

Irénée had no great love for Henry or the rest of the du Ponts. At best, he found them pompous—Henry especially, with his tall silk hat and somber, dark clothes. At worst, with their homes—small homes, really, compared to the great mansions of the South or the townhouses of New York—named after grand French estates, and their affectations of being landed gentry, the rulers of the Brandywine, Irénée considered his uncles and aunts, and most of his cousins, ridiculous. Secretly, he despised the airs of the du Ponts, his mother included. He was a powderman, perhaps the leader of powdermen, and his hands mixed the same sulfur, saltpeter, and charcoal as the workers' did. With the exception of his Uncle Alexis his relatives seemed thoroughly humorless, seemed even to hate the kind of gallows humor that punctuated the workers' conversation. His grandfather had been that kind of man, keeping the powder mills alive on sheer courage, and his father, as troubled by his responsibilities, had come to be the same: silent, unsmiling, unfeeling. Irénée vowed that he would never become aloof from the men who did his bidding, or unable to laugh with them over a glass of whiskey after a long day's work. Perhaps, even if it meant his losing their companionship, his young brothers would be better off by far away from the Brandywine.

Fred and Bidermann had decided to leave Eleutherian Mills while

Lammot sailed with his shipload of powder to Sevastopol. They had awaited his return before going, but Lammot's counsel had not been sought. He might have dissuaded them; the young boys looked up to their brother with love and respect and Lammot had always believed in family unity. Even more than Irénée himself, Lammot understood that their father had little time left to live after surrendering control of the mills to Henry. Yet Lammot had simply wished his brothers well in Kentucky. Something had happened in the Crimea to change Lammot's view of life on the Brandywine. He might never say so, but Lammot no longer hungered for the powder yards after his trek across the world, and privately he greeted Henry's orders and demands with disgust and blamed the Red Fellow for errors that at times cost the workers their lives.

Irénée had noticed the change most when three powder wagons, traveling to the wharf on the Delaware River, exploded in the streets of Wilmington. They were Conestogas, specially designed and lengthened to take one hundred fifty kegs of powder each. Loaded until they groaned with each turn of the wheels, the wagons had set off for the river close behind each other, under Henry's orders to go by the shortest route. A ship bound for Europe awaited them at the docks. Six mules pulled each wagon and a valuable man sat astride the drive mule of each Conestoga. The drivers had always been special to the family and firm, admired by the founder, praised and well paid by Alfred. All the wagoneers did was drive; even the task of unhitching and caring for the mules was left to others. Mule drivers needed more than courage to drive a wagon carrying three and a half tons of black powder; they had to be devoid of normal human nerves. Henry had ordered the three drivers to take their cargo through the streets of Wilmington, a saving of perhaps an hour, and a risk anyone else would have found unacceptable. The city streets were narrow, crowded with people at times, and filled with horses and wagons and men smoking cigars and pipes. A single spark and ten tons of gunpowder would go up, with it three drivers, eighteen mules, and perhaps half the city. Henry seemed not to care: time meant profit, and profit meant more cash for himself.

When the wagons blew, and the bodies of the three drivers were scattered into tiny bits, only two of Wilmington's residents were killed: a miracle of coincidence. The ground rumbled all the way back to the powder mills, five miles away. Within days newspapers across the nation damned the du Ponts for their disregard of human life. Powder wagons were banned from the streets of every major city between Boston and New Orleans. Henry merely scowled and ordered Alexis and Irénée to work the men harder and make up for the lost kegs of powder.

Working at the rough table his father had set up, Lammot could avoid Henry much of the time and, with Irénée and Alexis running the yards, devote himself to research. Henry's dictums came daily to the laboratory, and always they were the same: cut costs, make cheaper powder, find a way to circumvent the high price of importing saltpeter from India. A big, rawboned, homely man, Lammot took Henry's orders well, as did Irénée. They were born to the yards, and their loyalty was to their work, their men, and each other. Both single, Lammot and Irénée still lived in the house called Nemours with their parents and spent time with Alfred after the long workday ended, doing all they could to soothe their father's frazzled nerves. They kept from him, when they could, tales of the way Henry ran the powder mills.

Irénée hurried back into the yards after watching Fred and Bidermann ride west over the crest of the hill, past Sand Hole Woods and down onto the road that would take them south toward Baltimore. Soon Henry would leave the office near his home to inspect the mills at the end of the day, top hat on his head, his pants tucked into the high black boots he always wore. Irénée, Lammot, and their Uncle Alexis preferred the overalls of the powdermen. After Henry's inspection they would walk back to the office with him for the daily council Henry demanded, reporting on production, the workers, and shipping for the day. Henry, behind the desk that had been Alfred's and before that their father's, would sit quietly, tilted back in his chair, his feet on the edge of the desk, and tell his brother and nephews what he expected out of the mills the next day, what changes he had decided upon, what men he had found flagging in their efforts. He would not ask their advice on any matter, company or family, and they had learned soon after Henry took over that to offer it would be a useless waste of time. Henry had begun the ritual of the council the day after Alfred retired. In the thirty-nine years he ruled the company he never allowed it to change.

Alexis I. du Pont's hands, blistered and raw, hurt with the stabbing, searing pain only burns can bring. They would be useless for days, perhaps even weeks, and so would he. His wife, Joanna, would bandage them and cover the burns with salve, but Alexis knew from experience that he would lie awake for many nights: such was the agony of a

*Pierre Samuel Dupont de Nemours (1739–1817) fled Napoleon's France after a long government career to settle in America.* (DU PONT ROMANCE)

*Eleuthère Irénée du Pont (1771–1834) began the family gunpowder business on the Brandywine with borrowed money.* (BETTMANN ARCHIVE)

*E. I. du Pont moved his family into this cabin in 1802 while stonemasons and carpenters erected the first of the du Pont mansions.* (WIDE WORLD PHOTOS)

*The original du Pont powder mills had slanted roofs made of wood that allowed explosions to blow out over the Brandywine Creek.* (BETTMANN ARCHIVE)

*Alfred du Pont (1798–1856) took control of the powder mills after E. I. du Pont, his father, died. He was the eldest son of the company's founder.* (DU PONT ROMANCE)

*Henry du Pont (1812–1889), E. I. du Pont's second son, became head of the family business when Alfred, unable to cope with the dangerous work, retired.* (DU PONT ROMANCE)

*Lammot du Pont (1831–1884), a nephew of Henry du Pont, was the first of many excellent chemists who improved the making of gunpowder on the Brandywine.*
(DU PONT ROMANCE)

*Eugene du Pont (1840–1902) succeeded Henry as head of the family business in 1889.* (DU PONT ROMANCE)

*Thomas Coleman du Pont,*

*Alfred I. du Pont,*
*and*

*Pierre S. du Pont rescued the company from sale to a competitor by taking over after Eugene du Pont died in 1902.*   (WIDE WORLD PHOTOS)

The first office of the powder company, on the Brandywine, gave way to a large office building in Wilmington, Delaware, and an international chemical business. (DU PONT ROMANCE)

powder burn. The mills would function without him for a time, run well by his nephew Irénée, but it was small consolation; his place was with the powdermen. At least, and by the grace of God alone, he was alive.

The fire had been an eerie one, coming less than an hour after he and his brothers and sisters and nieces and nephews finished burying Alfred in Sand Hole Woods. The mills had been shut down for the funeral. Only a skeleton crew of watchmen and workers charged with overseeing operations that could continue without most of the men remained in the yards. The alarm gong had startled the du Ponts, some of them still praying at Alfred's graveside. In moments, from a small mill near the water, the fire had spread to the sawmill, inflamed piles of lumber, and crept toward the press mills, filled with powder ready to be packed and shipped.

One explosion had shattered Alfred's confidence, turning him into an old man at fifty, hastening his death. Now another threatened to destroy the very mills he had given his life and health to. Alexis ran from the graveyard to the powder yards, located the burning buildings, and leaped atop the press mill nearest the flames. Workers handed buckets of water up to him. Alexis spilled them across the flimsy wooden roof, hoping to dampen the boards enough to repel the fire. The roof would not hold his weight; he fell down through it, into a mixing vat filled with black powder, and his services were over for the day; the powdermen contained the fire without his help.

The blaze had started spontaneously. Alexis, who had been baptized into the Episcopal faith after Doctor Tom Smith's death, thought it an omen from God, as though the heavens understood what Alfred had given in the service of his family. Alfred had never joined the church. His wife insisted that the church bells ring at her husband's funeral anyway. Alexis approved heartily; he had spearheaded the family's attack upon Henry's lack of religious convictions, wresting from him the services of stonemasons to build a family church on company land. Christ Church, as it was called, became Victorine du Pont's special province, and after Doctor Tom's death, his widow Eleuthera's. Victorine had long sought to convince Henry that he should donate land and workers' time to building a church. She had found her influence with him as small as that of his other relatives, even though she still lived in his house, the house that had been their father's. Only Alexis seemed to have the slightest power over Henry, and that, Victorine guessed, was because Alexis controlled the daily operations of the powder mills. To Henry, the building of Christ Church was a small matter; he would exact repayment from Alexis in the yards. And he grudgingly approved of the powder workers' devotion to their Catholic faith. Religion disciplined them, made them better workers, and gave them someone other than the du Pont family to blame when tragedy struck. Perhaps the same would happen in his family; the discontent he sensed might be transferred to God and exorcised in their Sunday prayers.

With a certain degree of sadness Henry had watched shovelfuls of dirt cover Alfred's coffin. They had grown up together on the Brandywine. Henry was fourteen years the younger and until he left for West Point, Alfred had been his idol. Since Alfred's retirement he had posed no threat to Henry's authority. In fact, his weak nerves and frail health stood as an example to the rest of the family that Henry's rule was much better than the older brother's. But, with Alfred dead, Henry would find it much easier to control his nephews Irénée and Lammot. Alfred's other boys, Fred and Bidermann, amused more than threatened Henry.

The two younger brothers had journeyed home from Louisville for their father's funeral. Fred resembled Alfred in looks, manner, and disposition: he dressed like a pauper and rarely spoke. Bidermann, away from the Brandywine, had grown into a blustering fool of a man, Henry believed, too free with words, too empty-headed to succeed. Yet the brothers' paper business in Kentucky was going well, due very likely to young Fred's brains: he might prove more formidable than anyone suspected. Henry was pleased that Fred had left the Brandywine rather than take his offer of a job in the mills. He had enough difficulty keeping Irénée and Lammot in their places.

Nephews: if only his wife, Louisa, had borne more sons and fewer daughters. Their ninth child had just come into the world, months before Alfred's death, a boy finally, after seven girls. His firstborn was also a male, named Henry after himself. He would push his eldest child into the military if he could, to reap the honor he himself had sacrificed when he came home to the Brandywine. He would be a very old man before this youngest child, William, could be groomed to take over the family and company. But he knew, with the stubborn certainty he had inherited from his father and grandfather, he would never surrender his power over Eleutherian Mills to his brother's sons rather than his own.

Lammot du Pont strode lightly through the powder yards, a rare smile creasing his face. The sunlight, reflecting off the smooth water of the Brandywine, hurt his eyes. He lifted the steel-rimmed spectacles off his nose. Without them his eyes, a light, cool gray like his father's and grandfather's, usually looked bland and expressionless. Today they seemed on fire.

Through the small window in his office Henry could see Lammot approaching. It must be an emergency, a fire that the alarm gong had failed to signal, or an accident. Only then did Lammot venture outside his laboratory during the working day. Henry rushed from the office. Lammot's smile startled him. A few words from "our Chemist" and Henry's solemn expression broke into a smile, too.

Lammot de Pont had succeeded in changing the ingredients of gunpowder for the first time in seven hundred years. In time—although neither man could know it then—his discovery would change the face of the earth.

Working alone, using formulas scribbled in French on bits of paper by his grandfather, Eleuthère Irénée, Lammot had substituted sodium nitrate for potassium nitrate in black powder. For a half-century his family had searched the world for a supply of saltpeter that would free them from the expensive trade with India, where, for three hundred years, all the world's saltpeter—potassium nitrate—had been mined. Irvine Shubrick, Julia du Pont's navy husband, had once found a two-hundred-mile stretch of land in Peru where saltpeter abounded. But it had been sodium nitrate, not potassium nitrate, impure and so much less effective than the mineral from India that no one had ever bothered to mine it. Alfred du Pont had fiddled with the powder process for decades, to no avail. Lammot continued his father's work at the laboratory bench. After seven years of research he had found the answer: a change in the proportion of gunpowder's three ingredients and a slight alteration of the drying process after the powder was mixed and grained.

Peruvian saltpeter would cost less than half as much as the Indian mineral. Eleutherian Mills could produce powder made with sodium nitrate for the coal-mining trade in Pennsylvania, for the railroad companies throughout the United States, and for the gold prospectors of the Pacific Coast. Soda powder would not replace the older types for the military and sporting trade, but for blasting, where the explosive power of gunpowder counted more than its ability to propel bullets, Lammot's new formula would work even better than the old ones.

Henry ordered the mill machinery modified and Peruvian saltpeter imported in bulk. Hurriedly and without fanfare, he applied for a patent on the formula, in Lammot's name. In May, 1857, the reply came from

Washington: Lammot du Pont had been granted U.S. Patent Number 17,321 for the manufacture of gunpowder using salt of soda rather than salt of potash.

Within weeks the mills were geared to begin soda powder production. Peruvian saltpeter had already arrived at the docks in Wilmington. Men had been trained to operate the mills differently. Irénée and Alexis were thoroughly indoctrinated in the new powder's nuances. The nation, stricken with panic brought on by the boom and inflation after California's gold rush slowed to a halting walk, was tightening its economic belt, barely managing to keep the country's trousers hitched. Henry, with a million dollars in the bank from the Crimean War trade, plotted to expand into the coal fields of Pennsylvania. Less than a year after Lammot's discovery, when the Parrish, Silver and Company mills on Big Wapwallopen Creek in Luzerne County, Pennsylvania, collapsed in bankruptcy, Henry bought them with his ready cash, sent Lammot into the coal country to rebuild them for soda powder production, and spent long nights in his office near Sand Hole Woods writing the company agents that the new Eleutherian Mills blasting powder would soon reach their warehouses.

Profits, he knew, would soon begin cascading in, and with them urgent pleas from every other powder manufacturer for the du Pont secret to using Peruvian saltpeter. Soda powder would not make him the equal of John Jacob Astor, whose fortune was already worth more than twenty millions, or of Cornelius Vanderbilt, whose shipping business had earned him fifteen million dollars by 1853. They were a different sort of man, manipulators of dollars, not tied to a single factory that could produce only what the nation would buy. But with Lammot's new soda powder Henry would call the tune among the giants of commerce and finance, men for whom time and profit coincided: the less time it took to build railroads, open mines, or dredge canals, the higher the profit. Blasting powder from the mills near Big Wapwallopen Creek, vastly more efficient than any ever before manufactured, meant less time and more cash. And he did not intend to even license the new refining process.

A single problem clouded the future Henry envisioned. After he finished constructing the Wapwallopen Mills, Lammot would return to the Brandywine, to his laboratory, and to the praise and esteem of the family. Henry would find it difficult, perhaps impossible, to exclude Lammot from the partnership without risking a family mutiny that might bring his own reign to an end.

# *16*

ONE by one the powdermen of Eleutherian Mills stepped softly into Alexis I. du Pont's bedroom, their heads bowed, their denim hats in their hands. Pale, moaning in a low voice, a mangled leg covered by a blanket, bandages crisscrossing his chest, Alexis opened his eyes long enough to recognize each man, call out his name, and beckon him to his bedside.

Alexis knew all the powdermen by name, knew their wives, their children, even their pets. For twenty-two of his forty-one years he had worked among them. A few of the men had even joined his father in celebrating Alexis's birth in 1816. They had played with him in the powder yards, corraled him when he came too close to the dangerous mills, picked him up from the ground when he fell, sent him running home when his mother called him to dinner.

And, with his father, the founder, and his brother Alfred, they had trained Alexis to the powderman's trade, taught him to refine sulfur and saltpeter, to burn willow branches to just the proper degree, to press and grain and glaze the black powder until it met the standards his father had set. Finally, the powdermakers became Alexis du Pont's employees and, in a bond even Boss Henry could never break, his friends.

Every man at Eleutherian Mills trusted Alexis. Never did they need to check a task he had done; never did they fear that when he walked into a mill he might become careless and cost them their lives. Alexis was an alert, cautious man, his nerves steady, his disregard of danger and his willingness to risk his own life rather than the workers' the source of admiration the powdermen had shown no other du Pont. Any of the hundred men who had come to pay their last respects to Alexis would gladly have changed places with him, for they knew that, among all the du Ponts, only Mister Alexis cared more for the powdermen than the powder mills.

Now, saving their lives was about to cost him his.

On a Saturday afternoon Alexis had been overseeing the dismantling of a graining mill in the Hagley Yard. A heavy metal box, used to hold the powder that had been sifted into small round grains, had to be moved. Alexis had called a few men to help him. Together they slid the bin toward the door. Powder dust coating the metal caught fire from a spark, leaped to some stray grains of powder on the mill floor, and exploded. In seconds, three men died. Another wandered toward his home, only to fall dead at the feet of his wife. Alexis, thrown perhaps thirty yards, ran for the Brandywine with his clothes on fire, leaped into the water, and climbed back on shore. Burns covered most of his body.

Flaming brands from the graining mill had scattered everywhere, carried on the wind from the Creek. One landed on the roof of a press mill, the most dangerous of the powder yard buildings, where loose powder was compressed into flat slabs under tons of pressure. Alexis screamed for his workers to flee. As they ran, he climbed onto the press mill roof and reached for the burning scrap of wood. Before he could fling it away the building exploded.

Eugene, at seventeen Alexis's oldest son, found his father lying on the ground, his back broken, the bones of one leg sticking up through the thigh, two of his ribs cracked into a lung. The powdermen carried Alexis home on a window shutter. Joanna called the rector of Christ Church, the church Alexis had built, and doctors from Wilmington.

Alexis took the verdict of death calmly, sent the doctors away, spoke briefly with the minister, the Reverend Brinckle, and asked Joanna to summon the powder workers. It was, he told his wife, the best way to go: surrounded by all his lifelong friends.

A night and a day after the explosion, his farewells said, Alexis closed his eyes and died. His family carried the body to Christ Church, where throughout the Sunday the powdermen and their families had prayed for their friend. Bells in the tall church spire rang as another grave was opened in Sand Hole Woods.

A year earlier, while stonemasons were building the church, Alexis had happened by. The men were known to drink, at times on the job. When they saw the superintendent of the mills coming, the masons hid their bottle of whiskey in the wall they were putting up. Alexis had noticed the bottle being placed between the mortar and stone. He had settled on a rock a few yards away and watched as the stonemasons sealed their whiskey into the wall of Christ Church. Now he would be the first du Pont buried from inside it.

Henry led the mourners to his brother's grave. He was the last surviving son of Eleuthère Irénée du Pont, the only one of his father's children still active in the powder mills. His Uncle Victor's sons and grandsons cared little for the gunpowder business; their tastes had turned to politics and the practice of law. But the du Ponts from across the Brandywine often mingled socially with the du Ponts from the powder mills. Henry had noticed that some of the younger men and women seemed to have more than just a family interest in each other. Perhaps the family might benefit if a few more of his relatives were to marry each other. His sister Sophie and her husband, Sam Francis, seemed happy enough, although the navy kept him away much of the time, and she, an invalid, rarely ventured beyond the gardens near Louviers—except, of course, to attend Christ Church.

Still, his cousins across the water had their uses, even in their political lives. Charles, serving in the Delaware legislature, had helped Henry wangle a place for his son, Henry Algernon, at West Point. He would be asked to return the favor; perhaps he would find Charles's son, Charles Jr., a job in the powder mills. Knowing that a boy from across the Creek might rise above them would keep his nephews in line.

After the funeral, as was his custom each day, Henry ordered his buggy and horse from the stables near his office. Even though it was August, humid and hot, the storm curtains of the carriage were up. He rode away from the powder mills, across the gentle hills that spread out into rich farmland, over earth he had begun to buy and, with every spare dollar of company money, intended to continue adding to his estate. The Crimean War had made him wealthier than any du Pont before him. Now a nationwide panic was driving the price of land down. But the demand for Du Pont Powder continued to rise. Other men with money were taking advantage of the depression to acquire land at bargain prices, and to buy railroads and coal mines as well. They desperately needed his blasting powder to continue building while prices and wages were low. Soon the economy would turn, and the dredging of canals and tunneling out of mountains would slow as the financiers of Wall Street found better ways to invest. So, too, would the gunpowder trade drastically lessen. But before then, long before, Henry planned to own much of the countryside surrounding Eleutherian Mills. And, very likely, another war would rescue the mills before sales dropped—if not a war across the seas, then the war that Henry knew was coming to the United States, the war between slavery and freedom, as the politicians called the issue; the war between the manufacturers of the North and the planters of the South, as Henry knew it would be. Where, he wondered, would his own state stand? In the south of Delaware men planted cotton and owned slaves, and in the north factory wheels turned. And where would the gunpowder mills of du Pont place their loyalty? If nothing else, Eleutherian Mills must be on the winning side.

At three A.M., on the night of November 7, 1859, Henry du Pont sat in his small office awaiting the returns of the presidential election. A mist had come off the Brandywine earlier in the night, covering the mills with dampness, helping keep the powder wet. Often Henry stood on the piazza of the director's house, looking down into the powder yards, seeing only vague points of light where lanterns hung to illuminate the night's work. He could remember when, as a child, he had stood on the terrace with his father and grandfather, listening to them talk in French, not understanding their words, but knowing that his grandfather Pierre was filling his father's ear with reminiscences of France and the glory of the Bourbon kings.

The memory was dim; he had been only five when his grandfather died. But he could still hear the solemn note in his father's voice, the calm, amost serene way he answered Pierre, and his grandfather's excited, shrill tones. Henry knew he sounded more like his father than his grandfather. He liked it that way: Eleuthère Irénée du Pont had been a great, courageous man. Yet Henry sought to bring his grandfather's dreams to pass. His father had had no interest in building a kingdom of Pontiania in the United States.

Night mists came across the Brandywine even in winter when snow covered the ground. The mists bothered Henry at times: he could never tell at a glance what his workers were up to. And it seemed to Henry that he had grown less impervious to the Brandywine chill, especially in his office, with its cold rock walls. He could have had a fireplace built near his desk, but that would have been an outward sign of weakness and a frill. Except on election night, he rarely spent late hours in the office.

Henry took the old watch that had been his father's from a vest pocket, opened it, and held it up to the candle that lighted his work. The telegraph in his clerk's room had been clicking all night, bringing the outcome of local elections. His cousin Charles, running for the governorship of Delaware, had, surprisingly, lost. Perhaps his defeat would teach him not to support unpopular minorities, at least not publicly. Charles had come out strongly for the rights of Catholics to educate their children according to the tenets of the church in Rome. Delaware had long had public education for all who wished to attend public school, a movement the du Ponts had started by building a small schoolhouse for the children of the powder workers. Charles and his father, Victor, had supported the move toward public schooling, making Delaware the first state to pass free education laws. But Charles had gone too far: education was one thing, backing the Catholic church another, especially since Charles drew most of his support from Delaware's many devout Protestants. Henry thought Charles possessed too much principle to make a good politician: he had even refused to attend Christ Church on Sundays. He was no Episcopalian, Charles said, and did not intend to join the church solely for political reasons.

Charles's defeat was a blow. If, as Henry suspected, his candidate for President, John Bell, lost as well, all hope for peace was gone. Not that war boded ill for the powder mills: orders would flow in at their usual wartime rate. But it would be difficult to choose sides in a civil war. The South would be fighting for the survival of its way of life, on its home ground. The North would have to invade the South to enforce the constitution. Henry's son, nearing the end of his years at West Point, had written home that many of his fellow cadets were Southerners. Henry A. liked them, with their tradition of fine living and military glory, but he knew they would return to their plantations to lead battalions against the Union. Civil war was a certainty: the two ways of life would never learn to exist together. Du Pont agents in the South had hundreds of thousands of pounds of black powder in their storehouses, powder that must be sold or moved before the South decided to rebel. Otherwise it would be lost to Du Pont.

Delaware might go with the South, and Henry would be forced to place his mills at the disposal of the Confederate states. New Jersey and Pennsylvania were staunch Northern strongholds. Maryland, put to the test, must in the end support Washington. Eleutherian Mills, tucked in a corner of Delaware surrounded by the three states, might find itself under siege. The wreck of the mills would put an end to the fortunes of the family.

Of all the so-called border states, where slavery was practiced in some counties but not others, Delaware, with Eleutherian Mills, would be the most important to the South. Henry knew that only one small mill manufactured gunpowder in the South. Scattered through New England and the Pennsylvania coal fields, two hundred powder mills had sprung up since the California gold rush. None compared with Eleutherian Mills; the Brandywine yards turned out fully one-fifth of all the powder made in the United States. But their combined output would make the North substantially stronger than the South—unless Rebel soldiers occupied the Brandywine.

And so Henry awaited the returns of the presidential election. Delaware, like the du Pont family, had not gone solidly for any of the candidates. Henry urgently wanted John Bell in the White House. Charles had supported John C. Breckinridge, candidate of the Southern Democrats, to swing Delaware's lower two-thirds to his side. Sophie's husband, Sam Francis, a navy captain now, had pushed for Abraham Lincoln's election—the worst possible alternative, Henry believed. Lincoln meant war, and soon. No one in the family particularly wanted Stephen Douglas in office.

Shortly after three A.M. the wires clicked out the message: the Illinois lawyer had won, not by much, it seemed, but he would carry the electoral college with ease. Henry thought of his distant relatives in South Carolina, the descendants of Abraham Dupont, who had come to America in 1695. Abraham's son, Gideon, had made rice a profitable crop by introducing the flooding of paddies to do away with weeds. Gideon's great-grandchildren operated a successful plantation near Charleston and owned many slaves. They would be even less happy than Henry at Lincoln's election.

Henry snuffed out two of the three candles on his desk. The third, the shortest, he placed in the old square lantern that stood on the window ledge. It was another of his rituals, using three, and only three, candles to light his office, taking the shortest home in his lantern, replacing it the next day with a fresh taper. Many of his relatives would be in his parlor awaiting news of the election. Some would celebrate the nation's decision; others would scowl. One, his nephew Irénée's wife Charlotte, daughter of a Southern planter, would be sure to cry. Putting on his tall silk hat and trudging the short distance home, Henry hoped they would toast Lincoln's victory quickly and scatter to their own parlors and bedrooms. Dawn would soon arrive and Henry had work to do: Eleutherian Mills must prepare for war.

# 17

LATE on the night of April 17, 1861, news of the fall of Fort Sumter crossed the telegraph wires to the Brandywine. Henry du Pont immediately began writing his Southern agents of his decision: Eleutherian Mills would remain loyal to the United States of America and the Constitution. More than six hundred thousand pounds of Du Pont's best black powder lay unprotected in warehouses from Charleston to New Orleans. Not one ounce was for sale to the soldiers of the South. Jefferson Davis was certain to order raids on the warehouses; had he been in the Confederate president's place, trying to raise an army and supply it, Henry would have done the same. He had decided to forfeit the powder: it would be the last the Confederate States of America would get from Eleutherian Mills.

In a way, the attack on Fort Sumter had pleased Henry. Abraham Lincoln had turned out to be less a war hawk and more shrewd a politician than the Red Fellow had figured him to be. To the chagrin of many Northerners, the President seemed to have gone soft on the slavery issue after his election. Lincoln made his stand on constitutional grounds: no state had the right to secede. But secede the South had, and still Lincoln refused to attack, or even to form a military force that would crush the Confederacy quickly: he refused to become the aggressor. If he waited until the Rebels drew first blood, the people of the Union states would back whatever course their President followed and, after entering the White House with less than a popular majority, Lincoln would become the guardian of all the North held righteous and true.

Now that Fort Sumter had fallen, the President would be unable to withstand the pressure for war. War had to come soon; Eleutherian Mills could not stand the financial strain much longer. Early in the year Irénée had pleaded with his uncle for a reduction in the output of the mills and a layoff of at least some of the workers. Henry had quieted his nephew's first complaints with little more than a stare: how dare he suggest something to the senior partner?

Irénée was not easily silenced. When the economy of the North fell to depths unseen since the revolution, he demanded that Henry shut down the mills completely. The Red Fellow unleashed his anger at the younger man: Eleutherian Mills would never close. He used the one argument neither Irénée nor his brother Lammot could face: who would tell the five hundred men, many of them third-generation powdermakers, that they no longer had jobs or homes? War would come, and it would be difficult to hire his workers back after months of idleness. Many would drift into jobs at other powder factories, and he would have to break a cardinal rule of Eleutherian Mills: no powderman who ever worked for another company would ever enter the powder yards on the Brandywine. Henry held firm against Irénée: not a single man was to be fired, not a single mill closed. Enough profits remained from the Crimean War, he reminded his nephew, to carry Du Pont until the Civil War began.

On the day after Fort Sumter fell Henry stepped through the doors of the director's house wearing a neatly pressed black coat, an American flag under his arm, his jaw set. Every man of the name du Pont awaited him on the lawn. He had ordered them there in military fashion; a few of his relatives snickered that Boss Henry enjoyed war a good deal more than he did peace.

Together, Henry announced, they would march the short distance to Henry Clay Village, just outside the mills. He would hoist the American flag to the top of the pole on the village green. The time had come to end the ugly rumors that Eleutherian Mills was providing gunpowder to the soldiers of the Confederacy.

Henry conducted the ceremony and hurried his relatives back to the lawn before the director's house. He admonished them to remain loyal to the interests of Eleutherian Mills, even if they conflicted with their own, and to keep their families in line: no hint of Confederate sympathy was to reach a powderman's ears.

Irénée winced at his uncle's words: they were meant for him and his Southern-born wife. Since Lincoln's election he had broken up many fights between Charlotte and his mother, Margaretta. His mother seemed unable to keep her sentiments to herself; she seized upon any excuse to ridicule the South within Charlotte's hearing. When Charlotte refused to react, Margaretta took to beginning and ending family dinners with a few words about the possibility of Confederate spies within the powder yards: had not Henry warned of it? Irénée had stormed at his mother, demanding that she stop baiting Charlotte. His mother agreed with a smile and continued to harass her daughter-in-law.

Now Henry himself was pointing a finger at Irénée's wife. The Red Fellow regaled his partners in their nightly meeting with stories about his son, Henry Algernon. Word had come that Henry A. would graduate first in his class from West Point. The senior partner glowed with pride: at least one du Pont would carry the family's banner in the war. And his sister, Sophie, still living across the Creek at Louviers, brought news of Samuel Francis. The navy had ordered him to organize and lead the South Atlantic Blockading Squadron, charged with defeating the Confederacy at sea. Henry hoped privately that his sister's husband, cousin or not, would fail to eclipse his son with his war exploits. Out in the hills each afternoon, on his daily buggy ride, Henry had taken to calling his horses, regardless of their names, Frank, a nickname Sophie used for Samuel Francis.

Henry dismissed his family from his lawn and called Irénée and Lammot to him. They were to watch carefully over the powder yards for the next few days. He had telegraphed Washington that he wished to see the President, on urgent business concerning the output of Eleutherian Mills. He would leave at dawn, he told his nephews, and be gone three or four days. The call at the White House was a formality, to assure President Lincoln that the mills on the Brandywine stood squarely behind the Union. He had two other purposes in going to Washington: to secure war contracts for Eleutherian Mills and to convince the War Department that the du Ponts and their workers must be exempted from service in the nation's armed forces. He would tell the Secretary of War that Eleutherian Mills could supply all the gunpowder the North needed, given access to enough raw materials and the proper support from the United States government.

Victorine du Pont clipped the first roses of spring from their vines in her garden. How had she so quickly grown old? She remembered, nearly a half-century ago, sitting here among the flowers, reading the letters from Ferdinand, waiting so impatiently for his return. Had he really been dead for forty-nine years? She could close her eyes and conjure a picture of him, tall and fair and smiling, and of her father, seething at their desire to marry and banishing Ferdinand to Europe for two years. Or had it been Ferdinand's father who sent him away? No matter: it was so very long ago.

Victorine's gardens were magnificent, stretching in patches of green and lovely colors well away from the director's house and over the edge of the hill down toward the powder yards. Her father would have been proud of them. Irénée had been dead for twenty-seven years. Alfred and Alexis were gone, too. Life was not the same with Henry running the company. It was almost as if her brother had inherited their father's manner and their grandfather's principles. She could remember when her days were filled with trips into the powder yards to see to the workers' needs, to clean the barrackslike buildings the single powder-men lived in and cook their meals. Most of the men and their wives had spoken French then, her native tongue; now they all seemed to talk with that grating Irish accent, to swear in public and raise their children as Catholics. No matter how much Henry wished to give the impression that nothing had changed on the Brandywine, Victorine knew that everything had: the powder workers were no longer like a family, and the du Ponts little resembled kind uncles and aunts.

Except for walks to Christ Church and the powder workers' school, Victorine rarely ventured outside the house and gardens; she could see all she wished of the mills from the piazza on the hill. Here, in the rooms and few yards of lawn she had lived among for fifty years, the new war would hardly reach her. Her father and Uncle Victor had loathed the military way, recoiling from everything that had to do with men killing men—except the manufacture of black powder. Irénée had never let war touch his family or home, or his workers. Henry seemed to glory in it.

Even Henry's somber face could not hide the exhilaration he felt when Delaware's governor appointed him major general of the state militia. Victorine was certain Henry and the governor had made a deal. Delaware had strong sympathies with the South, and Henry had the firepower to keep the state in line with the Union. Ever since Henry had been called home from the army to help their aging father, a quarter-century ago, Victorine had sensed his disappointment in leaving the military life. For a simple guarantee that the people of Delaware would be kept loyal to the Union, Henry had won his military title back.

Her brother had openly told the family that his name would be changed from Mister Henry to General Henry among the powder workers. And he had even called the men together after a long day in the mills making powder for the Union to demand that they take an oath of loyalty to the North or lose their jobs. In their father's day it would have been unnecessary.

Nothing seemed to stop Henry's patriotic zeal. After all the powder workers swore fealty to the Union, Henry took his campaign to the streets of Wilmington. There, however, the citizens laughed at him, telling him to take his oaths and arms back to the Brandywine and keep his mouth shut. Henry had telegraphed the army commander in Baltimore that the state was about to secede by popular will and demanded federal troops to enforce loyalty to the Union. Nearly three thousand soldiers, in government dress, marched into Wilmington. Under General Henry's command the soldiers secured the city hall, then turned south to the state capital. Henry had seen to it that the people had no choice about which side they gave their energies to: Delaware would never join the Confederacy.

Victorine knew that soldiers would soon come to the Brandywine to protect the powder mills. The young women of the family would parade before them in the afternoons, strolling down the road to Camp Du Pont, as it was called whenever troops set up their tents in the fields a half-mile from the mills. She would stay in her garden, clipping flowers for her only male friend, the Reverend Brinckle of Christ Church. Her relatives believed she loved the minister. They were right, of course, but Victorine never so much as hinted at it in her speech or actions. The Reverend Brinckle was a man of God, and she would never taint his reputation. Besides, she must remain faithful to Ferdinand: it was the French way. This year, she decided, the best of her early roses would go to Christ Church, not to the hallway of her brother's house. Let the younger women of the Brandywine prance about laughing with the soldiers; she would stay in her gardens and receive the Reverend Brinckle each afternoon. After all, how many more springs would she live to watch the roses bloom?

Lammot du Pont ran a finger across the fringe of black beard that ringed his face and made him look older than his thirty years. The small mirror above his washstand in London's Hotel Morley did not lie: he truly was as ugly a man as Abraham Lincoln. But Lammot believed the resemblance ended there. Others did not: he had been mistaken for the American President a number of times since coming to England. If only he had Lincoln's power! He would not be pacing his room, wondering if he had convinced the British Prime Minister, Lord Palmerston, with his ultimatum. Let the saltpeter go, he had told the Englishman, or the United States would declare war on the British Empire.

Lammot laughed at the enormity of his bluff. The President had called him to Washington in the autumn of 1861 and urged him to travel to England, with diplomatic credentials sealed in his coat should a British ship stop his ship, to buy saltpeter for the gunpowder factories of the Union. Uncle Henry had convinced the President and his cabinet that the saltpeter crisis could cost the North the war. Only a few weeks' supply remained in Union storehouses. After that, the soldiers who wore the Union blue might as well throw rocks at the Confederates: their guns would be useless.

President Lincoln, a remarkably gentle and good-humored man, explained that buying saltpeter in London would be more than a matter of exchanging money for crushed rock. The British were nearly committed to joining the Confederacy in the war. If they were faced, quite openly, with someone spreading huge sums about the country on behalf of the United States government, their diplomatic relations with the Confederates would force them to stop the saltpeter from leaving England. Lincoln believed the British did not truly want to fight the Union. He asked Lammot to buy the saltpeter in his own name. The Treasury was preparing one-half million dollars in gold bullion to send across the Atlantic a few days after Lammot left. It would be at his disposal in London. The mission held a certain danger: if Britain entered the war against the North while Lammot was still in London he might be imprisoned and shot as a spy. The President could offer no guarantees for his safety or promise that the United States would invoke its diplomatic privileges in his behalf should he be arrested.

Lammot agreed to go on two conditions: the saltpeter was to be given to his company to refine—all of it—and, for the entire war, Eleutherian Mills was to be provided with saltpeter at the price Lammot paid for it in England. As for his own safety: how much worse could London be than Sevastopol?

The Atlantic winds had been brisk. By the middle of November Lammot had arrived in London and begun searching for storehouses of saltpeter throughout the British Isles. Merchants welcomed him. They knew his name, of course, and none suspected that Lammot's buying trip carried any more than normal importance for the Du Pont Company. Within ten days Lammot had bought over two thousand tons of saltpeter, the entire private stock in England, and all that was en route from India. Ships awaited the saltpeter in London, Liverpool, and Greenock. The sellers clamored for payment; he owed them nearly the entire half-million Lincoln had promised to send. But the gold had not yet arrived, and the mission had taken on a new, more important light. If he succeeded in spiriting the saltpeter away before Parliament got wind of it the British would be unable to fight alongside the Confederacy even if they chose to: their stock of saltpeter, kept in government warehouses, would not last a week. Lammot would bring Mr. Lincoln a bonus.

With thousands of bags of saltpeter sitting on wharves around England, the Union broke international law by taking prisoner two Confederate diplomats bound from Havana to England on a British mail ship. John Slidell, of Louisiana, and James Mason, of Virginia, were arrested as prisoners of war. Word reached London swiftly, and Lammot looked up from the docks to see a company of soldiers beckoning him to shore. He would accompany them, their commander said, to the customs house, to check on the legality of his documents. Lammot asked for a moment to consult with his ship's captain. Sail, Lammot ordered, at the next high tide, early the following morning before the sun rose. The captain nodded. Lammot walked off toward the customs office, looking back over his shoulder in dismay: soldiers were guarding the ship's ropes and planks. There would be no casting off at the next high tide.

Soon Lammot learned that Lord Palmerston had issued a letter of objection to the Union government. Mason and Slidell, aboard the mail packet *Trent*, had been under England's sovereign protection. When the U.S.S. *San Jacinto* fired broadsides across the *Trent's* bow, the Union had broken international law. Lammot du Pont would get no saltpeter until Mason and Slidell were released.

Lammot paced the floor in his room at Morley's. What could he do? Washington must be crazy! The balance of the war might very well hang upon his saltpeter. Even if Mason and Slidell convinced the British to enter the war, it would be too late. The saltpeter would be safely stored in the American North. He shrugged in disbelief at the stupidity of whoever commanded the *San Jacinto*. He remembered that it was one of the ships his uncle, Sam Francis, had assembled to blockade the South. While he tried to secure victory for the North, its most decorated naval commander might be making that success impossible! Lammot decided to set sail the next day for Washington.

Three weeks later, on the Brandywine, his relatives gathered around him over a day-late Christmas dinner. Where had he been, what had he been doing? Why the secrecy? they wanted to know. Lammot only smiled: it ws none of their business. His brother, Irénée, was shocked. Even he had not been told where Lammot was bound. Margaretta, who besides Henry was the only other du Pont informed of Lammot's mission, kept silent. If he would not tell them where he had gone, his relatives chimed, at least he had returned safely. They had missed him.

He was sorry to disappoint them, Lammot said, but he must leave again that very day. No, he could not say where he was bound, but he promised to bring them back a special gift—a gift for the entire Union. Lammot finished his dinner, conferred with Henry for a few moments, and mounted a horse for Wilmington, where a train awaited his arrival and would speed him to Washington.

Lammot hurried from Washington's train station to the White House. Behind locked doors Abraham Lincoln agonized over another crisis. He had been informed that the British had sent eight thousand men to Canada, ready to invade the Union should satisfaction not be given in the *Trent* affair. The officers of the *San Jacinto* were being hailed as heroes by the nation for capturing Mason and Slidell. In Boston a dinner was held in their honor, with toasts drunk to their grand success in stopping the South's diplomatic mission from reaching Europe. The public knew nothing of the saltpeter; Lincoln had done everything in his power to keep the sad state of American supplies from the people. Now England demanded the Rebels' release, in seven days or less, or war would be declared. If Lincoln gave in to the British the people would damn him; if he did not defeat was almost certain.

When the cabinet members rose for a brief recess, Secretary of State Seward came out to speak with Lammot. The President knew all that had transpired in London, Seward said, and he had reached his decision: he would order Mason and Slidell released. To the public outcry that would come, Lincoln could plead the need of the Union to comply with international law. Lincoln was well aware that even releasing the two Confederates might not prod England into letting Lammot's saltpeter go, especially if Parliament knew what the saltpeter meant to the Union cause and England's ability to make war. But the Parliament might not: greater blunders had been made by statesmen of larger stature than Lord Palmerston. Lammot's orders were simple: get the saltpeter. Seward would provide him with strong credentials and letters to the Union ambassador in England. Lammot was to do whatever, in his judgment, he must to secure the precious mineral.

Lammot sailed at once for London. The moment he landed he raced from the docks to 10 Downing Street and asked to see the Prime Minister. Lord Palmerston's secretary was sorry, but the Prime Minister was rather busy; perhaps if Mister du Pont returned the following day. Lammot replied that he most certainly would.

The next morning, and the next after that, Lammot sat in the Prime Minister's reception room, waiting to be admitted to Lord Palmerston's presence. On the fourth day, his patience gone, Lammot burst in upon the Prime Minister, pounded his fists on Palmerston's desk and roared a simple demand: *saltpeter or war*. Shaken, Palmerston assured Lammot that he would have an answer for him that afternoon. Lammot returned to his hotel room to await the Prime Minister's messenger. None came.

Leaving word that he would be in the hotel dining room, Lammot slipped down to dinner after sunset, brooding over what he would do next. Palmerston had not gone for the bait, it seemed, and his saltpeter-filled ships still lay at anchor, surrounded by British soldiers and ships. His appetite had gone. He sat gazing out the window while his food grew cold. Suddenly he turned to his plate, eating voraciously, obviously enjoying the meal, not a care on his mind. Through the window he had seen a carriage bearing the seal of the Prime Minister pull up. Lord Palmerston hurried through the door of the dining room, alone. He approached Lammot's table, cleared his throat to announce his presence, and when Lammot only stared, laid his gloves and top hat on the table and sat down. Haltingly, Palmerston apologized for not getting in touch with Lammot sooner. There were complications; Parliament was still angered by the Mason-Slidell affair. He had encountered opposition from his advisers. Some simply did not want to let the saltpeter go. England, after all, might have need of it. He had learned that Lammot's purchases all but wiped out England's supply; it would take a year to rebuild it. Of course, England wished the Union no ill will and, as a neutral nation, did not balk at taking the North's money.

Lammot stopped eating briefly, looking at Lord Palmerston only long enough to utter the same demand he had made earlier that day: saltpeter or war. Those were, he said, his instructions from President Lincoln.

In that case, Palmerston said, he was empowered to allow Lammot to sail. The formalities would take a bit of time, of course, but he was certain he could have the necessary papers ready by late the next afternoon.

Lammot gazed across the table. Was it a trick? Was the Prime Minister buying more time to consult his advisers, perhaps even Parliament, to construct a plausible reason why the saltpeter must not be allowed to travel across the Atlantic? Would the British really risk war with the Union over the mineral? Perhaps Palmerston had decided to bluff Lammot into giving him time to find a way out of the ultimatum. Lammot set his wine glass down on the table. Another day would not do, he said. Early the next morning he planned—in fact, he must—sail for the United States. If Lord Palmerston was not willing to give him the travel permit at once, then he supposed it would be war between his nation and England.

Palmerston crumbled. He drew a blank sheet of paper from within his coat and wrote out a special sailing permit for Lammot's ships, effective immediately, with no interference from either the customs department or British soldiers. When the Prime Minister finished, handed the paper to Lammot, and stood to leave, taking his gray top hat and gloves from the table, Lammot stood with him. His face red, Palmerston turned and walked from the hotel without a word.

Lammot swept the plates of cold food aside and ordered a hot meal and a bottle of the Morley's best wine. He had a celebration coming, he knew, and needed a stiff drink to stop his wobbling knees. He had bluffed England into helping the North win the Civil War and effectively neutralized the world's greatest navy. Lammot wondered what his lookalike, Abraham Lincoln, would do if he knew that a private citizen, with no authority, had, on behalf of the United States, threatened the Prime Minister of Great Britain with war.

# *18*

L AMMOT DU PONT rubbed the weariness from his eyes with the
  backs of his large, square hands, resting his spectacles on his head
for the moment. He was not really listening to Henry intone the production and shipping figures for the day; they interested him a good
deal less than a few hours' sleep.

Never had he felt so tired. Eleutherian Mills turned out gunpowder
twenty-four hours a day. The war fever had touched him even tucked
away in his laboratory. Irénée felt worse than he did. His brother rarely
left the powder yards before midnight; never did he arrive after dawn.
Even Irénée's sense of humor seemed to have fled in the face of the war.
Lammot had not seen a look of less than complete absorption on his
brother's face in months.

He wondered what weighed heavier on Irénée: the powder yards or
his wife's frayed, nearly collapsed nerves. Lammot could not help feeling disgust with their mother for her constant attacks upon Charlotte's
Southern heritage. But if Irénée's anger and cajoling could not stunt the
invective Margaretta poured on Charlotte, what could he do? Their
mother had always been a strong-willed woman, not about to take the
advice of her sons.

Rubbing his eyes did Lammot little good. He wished that Henry
would abandon the candles he used for kerosene lamps, but he knew
that nothing changed the General. The ancient quill pens, inkwell, and
curved blotter on the Red Fellow's desk had been inherited from Irénée
the first. Lammot doubted that Henry would ever even exchange the
inefficient quills for steel pens: his uncle revered tradition. He had been
more than a bit happy when Lammot and Irénée's sister, Mary Sophie,
chose a mate from among their cousins across the Brandywine. The
General had fairly glowed at the wedding; rumor had it that he would
make Mary's husband, Charles I., superintendent of the Upper Yard. All
the partners should have made such a decision, but Henry's love for
tradition ended where power over the company became involved.

Irénée could barely hold his head up through Henry's report for the day. Soon the meeting would be over and they would both be free to have supper before returning to the yards. Irénée longed to linger over dinner with his wife: Charlotte was pregnant. But he would take no longer than a few minutes to gulp down his food and stride back through the mill gates. Lammot shared Irénée's loyalty: while powdermen toiled on the Brandywine, nothing came before the mills.

Henry's voice stopped. Lammot broke from his reverie to see a rare smile on his uncle's face. They had cause for celebration, Henry was saying. The two goliaths of the Civil War, the new ironclads, *Monitor* and *Merrimac*, had clashed at sea. The *Monitor* had fairly blasted the Rebel ship out of the water. Both were clothed in sheets of steel; both had large guns. But the Union ship prevailed for one reason, and one reason only: Mammoth Powder. Lammot could be justly proud of his invention, as could they all. Irénée had manufactured the giant grains of black powder—some as big as baseballs—precisely and swiftly. The victory was certain to capture the imagination of the people and help raise the North's sagging morale. Henry instructed his nephews to compliment the men in the mills—not too much, just enough to make them feel they had done their part for the Union and the company. They would need the praise: new orders had come in from Washington, and word crossed the telegraph wires that Lincoln wanted hundreds of thousands of new recruits, by conscription if necessary, to enter the army for three years. The President had realized at last that the Civil War would not be won in weeks or months. Great days of achievement—and profit—lay ahead for the owners of Eleutherian Mills.

Shortly past noon on September 17, 1862, guards patrolling the perimeter of Eleutherian Mills captured two men hiding in woods within a half-mile of the powder yard gates. In their packs they carried complete sets of plans for the powder yards. Irénée questioned the men on the lawn near the director's house. One admitted to being a captain in the Confederate army; the other would say nothing.

The Rebel soldier, O'Keefe, denied repeatedly that they had been accompanied by any other Confederate troops. Irénée only half believed him. Early that morning Union and Confederate forces had clashed at Antietam in Maryland. If the Southerners commanded by Robert E. Lee won, Eleutherian Mills would be their next target: the spies were proof.

Irénée wished his Uncle Henry and Lammot had been on the Brandywine rather than in Washington consulting with the Secretary of War. Irénée sent the captured spies to Fort Delaware under guard, packed charges of blasting powder, and chose places in the yards where they would do the most damage: he was prepared to destroy Eleutherian Mills rather than turn it over to the Confederacy.

The telegraph in the company office clicked out a message from Henry in Washington: Lee had dispatched three thousand soldiers to capture Eleutherian Mills. Henry reacted predictably. Irénée was to ship all the powder stored in the grand magazine and abandon the mills. Irénée hardly believed what he read: a du Pont choosing to flee and leave the yards to the enemy rather than destroy them. He sensed beneath Henry's order a cowardice that disgusted him nearly as much as his mother's baiting of his wife.

Another cable came in from Washington. Secretary of War Stanton had decided that Eleutherian Mills was too valuable to either abandon or blow up. Two thousand five hundred Pennsylvania regulars had been dispatched to protect the mills from Lee's soldiers. They were all the men President Lincoln could spare from the battle in Maryland: if the Rebels won at Antietam the mills along the Brandywine would be indefensible anyway.

Lammot du Pont began planning the final defense of Eleutherian Mills on July 2, 1863. He called Eugene du Pont, his Uncle Alexis's oldest son, to him from the Hagley Yard. Eugene was just twenty-three; he had come to work in the powder yards after five years cloistered in the University of Pennsylvania studying chemistry. Eugene had less to lose than any other du Pont and whoever Lammot took with him to command half the Brandywine militia might very well lose everything.

At first Lammot had wanted Irénée at his side, but Charlotte had given birth to a baby girl a few months earlier and would need her husband. Irénée could not be spared from the powder yards; should the North somehow defeat Lee's troops at Gettysburg, as they had at Antietam, the mills must go on, and Irénée would be needed to run them. Cousin Charles, superintendent of the Upper Yard now, was married, too, and not much of a soldier. Eugene was the only du Pont left for Lammot to choose.

The defense of the Brandywine would begin at the western boundary of Delaware, a few miles from the mills. Lammot and Eugene would each lead a company of soldiers, all powdermen. Lammot asked Eugene to form the men into their units on the lawn outside the director's house while he stopped at the company office to tell Henry that they were ready to leave.

The Red Fellow was not at his desk writing letters or balancing accounts as he usually did each morning. His daughter Louisa, only eighteen, had died during the night, and for the first time in Lammot's memory Henry had not gone to his office at dawn. Inside the director's house Lammot told Henry that he was preparing the men to defend Eleutherian Mills; they would appreciate a few words from the General. He appealed to the Red Fellow with words Henry had himself often repeated: during war the du Ponts must stand more tall, be more strong, more sober, more level-headed than at any other time. Now the very life of the mills was at stake. Henry told Lammot to form the men into their platoons while he said a few words to his wife. He would address the workers on the lawn.

Walking out into the morning sun, Lammot could hear a distant train whistle, coming from Wilmington, where cars full of casualties passed on the way to New England. If the North prevailed at Gettysburg the women of Eleutherian Mills would pack huge baskets of fruit and sandwiches, carry them in buggies to the train station, and try to comfort the injured men while their trains stopped for fuel.

The powder workers formed into companies in front of himself and Eugene. Eugene looked nervous—unusual for him. He had reason to be: the powdermen were likely to fight this time and leave dead men in the hills to the west, unless the Union soldiers stopped Lee. Lammot hoped that Eugene's character need never be tested under fire and that some of the gunpowder his workers carried would be used to make fireworks to celebrate Independence Day, rather than to kill Confederate soldiers.

In the first three years of the Civil War Eleutherian Mills sold three million three hundred twenty-three thousand eleven dollars' worth of gunpowder to the army and navy of the United States. Henry believed the price had always been fair: never more than twenty-eight cents a pound for the best grades of black powder used in Union rifles, less for soda powder that blasted cannonballs from navy guns. He had heard rumors that the Confederates were paying up to one dollar a pound for powder from their own nonprofit mills. Imported powder, slipped through the Union's blockade of the Atlantic coast, brought more than three dollars a pound.

Henry took pride in not being one of the war profiteers of the North, who sold tons of rancid beef to the Union soldiers for high prices, then claimed they had not known the meat was bad, or provided shoes that fell apart the first time they were worn, or rifles that refused to fire. He would make a decent profit on the war, but not at the expense of the safety or health of Union men. He had been right to stick with the Union: the North would eventually win. Lincoln was proving to be a man of wisdom in the White House, supporting the manufacturers of the North, declaring the slaves of the South free. Henry knew that the Emancipation Proclamation had been an empty act: it freed slaves only in captured Confederate states and did not include those in Northern states such as Delaware. Since not a single Confederate state had been brought under Union control, no slaves were freed by Lincoln's words. But the President had chosen a shrewd moment to make his declaration: the South was strangling in its own cotton and the Confederate army was tiring quickly. The slaves, hearing Lincoln's promise of freedom, would undermine their masters in any way they could—and the best way was to continue picking cotton, filling warehouses to more than bursting, and refusing to fight in the Confederate army. The slaves had been promised liberty: they would settle for nothing less. President Lincoln had found a way to apply pressure from the outside, with his army and navy, and from inside, by proclaiming the freedom of the slaves.

Henry had decided to increase his share of the company's profits. None of his relatives would complain; every decision he had made was proving right. When the war ended he wanted a stranglehold on the company, to do with it as he pleased, and his pleasure would be to take over all the gunpowder plants that had fallen to explosions or enemy attack. There was a kingdom to be built on the Brandywine. It must rise from the ashes of the Civil War, or never rise at all.

Life on the Brandywine slowly returned to normal when the war ended. The powder workers abandoned their daily drill with weapons, and Henry's cries for more and more powder production eased. The Red Fellow still insisted on being called the General; no one in the family or company was in a position to object.

For the first time in five years children swam in the still pools above the Creek dams that diverted water into the millraces. The women who mourned dead husbands—forty-three workers had perished in explosions during the war—seemed to feel better now that the South had been defeated. Lincoln was the man of the hour; even Henry backed him for reelection.

The Red Fellow had been remarkably pleasant when the government asked him to cancel the last of the orders for powder to supply the military. The mills would not suffer: war, with all its devastation, always seemed to bring about a boom in the nation: rebuilding, expanding, building. Eleutherian Mills never lost business after a war. When orders from the government stopped, those from private concerns turning their attention back to peace picked up. Henry gloated over the millions of dollars that stood idle in the company's bank accounts: once the postwar boom ended and a depression set in, as it always did, Eleutherian Mills would be able to weather the economic storms easily, perhaps even expand. Lammot had come to respect his uncle's business methods during the war; the du Pont family did not want for money or luxuries. He would support the General in whatever direction he chose to move the powder company.

The end of the war had brought the women of the Brandywine out of hiding. Henry's edict against afternoon walks ended when Camp Du Pont was dismantled. Lammot suddenly realized how lonely the war had made him. He had traveled to Europe, led the men of the mills to the battlefield, worked ceaselessly in his laboratory. But he had not once allowed himself the luxury of a woman's company: his mind had locked out anything unnecessary to the production of gunpowder. Now he longed for the touch of a gentle hand and something to go home to after his day in the mills besides the rantings of his mother about her daughter-in-law Charlotte. His brother's wife had given birth again, to a strapping boy named Alfred after the infant's grandfather. Irénée confided to him that Charlotte had taken the end of the Civil War far worse than its beginning. She rarely smiled, spending her time sitting in a rocking chair on the porch of their home, Swamp Hall, holding her infant son. Margaretta's attacks had not ceased after the truce; she goaded Charlotte mercilessly about her Southern relatives. Irénée had decided to send his wife abroad for a year; nothing else would restore her emotional health. Lammot tried to calm Irénée's anger at their mother. It was useless: Irénée intended never to speak to Margaretta again.

Charlotte was not the only du Pont woman who bore children during the war. In Louisville, Bidermann's wife gave birth to a son, Thomas Coleman, early in the fighting, and to another boy just before the truce.

Fred was still unmarried and Lammot did not expect his eccentric brother ever to find a wife. Fred still lived in his single room at the Galt Hotel, but Bidermann had taken a house of his own. The brothers rarely came north during the conflict. Now they would journey to the Brandywine regularly.

Lammot might have an occasion to bring his brothers north sooner than they planned. He had been courting a woman in the Brandywine community, Mary Belin, the company bookkeeper's daughter. The unmarried men in the powder yards ignored her; at twenty-six Mary was considered an old maid. She had been in delicate health since contracting tuberculosis while nursing a sick sister. The men of the Brandywine put a premium on women who would bear children quickly and well; the nature of their work made their futures too uncertain to let nature take its course. Lammot's relatives felt the same way about childbearing. Mary Belin looked frail, but Lammot sensed that she would carry children easily. Marrying her would start another family war; Mary Belin was one-quarter Jewish. But, despite her heritage, Lammot felt himself falling in love with her. Unlike so many of the du Pont women, bred into the legacy of du Pont nobility and the constant danger of the mills, Mary had a sense of humor. And she also had a certain quiet pride about her, a legacy from her grandmother.

Mary Belin's great-grandfather had been a merchant in Philadelphia, with a large business that brought enough money to educate his children well. He was a Jew. Moses Homberg's eldest daughter had run away with a sea captain, Henry d'Andelot, a Frenchman. But she had not forsaken her Jewish faith. One of the d'Andelot children had married Henry Belin, from another French immigrant family. Henry had joined the powder company early in life, risen from clerk to bookkeeper, and earned even General Henry's grudging approval for his earnest work habits and sobriety. Mary had grown up on the Brandywine; she and Lammot had known each other almost from birth. He was nearly thirty-four now and wanted a mature woman to run his house and bring him children—and not one of his stuffed-shirt relatives or an Irish powderman's daughter.

Lammot had approached his mother about the match. She suggested they discuss it in one of the family councils General Henry liked to hold on such matters. Lammot refused; his life was his own. He would not surrender the right to choose his mate to the family. How was that different from what the slaves had been subjected to before the Civil

War? Margaretta was tolerant, to a point. Marry whom he wished, she said, but she would not live under the same roof with Mary Belin. She would move to a farmhouse away from the mills. Lammot could have the house his father had built. With both Irénée and Lammot marrying outside the family, she would have little say in the affairs of the Brandywine anyway: better that she leave than wander unheeded through the powder yards. Lammot did not object to his mother's plans.

He told the General that he planned to wed Mary Belin. The Red Fellow seemed pleased, if slightly insulted that his nephew had not come to him for advice before proposing. Mary would make a good wife, and Lammot would lose influence in the company by marrying a woman with Jewish blood in her veins. The family could be expected to ostracize Lammot and his bride. Henry would play the role of peacemaker. If, after a time, he openly accepted Mary himself, the family would follow suit. But before he did so, the damage to Lammot would be done.

Lammot's exploits in the war had brought him great favor, especially among the family's women, and Henry knew that the du Pont women influenced the du Pont men. Henry had plans for the millions in profits from the war. With Irénée preoccupied by his wife's increasing insanity, and Lammot's star fallen after a marriage to the Brandywine's only Jewess, Henry could do what he wished with the money. Lammot and Mary planned to wed in October, while the warm autumn sun still allowed a celebration out of doors. Perhaps Henry would wait until New Year's Day to bestow his approval of the new bride, stopping his carriage at her door with the traditional gift from the family's head. Two months would be long enough to build hatred for Mary, and disgust with Lammot, that would never go away. And two months would be a short enough period to allow an easy mending of Lammot's hurt feelings. Above all, Henry needed the family's chemist.

In the afternoons the General had resumed taking his buggy and hounds across the hills. He decided to begin buying land as soon as Lammot's wedding was over. Some farmers would sell out for very little, their spirits broken by the war, their debts so large that no amount of crops or cattle would carry them into the black. Others, not wishing to be surrounded by du Ponts, would sell just to escape the General's continuous prodding and offers. Lammot's marriage to Mary Belin suited Henry well. Only one man would rule the Pontiania he planned to establish on the Brandywine.

# 19

THE ENTIRE du Pont family gathered at the cemetery in Sand Hole Woods in late June, 1865, for the funeral of Admiral Samuel Francis du Pont, United States Navy. The line of mourners following the Admiral's flag-draped coffin as it left Christ Church had stretched from the woods all the way back to the powder yard gates. Young and old the du Ponts had come, from their homes on both sides of the Brandywine, to honor their favorite military son; the Admiral's grand-nephew, Victor, and his wife, Alice, had even brought their ten-day-old son, the Admiral's namesake, to Sand Hole Woods.

The Admiral's death had been both merciful and severe. On the night of June 22, while visiting Philadelphia with his wife, Sophie, Sam Francis had fallen ill and, by the morning, had died. His demise had, however, begun two years earlier, when the United States Navy dismissed him from command after a brilliant forty-year career on the seas, and Congress opened an official investigation into the charges that Samuel Francis had been personally responsible for the defeat of the Union navy at the battle of Charleston.

The evidence against Admiral du Pont had been damaging: in the attack on Charleston the flotilla he commanded, which had for months dealt crushing blows to the Confederacy up and down the Atlantic coast, fired only one hundred thirty-nine cannon rounds to more than three thousand for the Confederates. Samuel Francis had ordered his ships to retreat. He then twice ignored specific orders from President Lincoln to rejoin the battle and moved his flotilla out to sea. It appeared to the nation—and the people on the Brandywine—that their navy hero, one of the first Americans ever elevated to the rank of Admiral, had fallen prey to stupidity, at best, or, at worst, cowardice.

Samuel Francis had returned to the Brandywine to live quietly with Sophie at Louviers while Congress considered the charges against him. Disgrace, the Secretary of the Navy decided, was enough: no punishment was meted out aside from loss of his command. The family rallied around Sam Francis and Sophie; the world might condemn him, the du

Ponts did not. Behind the protective shield of the Brandywine's tight community the Admiral had wasted away, his robust body shriveling, his mind becoming strangely addled for a man who had commanded and been victorious in war. For many months Sophie had been preparing herself for her husband's death.

Sophie sat on a wooden chair at the gravesite. No honor guard had come from Washington for Sam's burial, but Sophie liked it that way: only the family had stood beside her husband in his disgrace. All the du Ponts were in the cemetery, standing in clumps near the turned earth. Henry and Louisa and their children, bright and refined in their manners, were the closest to her. The Admiral had always liked Henry, more than the rest of his relatives, and Louisa as well. Alfred's widow, Margaretta, had gathered most of her own children and their husbands and wives about her for the funeral; it was a strange scene: Margaretta and her children did not really get along. Irénée's wife, Charlotte, had been emotionally broken by her mother-in-law during the war. She was the single family member absent, away in Europe to get her health back. Fred and Bidermann had come up from Louisville. Bidermann's wife had already given him two children, beautiful, healthy young people. The boy, Thomas Coleman—T. C. everyone called him—stood surprisingly tall for his two and a half years; he would grow to be as tall as Irénée the first had been. Near Bidermann, Sophie could see Lammot and his girl, Mary Belin. The du Pont looks had bypassed Lammot; he was as ugly a man as had ever walked the Brandywine, with a plain face his beard did little to help. But Lammot had a certain humor. The children of the Brandywine loved him; they called him Uncle Big Man. He relished pulling bits of candy from his pocket to treat the youngsters with. Sophie wondered if the Admiral, had he lived a different life, would have been like that, or like Irénée, whose sense of humor rocked both the family and the powder workers with mirth. Irénée stood a bit apart from his mother and brothers; he and Margaretta had not spoken to each other in months.

Beyond Irénée stood the children of Sophie's brother Alexis. He had died so young! None of his five sons and daughters had been beyond school age when Alexis perished in an explosion. The youngest, Joanna, had been only three; she was barely eleven now, a pretty girl, almost the twin of her sister Eleuthera. They would grow into beauties, Sophie believed, and their brothers, Eugene, Alexis the second, and Francis G., would be tall, strong men. Gene was in the mills already; Lex would follow soon. Frank, just fifteen, seemed more than any of the others to have inherited the du Pont curse of fascination with gunpowder: not even Henry's edict that he stay home and study kept him from the powder yards.

Sophie let her eyes wander farther from the grave. Would there always be this split between the du Ponts of the powder mills and those from across the Creek? Even here, at a funeral, an invisible line kept them apart. Only one gunpowder du Pont stood with the cousins from across the Creek: Mary Sophie, who had married Charles I. Perhaps, Sophie thought, the two of them should straddle the Admiral's grave to make everything quite equitable.

So many du Ponts! Her grandfather, Pierre Samuel, had wished for a dynasty; he had indeed founded one. His two sons had fathered a dozen children; their children had brought thirty-nine men and women onto the earth. A few had strayed from the Brandywine; her sister-in-law, Julia, the Admiral's younger sister, even had one child who had entered a convent, Mother Mary Jerome. Old Pierre Samuel would not have approved of Catholicism in the family, or the marrying of Jewesses, as Lammot was about to do, but America was a different land than France, and Pierre would have understood his descendants' need of religion. France: Sophie had pledged to take a trip to her family's native soil, to see the old country house in Nemours her grandfather had lived in and to try to buy it back for the family. Antoine Bidermann had told her much about it; he had come to the funeral too. The Admiral would have appreciated Antoine's riding to Sand Hole Woods from his house, Winterthur. Since Evalina's death, in the second year of the war, Antoine had gone out little. He looked terribly pale, as theAdmiral had in the last months of his life. Would he live to see the new year? Probably not.

Sophie watched as the soil covered her husband's grave. She looked briefly up toward Pierre Samuel's marble marker, already worn from the Brandywine wind. A pyramid of du Ponts, together in death as in life. Her brother Henry came to ask if she needed anything. He was a strong man; no one else, Sophie knew, could have kept the family together during the Civil War. Not once had he uttered a bad word to her. Others on the Creek disliked his old ways, his formal traditions, even his management of the mills. But the family did not balk at growing rich, at the lovely homes—not mansions, really, more like country châteaux—that dotted the hills near the Brandywine, all built with powder company profits. She knew that the young du Ponts laughed behind General Henry's back, and even held mock family councils, with all the seriousness the General affected, to decide the most frivolous matters. They simply did not understand du Pont tradition, Sophie believed. They had been born into their homes, not carved them out of a wilderness. She could remember when she and her brothers and sisters had first played on the Brandywine's banks, when the mills were just a few crude buildings, when the only house was theirs, the director's house. In the last year of the Civil War her share of profits alone had come to more than three times what her father had invested to build the mills in 1802. The name du Pont had grown in stature throughout the nation over the years. Everyone knew that during the Civil War the North might never have conquered the Confederacy without powder from the Brandywine. And Henry had been the architect of Eleutherian Mills' success since Alfred retired in 1850.

True, outside the Brandywine, people believed the du Ponts were a strange, even mad group of men and women. The citizens of Wilmington had since her father's time cracked jokes at the du Pont family's expense. But the town's merchants never turned down the family's money. Henry had little time for outsiders; neither did Lammot or Irénée. Only she and her husband had taken the effort and care to build a circle of friends beyond the gates of the mills. Some of her relatives on the east bank of the Creek, not infected by the powder yards' strange attraction, had married into leading Delaware families. But in the powder yards, and around them, only du Ponts and powdermen existed. Henry had seen to that by expanding the lands he owned as the family grew. His relatives need never journey into the outside world; he would buy the outside world and bring it to them.

Sophie's relatives crowded around her, trying to distract her from the funeral, to carry her off to Henry's house, where Louisa's servants had prepared a meal. She told them she wished to be alone for a few moments with her husband. Looking at Sam Francis's grave Sophie made a silent pledge. For fifty years he had written to her daily, from Mexico or China or wherever his ship happened to be. The Admiral had been a brilliant naval warrior, brutalized by ambitious men who needed a scapegoat for their ineptitude and stupidity. She vowed that before she died the reputation of Admiral Samuel Francis du Pont would be resurrected.

Mary Belin surprised the du Pont family: childbearing agreed with her. In five years of marriage she had given Lammot two healthy daughters. After each birth Mary had been up and around in days, and healthier than ever. The pallor from her bout with tuberculosis had left while she nursed the girls. But her fertility and good health had not stopped the jeers about her heritage Lammot heard whispered behind his back.

Lammot chose to ignore them. When General Henry came to call on the first New Year's Day after their marriage, Lammot knew the rest of the family would follow suit, whatever their feelings: no du Pont dared argue with the Red Fellow's judgment. He could tolerate their sentiments toward Mary for the time being. Eventually, he and his family would leave the Brandywine. Until then, Mary would continue to bring children into the world—strong, active children whose tiny hands caressed even his most hating relatives. The du Pont women had always used Mary's shyness against her. They were startled by her affectionate little daughters but dared not show the slightest insincerity or coolness toward them: Henry would have crucified the first who did.

In 1869, Mary became pregnant with her third child. Lammot hoped —and believed—from the first that it would be a boy. Henry would never surrender control of the Du Pont Company to Lammot, no matter how old or feeble the Red Fellow became. But this child might someday rule the Brandywine. On January 15, 1870, when the doctor unlocked the door to Mary and Lammot's bedroom in their house, Nemours, and announced that the newly born infant was a healthy male, Lammot had on his lips the name he wished to give his son: Pierre Samuel du Pont. His firstborn son would bear the name of the family's founder, the first du Pont child to carry it. No one at Eleutherian Mills would doubt what Lammot had in mind for his son.

Lammot hated New York City—every city, in fact—and the Wall Street area of New York he hated the most of all, with its tall buildings and dirty winds streaming dust into his eyes. Spring was the best of the city's seasons, but April in New York was not April on the Brandywine. Lammot wished he could have refused Henry's order to travel with him to the company's Wall Street offices for a conference with the leaders of the nation's other large gunpowder manufacturers. But Lammot long ago had learned that there was no way to disobey the General's commands.

Henry had told him little about the meeting. The General had sent letters to the owners of five other powder companies, asking them to gather in New York for a discussion of the prices they charged and the territories where they sold gunpowder. Lammot had come to trust his uncle's business sense, but this seemed like folly.

Since the end of the Civil War, Henry had fumed about the situation in the powder business. While the fighting was on, Du Pont Powder had been unable to reach California, and the gold miners and railroad builders in the West had chipped in to start the California Powder Works. Shipping explosives around the tip of South America, or by rail and mule train across the Rocky Mountains, took weeks and cost a great deal. The California powdermakers stole what little remained of Du Pont's market with lower prices and immediate delivery. Lammot had engineered a partial takeover of the California company by 1869, but Henry remained unhappy. The next year the Red Fellow bought out four small Pennsylvania companies, to hold down competition in the coal fields. Yet he still worried over the other powdermakers' profits in the mining region.

Lammot believed that the General had no desire to join the Wall Street manipulators, stealing fortunes by watering stock and driving competitors into bankruptcy through proxy takeovers. The Red Fellow was a manufacturer, not a speculator, and Lammot did not think Henry would even consider using powder company funds to compete against the jackals of Wall Street. Yet Henry had called this meeting, an uncharacteristic act. Lammot had learned that when speculators began their dealings, business invariably grew throughout the country—paper business, most of it—but real enough expansion to require huge amounts of Du Pont blasting powder. Other companies had approximated Lammot's formula, and a few had begun to manufacture dynamite, the powerful explosive Alfred Nobel had developed. Lammot had already feuded with Henry over dynamite. The General had turned a bright red, his usual color during an argument, and silenced Lammot with a single word: no. Du Pont would never make anything but powder. Dynamite was too dangerous and would never catch on in America: leave it to the fools who wished for death in an explosion. Lammot had taken the only course open to him: silence. Sooner or later his time would come, and the Red Fellow would not be able to deny his vision of the future.

Lammot held the door to the Wall Street office open for his uncle. Henry greeted the other men briskly and sat down at the head of the table. He said he had called them together to discuss stabilizing the gunpowder industry in the United States. Washington was ruining them by selling off its leftover Civil War powder for as little as a nickel a pound—a full twenty-five cents below the best price Du Pont could give its customers. The little fellows of the business—nearly two hundred of them—sold inferior powder near their factories at low prices. They paid nothing in freight and had a minimum amount of overhead to worry about. He proposed that the major manufacturers divide up the country into protected territories, that they set prices in common, and that they levy a severe penalty against anyone who undersold them. The small manufacturers would either follow the price guidelines or the association would undercut them badly enough to bankrupt them. He did not intend that any small powdermaker who met their demands be driven out of business; the prices would be fair enough to yield decent profits for all. He suggested they band together formally into the Gunpowder Trade Association and elect Lammot, his nephew, president. The young chemist was respected throughout the industry, and no one would dare call a du Pont a manipulator.

The other powdermen heartily agreed. Henry brought out blank sheets of paper and they began hammering out territories and prices. Lammot noticed that the General took only a fair share for Eleutherian Mills; perhaps his uncle was sincere in wanting equality for all the powder companies. But he knew how astutely the Red Fellow analyzed the nation's economic situation. If the stock watering kept on, the country would find itself little more than a paper empire, and when bills came due businesses would begin to fold. It was the cycle after war that Henry had always expected and had taught Lammot and Irénée to be prepared to meet in the powder mills. Lammot sensed a deeper purpose in Henry's desire to band together with the other giants of the powder business. When the panic came, as it was sure to within a few months, Henry would do more than limit the price of powder; with the small manufacturers making only a slight profit, by edict of the Association, they would never be able to withstand a severe depression. Eleutherian Mills, fat on war profits to the tune of three million dollars, would pick up the pieces of the industry for pennies instead of thousands.

Lammot wondered if the General had chosen him as president of the Association for the reasons he had mentioned or to keep him away from the Brandywine as much as possible. It did not matter: Lammot had decided that dynamite was the wave of the future in the explosive business and if Henry would not let him manufacture it on the Brandywine, he would leave the only home he had ever known to make his fortune elsewhere.

Charlotte Henderson du Pont stepped from the carriage onto the lawn in front of Swamp Hall. She had a serene look about her, a calm her husband Irénée had not seen on her face in years. This second trip abroad may finally have worked a cure for his wife's illness.

He had always believed that if his mother had not baited Charlotte so badly she would never have lost her sanity. Eleven years had passed since the end of the Civil War and still Irénée would not speak to his mother or enter a room in which she sat. Charlotte had given birth to three more children, strong young people, and while she nursed them her sanity seemed to return. But once the boys and girls were turned over to the servants for care, Charlotte slipped into despair again, sat silently for hours, cried and raved, and forgot where she was or who was with her. Irénée had suffered immeasurably for his wife. He had immersed himself in running the powder yards as much as he could, knowing that he ignored his children at times, but realizing that he had to remain sound of mind for them. When the doctors gave up on his wife he had suggested another trip abroad, a long one like the first: it had helped then, perhaps it would now.

And here she was, finally home. Her children had missed her. They were rough-and-tumble kids who did not affect the aristocratic airs of their many cousins. Alfred, most of all, seemed to blend into the life of the powder workers. His friends were from across Breck's Lane and Long Row, where the workers' small cottages stood. He tagged along with Irénée to the yards almost daily and could be found scrapping with the strongest of the Irish boys. Irénée approved of Alfred's conduct, even if Henry did not; at eleven his son could hold his own with any boy. He had years enough ahead of him to learn the manners and traditions of the du Ponts.

Charlotte looked well. Irénée had always liked the way she wore her hair, in two buns pulled tight to the sides of her head. She was a great beauty; they had remained deeply in love even through her illness. He vowed to shield her from the family's venom this time. She would not slip back into her illness if he could help it.

Charlotte looked up at the windows of Swamp Hall. The house was plain, old boards nailed together, covered with enough coats of white-wash to cake in the summer sun. Irénée had named the place Swamp

Hall to mock his relatives' fine châteaux. Charlotte had accepted life there happily, rarely thinking of her family's great mansion in Virginia.

A crowd of powder workers, and even a few du Ponts, had gathered on the lawn to greet her. She liked the powdermen and their famlies, but she had only one desire: to see her children. They stood on the porch of Swamp Hall, dressed in clean clothes—a chore for Alfred—their faces scrubbed. Charlotte ran up the few steps to them, gathered them around her, and walked into the parlor. Irénée stood watching from the lawn, shaking his workers' hands and waiting for his brother Lammot to come up from the yards; he had noticed him approaching at the end of Breck's Lane. He saw little Louis, his youngest child, only six, disappear through the door to Swamp Hall clutching his mother's hand.

The powder workers slapped their superintendent on the back, congratulated him on how well Charlotte looked, and drew bottles of whiskey from their coveralls to celebrate. Their wives came to offer Mister Irénée any help he or Charlotte needed; she would want friends nearby, and they revered Irénée as they had Alexis before him. Coming up the hill, Lammot could see a celebration in process: Charlotte must be well.

Suddenly the noise of the homecoming dissolved into silence. The powdermen and their wives looked toward the house. A scream had come from inside, then another. Irénée charged through the door into his parlor. Lammot ran up Breck's Lane, across the lawn, and into the house.

Charlotte stood shaking in a corner. Louis, sitting on the sofa, had his shirt off. Great welts and scars crisscrossed his back. Irénée froze in the doorway. He demanded to know what had happened. Alfred said their mother had asked about the way the housekeeper, Emma, had treated them while she was gone. Louis had complained that she beat the children. Charlotte had not believed that the German girl would do such a thing. Louis had pulled off his jacket and shirt to show her the proof. She had screamed and started crying.

Irénée held his wife to his chest, trying to soothe her nerves and stop her sobs. He helped her up the stairs to their bedroom and ran for a doctor. In a few minutes she was under sedation and asleep.

Irénée found Emma and demanded the truth. She admitted striking the children; they had, evidently, lived in too much terror to tell even their father. Irénée threw the woman from his house. Charlotte's doctors were called from Wilmington and Philadelphia. Their verdict sent Irénée to fetch a carriage from the stables. His wife would be committed to a hospital in Philadelphia. Her nerves were shattered. The doctors felt it was the end of her years of mental agony: Charlotte would never again be able to live among her relatives, the family du Pont.

Mary Sophie and Charles I. du Pont, Jr., died within four years of each other, she in 1869, he in 1873. They had been the third set of cousins to marry on the Brandywine, and the family had welcomed the match, uniting as it did the powdermaking du Ponts and the du Ponts from across the Creek.

Mary and Charles left behind a daughter, Victorine Antoinette, who, in 1876, at the age of eleven, died, too. She had been their firstborn and, it was rumored on the Brandywine, a strange child from birth. A second daughter had died within a few days of being born; the powdermakers and their families whispered that its parents' common blood had brought forth a mental mutant incapable of living.

On the day of Victorine Antoinette's death General Henry called together the elders of the family and told them that he had decided to put a stop to the senseless births and deaths of children on the Brandywine. Death had touched the Red Fellow twice: one daughter had perished during the Civil War; another, aged twenty-two, in April of 1876. His son, Henry A., had lost a child that year as well, a girl only eleven months old. The toll of du Ponts was reaching devastating proportions.

He ordered his relatives to forbid their children to become involved with another member of the family: any du Pont found guilty of loving another du Pont would be banished from the Brandywine. He invited no discussion, and no rebuttal. His relatives were welcome to join him for dinner or free to go.

Henry ate silently in the dining room of the director's house and set off for the company office. He could hear the familiar humming of the mills from down the hill; they would be well into the second shift of workers. A panic had hit the nation and stilled many factories, but not his. Henry had another difficult decision to make that night. He had forced the owners of Hazard Powder, the nation's third largest powdermaker after Eleutherian Mills and Laflin and Rand, into a position that made it impossible for the company to continue operation. Should he buy the firm or let it die?

The Gunpowder Trade Association controlled ninety percent of the nation's powdermaking capacity. By taking over dying companies during the depression Henry ruled the Association. Lammot was pliant enough, doing what Henry bade him do, forcing on their competitors the prices Henry decided upon, slowly grabbing territories that produced large amounts of sales, giving away those that did not.

Henry would grab at Hazard quickly but for one fact: Laflin and Rand nearly equaled Eleutherian Mills in size. If its owners got wind of his takeover of Hazard a price war would result, and Henry might not win. He had bought every independent in the coal fields, after shutting down the first one he purchased as a lesson to the others. Near panic had hit the mines when his men started dismantling a factory he had just bought for one hundred thousand dollars. But it had disciplined the others, and they had buckled under quickly.

The California Powder Works had fallen to his price-fixing through the Association, too, and he now owned nearly seventy percent of California's stock. The South had been sewn up with the takeover of Sycamore Mills, which owned the old Confederate Powder Works in Augusta, Georgia. All that remained was the giant Lake Superior Powder Company in Michigan selling tons of explosives to the copper and iron ore miners of the Midwest. Laflin and Rand had designs on Lake Superior and had asked Hazard to join in its purchase.

Henry considered the young men to whom he had given shares of the Du Pont Company: Lammot and Irénée, Alfred's sons; and Eugene and Francis G., children of Alexis. All were nephews. He had convinced Henry Algernon, his own son, to give up the military life for a place on the Brandywine just a year earlier. But Henry A. had no powder experience; the best he had been able to do was make him head of the company's growing transportation department. His other son, William, was growing into a man worth rather little, more interested in spending his father's money than adding to it. He would join the company, eventually, but Henry realized he would never run it.

Henry would soon turn sixty-four; the red of his beard had begun turning gray. One day he would have to give up control of the company and the family, but he still felt strong and thrived on work: which of his young partners would return to the office after a day's work to write fifteen or twenty letters? He had started this building of a string of gunpowder firms across the nation, and he had to finish it, whether or not his own sons one day took it over from him. Riding over the hills of the Brandywine, Henry could not reach the end of his lands in a half-day's gallop. Even the old house at Winterthur had become his when Antoine Bidermann died, bought from his sister and brother-in-law's son, who had chosen to live in France.

The purchase of Hazard Powder was not really a matter of choice. Whatever the risks, Henry had set out to build Eleutherian Mills into an empire ruled by him from the Brandywine. He would not stop until it was complete.

# 20

ALFRED I. DU PONT hefted the shotgun to his shoulder, sighted down its long, dull gray barrel, and swept the horizon from the wooden porch of Swamp Hall. In the distance, coming across the fields from his Great-uncle Henry's house, Alfred could barely make out the figure of a man approaching slowly.

The time had come to defend his home. In a shrill, adolescent voice Alfred called to his brothers and sisters inside the house. Armed with axes, clubs, and kitchen knives, Anne, Marguerite, Maurice, and Louis piled out through Swamp Hall's front door and spread themselves across the porch, their weapons raised, awaiting whatever might come. In a meeting the night before, after their father Irénée's funeral, the five children had decided: they would not be moved from Swamp Hall.

Their father had been buried on a cloudy Wednesday afternoon, taken to Sand Hole Woods amid a crowd of relatives, nearly sixty in all, and laid to rest beside his wife. For days he had lain in agony on his bed, coughing up clots of dark blood, breathing heavily, clutching the hands of his children, asking between moans for his wife.

The doctors had advised against telling Irénée about Charlotte. She had died a month earlier, after more than a year in a Philadelphia mental hospital. The shock of her end would only speed Irénée's own, the physicians said. The family decided to follow the doctors' wishes.

Lammot had spent every spare moment at his brother's side, ignoring the mills except when an emergency beckoned, trying to help Irénée make amends with their mother, Margaretta. For twelve years Irénée had refused to speak to her, to spend any time in her presence, or to allow his children to communicate with their grandmother. Margaretta had moved away from the mills after Lammot's wedding, and it had been easier to ignore her. But when her son contracted tuberculosis, Margaretta had wanted to make peace with him. Irénée knew he was dying; the doctors had not tried to hide the seriousness of his illness from him. But, to the last, he had remained adamant: he would not speak to Margaretta. He did not want her in his bedroom, then or after he died. His mother had ruined his wife's health. He was sorry, he told Lammot, but the decision had been made more than a decade earlier. There would be no reconciliation.

Only Irénée's children had been allowed at his bedside. He had called Alfred to him last, pulled his son's ear down to his lips, and whispered a few words. Alfred had straightened, fought to choke back his tears, and grasped his father's hand in his own. Irénée had closed his eyes, turned away, and died.

The grave in Sand Hole Woods was the forty-fifth dug there since Pierre Samuel died sixty years earlier. Irénée's brothers Bidermann and Fred had brought their families north from Kentucky for the funeral. Relatives had come from every corner of Henry's land. Fred had been named executor of Irénée's will. He had not been surprised that his brother left an estate of more than a half-million dollars; since the beginning of the Civil War the partners in the powder company had grown wealthier each year. General Henry had shrewdly consolidated power in the powder industry until no name but Du Pont mattered.

Fred liked Irénée's children. They were respectful and well mannered without being pretentious, as were many of their cousins. After Irénée's funeral the Red Fellow had called a council of the family elders to decide what should be done with the five children. Henry had invited no suggestions, even though Fred and a relative from across the Creek were named guardians of Irénée's sons and daughters. The five boys and girls were not old enough to decide their own destiny. They would be sent, separately, to relatives' homes to live. The eldest, Annie, at seventeen needed guidance, or she would become as ill bred as the powdermen's daughters she associated with. Henry appointed Fred to tell the children of his decision and turned to the task of filling Irénée's place in the partnership. His chance had come; his older son, Colonel Henry A., had been with the company for two years. The younger boy, William, worked as overseer of his father's many farms. Henry decided to admit them both to the partnership; Lammot might object, but not for long. Henry had simply to stare him into silence.

It was Fred's disheveled figure that Alfred drew a bead on from the porch of Swamp Hall. Alfred knew he was a good shot; he could blow a hole through Uncle Fred at nearly two hundred yards. But, of all his relatives, Alfred I. trusted and admired his uncle from Louisville the most. He decided to let the man approach.

Fred had been walking with his face turned toward the ground. He looked up to cross Breck's Lane, saw the armed band of children on the porch of his brother's house, and stopped short. Alfred kept the shotgun at his shoulder; what, he shouted, did his uncle want?

Fred answered that he had come to tell them of Uncle Henry's decision about their future. Alfred yelled back that they need not be told anything: he would defend his home by force, if necessary, and so would his brothers and sisters. Fred feigned deep seriousness and asked for a truce to talk the situation over. He knew that Henry's word would be law: no one had ever known the Red Fellow to change his mind, least of all to bow to the wishes of children. And Henry controlled his brother's house. Irénée might have left a half-million dollars to his five children but that did not include many worldly goods. The company owned all but a horse, a mule, their clothes, and a lot of money. His brother's children had all been born in Swamp Hall, but, at any moment, the General could have them dispossessed and turn the rambling ten-bedroom house over to another member of the family—or have it razed. Yet Fred had some leverage over the Red Fellow. Most of Irénée's estate was represented by stock in the powder company. He could demand that it be paid for in cash, not securities, taking away most of the General's operating capital. He did not want to argue with his uncle—it would breed nothing but hatred for the children—but he would not see them lose their mother, their father, and their home in less than thirty days.

Fred approached the porch of Swamp Hall. Alfred signaled his brothers and sisters to drop their weapons. Fred herded them inside, listened to their pleas, and told them he would do what he could. Their desire was simple: to be allowed to stay together in Swamp Hall. Annie, at seventeen, could easily run the house with the help of servants. Marguerite, two years younger, would help. Alfred, the oldest boy, would make all decisions and they had agreed that his word would be law. The two youngest, Maurice and Louis, promised solemnly to listen to their brothers and sisters.

Fred walked slowly out the door of Swamp Hall, onto the porch, and down the steps. He strode across the fields above the powder yards, burst into Henry's office, and made his demands.

The Red Fellow listened silently. Fred had become an enormous success in Louisville running a number of businesses. His shabby clothes and frugal way of living hid a singular strength of purpose among the du Ponts. Fred would fight if he chose, and the family would split over the children's futures. The Red Fellow stroked his beard and agreed to give Irénée's children a trial at running their own home. They had seen enough tragedy for any young people; perhaps this gesture of generosity and understanding would further bring the family into line behind him and at the same time help the children. And Henry needed support for his appointment of his sons to the partnership. Never before had anyone risen to a share of the profits without first serving many years in the mills.

Another problem had come up that morning. He had told William about the partnership he would receive. His son had thanked him and then informed Henry that, threats of banishment or not, he intended to marry a cousin, Mary Lammot du Pont, from across the Creek. Henry had become furious, but he knew at once that his anger would lead to nothing: William was, in his own way, a stubborn man. If he chose to marry a cousin Henry could not stop him. The Red Fellow was rankled to see his orders defied twice in one day, but he could do little about it.

Fred ran back to Swamp Hall to tell the children of the General's change of heart. Alfred laid his shotgun aside; Annie set about cooking lunch. Fred sat in the parlor with them talking of their future. Alfred must return to school at the Reverend Shinn's in Waterford, New Jersey. Maurice and Louis would continue at the boys' school they attended near Philadelphia. Annie and Marguerite need not stop traveling to day classes in Wilmington each morning. One day each would inherit a large fortune. Until they turned twenty-one, or married, Fred would oversee the money, investing it as well as he could, and hand out allowances to them all. Annie would have a household budget. Fred would pay any large bills that came due. Although he was busy in Kentucky, Fred told them, he would come to the Brandywine often, and so would their Uncle Bidermann, with his children. Fred chided Alfred that Bidermann's son, Coly, had grown taller than his cousin, even though he was younger. He cautioned Alfred not to engage in his well-known passion for fistfights with Coly; he might end up with a bloody face and cauliflower ears. Alfred threw out his thirteen-year-old chest and reminded his Uncle Fred that he could lick any boy on or off the Brandywine. Fred laughed, shook his nephew's hand, and left to begin the long train ride back to Louisville.

When Henry du Pont bought into the California Powder Works, in 1873, Lammot had gone along without a murmur. Henry had expected his nephew to complain that they did not need to own California Powder; through the Gunpowder Trade Association they controlled the West Coast, and it would be difficult to manage a factory three thousand miles away. But Lammot had said nothing. The Red Fellow had congratulated himself on earning Lammot's acquiescence. Now he damned his own stupidity.

The California Powder Works made dynamite. More and more, the miners in the West found it far superior to gunpowder for blasting through rock. And the Gunpowder Trade Association controlled none of the dynamite market. The California people had been a thorn in the Association's side for years. Lammot, on Henry's orders, had for years been undercutting the price of gunpowder in the West. The Association's members had balked; they were losing profits daily. It would be easier simply to forget the Western trade. But Henry would not. Finally, after the Panic of 1873, California Powder accepted Henry's offer to shore up its sagging finances in return for nearly one-half the company's stock. By 1875, without telling the other members of the Powder Trust, Henry was ready to sign an agreement with them on behalf of the California Powder Works to set prices in the West. From his office on the Brandywine he controlled virtually every ounce of powder sold west of the Mississippi, as well as east of it.

But the General had failed to understand that California Powder made most of the dynamite in the West, as well as most of the gunpowder. Overnight, against what had always been his policy, he had become one of the largest manufacturers in the world of Alfred Nobel's discovery. When Lammot came to him with plans for a nitroglycerin and dynamite factory of their own, on the East Coast, Henry could find no reasonable excuse to turn him down. Lammot had used a certain tone of voice; Henry realized that if he said no, Lammot would leave the Brandywine anyway, to start his own company. His nephew had already bought a plot of land not far from Eleutherian Mills. If Henry did not support him, Lammot said, he would go it alone. The General decided to take the lesser of the evil routes: Du Pont would not manufacture dynamite, but he would help Lammot set up a company of his own, furnishing the money and influence with other powdermakers to see it through to success. He had one requirement: the nitroglycerin must be made far enough away from the Brandywine to ensure against an accident blowing the powder yards to smithereens. Lammot walked from their meeting smiling. He had found a way to keep his uncle's support and still leave the Brandywine. He had never intended to open a dynamite factory near the powder mills; in fact, he had chosen a site thirty miles from Eleutherian Mills, near Philadelphia, on the Repaupo River where it joined the Delaware.

Within a few days Lammot had made plans to leave the house where he had been born. Mary, pregnant with their ninth child, organized the children and the servants and journeyed to Philadelphia to find a home for her large brood. Lammot decided that if their next child was a son he would name him Lammot, after himself. This child, he believed, would inherit something he created, not the legacy of the Brandywine and Henry the Red.

Alfred I. du Pont sat in the window of his room at Phillips Academy in Andover, Massachusetts, playing the flute he had just unpacked from his suitcase. Uncle Fred had chosen this school for him: would he like it? His uncle's decisions were right more often than not, and he had supported Alfred and his brothers and sisters when the rest of the family would have allowed Uncle Henry to separate them.

They had been correct to stick together; General Henry had backed down. But, in one way, Uncle Fred had proven less than generous to his wards. Alfred's allowance was peanuts compared to what the other young du Ponts received. Uncle Fred refused to raise it; Alfred's allowance was higher than an apprentice powderman's salary, he explained. It would have to do. What other du Ponts did with their money was no concern of his. Alfred and his brothers and sisters would be rich soon enough. They must learn the value of a dollar now, or they never would.

Alfred sat playing his flute, looking over the hills near the academy. He wondered what the other boys at Phillips were like. They had greeted him well enough, trying not to stare at his misshapen nose—it had been broken diving with his friends into the shallow depths of the Brandywine. A few had made fun of his violin case. Now more of his fellow students had gathered beneath his window, jeering up at him to stop playing his silly flute. He had heard a nickname no one of the Brandywine had ever dared use: Dupee. Alfred laid aside his flute and looked into the mirror above his chest of drawers: sooner or later the others would have to learn that he was not to be laughed at for his music. He would be playing the piano, violin, and flute every day, and the other boys would haze him until he taught them a lesson. He decided that now was as good a time as any. He removed his coat and collar, changed his trousers for a pair of knickers, and walked down the stairs of the dormitory. He singled out the largest of the boys, challenged him to a fight over his right to play the flute, and in minutes knocked the boy unconscious. Alfred returned to his room, picked up the flute, and sat back down on the window ledge to play: there were no jeers from the yard below.

Lammot threw up his hands in frustration: his son would never become an athlete of any sort. He had tried, with lessons in the local gym, expensive lessons from the best teachers that could be hired. Pierre had balked, found excuses not to go, finally become ill over the matter. Lammot had given in but insisted that the boy take up horseback riding; it would harden his body and give him at least some sense of his physical self.

And now Pierre openly admitted that he had bribed one of his sisters to take the riding lessons for him. Lammot looked across the room at his son. He had a large nose, too large for his head, and a thick body, unlike his own lean frame. Never had he known a boy so young—he was only eleven in 1881—to have such a serious way about him. Back on the Brandywine everyone had tried to teach Pierre to swim. Nothing had worked until a triangle of light wood was strapped to his son's belly, keeping him afloat while he thrashed around. The others had made fun of him—Alfred I., especially, and Coly, when he visited from Louisville. Pierre had found friends among their relatives, at least, and, if nothing else, he excelled at the art of the slingshot. But while other boys rolled about the yards, dove into the Creek, and chased each other through the woods, Pierre seemed content to sit and read, or think.

Philadelphia had made no change in him. Perhaps Mary mothered Pierre too much; but Lammot knew that was untrue. She barely had time to pay the slightest special attention to any of the children, with nearly a dozen of them running around. No, it was simply his son's personality; there was little of the roughneck boy in him. He doubted if Pierre would ever enter the powder or dynamite business, pursuits that demanded strength and more courage than a man needed to ride a horse.

His son was a good student. The boy's headmaster had told Lammot that Pierre's mind was better than most, his desire to learn great. During one discussion the headmaster had let slip Pierre's nickname: Graveyard. The teacher himself had started using it, and the other boys had picked it up. Pierre did not seem to mind; he took the nickname, as he took everything else, soberly. Lammot believed he saw a bit of his own grandfather, Eleuthère Irénée, in the boy: even thirty miles and a world away from the Brandywine, his children could not escape their heritage.

Soon the family would be traveling to the Brandywine to celebrate the marriage of Irénée's daughter Marguerite. She had chosen to marry a lawyer from Virginia, Cazenove Gardner Lee, related, distantly, to Charlotte's family. Lammot could picture Alfred I. in his formal collar and coat, dressed up to give his sister away in holy matrimony, and hating every moment of it. Lammot was proud of the way his brother's children had conducted themselves in Swamp Hall after Irénée and Charlotte died. General Henry had been pleased. On the New Year's Day after Irénée died the Red Fellow had instructed his male relatives to call upon Annie as the female head of a du Pont household, the oldest family tradition that signified respect and regard. Fred, up from Kentucky for the festivities, had brought Annie a platter piled high with cookies and sweets. She had surprised everyone with her good sense and cautious care of the other children. To have the General stamp her household with his approval meant that the home of Irénée's children was safe forever.

The visit to celebrate Marguerite's wedding would not be all fun. Lammot had a message to give the General, and the Red Fellow would become angry at what he had to say. The dynamite plant was progressing well. Lammot had decided to end his ties to the Brandywine once and for all: he would resign his partnership in the powder mills. His brothers, Fred and Bidermann, were established in Louisville; they would not need his help ever, and the security of the partnership would bring him only memories of how the family had treated his wife after their marriage. For years his children had been the butt of jokes about their part-Jewish heritage. Lammot had decided that they would never need to return to the Brandywine. Henry and his sons could have the powder company.

Lammot was nearly fifty years old. For most of his life he had listened to and followed the Red Fellow's orders. His brother's wife, Charlotte, had been driven mad by her du Pont relatives. His own wife had been ostracized and insulted beyond endurance. He had watched his relatives court cousins and marry them, even after the Red Fellow forbade it. There was a certain life to the Brandywine Creek itself, beyond even the General's control, and it had made haughty, narrow people of the du

Ponts who lived on its shores. Lammot did not know which infuriated him more: the General's pretense of rule over his relatives' very souls, or the clucking of the du Ponts whenever one of the family deviated from the aristocratic life-style they affected. None of it mattered now: his children would not suffer in the shadow of Eleutherian Mills.

Alfred I. du Pont entered the Massachusetts Institute of Technology at his Uncle Fred's suggestion and moved into a room with his cousin, Thomas Coleman, who was in his second year at M.I.T. Coly's father, Bidermann, provided him with more cash than he needed. Alfred thought it cruel of Uncle Fred to limit his own funds to thirty dollars a month: it was 1882, and thirty dollars did not go far in the bars of Boston's Back Bay.

Coly had told him of their Uncle Fred's strange ways. He still lived in one shabby room at the old Galt Hotel, wore nearly the same clothes he had brought from the Brandywine in 1854, and was never known to squander a penny. Alfred could understand that his uncle might be out of touch with modern times, but his understanding did not put more cash in his pocket: he would have to find ways to earn money.

Alfred discovered that musicians could make money playing in theater orchestras and see plays and musicals for free. He joined a theater group and moved his violin into the string section. When winter came he took days off school to shovel walks. In the evenings he often stopped at Howard's Athenaeum, a burlesque house, where the burly chest and deep voice of the city's native hero, John L. Sullivan, challenged all comers for a thousand dollars in the ring, the boxing match to end only when he or his opponent lay unconscious on the mat. Sullivan boasted that he could knock out any opponent, in the ring or at the bar. Alfred could not box as well as John L. or drink him under the table, but the fighter revered higher education, and Alfred soon became one of Sullivan's regular cronies in the saloons on Boston's Washington Street. Sullivan admired Alfred's ability with his fists as much as his enrollment at M.I.T. Often the back room in a tavern would be filled with local drinkers betting on two amateur boxers. Alfred donned the gloves whenever John L. offered him a match, always with the better fighters, and took a cut of Sullivan's winnings. In his best suit, sporting a long cigar, his blond hair tousled across his forehead, Alfred would sit at John L.'s side while fans listened to the world champion expound on his title bouts. When the gang broke up for the night Alfred would help

John L. to his home, pushing him through the door and into a chair, and sit quietly while the champ's wife railed at him for drinking too much and earning too little. Then he and John L. would tip a last beer for the night, and Alfred would wander back to his room, where Coly, dressed in evening clothes, would be just returning from a night out with one of his many female friends.

Together, the college men laughed at the intrigues and bickering that entwined the du Ponts on the Brandywine. The powder yards seemed a long way off; Alfred's two sisters were married and gone, and his brothers were away at school themselves. Coly cared little for the Brandywine community. His family, in Louisville, had moved into a grand house, built by Uncle Fred on a wide plot of land in the best part of town. Fred had erected the mansion for himself but could not bear to exchange his spartan room at the Galt for its wide hallways and tall bay windows. He had offered it to Bidermann, whose wife had given birth seven times, because his brother needed the room. Coly loved the house; someday it would be his and he would raise his own children in it. Alfred listened to his cousin's tales of Louisville and thought how much unlike the Brandywine it must be.

When he left Boston to spend the summer of 1882 on the Brandywine, Alfred found his old friends among the powder workers' children grown into adulthood. Many had gone into the mills to learn their fathers' trades. He had always felt more like a powderman than a du Pont, but the difference in their births was beginning to show. He had splashed in the Creek with the powdermen's sons, ridden sleds down Breck's Lane with them when it iced over, taken potshots with his rubber sling at their sisters and his own. All that seemed gone now.

He had enjoyed his first year at M.I.T., particularly the shops where he could turn out practically anything on the best machine tools in the nation. He hated classrooms and refused to do any more studying than necessary to get passing grades. He had not followed the standard course of study; he had no doubts about what his life would be like when he left college. He had heard the last words his father had spoken on his deathbed: stay close to the powder mills; the family and company would one day have need of him. From that moment on Alfred had never intended to do anything with his life but make gunpowder at Eleutherian Mills.

Lammot du Pont sat tilted back in his desk chair, a small mirror in one hand, a pair of scissors in the other. Carefully, he trimmed the stray hairs from his black beard, clipping them off one by one, as he did each morning. Soon the business day would begin and he wanted to look well for his visitors. He took a few extra moments, brushing his beard back and forth until he was satisfied with its neatness. He had received a letter that morning from his nephew Alfred, telling him of his work in the machine shop at M.I.T. The letter had surprised him; Lammot thought Alfred was more rake than worker. Perhaps he had been wrong and the boy would one day turn out to be valuable to the family, at least on the Brandywine. Coly, his nephew from Louisville, had already left school to work in one of his father's businesses, a coal mine. He liked Bidermann's son. Coly had a way with people, a certain air of easy confidence about him that workingmen liked and even the du Ponts had been hard pressed to criticize. Coly had inherited the du Pont good looks. He was more handsome than most of his cousins and uncles and seemed to know it; women gave Coly whatever he asked of them. Yet Lammot had not been surprised that T. C. insisted on working in the mines to learn the business and get acquainted with the men: that was his way. Few enough du Ponts—his own sons included—were willing to dirty their hands with labor. He was pleased that, even away from General Henry's prodding in the powder yards, ambition had not altogether left the family.

Lammot returned the mirror and scissors to his desk drawer, drew on his coat, and greeted his visitor, a salesman from St. Louis. Together they walked to the laboratory of the factory, where Lammot began showing the salesman his newest developments. At that moment a workman came running from the mixing house, where pure nitroglycerin was made. Something had gone wrong with the mixture of raw ingredients; it was fuming and seemed about to boil in the steel vats. Lammot ran into the factory, ordered the workers out of the building, and tried to pour the nitroglycerin off into a water tank to cool it. The salesman from St. Louis, impatient at being kept waiting, walked from the laboratory just as the building exploded. He was at least a hundred yards away, but his neck was broken instantly. Flying timber and metal killed four others. Lammot's body remained buried under ten feet of rubble and earth until hours later when workmen managed to dig his crushed bones from beneath the wrecked building. He was taken across the Delaware River by boat, then to his home in Philadelphia. Mary, pregnant with their twelfth child, prepared the house for a funeral. Lammot's relatives came from the Brandywine to pay their last respects. They rode with his body to the cemetery in Sand Hole Woods.

After the funeral Mary and her children returned to Philadelphia. She noticed that the parlor window shades had been left open and began to draw them down. Pierre, barely fourteen years old, stopped his mother and asked her to rest: he was the man of the family now and covering the windows was his task. From this day on, he announced, he would be the father to his brothers and sisters; they were to call him Dad. Mary touched the bulge beneath her black dress and left the parlor to climb the stairs to her bedroom: perhaps it would be best for them all if her son became head of the family. She decided to tell her other children, even the oldest, Louisa, to call Pierre Dad, and to respect his wishes as though they were Lammot's. With her husband dead, she need never return to the Brandywine, to the prejudice and hatred of the du Ponts. But her children might one day desire the life of Eleutherian Mills. Her son Pierre Samuel, named for the family's founder, might make that life possible for them.

# 21

ON A LATE spring morning in 1889, General Henry du Pont, who had for a half-century risen at dawn to begin his day on the Brandywine, was unable to lift himself from his bed. His wife, Louisa, ordered breakfast sent up to him in their bedroom, for the first time in fifty-two years of married life. A clerk from the company office brought a portfolio of papers to Henry's bedside and, by the light from his bedroom window, he performed the day's work, writing letters, balancing accounts, planning the continued expansion and prosperity of Eleutherian Mills.

Old age had crept up on the Red Fellow swiftly, invading his body the way the sulfur smell of the mills invaded his nose: once there, he failed to notice it. Henry had not sensed himself faltering or his body weakening. In the first few days of his infirmity he missed his daily ride across the hills to see his lands; he missed, too, inspecting the powder yards at dusk. But after a few weeks even the desire to watch his powdermen work had gone, and he was content simply to write a few letters each day and speak with his partners each evening. From his bedroom he could hear the humming sound of the mill wheels. He propped himself up in the oak bed that had been his for fifty years. On a table nearby a portfolio of letters awaited his attention. He felt good, at the age of seventy-nine, having the comforts of a lifetime surrounding him.

The Red Fellow knew that he would die soon. He thought of the future of Eleutherian Mills. There were always many infants on the Brandywine. Most were born strong, sending their cries above the Creek, harkening to the future. A few, like the children of his son, Henry A., were less fortunate. Henry and his wife had lost five of their seven children in infancy. Two, twin boys, had especially hurt Henry; they had been the first twins born on the Brandywine. One had lived only a day; the other had died within his first year of life. The Brandywine, Henry believed, held a particular cruelty. He had been given—no, taken—power over the powder mills and the du Pont family. And he had been robbed of the many male descendants his brothers and nephews and cousins produced, as though by giving his life to the mills he had surrendered the male portion of his future generations.

Henry had found in the Brandywine's legacy to him all the more reason to ride herd on his relatives. They, not he, would raise the leaders of Eleutherian Mills. His sons, Henry A. and William, were good, solid men, but they were not powdermen. Henry had bought the stock in Lammot's dynamite company after his nephew's death and given it to William. But his younger son was more playboy than manufacturer. William realized his own failings; he had hired competent managers for the dynamite factory and rarely emerged from his office. Henry A. had become more interested in railroads than gunpowder; he would become a wealthy man, but he would not inherit the mantle of rule over the Brandywine. The Red Fellow sensed in Henry A. a hunger for the public life. He would leave his son enough of a fortune to indulge his fervor for politics, but it was a flaw in Henry A.: no man who ruled Eleutherian Mills could care for the empty jabber of politicians.

Who would rule the kingdom he had built? Not being able to pass the scepter on to his own sons bothered Henry much. Yet many sober, dedicated du Ponts still listened to the rustling of the Brandywine's winds. One would emerge, the right one, as had always happened among the du Ponts, to keep his kingdom intact. As a child Henry had needed only a few minutes to walk the length and breadth of his father's land. Now a man could not ride across his land in a day. Everything, and nothing, had changed.

Six years ago Henry had noticed a mill wheel sparking down near the Creek. He had taken off his top hat, run to the millrace, and filled it with water to douse the sparks. Had he saved lives? Perhaps; only his action mattered. It was the du Pont way, caring for the safety of the mills, always alert, ever ready to stop a fire, to avert a disaster. Henry had run a safe factory. His brother Alexis's son, Francis G., as fine a chemist as Lammot, and a better powderman, had written down all the explosions of two decades and, as time went on, fewer workmen were killed in accidents. Henry was proud that the Brandywine legacy of death had eased under his guidance.

The Red Fellow did not fear death. He had lived with the ghost of death all his life, every day knowing that at any moment he might be blown—what was it the old powdermen used to say?—across the Creek.

The cemetery near St. Joseph's Catholic Church was filled with powdermen who had died in explosions; his family's burial ground had its share, too. Many times he had walked from his office to Sand Hole Woods to mark out the place where he would be buried, at the left side of his father, Eleuthère Irénée. How much of his blood rested in Sand Hole Woods? Fifty relatives? Sixty? He was the last grandchild of Pierre Samuel alive. His sister Sophie had gone the year before, in 1888. She had spent twenty-five years struggling to resurrect her husband's reputation from the deep hole Congress had placed it in after the Civil War. The Admiral would have been proud of his wife, working tirelessly for him long after he died, never ceasing to write letters, to harp at Congressmen over Sam Francis's navy record. Henry had known that Sophie would fail. After a war a nation wanted only to forget. It had always helped the powder mills, this forgetfulness; after a time the outcries against war profiteers ceased, never to be brought up again. But Sophie's letters, her campaign to clear Sam Francis's name, had kept her alive. Just as the powder mills had kept him alive.

For thirty-nine years Henry had run Eleutherian Mills his way. His nephews and nieces—especially Irénée's son Alfred I.—had wanted change. Change! The ways of his father had always been good enough for him. Alfred, after visiting Thomas Edison in New Jersey, had wanted electricity installed in the mills. Henry had vetoed that; Alfred could have all the electric lights he wanted in his own house, but not in the powder yards. Kerosene had been efficient enough in the Civil War; it would do forever. His grand-nephew was a good powderman, though, even if he had inherited his father's love for the company of workers rather than the company of du Ponts. Alfred I. was a bit of a wild man, charging around the Brandywine on that silly contraption he called a bicycle, with a giant wheel at the front and a tiny one on the rear.

Henry was glad there were more sober men on the Brandywine, men like his grand-nephew Pierre S. The boy was odd-looking for a du Pont, with only a trace of the cleft chin most of them inherited. Perhaps it was the Jewish blood his mother had given him. But he had done well at M.I.T., and Henry saw in him the possibility of leadership. Pierre seemed earnest about learning the gunpowder business. He rarely went to the dances the young people held at Breck's Mill, across the Brandywine, in what had been his Uncle Victor's woolen mill a half-century ago.

Henry could recall the day Pierre's father, Lammot, had come to him with his choice of a wife, Mary Belin. The wedding had been a huge affair, with ten attendants. Lammot had believed deeply in keeping his family together, before he left to open his dynamite factory, and when the wedding celebraton ended, he invited all ten friends along on the honeymoon trip to Niagara Falls. There had been many bright days on the Brandywine, and many wars with his relatives. But the wars had brought his family together, and with the du Ponts behind him he had built the largest gunpowder and explosives company in the world. He could not count the number of smaller, weaker firms he had bought or driven out of business; it must be well over a hundred. When the government in Washington wanted something new for the army or navy, it came to Eleutherian Mills, as it had earlier that year, asking Alfred I. to journey to Europe to buy—or, if necessary, steal—the French formula for smokeless gunpowder. Alfred had gone, reluctantly, and been turned down by the French; they would not even allow him to tour their explosives plants. But in Belgium, Alfred had shown some of his Uncle Lammot's spunk and disguised himself as a powder worker to get inside the Coopal gunpowder works. Later, after confronting the factory's owners with what he knew, he had come away with a licensing agreement for the most revolutionary change in gunpowder since Lammot's soda formula. For centuries, when a soldier fired his weapon the smoke gave away his position. With smokeless power any rifle could be fired undetected—and cannon, as well. Henry had pressed his influence upon Washington; the du Ponts would make smokeless powder only if the federal treasury picked up the tab for the royalties owed to Belgium. Henry had known the War Department would agree. But the formula from Belgium proved defective, and he had set Francis G. to discovering his own. In the end Alfred had botched his mission. It had given Henry an excuse not to promote the boy beyond superintendent of one of the yards.

Henry could not set aside the question of who would run Eleutherian Mills after his death. Would it be Eugene, his nephew Alexis's son? Gene ran the yards, diligently and well, but he was not a tough man, and to keep the family together required enormous strength. Certainly Eugene had the best qualifications. No one knew the manufacture of powder as well as he. Perhaps Eugene would not need as much toughness as Henry believed. In his thirty-nine years running the family and firm, Henry had built into his relatives a pride and discipline that would never falter—no matter whom the powder workers called Boss.

Henry stroked his beard, fully gray now where it had been red, and lifted the file of letters from his table. He was not dead yet, and there were decisions to be made. He had written six thousand letters a year, all of them in longhand, all of them on plain white paper without even the name of the company at its head, since he took over the company. He could write a few more, even here in his bedroom, even in the August heat of the Brandywine. When the time came—and it had not yet—he would choose an heir to his throne.

On the day Henry was born, seventy-nine years earlier, the Brandywine's current had turned the mills to make black powder. He supposed the current would not stop for his death. The Red Fellow wanted it that way: he had dedicated his life to turning the wheels, in war and peace. Even on the days when many of his relatives died the mills had turned. Darkness or light, through sunrise and sunset, Eleutherian Mills had turned out his gunpowder. Henry would not let them stop just to mark his passing.

After two months of living in his bed, General Henry du Pont died and was buried in the cemetery in Sand Hole Woods. Eugene du Pont, the son of Alexis, took the reins of the powder company, with reluctance, to end a bitter family struggle for control of Eleutherian Mills. Henry A. had wanted them; so had his brother William. Francis G., Eugene's younger brother, enjoyed laboring in the powder yards more than administration but refused to allow the General's son to take over. His other brother, Alexis I. the second, a doctor by training, had joined the company but had little experience in the yards. Alfred I. and Pierre S., both good powdermen, were too young to command the respect of the family. Eugene, fifty years old, seemed the only choice. He accepted the senior partnership in the hope that he could at last bring the Du Pont Company into the modern age.

Eugene immediately began construction of new offices for the company. Soon workers hurried through corridors on five floors; the Red Fellow had had fewer than five administrative employees in all the thirty-nine years he ran the mills. With Henry's death, Eugene proclaimed, an era had come to a close. The master of Eleutherian Mills would no longer travel like some feudal baron over his lands, hunting dogs barking his coming, a whip in his hands, his trousers tucked into tall black boots.

Since the end of the Civil War, American life had slowly changed.

Most of the du Ponts liked the conveniences modern life brought—electricity, steam, even a hint of what everyone called a horseless carriage. But change had bypassed General Henry by his own choice. The Du Pont Company was the most successful of its kind in the world, and Eugene knew he had to bring it into the modern age if it was to survive. The Red Fellow had built the mills into an empire and had done much for the family, piling riches into the company bank accounts, acquiring land that, suddenly, had become preciously expensive after Henry stopped buying. Nearly four hundred relatives had lived under the General's rules not really liking them. They appreciated the string of fifteen large houses along the Brandywine but they had laughed behind the Red Fellow's back at his archaic manners and stern discipline.

Eugene had abandoned the General's methods. He had brought younger blood into the partnership—Alfred I., Charles I. from across the Creek, and his own brother Alexis. He had ordered electric lights strung throughout the powder yards, a rail spur built to join the Brandywine to Wilmington, telephone lines installed in all the partners' houses. The General had left Eugene a dynasty to rule, hundreds of du Ponts who looked to him for guidance and decisions. But Eugene believed in allowing his relatives to run their own lives; the powder company was enough to consume his time and thoughts. What little energy the business left over, he wanted to devote to his children. His wife, Amelia, who was also his cousin, enjoyed dealing with the huge du Pont family on the Brandywine. In truth, Eugene did not; he spent enough time among relatives during the business day. But he had inherited the General's position, and that included running the family as well as the powder mills. He had not inherited the Red Fellow's relish for personal power, and within months of Henry's death Eugene's weaknesses had surfaced.

Although the company was doing well, better in fact than ever before, the family had fallen apart. The name du Pont, for the first time, had emerged on the front pages of newspapers. Since Henry's death his relatives had started venturing into the outside world, not fearing that Eugene might throw them from their homes if they did, or cut their allowances, or fail to answer their requests for money. They had begun to travel, to mix with other families who owned giant industrial complexes, to find their ways into politics and public affairs. They had begun to see what money, such as the money they knew the family collectively controlled, could buy. Trips to New York, to Paris, to the

West Coast became weekly events for some members of the family. Alfred I. bought a luxurious yacht. Others began breeding racehorses or bought hunting lodges in the best resort areas.

Eugene did not really mind the du Ponts' pastimes. Over a thick cigar after dinner he often even relished the stories of his relatives' latest escapades. It pleased him that the Brandywine remained the center of their lives and that children still fished and swam in the Creek. He enjoyed seeing the physical characteristics he had inherited, the deeply cleft chin, high forehead, and gray eyes, emerge in his younger relatives. Yet with the physical heritage, at times, a strain of something approaching lunacy also surfaced. Alfred I.'s brother Maurice had made headlines all over the East Coast with his marriage to an Irish barmaid he met while traveling. Eugene had known Maurice's mother, Charlotte, well and had seen her driven insane by Margaretta. But did the seed of Maurice's wild act come from his mother or his father? All that mattered, really, was the scandal that had plagued his family. Never before had a du Pont brought such publicity down on the heads of his relatives. Maurice had not even bothered to telegraph from Europe before the wedding. Many du Ponts doubted that Maurice would have dared do such a disservice to the family while General Henry had been alive.

Eugene's problems began when he and his brother Francis G. fought with the General's sons over the senior partnership. Eugene led the company and family only by a compromise between the other partners, a fact he never forgot. He had recognized two factions within the family: those who wanted to continue Henry's ways and those who desired to push as swiftly as possible into the future. Naturally, the younger men wanted change; most of all they wished for an easier path to leadership and responsibility in the company. Eugene could never allow that to happen; the other partners would cause a ruckus that might split the family apart. He had settled for changes in the company that made business dealings more efficient, and placated his younger relatives with vague promises.

Even Eugene's modernizing of the powder yards had caused trouble. When Henry died Eugene found dozens of masons and carpenters on the payroll who had little work to do. He dismissed them. A series of fires broke out in the yards. Only the partners knew that Eugene suspected a few of the employees he had let go of setting them. For months he lived in the fear that tons of powder might go off at any time, not by the hand of fate, but by the device of a bitter worker. Eugene had hired detectives to pose as powdermen, infiltrating every corner of the yards, with orders to report anything that resembled discontent among the workers. Eventually, the arsonists were caught, disgruntled workers as Eugene had thought, and the fires ceased, but not before an enormous explosion devastated the mills, destroying the old Upper Yard completely and killing twelve people, including a woman and infant who were crushed under the debris of their small cottage. At least one hundred fifty tons of powder had gone up; three years after the explosion the Upper Yard was still being rebuilt. The arsonists caught by the undercover detectives—a carpenter, a mule driver, and his wife—went to prison, but not for setting off the great explosion. Francis G., investigating the blast, was never able to prove how it had begun.

Eugene was finding running the family more and more difficult. And the family's problems were invading his concentration at the office. He must take his relatives firmly in hand or the scandals that had begun to shout from newspaper headlines might continue. But Eugene did not: he could not rule the Brandywine as General Henry had.

The Red Fellow had treated his workers like vassals, his relatives as valets. Not long after his death the General's widow, Louisa, had left their home to move away from the Brandywine. The director's grand old house, with its tall dormers, giant piazza, and the lovely gardens du Ponts had tended for ninety years, stood empty. Eugene had offered it to any relative with a large family; he found no takers. Francis G. suggested that the director's house be turned into a club for the workers. In the parlor, where four generations of du Ponts had sat listening to gentle piano music, powdermen now drank and spat tobacco juice into brass spittoons. In the dining room, where Eugene's grandfather and great-grandfather had discussed France and the American Revolution, bearded workers played billiards. The dispositon of the director's house had been the family's way of memorializing General Henry's life and placing their final judgment on his reign over the family. Eugene's six children united in their veins the two sides of the du Pont family, Eleuthère Irénée's, through him, and Victor's, through Amelia. Eugene, more caretaker than king of the Brandywine, would allow the du Pont family to dissolve before bequeathing his children the legacy of bitterness and dislike General Henry had left his.

# 22

LOUIS DU PONT, the youngest son of Eleuthère Irénée du Pont the second and Charlotte Henderson, committed suicide on December 2, 1892. He walked from the Brandywine's chilly winter air into the private Wilmington Club, chose a comfortable armchair in its parlor, drew a revolver from his coat pocket, placed it against his temple, and pulled the trigger. He found a way out of the mental torture he had suffered for the last six of his twenty-four years.

The trouble had begun on another winter day on the Brandywine, the wedding day of Louis's brother, Alfred I. Louis had worn a mask of pleasure to the ceremony and party, not wishing anyone to see his anguish. Alfred's new wife, Bessie Gardner, was a beautiful woman, too beautiful, Louis knew. He had loved Bessie for years, after meeting her while he studied at Yale. He had introduced her to Alfred I. on one of his brother's frequent visits to the school. At first, Louis had enjoyed the closeness Alfred and Bessie showed; he revered his brother. After their father and mother died Alfred had been a brother, father, and adviser to him, even more than Uncle Fred in Louisville. He had kept his plan to marry Bessie Gardner a secret from Alfred, waiting for his graduation from college to announce his intentions, even to Bessie. She was from a fine old Virginia family—relatives of hers had already married du Ponts—and Louis wished everything to be as genteel as Bessie's Southern manners. But soon after Alfred and Bessie met, his brother had come to Yale to tell him that they planned to marry. Louis had been speechless: did Alfred really not sense what he felt for Bessie? Yet, it seemed, his girl wanted to marry Alfred. Louis could do little but keep his feelings to himself.

Nothing had gone well for him after Alfred and Bessie's marriage. Louis began drinking heavily. His grades fell off. Finally, after three years in the senior class, he left Yale without his degree and entered law school. It was a pretense; never did he come home early enough from the night's drinking and carousing to attend classes the next morning at Harvard Law. After a year he had packed his bags and left; why bother trying to study? Life could be gayer in New York, and he had reached his majority, giving him his share of his father's estate. He could spend the income from it any way he chose, work not at all, and forever remain comfortable. Rarely did he journey to the Brandywine. He could not escape visiting Alfred and Bessie at Swamp Hall, and he could not bear seeing them together. When he did ride the train from New York to Wilmington, he spent his time at the Wilmington Club, where he could attend the dances the club gave each week, drink his fill without being bothered, and see as little of Alfred and Bessie as possible.

Alfred and Bessie were happy together, as far as Louis could tell. Bessie loved to sit on the steps of Swamp Hall reading while Alfred and his friends formed an impromptu orchestra on the lawn. They had two daughters, beautiful children. Alfred had entered the mills, the only one of Irénée's children to take up the powderman's trade. It was the life Louis had hoped he himself would lead, with the same woman, the same home, the very same job. Louis could not look at Bessie without his heart jumping; he had never reconciled his loss of her. Yet he had managed to keep his feelings secret from Bessie over the years. But it had become too much to bear: he had botched his life, and hated his brother, and become disgusted with himself for his hatred. His family made gunpowder; he had decided to use a few grains of it to stop, forever, the emptiness of his life and the torments of his heart.

William du Pont, after enduring a bad marriage to his cousin, Mary Lammot du Pont, for fourteen years, journeyed to North Dakota in 1892 to establish legal residence and secure a divorce. He had wed Mary in 1878, at the height of his father's reign, against the Red Fellow's wishes and under his threat to banish from the Brandywine any du Pont found loving another du Pont.

William had respected and liked his father. Why had he challenged his authority? Had he needed to rebel against the General? His brother, Henry A., had not married within the family. Perhaps that was it; Henry A., seventeen years older than he, had returned to the Brandywine from the Civil War a colonel and a hero. William had always looked up to his brother, but he had hated the attention his sisters and cousins lavished on Henry A. Did he marry a cousin to take some of the limelight from Henry's military carriage and sparkling uniform?

Perhaps. Yet the General had always been more of a presence than his brother had. And he had good reason to want more of his father's attention. The General devoted nearly every waking hour to the powder mills. He had been forty-three when William was born, long unused to jostling an infant on his knee. William had seen what the General did to the other members of the powder company partnership, ignoring them more than listening, rarely taking their advice, making them follow precisely his orders on the simplest matter, giving them nothing—money, property, or responsibility—that he could keep for himself. William, from the time he was a small boy, had had no better luck earning his father's respect. The General seemed to care little more for his own children than his cousins and nephews.

At first, William had loved Mary, or at least thought he had. She was an attractive woman, and they had grown up together, crossing the Brandywine on frequent visits, attending the same church, wandering the same hills and woods. But he had spent as much of his time with other female cousins, and he had never felt for them the lust that had drawn him to Mary. He had had other girls who excited him as much, yet Mary was somehow different. Perhaps it was that her life—her heritage—so closely resembled his. Mary had been a safe choice. His father had never taught him to accept responsibility; it would have meant surrendering some of the General's own. Mary, bred to the Brandywine, attached, as William himself was, to the traditions and legends of the family, would be easy to build a life with. All he had to do was follow in the footsteps of dozens of his relatives, take his large share of the estate his father would leave, perhaps enter the powder company's service, and move into a mansion near the Brandywine. He and Mary would raise a brood of children to rival any on the Creek and live their lives out among friends and relatives who would adore them for bringing the two halves of the family together.

It seemed so long ago now. A few relatives had rebelled against his father before William decided to challenge the edict against wedding cousins. His cousin Irénée's children had staked their claim to Swamp Hall after their parents died, and the General had been unable to uproot them. Fred and Bidermann, making their fortunes in Kentucky, had done as they pleased with their lives. Lammot, for years the butt of the General's whims, had married a daughter of one of the company employees and forced the General to enter the dynamite business, something the old fellow had vowed never to do. William had judged his father's armor not quite invincible.

Yet he did not feel comfortable blaming youthful rebellion for his marriage, or even the need to make his father take notice of him. Something deeper had been involved, something invisible even after his marriage turned sour. It had been the family, the insistent, encompassing common soul shared by the du Ponts, the *ego* attached to them all. Somewhere across the years they had grown different from others. He knew the obvious things, the soberness that hung above them living near the powder mills, the nonchalance they all seemed to exhibit in the face of danger. But there was more. In the shadow of his father he had gone nearly unnoticed on the Brandywine, even after his marriage, especially when Mary failed to become pregnant as the years wore on, and he had been able to observe his relatives from a sheltered sort of place—within the family yet detached from it. His relatives had amused him, with their common looks, their common mannerisms, even their nearly identical personalities. Two strains of character ran through them all, either the deep sobriety and sense of tragedy the powdermakers had, or the lightheartedness and frivolity his cousins across the Creek had inherited from the first Victor.

William had been young during the Civil War, only ten when it ended, and it had all seemed so romantic to him, the marching and parades, the tearful goodbyes as men left for the fighting, the grieving when some died and others came home crippled. Through it all he had watched the du Ponts make their gunpowder, and years later, when he thought back to the war, he realized that his family thought little about the soldiers or the emancipation of slaves. Isolated on the Brandywine, they filled the government's needs for gunpowder less out of patriotism than out of a sort of *noblesse oblige,* as though the du Ponts were an aristocracy more lasting, more durable, and more important than the United States—or for that matter, any government. To have joined two branches of the family by marriage was merely an extension of the family's belief in the superiority of du Ponts: where away from the Brandywine could William have found a suitable mate?

Throughout his youth William had heard stories of his ancestors, particularly Pierre Samuel du Pont de Nemours, a French nobleman of the highest order, confidant and defender of kings, driven from his homeland by the radicals of the French Revolution, arriving poor and old on America's shores, sending out his two sons to make the family's fortunes. The family crest read *Rectitudine Sto* beneath a vertical column: Be Upright. William had loved Annie Zinn, a widow from a town near the Brandywine, for years. When his divorce was declared final, he planned to marry Annie and leave the Brandywine forever, just as his wife, Mary, would wed Willard Saulsbury, her father's law partner. For now, the family stood behind William's wife, thinking him terrible for divorcing a faithful and loving woman. How many columns, on how many family crests, would totter just the slightest bit when his relatives discovered that his wife had long kept a lover of her own?

Alfred Victor du Pont switched off the light in Room 422 of the Galt Hotel, pulled the door of the room closed behind him, and turned his key in the lock. He had never tired of the simple furnishings in his room, of the faded rug on the floor, or the misshapen cushions of his reading chair. He wondered to himself why he had even started to build a large house in Louisville's best section; he would never leave Room 422 of the Galt. It had been his home for nearly forty years. The closest he had to a family were his brother Irénée's five children on the Brandywine. Now they were all raising families of their own, except for Louis, who had killed himself. He had no need for a mansion.

Fred walked through the small lobby of the hotel, nodded to the desk clerk, and emerged into the spring sunshine. He enjoyed walking the streets of Louisville on a spring morning, when the air was clean and smelled of new flowers. This particular morning, however, might be a bit less than pleasant.

The people of Louisville, hurrying to their jobs or the market, stopped to wish Alfred Victor well. He was known everywhere for the many generous gifts he had given to Louisville, most recently a sparkling new high school and public park, worth nearly a half-million dollars, in the very center of town. Many merchants had borrowed money from A. V. du Pont's bank, the First National of Louisville; many more worked in his paper factory, or his street railway system, or his coal and iron firm.

A few blocks from the Galt, Fred turned into West York Street, looking around carefully to make certain no one saw him. He knocked at a small house, watched the door open slightly, and slipped inside. The woman who had let him in began to argue. He had to face his responsibilities, she said, and provide for the child he had fathered. Fred was rich, the wealthiest man in Louisville; what would it take for him to properly support his own son? Fred had made up his mind: he would not spend a single cent on the baby, his or not. How was he to know that Maggie Payne, madam of the most popular whorehouse in Louisville, had indeed given birth to a child by him? What proof might she provide him?

The argument exploded into a fight. The woman drew a gun, aimed at Fred, and shot. He fell to the carpet, dead.

Later that day a doctor signed a death certificate in Maggie Payne's house for James G. Johnson, aged seventy-six, and called an undertaker to remove the body to the train station for shipment to relatives in Bowling Green, Kentucky. But the hearse moved no farther than the mansion Fred had built and given to his brother Bidermann. Quietly, by night, Fred's body was taken to the Louisville train depot and placed aboard a car bound for Wilmington and the Brandywine. Alfred Victor would be buried in Sand Hole Woods.

The following morning the Louisville *Courier-Journal* reported that the city's leading citizen, A. V. du Pont, had died of a heart attack while he stood on the sidewalk outside the Galt Hotel. He was pronounced dead in his room. Louisville would mourn the demise of so generous and unselfish a man.

Two days later a Cincinnati newspaper broke the real story. Alfred I., on the Brandywine, telephoned his cousin Coleman in Louisville, demanding the truth. Coly told him that the editor of the *Courier-Journal* had been heavily in debt to Uncle Fred, and that he had paid off the debt with the coverup of the old man's death. Somehow, a reporter from Cincinnati had discovered what really happened. Coleman said there would be no escaping the story. Alfred said he would try to calm Eugene but it would be difficult: the scandals of the last few years had made him less than tolerant of publicity. Coly promised to keep the *Courier-Journal* in line, if it would help, and to make certain that the paper printed stories emphasizing the good Uncle Fred had done in his life. He rang off with a promise to see his cousin soon on the Brandywine.

Eugene du Pont's relatives had brought little except scandal down upon the family name since General Henry's death. William's divorce had been bad, Fred's death in a bordello worse. Now, in 1873, Mary, William's ex-wife, announced her intention to wed Willard Saulsbury. Eugene liked Willard; he had written wills for the family and shaped legal documents for the company. However, the newspapers gloated over every move any du Pont made and Eugene found it more difficult to buy up powder companies each time one of his relatives made headlines.

And William had announced that he would take the widow Annie Zinn as his second wife, another public disgrace. Something had to be done about William; Eugene could not allow his cousin's reputation to ruin the dynamite business he ran for the company. Eugene had plans to consolidate his family's control over the high-explosives industry as the General had over the gunpowder trade. Publicity was the last thing he wanted when all over the nation politicians were crying out against the trusts that ran other industries with an iron hand—steel, coal, oil. He had used the General's strategy well so far, offering to buy out smaller concerns, underselling them until they starved if they refused. William's divorce would keep his name in the papers. Eugene decided to buy his cousin out; it was the only way to detach his scandalous personal life from the family's businesses.

A little good news filtered through the bad. Francis G. and Pierre S. had finally broken the mystery of smokeless powder. The patent had just come through, and the partners had decided to go into the smokeless trade. No one else in the United States knew how to manufacture the powder; the Du Pont Company would have a monopoly until it decided to license the patent to others, at an exorbitant rate. Smokeless powder could be made in any color; Francis G. had dyed the samples red, green, and blue. It would be no less lethal than the old black powder, but much nicer to look at.

Eugene had bought a tract of land across the Delaware River and up from Wilmington, called Carney's Point. He would name Pierre S. superintendent of the smokeless plant; the young man had earned the responsibility, and perhaps it would quiet his frequent nagging for a portion of the company profits. Other du Ponts shared Pierre's feelings; they wanted a larger stake in the family and company riches. Even Alfred I., who had worked his way up in the yards after leaving college and been given a junior partnership when the General died, regularly demanded more money and a larger say in how the firm was run. Eugene wished he had the General's icy stare and commanding voice. He had lost control of the du Pont family; it would not be long before he lost control of Eleutherian Mills, too.

Alfred I. du Pont had sensed his wife's unhappiness when Bessie first moved into Swamp Hall soon after their wedding in 1887. As the years passed they drew farther and farther apart. In the first four years of their wedded life Bessie gave birth to two daughters; not until eleven years later did she bear another child, a son, whom Alfred I. named Alfred Victor.

Even the coming of the son he had long wanted did not reconcile Alfred I. to his married life. He found himself unable to speak to Bessie in civil tones, and the thought that his brother Louis had killed himself over her burned constantly inside him.

Bessie had never been able to accept the simple, overriding fact of her husband's life: he was a powderman. She wanted to know why he needed to dirty himself in the mills, why he enjoyed the company of powdermen more than du Ponts, why he could not exchange his rough manners for more refined ways—as most of his relatives had.

In turn, Alfred I.'s sisters hated his wife; they stopped coming to Swamp Hall. Yet some of the du Ponts liked Bessie, for her Southern manners and her attempt to instill a measure of courtliness into Alfred's rough ways.

To escape Bessie's harangues Alfred had turned his attention more and more to the powder yards and to his music, organizing an orchestra among the family members and workers who played instruments. The music brought him a little relaxation, and the powder firm demanded most of his time from dawn to dusk. He did not have much of a say in the larger matters of the company, but he was the best powderman the family had, and at any moment, should war break out in the world, Eugene would come to him to take complete control of the mills. He and his cousin Pierre S. had talked often of how they might grab a larger share of the company from Eugene and Francis G. and Colonel Henry A. Alfred had begun a campaign to force Eugene into reorganizing the company; the senior partner's inefficiency was well known to the other owners. Eugene had neither the brains nor the talent to run Eleutherian Mills effectively, especially since whoever ruled the Brandywine now controlled both the powder and the dynamite trades in the United States.

Eugene was not a strong-willed man. Alfred believed that he would soon give in and take someone younger into his office to help with the administrative duties. It would amount to only a foot in the door, but once Eugene's ineptitude was proven, his downfall would be only a matter of time.

In 1898 the Spanish-American War gave Alfred I. the opening he sought to challenge Eugene du Pont's supremacy on the Brandywine. Eugene had already succumbed to the pressure from Alfred and Pierre S. and brought a younger man into the company office. Granted, it was his own son, Eugene Jr., but it was, at least, a step in the right direction.

Alfred I. had been correct about what would happen in wartime. He had frustrated and frightened Eugene by going to Washington to offer his services as an engineer. The Secretary of War, not knowing that without Alfred the du Ponts could never meet the nation's needs for powder, had offered him a commission as a major in the Corps of Engineers.

When government ordnance men arrived on the Brandywine to tell Eugene that they wanted only smokeless powder to fight with, the senior partner had panicked. The company could produce only three thousand pounds of powder a day; the army needed at least seven times that. Only one man had the knowledge to speed up the mills that much, and only the same man, Alfred I., had the trust of the workers: they would give their best for no one else. Alfred demanded complete control over the powder mills—all of them—in return for refusing the army commission. Eugene and Francis G., who ran the mills, had no choice but to give in to their junior partner. In sixty days the mills were churning at the rate of twenty thousand pounds of smokeless powder a day. Within four months Alfred delivered nearly a quarter-million pounds to the army and navy. It had been a return to the old days, and Alfred had loved it, keeping his two daughters with him in the yards while he worked, showing the powdermen that he was willing to risk his own life, and the lives of his family, to stand behind the government. Bessie had railed at him for taking little girls into the company of the rough powder workers, but Alfred had stood firm: the morale of the men meant more than his own life and, if need be, the lives of his children.

When the war ended, a few months after it began, Eugene told Alfred that he would no longer run all the company's mills; the firm would return to its prewar way of operating. Alfred had fumed and then gone on a winter hunting trip to Ball's Neck, Virginia, where he met a young woman of the Ball family, Jessie. He returned in a calmer mood, quieted by the days in the woods and Jessie Ball's company. He found Eugene in a more cooperative mood.

The senior partner had decided to set up a corporation; the old partnership simply was not workable for the giant Eleutherian Mills had become, with its dozens of plants strung across the United States. Alfred I. received only ten percent of the stock in the new corporation—control remained with Eugene, Francis G., Colonel Henry A., and Doctor

Alexis—but he had not been entirely excluded. In time, he told Pierre S., Eugene would have to step down, and they would move to take over the company.

Pierre disagreed violently with what Eugene had done. He came to Swamp Hall one evening to tell Alfred that he was through doing Eugene's bidding. Coleman, in Ohio, had offered him the presidency of the Johnson Company. He did not need his salary from the powder firm; his father, Lammot, had left him a fortune. He was tired of sitting idly by while Eugene and the others ruined the powder company with bad management. Eugene had allowed Francis G. to take in two of his sons, and the two boys, barely out of school, had moved into positions of responsibility greater than Pierre's. Coleman wanted a free hand to travel east and deal in the stock market in New York. He had told Pierre that he planned to buy a house in Wilmington. Pierre told Alfred I. that he had had enough of the du Pont family. A stint in Ohio would clear his head.

Alfred tried to dissuade Pierre from leaving, knowing in advance that he would not succeed. He did not bother to raise the principle of faithfulness to the Brandywine, to the family, or to the powder mills. It had been many years since even Alfred himself had felt the power of the old clubs General Henry had held over the heads of his relatives to keep them in line. The du Pont family had traveled far since the Red Fellow had last inspected the powder yards in his long black coat and silk top hat.

After Pierre's visit Alfred I. listened in the winter stillness to the humming of the steam generators that, finally, had replaced the Brandywine's current as a source of power for the mills. At any hour, while the mill wheels turned, a du Pont could be found in the yards, directing the work, straining alongside the powdermen, or learning the business. But for every one of his relatives who entered the yards, showing a pass to the watchmen at the gates, drawing a check at the end of each month in the company payroll office, five had left the Brandywine to build lives elsewhere.

On New Year's Day, 1900, the family would hold a glorious celebration, marking to the very day a century since the du Ponts first stepped on the soil of Newport, Rhode Island, and stole their first meal in America. Hundreds of his relatives would converge on the Brandywine, people he had never even seen, distant cousins who carried more different names than he could ever hope to remember. In common they would have the blood that ran through his veins. Many would look at him in awe, the eldest son of the eldest son of the eldest son of the founder, Eleuthère Irénée. But, aside from the very diluted genes of their ancestors, and the family fortune that in some measure touched each of their lives, they would have little to draw them together. Alfred wondered if, really, the family du Pont had any cause to celebrate.

# *Part Four*

# ALL RIGHTS OF HERITAGE

# 23

DURING the century from 1801 to 1901 men of enormous will and personal strength ruled the Brandywine, each in his own way building the fortune and legend of the du Pont family ever greater. Eleuthère Irénée the first, Alfred, his son, Henry, another son, and finally Eugene, a grandson, transformed Eleutherian Mills from an idea to a reality to an empire.

But with the turn of the nineteenth century into the twentieth, the seeds sown by these men, their roots complete in the soil of the Brandywine, pushed up through the fertile earth and saw the light of day and it seemed, to the du Ponts, that men of the stature of Irénée, Alfred, Henry, and even Eugene no longer could be found. The seeds were discontent; the roots jealousy, bitterness, and at times one du Pont's hatred toward another. What threatened to flower was the end of the du Pont family and legacy as it had stood for a century.

On January 28, 1902, Eugene du Pont died after a week-long bout with pneumonia, suddenly leaving Eleutherian Mills without a leader. Eugene, in a dozen years of rule over the du Pont family and company, had not been the equal of his ancestors. He had neither the singleness of purpose that had enabled Eleuthère Irénée the first to carve a small powder mill out of the wilderness, nor the dedication of Alfred to the men in the yards, nor the ego and strength of General Henry to make himself the only force of consequence on the Brandywine.

Eugene had wished deeply to bring Eleutherian Mills into the present as a company, to expand its horizons in the industrial world, but never, in the process, to sacrifice the traditions of the du Pont family. He had failed: the company progressed little under his control, and the family, compared with the tight unit it had been for a century, had disintegrated.

Eugene had never worn the traditional mantle of blood inheritance that distinguished the rulers of the Brandywine. His father, Alexis, had been the youngest son of Eleuthère Irénée the first. He was not his father's eldest son, but the second. Still, Eugene believed firmly in the ancient family traditions and had taken a cousin from across the Creek, Amelia Elizabeth du Pont, as a wife. With her he fathered six children, who had united in their veins the two branches of the du Pont family and, it could be hoped, would become the new leaders of Eleutherian Mills when their father died. It was an honored belief among the du Ponts; it was not to be.

In the passage of time, and in the thinning of the blood that had flowed through Eleuthère Irénée du Pont's veins, what had once been the du Pont way had changed. No longer did children strive to follow their fathers into the powder yards. No longer did du Pont women devote their lives to the church and the gardens along the Brandywine. No longer did the children of the founder decide who would inherit a portion of the profits of the powder mills; the family had grown too large and too wealthy for any du Pont to respect such decisions, even if anyone dared attempt to make them, which no du Pont did.

Eugene du Pont left behind, when he died, three men in control of Eleutherian Mills, none of whom was capable of running the powder company or really wanted the burdens leadership of the du Pont family entailed. Of the three, Henry Algernon du Pont, the son of the General, most nearly would fit into the du Pont tradition of passing Eleutherian Mills on from father to son. But Henry A., grown rich in the railroad business, cared little for gunpowder. He had lived up to his father's expectations and was, at the moment of Eugene's death, locked in a struggle for one of Delaware's seats in the United States Senate. The second owner, Francis G. du Pont, a younger brother to Eugene, had been a practical powderman all his life and was more than fifty years old when his brother died. He had been in less than good health for years. He had neither the desire nor the ability to run Eleutherian Mills. The third owner, Doctor Alexis I. du Pont, another of Eugene's brothers, had never been a powderman, knew little about the business, and was, like Francis G., not completely healthy.

Together, after Eugene's death, in the new offices he had built these three men met to decide the fate of Eleutherian Mills. They chose, after a century of sacrifice by themselves and their predecessors, to sell the gunpowder and dynamite empire built by four generations of du Ponts.

Pierre S. du Pont stared out the train station's tall windows at the swirling snow. For a day and night leaden flakes had fallen, crusting Philadelphia's gray buildings in white, stranding Pierre in the station waiting room. He had watched the sky darken as his train snaked into the Pennsylvania hills from the flatlands of Ohio. The blizzard had beaten him to Philadelphia by several hours. The roads to the Brandywine were impassable. Pierre had no choice but to join the milling crowd waiting out the storm.

He glanced over at his traveling companion, John Raskob. Raskob flipped through the day-old Sunday newspaper they had both read more than once. Pierre liked the slight, dapper man he had hired as his private secretary in Ohio. Raskob spoke only when words were a necessity. Pierre had learned to listen carefully; Raskob was rarely wrong about anything. His temperament matched Pierre's own: quiet, sober, cautious. And Pierre had found Raskob possessed of a fine business brain. He would be a decided asset in the coming takeover of the powder company.

Pierre had waited two years for the moment when he could return to the Brandywine from his self-imposed exile. He remembered the day he had told his cousin Alfred I. that he was leaving the Creek and the family business.

What had he felt then? Frustration, bitterness, even hatred. He had tried, desperately, to claim a place for himself in the powder mills. Older, richer relatives had thrown up walls of stone to blunt his ambition: responsibility or power in the company was elusive. He had left Delaware for his cousin Coleman's steel company in Ohio. Coly and his associates had flattered him with the presidency of the Johnson Company, but it had been an empty honor: the company had been edging toward bankruptcy for years. Pierre had done little more than preside over the sale of its assets to Federal Steel, and then seen Federal gobbled up by the new giant, United States Steel. It had been a bitter lesson in the dangers of corporate finance: most of his funds, and the thousands of dollars he held in trust for his nine younger brothers and sisters, were invested in Coly's company. Only his family's complete confidence in him had eased the embarrassment of telling them that he had lost a part of their inheritance.

Pierre and Raskob had worked out the strategy they would use to wrest the powder company from the older du Ponts who owned it. Pierre knew their words amounted to idle chatter: the takeover would be planned and executed by Coleman. He would add little but the facts and figures Coly would need to make his ideas work.

He had picked up his office telephone on Friday afternoon, three days ago. Coleman's deep, rolling voice had fairly exploded over the scratchy static on the line. The owners of the powder company had decided to sell out to Laflin and Rand, their largest competitor. At the meeting called to decide on a price Alfred I. had pushed through an amendment to the owners' resolution: E. I. du Pont de Nemours and Company was to be sold to the highest bidder. After the meeting adjourned, but before anyone left the room, Al had jumped to his feet and said he would buy the company. Naturally, the older du Ponts had nearly burst out laughing: old Francis G., who had never liked Alfred, told him he simply could not have the company. Al had lost his temper, as he usually did with Francis G., and shouted that his relatives should sell the company to someone—himself—who could run it, if they could not. Frank G. had stomped out of the room, Coly told Pierre, his face flushed. But Colonel Henry A., the old war horse, said he admired Alfred's spunk and sentiment about not letting the company go to outsiders: he would back Al's bid to buy the business. He had convinced the old owners to give Al a week to raise the twelve million dollars—in cash—they planned to ask for from Laflin and Rand.

Alfred had burst into his house immediately after the meeting, out of breath and brimming with the news, to ask Coly if he would go in with him to buy the company. Coleman had hedged about joining his cousin, using the excuse that he had to ask his wife, Elsie, for her approval.

Pierre had known at once why Coleman put Alfred off: Coly was broke. The failure of the steel company had left him with millions in paper assets and no hard cash. He had gone to Wilmington to open a button factory and rifle assembly plant. He had credit, but barely enough money to live on. Neither had succeeded: his workers failed to turn out a single button, and the rifles they did manage to finish could not be sold at a profit. Coleman was a genius at buying companies, but a failure at running them. He had dodged Alfred's request that he make up his mind immediately to buy time for the Ohio call: Coleman would go in with Al only if Pierre would join him, to handle the powder company's books and day-to-day operations. They had only seven days to make their offer to the older du Ponts: what, he had asked, was Pierre's answer?

The word had leaped to Pierre's lips: yes. He would pack a bag at once and catch the first train east. He rang off with a promise to telephone Coly the moment he reached Wilmington.

And now the worst blizzard in a decade had stopped Pierre. He had always prided himself on being cautious, especially in business. Why had he been so eager to return to Delaware, to try to buy a company rooted in the paternalism of pre-Civil War years, a family concern riddled with all the petty jealousies his relatives were capable of—worst of all, a business that had no idea how much land it owned, or even how much money it had in the bank?

The Brandywine, that was why. His father, Lammot, had fled the Brandywine with his wife and children, escaped the clenched fist General Henry had used to rule the company and the family. Lammot had revolutionized gunpowder manufacture with his discovery of soda powder and had almost single-handedly saved the Union by buying up all of England's saltpeter during the Civil War. He had put the company into the dynamite business even after General Henry had forbade him to do so. He had run the Gunpowder Trade Association for decades, keeping the other powdermakers in line with the General's wishes. Until his death Lammot had never uttered a word against the General or any other du Pont. And still, because he had chosen to marry a woman with Jewish blood in her veins, Lammot—and his children—had been ridiculed and looked down upon by their self-righteous, bigoted cousins and uncles and aunts. For years the words "Jew-boy" had echoed in Pierre's ears. He had been made to feel inferior, unwanted, impure: a second-rate du Pont. Yet he had fought for a place in the powder yards, worked diligently for years to earn the respect of his elders. And he had failed, grown embittered, left.

But when Coly called he had not hesitated a second in saying yes. He had known, since his first days in the powder yards, that a crisis would come for the du Ponts. General Henry had ruled alone: he had taught no one the techniques needed to keep the powder mills running well, to keep the company growing. Eugene had certainly tried: in ten years he had done more to modernize the company than the General had accomplished in forty. But Eugene had made the same mistake the General had: neither man cared to bring younger, brighter, more tenacious du Ponts into the firm. Alfred I. had a piece of the business, ten percent in fact, but only by inheritance. His stock had brought him no responsibility, no power, no say in company affairs.

Pierre had realized that joining Coleman did not mean he would run the Du Pont Company. Coly had made plain his conditions for coming in on the deal: he was to be given the largest bloc of stock in the company, the presidency, and unquestioned final say in all corporate decisions. But Pierre knew that his cousin would soon grow tired of the powder business, restless to move on to something more glamorous and new. And Coleman had not been born or raised on the Brandywine: its current did not run in his blood in quite the same way it surged through Pierre's.

What of Alfred I.? He had known his other new partner all his life. Al had been a fighter as a boy, a roughneck who found the company of powdermen's sons far preferable to that of the du Ponts. Alfred was a hothead even now, impetuous and aggressive—immensely talented at making black powder, to be sure, and capable of exacting the last ounce of effort from the workers—but far from at home behind a desk or in a board meeting. Pierre knew that he could dispense with Alfred at any time he chose: his cousin had no talent for the fine art of manipulating blocs of stock or managing proxy fights.

Pierre could almost hear the rush of air sucked into hundreds of du Pont lungs when the family learned that he and his cousins were going to buy the powder company: Coleman, a du Pont with no allegiance to the Brandywine; Alfred, the most rebellious of the du Ponts, still living inside the peeling wooden walls of Swamp Hall while his relatives built fine mansions of stone; and he himself, named after the family's founder, Pierre Samuel, but the oldest son of the Brandywine's only Jewess. All his life Pierre had heard legends of the founder of the du Ponts; du Pont de Nemours had cherished one wish: to unite his family in America, far from the horrors of the French Revolution. The wish would have to wait five generations before coming true, but, at least, it would be a Pierre Samuel that did the uniting.

Pierre looked at the darkening evening sky. Night would be upon them soon, and even if the snow stopped falling, there would be little use in attempting to reach the Brandywine over unrecognizable roads in the darkness. He and Raskob would wait until morning to hire a carriage to take them to Wilmington. The extra few hours would not matter: he did not need a week to buy the powder company from his old and tottering relatives. As Alfred had told the board of directors when they asked why he wished to take over the company: Eleutherian Mills belonged to him by all the rights of heritage. Pierre believed he was returning to the Brandywine to claim his birthright.

Thomas Coleman du Pont gripped the edge of the washbasin, resting his two hundred fifty pounds on one arm: his legs had gone limp. In the pit of his stomach he could feel the shaking begin, the gnawing rise and penetrate his chest with a hot ache that turned into stabs of pain. With his free hand he reached for a towel, dipped it into the lukewarm water in the basin, and mopped his forehead. Another attack had begun.

Knowing before she saw him what had happened, Elsie du Pont ran up the staircase to her husband. After thirteen years of marriage she had learned to sense her husband's stomach attacks before they began: a certain amount of tension, the need to confront people, to convince them they should take part in one of his business schemes, and within a few hours Coleman would be screaming in pain. Often the attacks came when her husband was alone, hundreds of miles away from home. Elsie had long ago decided to keep a suitcase packed and ready for the frantic rush to Coly's side when his agonized voice came over the telephone.

Elsie opened the bathroom door, placed her small hands on Coleman's large back, and began massaging away his fears. Long ago she had urged him to see a doctor, and he had, many times. Medicine could do little, he had been told: the attacks were symptoms of his way of life. Coly had urged her to keep them secret; it would not do for the world to know that T. Coleman du Pont, six feet four inches tall, the image of easy, relaxed control, shook like a baby nearly every time he became involved in a business deal. Coly's confidence in his wife had given her the power to calm him when the pain came. Elsie barely reached her husband's shoulder when they both stood erect.

That morning Coly had faced the board of directors of Eleutherian Mills, all the du Ponts, and in a voice more quiet than usual, in a tone with just the proper amount of reverence for the old men, had explained his plan: the three cousins, Alfred I., Pierre S., and himself, would take control of the powder company, and ownership of its stock, and give the old owners twelve million dollars' worth of bonds in return. The annual income on the bonds would more than equal what they now took home in salaries and dividends. In addition, the cousins would issue their relatives a bonus of three million dollars' worth of the new stock they planned to create. The company would be reorganized on more modern corporate lines. He would become its president, Alfred vice-president, and Pierre treasurer. The former owners would take no risk: their bonds would be backed by company stock they would hold as collateral. All he wanted was a free hand to run Eleutherian Mills as he chose.

The older generation had taken the bait and now the three cousins owned the company. Pierre had made a quick inventory of the firm's assets: they added up to nearly twenty-four million dollars. The older du Ponts had no idea what they owned. Even at the purchase price of fifteen million dollars the company was a true bargain. Pierre was arranging a new stock issue, which would give each of the cousins millions of dollars in bonuses—for negotiating the purchase. Elsie could begin looking for a new house, not to rent, this time, but to buy. Their days of living in fifty-dollar-a-month quarters were over.

Alfred I. and Pierre S. and Thomas Coleman du Pont saved Eleutherian Mills from being sold to outsiders in June of 1902. Within weeks the wrath of the du Pont family turned against Alfred I. for daring to seek the companionship of a beautiful young woman, Mary Alicia Heyward Bradford, as a way to escape the sadness of his own marriage to Bessie Gardner. Alicia, as Alfred called her, had taken much of the burden of Alfred's marriage from his shoulders. Alfred had been seeing Alicia openly on the Brandywine for months, taking her for rides in his new French automobile, drawing the attention of many of his relatives as he drove the roads near the Brandywine, stopping to picnic in a clearing beneath the Creek's willow trees.

Alicia and Alfred were cousins. Her mother, Eleuthera du Pont, a sister of Eugene, Francis G., and Doctor Alexis, had married Edward Green Bradford. Bradford, a judge, had chosen to live near the Brandywine, to be near his half-sister, Elizabeth Canby Bradford, who was married to Doctor Alexis. Alfred knew how the family's displeasure had come about. Doctor Alexis's wife had called Henry A. to her home for a conference about Alfred's affair with Alicia. Elizabeth had very likely told Henry A. that her interest in Alicia went beyond considerations of propriety or family reputation. She was Alicia's aunt on both sides.

But Elizabeth's double aunthood was only a guise for her true feelings. She hated seeing the three cousins take over the powder company. Doctor Alexis had inherited a large share in the powder mills from his father, Alexis, the youngest son of Eleuthère Irénée the first. After Eugene died Doctor Alexis should have taken over the senior partner's office, with all its prerogatives of rule over the family. His wife would have become the grande dame of the Brandywine. But the doctor was sickly, unable to cope with running the company, and without practical powdermaking experience. Elizabeth had been relegated to a minor place among the women of Eleutherian Mills.

And, Alfred believed, she had always hated him, and his brothers and sisters. Elizabeth was the picture of old du Pont grace, decorating her life with ancient French mannerisms and customs, holding fast to the legend of nobility that had filtered through the decades from the first du Pont. Alfred had wondered often at the du Ponts' ability to pretend the dirt and grime of the powder mills did not touch them, that they earned their ample luxuries simply by being named du Pont. Elizabeth had since his earliest years looked down her nose at him; Alfred knew that his rebellious streak disgusted her—as it did many of the women on the Brandywine.

Colonel Henry had become the acknowledged head of the family after Eugene's death, but Elizabeth worked very hard to influence him. She could not bear the thought of Al and Coly and Pierre dictating jobs, promotions, even the assignment of homes to their relatives: it meant the end of Elizabeth's reign, such as it had been. By attacking Alfred for his affair with Alicia she might be able to undermine his authority—and keep the rest of the family's dislike for him at a high pitch.

Alfred realized he could not fight Elizabeth's will when it came to his relationship with Alicia. He was in love with her, and he had seen the havoc a divorce brought to the Brandywine. His cousin William had been thoroughly ostracized after he divorced Mary to wed Annie Zinn. Alfred liked Willie; he alone among the du Ponts had stood behind William during the divorce, bearing the brunt of family ridicule while his cousin lived in South Dakota for six months to establish legal residence and file proceedings against his wife. The family had driven Willie into exile, taken from him his job as president of the dynamite company at Repaupo, shut their doors to his face. Willie seemed happy enough, restoring Montpelier, James Madison's old plantation in Virginia: he and the woman he loved were together. And Willie would never want for money. He had inherited a substantial interest in the powder company from his father, General Henry. But the family's ostracism was complete; even his own brother, Colonel Henry A., had turned against him, vowing to outlive Willie, if only to see that he was not buried in the cemetery in Sand Hole Woods. Alfred had heard the vow and laughed: it would be a tremendous feat on the Colonel's part. Henry A. was nearly twenty years William's senior.

Alfred would gladly have followed Willie's lead, ending his marriage to Bessie and the anguish she brought him. Even their children gave him little pleasure in the company of their mother; he had grown apart from his own son, Alfred Victor, the son he had longed for since his wedding. But he could not leave Bessie; the scandal would ruin his reputation on the Brandywine for all time. He had finally become an important force in the Du Pont company; he could not bring himself to follow Willie into exile.

And so he had settled for horseback rides and picnics with Alicia, for stolen hours concealed as well as they could be from the ever-prying eyes of relatives. Henry A. had spoken to him at length about the problem: Alfred's affair could undermine the entire Brandywine community, at the precise moment that the family must be convinced of the rightness of the three cousins' takeover of the mills. He owed the Colonel much: when the rest of the old guard laughed at his desire to buy the company, Henry A. had, at the expense of his own reputation, taken Alfred's side, both publicly and in secret meetings with Doctor Alexis and Francis G. Without the Colonel's support Alfred and Coly and Pierre would never have been successful. He could not turn down Henry A.'s request that he stop seeing Alicia. He had given his cousin his word that the affair would soon end.

Alfred had found his promise hard to fulfill. He needed Alicia; without her, life on the Brandywine consisted of little more than day after day of hard labor in the powder yards. His hearing had been failing for years; he had given up the violin when its sounds came to his ears terribly distorted. Everywhere he went he carried a black box which plugged into his ear by a long cord and made others' words understandable. In the powder yards the workers shouted at him through a long brass trumpet, their lips close to its splayed end. The doctors he had consulted in New York attributed his hearing loss to breaking his nose while diving into the Brandywine Creek as a boy: another legacy of the flowing water. At times—when Bessie began one of her lectures about his bad manners and expletive-littered language—he did not mind being deaf. But his lost hearing had isolated him even more, and only Alicia's touch seemed to break the silence. She was his only escape from the life he hated: what would he do without her?

He had sat for many long, sleepless nights in the parlor of Swamp Hall after his talk with Colonel Henry A., searching for a way to keep Alicia near him and still turn aside the family's criticism. He had decided that if he could not leave Bessie for her, he would at least see to it that she was never taken from the Brandywine. He had introduced her to his newly hired secretary, George Amory Maddox. Maddox was not very bright, but he was handsome in a way, although women rarely paid attention to him after realizing how little backed his well-cut figure and face. Alfred had taken Maddox from poverty and given him a good job—a "drag" job, as the du Ponts called positions reserved for family members with little business talent. George and Alicia had hit it off, as Alfred knew they would, if only because he prodded Alicia into caring for the man. Judge Bradford had seethed and raged—his usual manner of expression outside a courtroom—at both Alicia and Alfred. Maddox, he believed, was unworthy of his daughter, in brains and wealth and prospects and even looks. Al agreed with the judge, in all but one category: he had decided that after George and Alicia were married his secretary would make an excellent traveling inspector for Du Pont. It would keep him on the road, away from Alicia, and leave Alfred free to see his lover. Alfred had taken on the judge's anger, arranging secret meetings for Alicia and George and sanctioning their marriage on the du Pont family's behalf. He had even committed Christ Church for the wedding—although the judge would not be in attendance and had forbidden his wife to so much as speak with her daughter—and planned to give the bride away.

He had decided on a wedding gift for Alicia and George: a home near the Brandywine. With his ownership in the powder company had come the power to delegate homes; Coleman cared little about which du Pont lived where. Alfred had bought Swamp Hall, and more than fifty acres around it, for the sum of five dollars. And he had taken personal charge of the mansions near the Creek. Alicia and Maddox would reside in Upper Louviers, where Admiral Sam Francis and Sophie had lived out their last years. The family would grumble, loudly, but do nothing: none of the du Ponts wished to be evicted. And it was time that his relatives understood that he did not intend to serve forever as the scapegoat for all the petty jealousies that hung in the air above Eleutherian Mills.

The powdermakers of Eleutherian Mills discovered soon after the three cousins took over that Coleman du Pont was not, like General Henry, aloof, distant, and harsh. On the Fourth of July, 1902, at the traditional company picnic, the workers found that Mister Coleman was the most accessible ruler the Brandywine had ever had.

Coleman shook with laughter at the picnic. These were good men: he had known many like them, honest workers who toiled each day for a day's wages and went home to their wives and families each night after a few whiskeys at the local tavern. He had worked alongside them in the coal mines of Kentucky, when he first entered his father's business, and he had joined a union with them, the Knights of Labor, when the organizers came into the coal fields.

Soon, he hoped, he would put most of the men gathered in the powder yards for the Fourth of July celebration out of their jobs and close the old powder mills. Times changed: in Kentucky, when he left the mines to take a desk near his father's, he had called in strike breakers to beat the Knights of Labor into submission. There were no unions on the Brandywine; he would not have to starve the men out, simply fire them.

Still, he liked them, and as the day wore on, with the fireworks and huge spread of food on tables under the trees, he believed they liked him as well. He had brought along his bag of tricks, a deck of cards he fingered in his coat pocket, and his good humor. The men were fascinated when he asked them to pick a card, any card, and then told them which one it was. The men feared him a bit, after learning that he was to be the new boss of the powder company, but he had instructed Alfred to explain the new setup. The men had been relieved to find out that he would rarely venture from the new company offices in Wilmington to the yards.

He would have to fight to close the powder yards, Coleman realized. Alfred would balk; the old mills and the powdermen were precious to him. Coly figured Pierre to join Al on this one; Pierre believed the yards were the key to keeping the du Pont family together. He himself cared little whether most of his relatives lived or died. To make the company pay, and pay well, he needed efficiency, and Eleutherian Mills was the least efficient of the company's many factories across the nation.

Coly enjoyed watching his relatives arrive in carriages for the traditional celebration. They made straight for him; he held the power now, and each and every one of his three or four hundred cousins would do their best to stay in his good graces. He had made them believe he cared about all their little interests—their gardens and stables and country retreats. It would give them a sense of security, a respect for him, and if he needed to call upon the few who owned a significant number of shares in the company, he would find them acquiescent to his wishes.

Coleman noticed a carriage arriving with Alfred's new traveling inspector, George Maddox, and his wife Alicia. Alicia would not come to pay her respects to the new company president; she had long ago turned down the passes Coly had made at her. He watched as she climbed carefully to the ground. It amused him that she was pregnant so soon after the wedding. Most of the du Ponts wondered who the child would resemble more, its du Pont ancestry or the Maddox family. For Alfred's sake, he hoped the baby did not come into the world with a cleft chin like the one that graced his cousin's face.

Al had made quite a show of Bessie's own swollen belly at the celebration, as if to signal that all was well at Swamp Hall. Coly and Pierre, who saw Alfred each day, knew that all was far from well: while Maddox traveled, Alfred spent many afternoons away from his desk and the powder yards. And Alicia did not turn down his visits. Coleman wondered what the lovely young woman saw in his deaf cousin that she did not see in him.

Coly wandered over to where Pierre stood talking quietly with his assistant, John Raskob. He approached them slowly. Pierre was the soul of politeness and fine du Pont manners. He would never interrupt a conversation between Coleman and anyone else, and Coly had learned to respect his cousin's ways. Pierre had already proven himself vital to the powder company's success. Coleman had given him ideas on turning the powder company into a holding company for their stock and taking a large percentage for themselves. Pierre had made his ideas work with a minimum of fuss and absolutely no complaints from the family.

Pierre had seen him coming. Coly waited a little apart for the two men to stop talking. Looking at his cousin, he wondered about his personal life. Pierre seemed not to be interested in women at all; as far as Coly knew, his cousin had never in his life had a girl—and he would soon be thirty-three. But then, Pierre had been thrust as a boy into the position of his family's leader: his brothers and sisters even called him Dad. Perhaps Pierre had come to enjoy being the patriarch among eleven brothers and sisters and needed no wife or children of his own. He had always been excellent at forming close relationships with men; they respected his business sense and knew that his shy—almost painfully shy—manner posed no threat to their manhood. And Pierre seemed to be taking on the care and feeding of his brothers' and sisters' children. Just now, one of his brothers, Henry B., was fighting the last of a long battle with tuberculosis. He would die soon and leave a son and wife Pierre would feel compelled to take under his wing.

Coleman tapped Pierre softly on the shoulder. His cousin turned, said hello, and listened to Coleman's flood of words. He had added up the figures Pierre gave him, Coly said. The powder company produced a third of all the blasting explosives in the nation, and through the Gunpowder Trade Association controlled prices across the United States. He had made a decision: they must buy up the entire powder and dynamite industry. Men were doing it in other fields: oil, steel, tobacco. Coly had promoted one of the company's sales agents, Bob Waddell, to manager over all company outlets and representatives. He wanted to give his new man a chance to sell all the powder used in the country. He and Pierre would discuss specifics the next morning in his office. In the meantime Pierre could begin thinking out how they could talk their largest competitor, Laflin and Rand, into selling. Coleman let out one of his giant laughs: wouldn't it just rip the old owners of Eleutherian Mills to know he planned to take control of the very company they had wanted to sell the company to? Coly shook with mirth and turned back to the celebration.

Pierre watched his cousin walk downhill toward the Brandywine and headed the other way, to Sand Hole Woods. He did not often have an opportunity to visit his father's grave in the family cemetery. With Coleman's new plan he would very likely be spending much of his time away from the Brandywine, even away from the new company offices in Wilmington's Equitable Building. Pierre noticed the old company office ahead of him. He unlatched the plain wooden door and walked in.

Everything was in its place, as though General Henry, or Alfred Victor, or even Eleuthère Irénée himself, might at any moment walk in and sit down to write out letters in longhand. On the windowsill the General's iron candlesticks stood three abreast, fresh tapers in two, a half-used tallow stick in the third, the very way Henry had left them. Throughout the years the powder company had been known by the name of the man who headed it, as "Henry's Company," then "Eugene's Company." Earlier that day Pierre had heard a powder worker call it "Coleman's Company." For a time, until Coleman finished building his monopoly over the powder industry, it would be. But in the end Eleutherian Mills would come to be known, forever, as "Pierre's Company."

# 24

ALFRED I. DU PONT felt a warm, small hand close around his own. Like distant, soft thunder, he could barely hear the sound of someone sobbing. The lid of his right eye flickered open. He tried to raise his head, could not, and let it fall back against the pillow. At the foot of his bed he could see the shape of his wife, Bessie. Beside him, holding his hand in hers, crying into a kerchief, stood his oldest daughter, Madeleine.

Alfred raised his left hand, felt the swaths of gauze circling his forehead, and attempted to remember what had happened.

He had been hunting in Virginia, taking in some bird shooting just after dawn, before breakfast with the Ball family. He and Frank Mathewson and Bill Scott, powder company men who often went hunting with him, had spread out along a hedge to flush their prey. He had heard a shot—from Bill's gun, yes—and he had fallen to the ground, struck in the eye. He had felt his own warm blood oozing down his face, and then he had blacked out.

Where was he now? He remembered: a hospital in Philadelphia. The days had passed in a haze of morphine and sedatives. How long had he been there? A week? No, it must be longer. Bessie was standing at his bedside—damn her!—and she had been in Europe, in Brussels. He had asked that she be wired about his accident, to avoid frightening the children with careless accounts the newspapers were sure to print. Why had she come? His wife cared little for his health—or his life. Perhaps the doctors had telegraphed that his condition was critical and she had returned from Belgium to preside over his funeral.

His daughter's sobs became clearer in his mind. Alfred reached up to touch her cheek, felt the tears running down her face, and tried to calm her. He had last seen his family in late summer when Bessie herded them aboard a ship, saying that she planned to live in Europe forever, never to see him or the Brandywine again.

Bessie had given birth to their fourth and last child late in 1903. It had been a girl. Alfred named her Victorine, an old family name first given to a du Pont when the family was about to flee the French Revolution: it was a name rooted in hope. Alfred had hoped that the baby would change his wife and end their marital troubles. Alicia Bradford had given birth, too, not long after Bessie, to a girl also, and named her Alicia. The whispers had begun immediately: Alicia's child looked remarkably like a du Pont, with the prominent, cleft chin, high forehead, and large nose that distinguished Alfred's branch of the family especially.

Who, the women of the Brandywine wanted to know, was the child's father, George Maddox or Alfred I. du Pont? Maddox traveled quite a lot, and Alfred found the road to Upper Louviers a convenient path in his wanderings to escape Bessie. Alfred had heard the rumors and stormed at his relatives whenever he saw them, causing the stories to flare. Bessie had heard them, too, and railed at her husband for his stupidity and unfaithfulness. She demanded an explanation. Alfred answered that none was needed. Carrying little Victorine at her breast, Bessie had boarded the ship to Europe. Alfred made no attempt to stop her.

Alfred felt the throbbing in his skull begin again. He had begun to recover, in the Philadelphia hospital, with Alicia spending her days at his side, soothing his pain, not talking, but always staying within earshot should he wish to speak, touching him lovingly when he moaned. The doctors were still trying to save his eye; it could be done, they said, if he had complete quiet, weeks of rest, and no emotional strain. He had been doing well until word came that Bessie had booked passage on a ship bound for the United States. Even the pain had nearly gone; now it returned, worse than right after the accident, and he had been unable to retain the calm Alicia's company had brought him.

What did Bessie really want? She had not come running into his room, not fallen across his bed in tears. She had walked in, stood near the door staring at him, and not even bothered to speak. Perhaps she thought her visit would make him increase the allowance he gave her; it would not. He could see that Bessie's attitude was tearing Madeleine apart. He wanted the woman gone, from his hospital room and from his life. He could think of nothing more repulsive than being forced to have Bessie near him while Alicia stayed away.

Alfred worked to quiet his anger. He was unable to bear the thought of losing his eye: how would he function with no ears and a single eye?

Soon after coming to the hospital he had remembered an old family legend of the first du Pont, Pierre Samuel, whose eyes had been damaged in a bout with smallpox. His ancestor had decided that having one very nearsighted and one extremely farsighted eye distinguished him from other men, who had eyes that only duplicated each other. He had called them his eye for war and his eye for peace. Alfred believed he, too, could survive with damaged vision but he was far from certain that only one eye, however good it was, would be enough. And, he believed, if Bessie did not leave him alone he would be faced with the problem.

Alfred pushed his body up against the pillows. He felt a moan rising within him, struggled to stifle its sound, and could not. A nurse appeared with a tray, edged Madie aside, and set it on the table near the bed. It was more morphine. He would try to withstand the drug's dulling effects, but it would do no good; in a few minutes he would sink into a half-slumber, and Bessie's face would soften into a mesh of colors. Then the pain would ease, and he would sleep.

Through the window of his room Alfred could see snow falling. It would be Christmas in a few days, and he would leave the hospital to return to the Brandywine. He had decided to give a party for the children of the powder workers. Bessie would leave for Europe when she realized he would survive and that she need not stand over his grave in Sand Hole Woods.

Alfred realized that he had seen only one of his four children at the hospital; Bessie had left the others in Brussels. He would not even be able to wish them a Merry Christmas, bounce them on his knee, or present them with gifts for the holiday. It did not matter: what, after all, did one Christmas mean when he might never see them again anyway? And the rooms of Swamp Hall would still ring with laughter, the laughter of powdermen's daughters and sons, on Christmas Eve.

Colonel Henry A. du Pont glared across the crowd of du Ponts at his brother William, caught himself, and lowered his eyes to the ground. A family funeral was not the proper place for the leader of the family to display ill will toward any relative. The minister had nearly finished his long eulogy; the family would trudge from the cemetery to their waiting carriages, drive in single file down past Sand Hole Woods, and scatter to their homes. An hour would pass before all the buggies were out of sight and nearly four hundred members of the family had said their goodbyes.

Henry loathed funerals, and this was the second one in less than a month. Francis G. had died in the first week of November, 1903; his brother, Doctor Alexis, had breathed his last only nineteen days later. Both had been unwell for years, but Henry believed it had been the takeover of the powder company by the three cousins that killed them. Both men had lingered for years with their illnesses. Only in the months since Alfred, Coleman, and Pierre moved into the company offices did they begin the sharp decline toward death.

Henry stroked his Van Dyke beard impatiently, removed his pince-nez from his face, wiped the lenses on his coat, and clamped it back on his nose. He searched the mourners for Coleman; he had much to discuss with the company president. He wanted to compliment Coly on the strategy he had worked out to win back the U.S. Senate seat Henry had lost a year earlier in a bitter feud with "Gas" Addicks, a robber baron from New England who wanted a place in Washington as a power base. He had asked Coleman to take over his campaign soon after the young man assumed control over the powder mills. Coly had agreed, with his usual proviso about being given a free hand to do what he chose. Henry A. trusted his cousin; his methods would be little different from the opposition's, buying votes with money, women, and promises of political office and influence, once Henry Algernon du Pont journeyed to Washington. Unlike Addicks, whose lieutenants made no secret of their objectives, Coleman would buy the Senate seat for him with a modicum of dignity. Henry had learned that underneath Coleman's rough exterior hid a shrewd mind. The gunpowder industry had learned, also. Coly and Pierre had bought up virtually all the companies in the United States that manufactured any significant amount of gunpowder or dynamite. They had walked out on the Gunpowder Trade Association; two weeks later it collapsed—its treasury richer to the tune of nearly a quarter-million dollars Coleman had used to convince the other members he had no intention of letting the Powder Trust fall.

Every time Coleman struck he came away with millions in assets without spending a cent. Laflin and Rand had been absorbed into Du Pont for the price of legal fees covering a bond issue to the old owners. And Coly was no fool when it came to men: he hired the top executives of the companies he bought, brought them to Wilmington, and integrated them into the Du Pont Company.

Henry did not quite understand how Coleman managed to persuade men to give up the products of a life's work for his bonds and promises;

perhaps he dazzled them with card tricks and exploding cigars first, mesmerizing them into agreement. Only Pierre knew Coly's methods, and Pierre was a silent and loyal man. The two of them worked together—the carrot and the stick—Pierre softly listing figures and facts, Coleman thundering after him with promises of a piece of the sky in return for a few thousand shares of stock. Henry A. had noticed that Coleman and Pierre kept their dealings secret from Alfred I. He understood their feelings: Al had little grasp of high finance, and less willingness to observe the rules of corporate diplomacy. But ignoring the third partner might prove dangerous in the future. Alfred owned a huge share in the powder company, and he cared little for the time-honored politeness du Ponts rendered to each other. If he convinced himself that his cousins were shutting him out of the company's most important affairs he might raise quite a row on the Brandywine. Alfred was capable of exploding like one of Coly's trick cigars at the slightest provocation.

The Colonel saw Coleman edging toward the cemetery gates. He hurried to join him, taking the tall man's arm as they emerged onto the road. Coly had come to him weeks earlier proposing that they buy a bit of influence in Washington with a large contribution to Theodore Roosevelt's reelection campaign. He had not understood Coleman's motives; Roosevelt was the greatest opponent the manufacturers of the East had, and he would win reelection easily without du Pont money. Why bother? Coleman. had been adamant: think over, he said, what it might mean to be on TR's side if war broke out and the powder company's product became urgently needed. And, Coleman added, think what might happen if the President decided to go after big business with his famed Big Stick. Finally, TR was pursuing his ideal of an American empire. Coly wanted the du Ponts in for a cut of the markets American troops would open up should they invade other nations: look what had happened since the government decided to buy only Du Pont blasting powder and dynamite to dig the Panama Canal.

Henry had come up with a reason of his own to impress President Roosevelt with the family's support of his reelection. With Coleman swallowing powder and dynamite companies whole, it would be best if the government did not look too closely at his methods. Henry walked Coleman to his carriage. He had decided, he told his cousin, to contribute heavily to the seventy thousand dollars Coly wished to place in the hands of Roosevelt's campaign chairman. Coleman's eyes twinkled from above his long nose and trim mustache: he was pleased that Colonel

Henry A. had the best interests of Eleutherian Mills—and the nation, of course—at heart.

Pierre swung his brother's lifeless body up into his arms, turned away from the sofa William K. had died upon, and walked toward the staircase that led to his brother's bedroom. The body was surprisingly light: Bill had always been a solid, robust man. Pierre choked back a sob and hurried past his brother's wife and three children. His tears would do them no good.

William K.'s battle against death had been swift; the doctors had diagnosed his fever and weakness as typhus only two months earlier. Pierre had planned to bring Bill into the powder business, as he had two other brothers, Irénée and Lammot. Now William K. would go instead to Sand Hole Woods, to a grave beside Henry B., still another brother whose life had been claimed by illness. It would be difficult to give his brothers a piece of the Brandywine larger than a burial plot.

Pierre rested his brother's body gently on the bed, bent over to brush his light brown hair back from his forehead, and walked softly from the room. He had a duty to perform, the duty that came to him as head of his family. His mother, Mary, would be waiting at her home, St. Amour, for word of her ill son. Pierre must take her the news of William K.'s death. He lingered a moment at the bottom of the stairs to tell Ethel, Bill's wife, that he would make the funeral arrangements and return as soon as possible.

Pierre buttoned his overcoat, wound his muffler high around his neck, and stepped out into the December cold. It was a clear, crisply bright day; the streets near his brother's Wilmington house were covered with a blanket of fresh snow. The roads out of the city, along the Brandywine up to St. Amour, would be slick and the ride would take at least an hour. A flush of tears fell on his cheeks as he mounted his carriage; he had loved William K., as he did all his brothers and sisters. Now, with two of them gone, he must act as father to four nieces and nephews. He had done well for his family in the five years since his return to Wilmington. Three sisters had married men high in the Du Pont Company hierarchy, promising executives Pierre had groomed to lead the company alongside Irénée, Lammot, and himself. Their father would have been pleased with the way he had raised and advised all three children.

The slow ride and bracing wind would give him time to prepare for the ordeal with his mother. Mary would take William K.'s death well, better in some ways than he was. But Mary would show her emotions, as he could not, and her flood of tears would make him feel helpless. He had never learned to cope with the way women so easily displayed their feelings.

And the long ride would give him time to think about what he would do now with the powder company. Coleman had done his job as president well; Du Pont now owned at least three-quarters of the powder and explosives manufacturing capability of the United States. Every major, and most minor, powder and dynamite companies had either been bought up or at least bought into. Coly had an uncanny sense of how men might be swayed; he seemed inwardly to know where their truest instincts lay, no matter what they said. And—it was Coleman's finest achievement—Du Pont Company plants turned out virtually *all* the military smokeless powder in the nation. If the United States desired to arm its soldiers and ships, Washington would have to pay whatever price Pierre and his aides in the treasurer's office set.

But the days of acquiring companies were over, at least in the gunpowder field: there were simply no more to be had. Growth must be the key to a river of gold to replace the Brandywine's green current. There was a limit to the amount of gunpowder and dynamite a nation could consume. A time of decision had arrived: was it to be foreign expansion, as Coleman urged, or diversification into new products, as he thought best?

A fork in the road loomed ahead of Pierre's carriage. St. Amour lay to the right, up winding roads into the hills near the Brandywine. To the left was the large Pierce farm Pierre had visited many times in the last months. He had decided to buy the two hundred acres and build upon them a retreat from the rigors of his work. He had pictured in his mind the gardens he would set in on the Pierce land, the still pools and rushing brooks, the acres of flowers and bubbling fountains. Once, walking with an older relative near the first director's house, now an employee's club, he had been told of the magnificent gardens Eleuthère Irénée du Pont and his daughter Victorine had tended there. A love for the delicate yields of the soil must be in his blood, just as the overwhelming desire to make gunpowder infected him and his cousins. Perhaps the du Ponts' need to make things grow compensated for the destruction their explosives had brought to mankind. And perhaps those of his relatives who found no solace in the soil were driven to madness. Surely there must be some explanation for whatever it was that took hold of someone such as Alfred I. and made him do whatever was in his power to defame the du Pont name.

Pierre had Coleman to thank for his plan to build an estate. Coly might be reckless at times, but he had proven himself right when it came to the powder business. Pierre had long disapproved of Coleman's forays into politics: it might draw attention to the ever-increasing stranglehold he and his relatives had over the explosives industry. But Coleman's political instincts had proven as accurate as his business sense. President Roosevelt, hot on the tails of the largest industrial firms, was tackling Standard Oil and American Tobacco. Du Pont would be easily broken by TR's Big Stick if the President chose to apply it. Somehow, up to now, the du Ponts had been overlooked. Perhaps Coly's contributions to TR's reelection campaign had helped. Coleman had expected a cabinet appointment for one of his political cronies in return for the seventy thousand dollars he gave TR, but that had not come about: the Rough Rider could not afford to taint his administration's image as a hunter of big corporate game.

And when, a year earlier, Colonel Henry A. had been reelected to the U.S. Senate, the President had sent a letter of congratulations to the people of Delaware—after attacking the Colonel publicly only three years earlier. Roosevelt's congratulations had failed to silence the repercussions of Henry's election among the du Ponts. Pierre knew that certain relatives, and husbands of relatives, hated Coleman and himself. Willard Saulsbury, especially, seemed fond of calling the du Ponts "that god-damned tribe" in public. Saulsbury was married to a du Pont but owed little to the family; his father and uncle had been United States Senators. His family, in fact, had come to Delaware before the du Ponts. It was much better to marry du Pont women to poor, low-born company employees: the ultimate reward for faithfulness to the du Ponts.

Years earlier, he had seen a fight brewing when Will Saulsbury represented Mary du Pont in her divorce from the Colonel's brother, Willie, and then married her soon after the decree was handed down. Willie and Saulsbury did not speak to each other, had not for years. Mary was the sister of Coleman's wife, Elsie. Coly had supported the Colonel against Saulsbury's forces in the election, and now the two of them were not talking. Even Mary and Elsie rarely saw each other, and their meetings inevitably ended in fights. Such were the fruits of intermarriage.

If the family feuds had ended there they would be easy to bury, the warring du Ponts not difficult to reconcile. But now, after years of bickering with nearly all his relatives, Alfred I. had blown the lid off the family's tempers with his marital problems. Pierre glanced up from the road to the tall Brandywine trees, bare and stark in the winter cold. No one would guess they stood as silent sentinels over armed camps down the pretty winding lanes. Alfred: his cousin's very name was enough to set du Pont tongues wagging, bring red blotches to their fair cheeks, inflame their long noses. What had possessed his cousin to stomp out on Bessie, after she had agreed to return from Europe with the children to try once more to mend their tattered marriage? What had taken over his brain, what kind of madness was it? A divorce! Alfred had risked public scandal, and private ridicule, for a woman. And the feuding on the Brandywine was not over yet.

In three years following the cousins' takeover of Eleutherian Mills, Coleman du Pont purchased and merged sixty-four companies into Du Pont. Running the powder company, after he had eliminated all the competition in the United States, had become a dull chore, and he had turned to politics, and Colonel Henry A.'s Senate campaign, as a diversion, leaving to Pierre S. the daily overseeing of the powder company.

But, in 1906, Coleman decided to take Eleutherian Mills in hand once again. A new field for his talents had opened up. In 1897 the major powder manufacturers of the world had signed the Jamesburg Agreement, dividing up the earth into spheres of sales, guaranteeing to each other that a protected territory would not be invaded by a rival. The Jamesburg Agreement was about to expire, and Coleman wanted Mexico for the company, free of interference from anyone on the other side of the Atlantic. And he wanted an end to the tight-lipped attitude of his British and German counterparts when it came to new technical developments; there was to be a free flow of information among the giants of the industry.

Pierre could not be trusted with the delicate negotiations. He was a wizard with figures and stock manipulations, but he had never showed the ruthlessness needed to wrest concessions from the European powdermakers. Colemen decided that, if the Europeans balked, Du Pont would simply battle for whatever markets there were—anywhere in the world.

Pierre had no taste for Coleman's methods. He had objected when Coly decided to raise the price of smokeless military powder to the government. What could Washington do? Build massive new powder plants of its own? Teddy Roosevelt's policy had been to regulate big business, not compete with it. So what if the United States paid seventy-two cents a pound for powder that cost only thirty-two to make? Coleman had Roosevelt just where he wanted him: unable to attack Du Pont without offering alternatives that made him look just like the European despots he professed to hate. The world trade in gunpowder could not be left to someone with Pierre's lack of toughness.

Coleman wished that all his problems were with the government and foreign powder companies. He had become embroiled in the stupid feuding over Henry A.'s Senate seat and Will Saulsbury's political ambitions. Elsie had obeyed his wishes, ignoring her sister, Saulsbury's wife, when she could. But that was no answer: the family had become polarized by the fight. Some du Ponts who owned large blocs of stock—Willie especially—had professed their hatred for Henry A. and were applying pressure on Coleman to clean up the mess.

Now Alfred I. was going to rip the family apart. If Alfred's divorce plans—he had finally decided to end his marriage to Bessie—reached the press, as they were sure to, attention would be drawn to the family just when Coleman needed it least: in the midst of his negotiations with European powdermakers. Al had told Coly about the divorce, and Coleman had given his cousin a plausible excuse to journey all the way to South Dakota. But the newspapers would be satisfied for only so long: how much time could a man spend looking for new plant sites? Certainly not the six months Alfred needed to get a divorce.

The gunshot wound seemed to have taken away part of Alfred's brain. Coly was sorry that Alfred had lost his eye, a pity to be sure, but no excuse for the foolishness which had followed: firing men on the spot, rehiring them the next moment, walking about the powder yards in knickers, shouting orders here, there, everywhere, orders that made no sense. Coleman had heard that one of the foremen had refused to do anything Alfred commanded unless it came to him in writing.

Coleman had urged Alfred to go to Florida for a rest and he had, but it did little except aggravate his insanity. Still, had he been Pierre, Coly would never have taken Bessie's side in the affair, offering to serve as trustee over the funds Al had given her as a property settlement. He understood Pierre's motives; taking Bessie under his wing had put a quick stop to any rantings among family members over Al's leaving out in the cold, with only a few hundred thousand dollars to support herself on, a woman who had faithfully been his wife and brought him healthy, bright children, while he played around. But Al was so damned unpredictable; it was impossible to tell what he might do next. He was even capable of supporting that fool Robert Waddell, who was making public charges about the stranglehold Coleman's company had on the gunpowder business.

Bob Waddell's campaign against the du Ponts was incredible: the man had charged the company, publicly, with breaking the Sherman Anti-Trust Law. Coly wished now that he had never taken Waddell from his job as a salesman in the Midwest and made him head of all the company's agents. He had lasted less than a year in the job, anyway, leaving in a huff over what he called Coleman's underhanded tactics. Waddell had started his own powder company, Buckeye, in Indiana, and had done well. Now he was screaming about unfair competition and presenting Congress with correspondence he had pirated from the Du Pont Company files years earlier. Proof, he said, that Du Pont was a monopoly in violation of federal laws.

Pierre was more alarmed at Waddell's charges than Coleman was. Coly had tried to calm his cousin; they had Washington in their pocket, with Henry A. on Capitol Hill overseeing the Senate committee that made appropriations to the War Department. Still, Pierre worried. Coleman admired his cousin's cool exterior a good deal and had always thought it extended far inside him. Never had he heard Pierre utter an impolite word, fail to be obsequiously considerate of others' feelings, or lose his temper—in public or private. Why, then, was he so worked up over the Waddell situation?

Nothing seemed to soothe Pierre, not even Coleman's statement that he had the future well in hand, since Big Bill Taft had become Roosevelt's heir apparent. He and Taft were longtime friends; Coly had done much for him as chairman of the Republican National Committee's Speaker's Bureau. And Colonel Henry A. and Big Bill were tight, too; they dined together often and even traveled the country together for the party. No, the du Ponts had nothing to fear if Taft became President. Perhaps Pierre fretted over the notice they had received that the attorney general's office was considering filing suit against Du Pont under the antitrust statutes.

With Taft in the White House, Coly believed he might be able to make the suit disappear, just the way Alfred had made George Maddox, Alicia's husband, become invisible. He wondered if there was any truth to the rumor that Maddox had embarked for Europe, permanently, with a million of Al's dollars in his pocket, the price for never again setting foot in the United States—and for dropping the lawsuit, charging alienation of affection, he had brought against Al.

Alfred must really have loved Alicia, enough to pay off the husband he had bought for her in the first place. Al certainly had found strange uses for the money that had come his way after the cousins took over Eleutherian Mills. He would have been far better off following the Colonel's lead; at least his millions had carried him into the Senate and bought him Wilmington's largest newspaper, the *Evening Journal*, to use in his political wars.

Power was something worth fighting for, Coleman believed; women were not. One could either stay away from them, as Pierre had, or use them lightly and get rid of them, as he himself had learned to do. But never, ever, did a man need to surrender his power over something like the powder company, as Alfred had, just for the affections of some little thing such as Alicia.

Still, Alfred's aberrations might be useful to him. Coleman wanted a larger share of the powder company now, what with the chance to go international. Pierre he needed; Al he did not. And if his deaf cousin persisted in igniting the family's passions, he might very well be able to force him right off the Brandywine.

Alicia closed the heavy oak door to Judge Sadler's chambers softly behind her. Finally she was free! Alfred had been correct: the judge, after hearing how George had abandoned her and fled to Europe, had granted the divorce at once. Now she could stop hiding behind the curtains of an empty mansion in Carlisle, Pennsylvania, and return to the Brandywine to claim Alfred. She hoped they would be married at once: Al had promised her that, and he had never broken his word.

Mrs. Mary Alicia Heyward Bradford Maddox du Pont. She would drop the Maddox, at least, from her new name. Alicia du Pont sounded fine enough all by itself; no du Pont had ever been given the name Alicia. As if she needed something as superficial as a name to separate her from the du Ponts.

Alicia strolled back to the house she had occupied for the last six months. She had learned the agonies of loneliness Alfred had described in his letters from South Dakota while he awaited his divorce decree. The waiting had become interminable. But now she felt curiously at ease, almost unwilling to let the moment of freedom go. She had packed the night before, in a rush to prepare to leave Carlisle, certain that the judge would look kindly upon the tearful story of a fellow jurist's daughter. What would Judge Sadler have done had he known how deeply she hated her father? Since her earliest childhood Alicia had sensed her father's disappointment that she had not been born a boy; ridicule for typically girlish behavior had been his way of communicating it. She could not remember ever earning his approval. And she had tried desperately to fulfill Judge Bradford's expectations. But she had grown into a strikingly beautiful woman, a fact she had loathed for years. She had decided to become the equal of any man, simply to now and then earn a grudging smile from the Judge. Now other women hated her for both her looks and brains, and most men feared her sharp tongue.

Bed, board, and name: was that why she loved Alfred so? For his name, his wealth, his—touch? Or was it his own quick wit, his own intemperate tongue? No, there was more; when, a few months earlier, she had lost a child, a baby that emerged from her womb already dead, she had needed Alfred for his depth, his compassion, his understanding. Without his support, she knew, she might very well have gone insane. He was inventive, imaginative, spirited, so unlike the dolt she had been married to. Good riddance to George!

Alicia caught sight of her reflection in a shop window. Her pregnancies had not cost her much. She would give Alfred many years of happiness and, finally, children they could raise as their own. What plans they had made!

Hour upon hour they had sat beneath the five poplars at Rock Farms, where Al had moved after Bessie forced herself back into Swamp Hall with the children. They had dreamed and built of clouds the home they would erect, a mansion for all the du Ponts to envy, with tall pillars of stone and dozens of windows and rooms rich with warm woods and exquisite carpets. Alfred had lived for long enough amid the sparse furnishings—both physically and emotionally—of Swamp Hall. His divorce complaint against Bessie had charged "barbarous and inhuman punishment." Bessie could have the Swamp, as Al called it; they would build a new home to go with their new life.

How soon would word of her divorce reach the Brandywine? Not soon enough. The du Pont women had disliked Alfred for years; now they had an excuse to hate him. Often Al had sat with her late into the night, talking of his childhood, his father Irénée, his struggle to keep his brothers and sisters together after Irénée's death, his mother's mental illness and tragic end. His words had never carried condemnation of the du Pont family, but Alicia sensed his pain at their coldness toward him.

Twice he had rescued the company, the first time during the Spanish-American War, then when the old men wanted to sell out after Eugene du Pont's death. During the war Alfred's running of the powder yards had made du Pont a hallowed name in Washington; without them, Roosevelt would never have charged San Juan Hill. But to the du Ponts a hero was someone like their relative who had been an admiral in the Civil War—Samuel Francis—someone who had been disgraced for refusing to obey the orders of the President of the United States. To defy a President, in the family's view, merely showed how right and powerful a du Pont could be; to defy the family, as Alfred had done, was blasphemy. Alicia had marveled that her father, a federal judge, could have married into a family that considered its name and heritage law enough for any man, woman, or child to live under.

What had made the du Ponts that way? Alfred was so unlike them, not a haughty man such as Coleman or aloof like Pierre, whose head seemed forever filled with thoughts that filtered down from some corporate Olympus only he occupied. They were men who spent their days dreaming of empire, of riches beyond what had ever been spread among other mortals. Often, Alicia had found herself hating them as much as they detested her. Now that she and Alfred were finally to be married, few words of good cheer would pass between herself and the rest of the du Ponts. She would ask Alfred to build them a mansion greater than any ever imagined on the Brandywine, with a high tower to hold a giant, pealing bell that could be seen and heard the length and breadth of the du Pont family lands, and sounded like laughter. She would have it rung each day at sunrise and dusk, whether she and Alfred were at home or not. It would be her final answer to the women of the Brandywine.

Alfred and Alicia called the home they built Nemours. The new mansion was lonely, its seventy-seven rooms used more by servants than du Ponts. Alicia's brother, Edward Junior, came often; few others did. Al had decided to build a nine-foot-high wall around his land. When it was finished he sealed his fate with the family by topping the wall with broken glass and announcing publicly that he had done so to prevent anyone of the name du Pont from sneaking a look at his happy new life. The du Ponts had driven his mother insane; they would not bother Alicia with casual visits and caustic words. Nemours's two giant gates, one from Wimbledon Manor, the other from the palace of Catherine the Great, would forever remain locked to his relatives.

After he moved into Nemours, Alfred ordered workmen from Eleutherian Mills to tear down Swamp Hall, until nothing remained of his life with Bessie. He had loved Swamp Hall, once even vowed never to leave it, but Bessie had turned all that sour: he seemed able to recall only the bad times. When the last timber of his childhood home was demolished, Alfred drove to where the porch of the house had been. He could recall himself and his brothers and sisters standing there, weapons in their hands, ready to defend their home against the family's decision that they be split up among various relatives. He could still hear his father's weak voice in his ear just before he died, telling him that the company and family would need him someday. And he could remember, as clearly as though it had happened that very day, the screams from his mother's lips when she saw the scars and welts crossing her children's backs, souvenirs of the beatings a servant had given them while their mother traveled Europe to regain her health.

From where the rear wall of Swamp Hall had stood Alfred could see groups of powdermen walking down Long Row, their workday over, headed for the two taverns a half-mile downstream. He had walked Long Row with them for years, in the old days when he worked as superintendent of the Lower Yard. Now he was confined to the new office building in Wilmington. He had hung up for good the powderman's overalls and wooden-pegged boots he had worn for twenty years. Still, more often than he needed to for business reasons, he went down into the mills, taking the time to slip into the workers' jargon, extending his visits until shifts changed and he could join the men for a drink.

Alfred hoped that destroying Swamp Hall would end the feuding on the Brandywine; he wanted only to live quietly and happily with Alicia at Nemours and to continue his work in the company. But his cousin Coleman had other ideas. Coly had told Alfred to sell out only two weeks after he married Alicia. Alfred had admired Coly since their college days, even picking him to go in on the purchase of the powder company a decade earlier. He had trusted Coly as well, even when he and Pierre made decisions without consulting him. Alfred did not share Coleman's love for politics; when Coly came to him collecting campaign contributions for William Taft he had gone along simply because his cousin's methods with politicians seemed to work. Taft had refused the twenty thousand dollars Coleman offered but remembered the gesture, appointing a former Du Pont Company lawyer, George Wickersham, as his attorney general. Even so, Coly's open pocketbook had backfired this time; Taft and his new attorney general had continued the prosecution of the company on antitrust grounds. Alfred knew the company was guilty as charged: his bank accounts clearly showed the results of Coleman's buying up of the entire powder and explosives industry. Coly had tried to lay the blame at his and Pierre's feet, taking sick—his gall bladder this time—as soon as the government called him in to testify. He had dumped the defense in Pierre's lap, and Alfred had decided to do the same, petitioning the government to separate his case from that of the others. Alfred claimed in court that he had never been in on the workings of either the Powder Trust or Coleman's takeover of the industry. The judges had accepted his word, severed his case from the one against the company, and found him innocent of wrongdoing. The implications of his testimony were that if he was not guilty, then the company, and Pierre, were. It was a lesson to his silent cousin that taking Bessie's side against him could be dangerous.

And Alfred had seen that Pierre was slowly ousting even Coleman from the center of power, first by bringing his brothers into the Wilmington offices, then appropriating the president's chair—temporarily, Pierre had claimed. His cousin had already served nearly three years as "temporary" president of Du Pont.

How ridiculous it had all become: lawsuits, countersuits, scandalous newspaper articles reporting that virtually every du Pont hated every other du Pont. "The War of Women," one Philadelphia daily had even dared call it—as though women ruled the Brandywine. Alfred was thankful that Alicia had a cooler head then he, that she was able to convince him that dragging the family's injured pride into open court would serve only to inflame the du Pont tempers even more.

After two years of fighting Alicia had wanted a truce. He had gone along—to a point. He had started two lawsuits against female relatives, planning to charge them with defamation of character, with slander, with whatever would stop their needling and whispering about Alicia and him. Alicia had firmly stood in his way—he had not understood why, at first—and he dropped the suits before filing bills of particulars. But he would never speak to anyone in his family again unless business made it necessary, and the gates to Nemours would remain forever locked to them. He had noticed the power the newspapers carried, and he had been impressed. Colonel Henry A. owned one of Wilmington's two large papers. He had decided to buy the other, through a third party. For a bit more than one hundred thousand dollars the Wilmington *Morning News* had become his. He did not intend to carry the family feud to its pages, but he believed the truce that had been called would not last. When the fighting began anew he wanted his own headlines, not in Philadelphia, but in Wilmington, where all his relatives would see them.

Alfred had decided to tear down the Swamp not just to insult Bessie, but to have the last word with his family. He wished he could have been present when Bessie opened Swamp Hall's front door to find a sheriff's deputy waiting with an eviction notice. Alfred believed he had been fair in raising Bessie's allowance by enough money to rent a fine house in Wilmington. As long as he controlled the houses on the Brandywine she would never live in one: if he must dwell away from the Creek, so must she. While they were married the du Ponts had shown no special liking for Bessie. Now they flocked to her side. He had had no choice but to throw her, and his children, out of Swamp Hall and tear it down. The people on the Brandywine must know that Alfred Irénée du Pont would not be pushed around.

Over the last five years he had become more and more disenchanted with the workings of the powder company. He did not need the money from his salary—dividends on his stock alone came to more than a half-million dollars a year—and he did not like what had become of the old powder firm. Where once the owners sat in council to decide major matters, now a number of committees looked after everything and reported to Pierre—and to Pierre alone. True, Alfred still sat on the vital finance committee and voiced his opinion when large sums of money were concerned, but most business matters never even reached his attention. And Pierre had grown covetous of important positions within the firm's management, awarding them to his brothers or the husbands of his sisters. His quiet cousin had even fought with Coleman over a place on the board of directors for Willie, who owned nearly as much stock as Pierre himself did. Pierre had disliked Willie since his divorce and wanted one of his own brothers-in-law appointed instead. Coleman, for no apparent reason but a rare display of sentiment, pushed for Willie's appointment and won. The two cousins had split—for the first time in

Alfred's memory—over a rather minor issue: membership on the board of directors implied no real power in the company. Alfred believed that Pierre had used the issue as a stage for displaying his power, even over Coleman; Pierre's pettiness seemed to increase with each step he took toward total control over Eleutherian Mills.

# *25*

I N JUNE, 1911, the federal district court in Delaware, after four years
of litigation, found the Du Pont Company guilty of holding a monopoly over the gunpowder industry in the United States and ordered that it
be dissolved. However, in the years since the three cousins took control
of the company so many small firms had been bought and absorbed that
to restore them would have been impossible. And so the court ordered
the owners of Du Pont, along with the government prosecutors, to work
out a formula to split the company into competitive units.

Coleman du Pont refused to accept the court's guilty verdict. He
threw the full weight of his political influence toward the White House,
where President William Howard Taft sat as the heir to Theodore
Roosevelt. Coleman became irrational, demanding that Taft overrule the
court, unable to accept that the President could not. Soon Taft, whom
Coly had helped elect, barred the powder company president from his
presence and refused to communicate with him.

Pierre, with a cooler head, prepared to split the company into three
separate corporations that, although they would give the impression of
being in competition, would all still be controlled by the du Pont family. Pierre was resigned to accepting the court's verdict and cooperating,
except in one area. He wanted the single most important portion of the
Du Pont Company's business, the manufacture of smokeless powder, to
remain under one corporate roof: in the event of war, the monopoly
over smokeless powder production would prove far more valuable than
all other manufacturing combined. Although President Taft could not
reverse the court's ruling, he might very well influence the disposition
of the smokeless powder issue. Pierre dispatched Alfred to see Taft at
the White House.

The President received Alfred in his office, his three-hundred-pound
bulk stuffed into a wide armchair. After a few minutes of discussion a
blotchy red flush rose to his cheeks. He lowered his voice nearly to a
whisper and demanded to know if the visitor to the White House was
indeed threatening the government of the United States.

Alfred turned the brim of his silk top hat through his fingers. He had meant no threat, he said. But he must make clear to the President that, should the court decree against Du Pont be carried out, he and his family would simply stop making gunpowder and explosives. He did not, as Coleman had, contest the company's guilt. But the President had threatened to throw Du Pont into receivership; to do so would seal the fate of both the du Ponts and the United States' ability to wage war—or defend the peace. America would find it difficult, if not impossible, to continue its policy of armed intervention in the Caribbean and South America with no gunpowder to propel bullets or fire cannon.

The President slumped back in his chair. He liked Alfred du Pont—more, at least, than he liked his cousins Coleman and Pierre. Taft considered Coleman a slippery, sly political operator, capable of any deed, no matter how underhanded, to get his way. He had refused to discuss the court's guilty verdict with him, even though his own brother, Charles, was one of Coleman du Pont's partners in a number of New York real estate ventures. Pierre was an unknown quantity, a sober, silent man who seemed to fade into the woodwork, but whose brain was behind Du Pont. He had agreed to see Alfred du Pont because he knew of no political ambitions in the man and because the Du Pont situation had reached crisis proportions: the nation's newspapers were calling for just punishment against the company and family. At least, he could be reasonably certain that whatever Alfred said would reflect the realities of the problem, not political interests.

And Taft knew how badly the government needed the du Ponts' cooperation. He had read the transcripts of the trial; it had not surprised him that the Du Pont Company held a monopoly on the manufacture of smokeless powder for military use. He had come into office determined to carry through the program of legal attacks Teddy Roosevelt had started against the major corporations that dominated big business. He had succeeded, to a point, against Standard Oil and American Tobacco. Du Pont was different: to inflict his will on the family that owned the company might leave the United States unable to continue shaking the Big Stick Roosevelt had also willed him. Granted, Taft's motives in pressing the courts for convictions against the oil and steel companies had been political: they had been let off with a mere slap on the wrist. But the convictions had the desired effect: the people believed he supported them against big business. But reality was far different: the nation needed big business for its economic health and growth. Standard Oil and American Tobacco had accepted the ruse; only Coleman du

Pont dared flaunt his company's importance, refusing to accept the court's verdict.

Taft had even been lenient with Du Pont, instructing the court to allow the company to work out its own dissolution along with the government prosecutors, as long as it met the approval of the judges. But Coleman du Pont refused to see broken up what he had spent a decade building. Taft had been hard pressed to believe Coleman's rantings about "My Baby," the Du Pont Company. Was it madness or an attack of acute ego? Either way, the du Ponts could not have asked for more congenial terms. They would not have to give away their fortunes, merely split them up to give at least the appearance of competition in the explosives industry. It must be madness: what did it matter whether the du Ponts kept the manufacture of smokeless powder under their name, or under another, as long as they reaped the profits?

At least Alfred du Pont seemed more reasonable than Coleman. Coleman actually believed the President could reverse a court's decree. The President had heard that the du Ponts were strange people, affected by decades of living too close to each other, of intermarrying until a man had the same people on both sides of his family. Coly's midnight calls to the White House and Attorney General Wickersham had become more than annoying; if Alfred offered no way out of the dilemma he would throw the full weight of his office at the du Ponts. Then they would see which was stronger: their laws or the law of the land.

Taft turned his attention back to Alfred du Pont. The powdermaker had been chatting with the other men in his office, Wickersham and his chief assistant, Bill Glasgow. He moved his black hearing box back around to face the President. Alfred said he would arrange for the top men in the army and navy to appear before the judges, to testify that it was vital to the security of the United States that the Du Pont Company be allowed to continue its monopoly over smokeless powder. That should blunt any public criticism. If the President would see to it that the court agreed with the du Ponts' viewpoint—by appearing in open court himself to voice his own agreement with the generals and admirals —Alfred would bring Coleman and Pierre into line, and the matter would end there. The remainder of the Du Pont Company would be split into three firms, separate in management, but of course owned by the du Pont family. There was no way, Alfred concluded, to rebuild the nearly one hundred companies Coly and Pierre had absorbed and then dissolved over the years.

Taft agreed quickly; an end to the publicity over the case had to come soon, or he might lose the presidential election in 1912. He knew that TR planned to run again, and the Rough Rider would just love to have an issue like Taft's inability to handle the big corporations to take to the campaign stump. Alfred's plan to have military men testify in public would soothe any public anger over the du Ponts getting off so easily: no citizen could tamper with the cry of national security. Wickersham had told him about the possibility of splitting Du Pont into three companies, one called Hercules, the second Atlas, the third Du Pont. If men not of the du Pont name were appointed to run the two new firms the public would never know who really controlled or owned them. Taft told Alfred he would travel to Philadelphia to appear on the du Ponts' behalf. He had but one condition: keep Coleman du Pont away from him, completely, and end his midnight calls.

Alfred smiled. He would do that, of course. Coleman was terribly busy in New York, when he was not on his new Maryland estate hunting or sailing or fishing. Alfred stood, straightened his black morning coat, wrapped the wire of the hearing device around its box, and shook hands with Taft and Wickersham.

Outside the White House Alfred allowed himself a broad grin and gales of laughter. Big Bill Taft was as advertised: all bluff. He was lazy and timid and easy to persuade. Perhaps that was why the President had refused to see Coly; his cousin was obviously too strong for Taft to contend with. Or for he himself to contend with, Alfred reflected.

Barely six months earlier Coleman and Pierre had plotted to oust him from the operations of the company. They had kicked him upstairs to a vice-presidency and taken away his precious black powder department, giving it to one of Pierre's in-laws. Pierre insisted he had done it in the name of efficiency. The black powder division had to be consolidated with other operating departments. Over the last ten years black powder sales had grown only a bit, while dynamite sales were up over three hundred percent. Pierre had told him, frankly, that he was a powderman, not an administrator. As vice-president he could roam the nation freely, looking into matters that had long gone unattended. It was a question of efficiency—and profit.

Alfred had become angry with Pierre. For years both he and Coleman had ignored Alicia's very existence. When Alicia gave birth to a daughter who lived only a few days, neither of his cousins had so much as offered condolences. He and Alicia decided to bury the child, named Eleuthera Paulina, beneath one of Nemours's old poplars. The rest of the family could have Sand Hole Woods to themselves.

And as if that had not been enough, Coly and Pierre were making important financial decisions without even consulting him. First came the nitrate plant in Chile. Pierre had wanted to stay away from foreign investment, but Coly forced him to recognize that the company needed a reliable source of nitrates or it might not be able to meet its orders. Pierre had set up Oficina Delaware, not far from the Chilean port of Taltal, after years of negotiations. Alfred learned of it only after reading a company report.

Then had begun the business of buying companies that had little to do with the manufacture of explosives. Pierre had explained away the purchase of the Fabrikoid Company, which made artificial leather, by saying that the company needed an outlet for its excess refined nitrate production. He even admitted to Alfred that the negotiations to buy Fabrikoid had gone on for five months before he was told of them—and then only in a slip of the tongue by one of Pierre's underlings.

And smaller, more personal disagreements had begun to sprout among the three of them, between Alfred and Coly, really, since Pierre never actually fought. When Alfred had shown an interest in buying some land along the Brandywine Coleman immediately entered a higher bid. Then, when Alfred's daughter Madie and Alicia quarreled, Coleman and Elsie had given the girl money for a trip to Europe. Coleman knew that Alfred wanted Madeleine to stay away from Europe, where she had fled soon after he and Alicia married, eloping with the son of a woolen cloth manufacturer in Wilmington. The marriage had ended in disaster; Madie's husband had charged her with adultery, naming a young German as her lover. The family had hushed the matter up, after Alicia threatened to reveal publicly all she knew about the du Ponts' strange ways, and Madie came home. Now she had returned to her German lover, with Coly's money in her pocketbook.

Pierre's reorganization had not been meant to give Alfred a larger say in company affairs: soon after he emptied his desk in the powder department, every man he had brought into his area of the business had been fired by Pierre. Alfred could not quarrel with Pierre's pleas for efficiency; his cousin had proven himself right in money matters, hiking the company's sales to over thirty-six million dollars in 1912, half again what the entire firm had been worth only ten years earlier. But, he believed, profit was not a worthy motive for shoving him out of the mainstream of the family business.

Alfred hailed a passing hansom and directed the driver to take him to Union Station. He would catch the very next train for Wilmington. He relished turning up in Pierre's office that afternoon with news of how well the conversation with President Taft had gone. Pierre would have no choice but to bring him back into the inner sanctum of company power. He, and he alone, now held the key to keeping intact the power and wealth Pierre had struggled for ten years to build. And he had waited long enough to throw his cousin's insults to Alicia back in his face. But he had no intention of starting even the slightest argument with Pierre or Coleman. He would strike back at them in the way they understood most: by taking control of the Du Pont Company out of their hands.

Coleman du Pont held his throbbing head between both hands. It must be noon, he thought. When had the party ended? It did not matter. He pushed himself up from the bed in his suite, switched on a light, and looked about the room.

Coleman saw a flimsy woman's negligee draped across a chair. He heard a knock at the door, a bellhop wondering if he could do anything for Mister du Pont. Coly thought a minute, then gave the man the empty negligee and told him to have it filled. He closed the door laughing.

Coleman stretched his arms, pulled the shades on his bedroom windows up, and headed for the bath. He enjoyed looking down upon New York. The view—and money—had been his reasons for joining Charles Taft in building the McAlpin Hotel. Since his gall bladder operation the powder company had appealed to him less and less. He was tiring of Wilmington: not enough to do there, and certainly no new fields of business to conquer. The Du Pont Company had reached the limit of its growth. Even Pierre's crafty figuring could take it no farther. And he was tiring of his wife. She seemed happy enough on their new country estate in Maryland. The New York society columnists had noticed that Mrs. du Pont was never seen at the McAlpin. Elsie was a good woman, and mother, but she would certainly cramp Coleman's style in New York City.

Coleman trimmed his neat mustache in front of the bathroom mirror: not a bad face for a man of fifty. And certainly not bad for a man who had been through what he had with his stomach. The telephone near his bed rang: Pierre, from Wilmington. Alfred had met with Taft, Pierre said, and worked out an answer to the antitrust problem. Coleman should know that the government would not set aside the conviction but that the results of the verdict would be nearly painless. Coleman listened to the terms Alfred had reached with Taft and agreed to them quickly. Pierre said they would have to let Al back on the finance committee now and listen to him occasionally. The sacrifice was not large in return for keeping their monopoly on military powder. The cousins hung up.

Coleman had more than powder company affairs on his mind. Now that the suit would be decided in Du Pont's favor—whatever the judges said—he could go ahead with his plans for once again jumping into the public eye. His long recuperation from a gall bladder operation had given him time to think about the future. The Republican party's bosses believed he wanted to push Colonel Henry A. du Pont into the White House. They must be persuaded that he had no such intention. He would hold a news conference to announce his latest philanthropy to the people of the State of Delaware. The McAlpin stood very high above the streets of New York, he would tell the reporters, and his new Equitable Building, when it was completed, would be even taller—forty stories to the top. But they were not large enough to suit T. Coleman du Pont. And so he had decided to build a monument one hundred miles high and lay it down on the ground for all to see.

Delaware needed a good road to link Wilmington with Maryland to the south. He intended to build the straightest, finest highway in the United States and donate it to Delaware. It just happened that the state was—more or less—one hundred miles long. He supposed the citizens would insist that he call it the T. Coleman du Pont Highway.

The road would serve notice on all the political bosses in Delaware that he had not made Henry A. a U.S. Senator out of the kindness of his du Pont heart; they could expect him to ask for a return on his outlay of political savvy and hard cash. In fact, the Colonel had just been re-elected to the Senate, thanks to the Republican machine Coleman had put together after the Addicks debacle.

Coleman believed Henry A. was on his last political legs. He had soiled his good name during the antitrust suit, through no real fault of his own. Ever since 1906, Robert Waddell had been charging that Colonel Henry was the brains behind the Powder Trust. Coleman knew differently: a strong arm, maybe, but never the brains—of anything. And Waddell's complaint that Henry A. had also been the man behind the consolidation of the powder industry could not be farther from the truth; it was, in fact, a backhanded insult to Coleman's own hard work.

Bob Waddell's public attack on the Colonel had dredged up the old business about his having kept Delaware from proper representation in the Senate for three years. Old Henry A.—over seventy now—could never survive another election. Coly's own loyal followers among the Delaware Republicans would turn to him as their new leader. He himself had not been tarnished by the antitrust suit; a bad gall bladder could be a decided political asset.

Even the workingmen of Delaware liked him. He had pushed, years earlier, for the passage of the eight-hour wage bill that had come before Congress. It had appealed to him as a way to diffuse the power of the labor unions. Al had been against him; his cousin said it should not be up to the workers how long they toiled each day, but the prerogative of the owners. As usual, Alfred had been shortsighted, not seeing that to give in on the issue would avoid a good deal of strife when union organizers brought their propaganda—Red propaganda, Coleman believed— to the Brandywine and other Du Pont plants. The bill had failed to clear Congress, but the working men and women of Delaware still considered T. C. du Pont their friend.

All the new construction Coleman backed was putting his face on the front pages of newspapers across the country. He was, the press had decided, a man who believed in the future of America and put his large fortune behind that belief. With the antitrust suit out of the way he could have Colonel Henry A.'s Senate seat any time he wanted it. But he might have more than that, much more. He had nearly decided to give up the presidency of the Du Pont Company for good, to clear out of Wilmington except for the house he kept there to insure legal residence. Pierre wanted to rule the company himself, and the entire explosives industry with it. If his business affairs kept on soaring upward—just as the Equitable Building would—and his reputation continued to spread, the people of the United States might just want T. Coleman du Pont to fill quite another kind of president's chair.

Pierre S. du Pont dined alone on the day of his mother's funeral in June, 1913. Rarely did he find enjoyment in the company of others at meals; his mother's death did not change that. Since moving into Long- wood, Pierre had made order out of his life, order and quiet among the gardens he had designed. The acres around his house reflected his love for system, extended even to nature. Formal gardens radiated from the house, with bushes pruned into stark shapes, sharp paths cut across the lawns, arches of vines trimmed into half-circle perfection.

Pierre relished the silence of his dining room. The crowd of du Ponts at the cemetery had bothered him. Never during his mother's lifetime had the family paid her homage. Had they attended the funeral because of his position in the company? Very likely. He would never have accused them of it aloud, but he felt the words circle in the air above Sand Hole Woods like some pagan chant: *the Jewess is dead, the Jewess is dead.* Mary Belin du Pont had been a blot on the family name since his father married her; Pierre knew it bit deeply into the pride of many du Ponts that her sons were coming into complete control of the Du Pont Company. It was all so foolish! Mary Belin du Pont had never followed the Jewish faith; neither had Pierre or any of his brothers and sisters. Now that his mother was gone, he hoped the sentiment against her would be buried, too—for the good of all the du Ponts.

Had he gone out of his way to keep Jews from joining the company? Perhaps. Certainly many talented Jewish executives were available who could have added much to the running of the Du Pont Company. But he had found it convenient to hire others, men who, should they become vital to the company's health, would be acceptable as du Pont in-laws. He had used marriage into the family as the final link—and reward—for his best employees. And he even liked the four men, all company executives, who had married his sisters.

Pierre felt the loneliness of his large dining room close in about him. He wished, at times, that he could enjoy the company of others more—but certainly not tonight. He had wanted his mother to be the mistress of Longwood, swirling through its long halls, listening to the huge organ that played every afternoon in the conservatory. But Mary du Pont had been content to live in St. Amour; she enjoyed being near her in-laws even if they found her company less than desirable. Pierre did not mind tending to the details of running a home; he rather relished the long hours he spent in the wine cellar. And, of course, the gardens would always be under his personal eye. He had heard that Alfred's home was grander than his own, and that he had done wonders with the grounds. What was Nemours like? Al had never invited him to visit it, and he had no interest in seeing Alicia. But the gardens made him curious. He could not imagine either Alfred or Alicia having the delicacy of taste it took to lay in magnificent grounds.

Why, suddenly, did Longwood feel so empty? Perhaps he carried Mary's presence with him more than he knew. For years, in the same way, the powder company had traveled with him, filling his head with constant plans and worries. He had needed Longwood to divert his attention. He was six miles from the Brandywine when he passed through Longwood's gates, yet he might as well have merely entered the old director's house; never was he able to leave his work behind. And, in the last analysis, the iron gates to Longwood had also failed to carry him away from the family feuds.

He had little appetite this night, but the servants expected him to finish the six-course meal he consumed each evening. Over the last few weeks family troubles had distracted him, especially the large fight he sensed in the making. Alfred had refused to drop the matter of the family's snub of Alicia. He still saw Alfred each day in the normal course of business and, on rare occasions when he descended from his office to the plush restaurants and lounges in the new wing of the Du Pont Building, even spoke with him pleasantly about matters other than work. But Pierre sensed a bitterness about Alfred, a distinct hatred of those du Ponts who had turned their backs on him. It had been most pronounced after Alicia lost a child and none of the family—including himself—paid their respects. He may have erred in supporting Bessie over the years, but he had done it to keep the family's tempers from boiling over. He could remember a time when he cared little for the sentiments and feelings of the Brandywine du Ponts, a time long ago, before he and Alfred and Coleman bought the powder company. Now he seemed to have become a pawn in the family's struggles with each other. And soon the feud would come to a head again.

Running the company and keeping the family quiet had become a burden. Pierre would gladly have given the president's office back to Coleman if only he could convince his cousin to return to Wilmington. He had been grooming his brothers to take over, but they were not yet ready. He felt older than his forty-five years, and what energy he had left over from work he wanted to devote to his gardens, not the problems of his relatives. It was time, too, for Longwood to have a true mistress. But who could he find to run a large estate, and to understand how he felt about the family?

Pierre smiled slightly. Who but a du Pont? He would very likely marry a relative in the end. They would not have children, of course: a few of his relatives had found out only too tragically what could happen when cousins bred, the deformities of mind that could result in off-spring. Yet others, notably Coleman, had normal children. Pure chance, a chance that did not fit in with his ideas on how life should be organized.

No woman on the Brandywine would refuse to marry Pierre and turn down a chance to rule her relatives. But could he find a du Pont female who had engendered no ill will among the hundreds of du Ponts? He would try. For more than a century the du Ponts had been breeding among themselves, bearing children who grew up, lived, worked, and died within miles of the powder mills. Only such a woman would know what it meant to lead the du Ponts; it was the best reason for marrying a relative.

And after he married he would quit the presidency of Du Pont. He had enough wealth to last his lifetime and no children to leave his fortune to. Something terrible was brewing in the world, something that mankind had never before seen. The cycle had come as it always came, boom and recession, and the buildup for war to bring the nation out of its economic doldrums. He had heard the legends of du Ponts, such as General Henry, who could feel in the wind of the Brandywine the tension brewing halfway around the earth. He had doubted the legend; now he felt the same emotion inside himself. Long ago he had forsaken powdermen's overalls for the stiff collar of management, yet the feeling came to him still. The jealous nations of Europe needed but an excuse to start a war. And the men in Washington were reacting with huge orders for powder and explosives, more than could be used except in time of war, never once balking at the high prices he charged.

But what if the old laws and cycles no longer held true? The world had changed since Pierre's boyhood. He could remember cringing in fear when his father ordered him to learn to ride a horse; now one of his relatives was contemplating going into the automobile business, to make a car called the Du Pont. And another fooled with aeroplanes. Pierre remembered the marvel he had felt when Alfred first lit Swamp Hall with electric light bulbs, and General Henry had vetoed electricity as a way to power the mill wheels in the powder yards. Now turbines whined in every du Pont family plant in the nation.

Pierre enjoyed being remote from these new things, able to leave them for the simpler world of Longwood, where he might be closer to the earth. Many of his relatives were like that. He had even heard of a du Pont who wrote poetry, bad poetry, but verse nonetheless, after he left the powder company offices each day. Their ancestor, his namesake, the first du Pont, had been something of a poet, too, and a bad one. And he had been an economist, as Pierre supposed he himself was today, preferring sheets covered with figures to the grueling work in the mills. The family had even feuded in its first years on the Brandywine, much as it did now, not speaking to each other, coveting each other's prestige or friendships with other du Ponts or control over the company. Little but years separated him from the first du Pont.

Pierre moved from the dining table to a comfortable armchair, a delicate cup of bone china, smoking with black coffee, in his hand. He had detected his servants' wonder at his calm exterior even on the day of his mother's funeral. Did they expect tears to flow down his cheeks? Sentiment, blustering, open sentiment, was Coleman's realm, not his. He liked both his brothers, Irénée and Lammot, for the cool exteriors they too displayed. Neither ever showed emotion; both would someday make good presidents for the Du Pont Company, once Coleman gave up the company for good.

Pierre had learned with great difficulty to cope with Coleman's attitudes toward the succession of leadership in the family. Coly insisted, even in correspondence, that the company was his infant. And he had refused to see some matters realistically, such as the antitrust suit. Pierre wanted Coleman either all the way in or all the way out of the business. He disliked having to deal with a large stockholder—as he had to do with Willie—who was often absent from the company offices. Coleman could run the company well if he chose to, a fact that had surprised Pierre in the past. But his cousin needed to build monuments to himself, and he would not leave New York until the Equitable Building was finished.

If he could convince Coly to return to Delaware perhaps the flood of gossip and scandal about his personal life would end. Alfred's continuous outrages against family tradition were bad enough, and Pierre had long since convinced himself to cease trying to stop them. But while Alfred isolated himself at Nemours, Coly led the press about like a fox fleeing good hounds, never letting the newspapers forget that he was the president of Du Pont, no matter how little time he spent in Wilmington. Pierre hated the press, and in public he would never deign to fight Coleman's outrageous claims about his running of the Du Pont Company. But it was he, not Coleman, who ran the company astutely, ever increasing profits, ever expanding into new fields. He wanted no glory for himself, but he wanted no one else to live off his hard work. If Coleman did not soon come back to the Brandywine to earn the acclaim he presented himself, Pierre decided, he might have to keep his cousin away from it permanently.

Alfred I. du Pont decided in February, 1913, that he no longer wanted the son Bessie had given him, Alfred Victor du Pont, to carry the name he himself bore. Only a special act of the Delaware legislature could legally change the child's name, so Alfred asked a Delaware senator to place before the lawmaking body a bill to have his son's name changed from Alfred Victor to Gardner Cazenove. Alfred assured the legislator that his former wife knew of and agreed to the change. It was a lie, of course; Alfred could not imagine Bessie agreeing with him about anything.

But Alfred believed that since he had named the boy, he could unname him if he wished. He had not seen his son in nearly ten years; Bessie had made certain of that, and he had never protested. All that really mattered was that Alfred Victor was no more of a son to him than the poplars outside Nemours. His only true offspring, a daughter by Alicia, lay dead under one of those trees, in a tiny grave. And he suspected that Alicia was pregnant again; he might very well wish to use the name for their next child. In the years since little Eleuthera Paulina had died he had thought much about his children by Bessie. What would they be like? Surely they would grow up hating their father; Bessie was not about to leave their minds untainted against him. And his good cousin Pierre would help that along, he was certain. Alfred's son carried a name sacred to him, his own name, the name of his grandfather. He wanted it back.

He had told the men in Dover as much as he cared to about his reasons; it should be sufficient that he believed the child might disgrace his name. What more could they ask? Edward Bradford, his brother-in-law, had promised to use his position as president pro temp of the state senate to push the bill through. Now, his brother-in-law had failed.

He had heard about the tactics Bessie's lawyers used before the committee, bringing her in to testify that she knew nothing about the name change, then, to assure defeat of the bill, reading a letter from the boy, or *supposedly* from the boy, wondering why his father wished to take his name away from him. When the legislature voted, the bill had been more than soundly defeated. He could not fault Edward; it had been a bad idea in the first place. But he could take no more of his family's ridicule, even if it was the same old campaign of silence. He had been humiliated even in the family business when Pierre relieved him of his responsibilities as a vice-president. Alfred believed it was the Spanish-American War all over again, with his relatives using his talents to win huge victories, then shutting him out of the business as soon as they could.

He and Alicia would go to Europe now and get the du Ponts out of their systems. He had a few matters to take care of first, in the basement of Nemours where he kept his collection of guns and toy cannon, and the small workshop where he designed ornate jewelry for Alicia. He wanted to finish drawing the new ring he had in mind for her and drop it off at the New York jewelers on their way to Europe. And he had to write out a check for the hospital in Maryland Alicia had visited and come away from horrified by the conditions of the maternity department. He had decided to give the hospital an entire new wing; work on it could be started immediately.

Perhaps Alicia would even go there when the time came to have another child. Alfred liked his wife's daughter, little Alicia, well enough, but he desperately wanted a son. Coleman's rule over the Brandywine was coming to an end; his cousin rarely even bothered to attend finance committee meetings. And Pierre, even though he and his brothers held the real power over the family company, had no children. What would Pierre's sophisticated ways with corporate finance matter in a few years, when he was too old to sit in the president's chair? Alfred believed that if he could father a son and bring him up in the tradition of the Brandywine, he would one day rule the company. The boy would be the fifth generation of his line to take charge of the powder mills of du Pont.

It was a pity that the Delaware legislature had turned down his attempt to change Alfred Victor's name, but Alfred I. would have to let the matter rest there. He could never reveal in public that he wanted the name back so that he might use it to anoint a new ruler for Eleutherian Mills.

# 26

EARLY in the summer of 1914, Alicia du Pont, her daughter, and her brother, Edward Bradford, departed from the United States to begin a European vacation Alfred I. had planned. Alfred remained on the Brandywine, intending to join his wife in France late in the summer. Alicia did not like leaving Alfred behind; the family quarrels had taken their toll on him, hardening the lines around his mouth into bitterness, driving him into a melancholy even Alicia had been unable to break. Her husband looked older than his fifty years. And Alicia was pregnant, with the second child she and Alfred had conceived.

Alicia and her daughter traveled to the south of France. She wired Alfred that they had found a pleasant patch of French countryside to spend their summer in; she would wait for him to join her there. Her brother had gone alone on an extended tour of France's wine country.

And then on June 28, 1914, Gavrilo Princip assassinated Archduke Franz Ferdinand at Sarajevo and gave Austria an excuse to begin World War I. Alicia, isolated among the simple peasants of rural France, heard little of what had happened in the world. No newspapers came to the inn she had made her summer home; at the tiny café where she dined each day she learned that the various allies of Austria and Belgium were declaring war. The people around her were farmers who understood only that, in the four days after August 1, Russia, France, and Great Britain had gone to war, and German troops had crashed into France. Alicia could hear the crackle of gunfire only a few miles away. What a prize she would make for the Kaiser: the wife of an owner of America's largest gunpowder and explosives company. Would they hold her hostage, demanding gunpowder and dynamite as the price for her life? She would be worth nothing to the Germans in ransom; the du Pont family would not trade one ounce of black powder for her safety.

Alfred, on the Brandywine, was frantic, pacing the great drawing room at Nemours, firing off telegrams that would never reach his wife. She had written daily of the delights of her trip, the beautiful countryside, the gentle people who had become her friends. She had told him how good the journey was for her, and how fine it would be for their new child. Alicia wondered if she should write again now, a farewell, apologizing for being caught up in the war.

Before the first week of August ended Alicia's brother arrived breathlessly and told her they must leave at once: German soldiers were on their way to the tiny village. Edward had cabled Alfred that they would take the first ship for home. Alicia gathered her daughter and clothes and set off for the coast of France. Alfred had made arrangements, with much difficulty and arm twisting, to have them board the next vessel bound for New York. Alicia stood silently at its rail as the coast of France dipped beneath the horizon. The child within her womb moved. She thought, with a smile, that the women of the Brandywine might not yet have the final say.

Pierre gently plucked the document out of Irénée's, hands. He had seen it before, without the signatures it now bore, had, indeed, constructed every phrase within it. Irénée had been given the task of seeing that the paper was signed. He had, as he always did, performed his brother's bidding well.

The signatures that had been scrawled on the paper made the French order for eight million pounds of gunpowder official. Pierre and Irénée had discussed the possibility of a European war many times: how they would cope with the orders, to whom they would sell, what might happen if they provided powder to both sides and the United States then became involved. Pierre had had ready answers: they would do what had been done by generations of du Ponts before them: expand production as fast as necessary, sell to anyone with the cash to buy, make certain the United States would remain neutral.

Pierre looked up at his brother. They said little, now or ever. Words were unnecessary between two minds that functioned as closely as theirs. Irénée had not questioned the terms Pierre wished to force upon the French government, as he never doubted anything his older brother did. Pierre was forty-five, Irénée six years younger. They might have been twins; both were just over six feet tall, both carried the prominent nose some called a heritage of the du Ponts and others maligned as evidence of their Jewish blood, and both had a hint of the cleft chin that could be only a du Pont hallmark. They shared sandy, light hair which thinned early.

Irénée had followed Pierre into the company's employ soon after his brother and their cousins took over the firm, biding his time, until one day Pierre called him from the factories into the treasurer's office as his assistant. And then, without the slightest protest, Irénée had followed Pierre's orders to quit his comfortable offices in the Du Pont Building and take over the development department, heading up the search for new products the company might manufacture with the excess refined materials from making explosives. Never had Pierre kept Irénée from the inner circle of men who decided what would become of the company.

When war broke out in August, Pierre had made the decision to fill orders on a fifty-percent-cash-down basis only; otherwise, should the nations they supplied lose, the company might go bankrupt just from building new plants. Pierre had instructed Irénée to bargain with France and Russia under that condition; Irénée had won with surprising ease. The weakness of the Allies had become instantly apparent: without Du Pont, neither France nor England nor Russia could wage even a short war.

Irénée secretly disliked the idea of war. He did not particularly care what became of the European nations, what despot ruled which lands, what flag flew over which country. War presented problems to Du Pont. The fighting could begin, and end, without warning; they had all seen the Spanish-American War fizzle within months after it started. And Irénée believed that this European war would be short-lived, much like the recent Franco-Prussian conflict. Pierre had agreed: the hostilities might cease unexpectedly and leave the Du Pont Company with millions in unfilled orders and idle plants and workers across the United States.

But, within a few weeks after the Archduke's assassination, the war had escalated into a continent-wide conflict. Pierre had called a hasty meeting of the executive committee. Europe could not meet its needs for gunpowder, TNT, or the picric acid used to fill armor-piercing shells; soon the Allies must come hat-in-hand to the Brandywine. And so might the Kaiser. Company policy would be simple. Any and every order, regardless of the nation it came from, was to be filled on the same basis, at the same price: one dollar per pound for cannon powder, precisely twice the price charged the United States government. Fifty percent of the cost was to be deposited in American banks before any manufacturing began. The Allies would balk, Pierre realized, but give in, since the raw materials needed to make war materials came from South America and every available European ship had been pressed into combat service. The Allies, in particular, had no way to bring nitrates from Chile to Europe. Even if, as the war went on, they did find a way, Du Pont owned the most productive nitrate fields along South America's west coast; they could simply refuse to sell it to any European nation.

Washington's stand, both in public and private, as Colonel Henry A. had assured Pierre from his position on the Senate's War Appropriations Committee, was one of neutrality: it was to be Europe's war. Pierre did not anticipate any orders coming from the German side, but if they did, the company would fill them: Eleutherian Mills had been called upon in the past to fuel both sides in a war, and it could happen again.

Irénée sensed, now that the first contract with an Ally had been signed, that Pierre inwardly disliked the war business. It would be sloppy, from his brother's point of view, with daily expansion that would cost millions and a question mark where Pierre always penciled in company profits on his weekly reports. Pierre's special brilliance lay in being able to envision what the corporate future held before spending the money needed to increase production capacity. War, with its changing tides of battle dictating the frequency and size of orders, made that kind of prediction impossible and upset Pierre no end. He was, above all, a fastidious man.

Irénée sealed the French contract in an envelope, marked it for the office safe, and suggested to Pierre that he join him and his family for dinner. Pierre declined, as he usually did these days. Irénée knew why; Pierre was seeing a cousin, Alice Belin, the daughter of their mother's brother. Rumor on the Brandywine had it that his brother and Alice would soon marry—and the Brandywine had been sent into shock by the very idea. Alice carried in her veins the same amount of Jewish blood as Pierre did; it would be a subtle breach of faith for him to marry her.

Irénée well understood his brother's desire to make Alice Belin his wife. She was a relative who had grown up near the Brandywine and knew well the tensions and strains Pierre lived under. Yet she was not literally a du Pont and had taken no part in the family squabbles of recent years; Pierre would antagonize no one from that point of view. And, most important of all, with her shared Jewish blood, she had, like Pierre, grown up under the shadow of the du Pont's prejudice and could understand fully how Pierre felt about his heritage. Pierre had made a magnificent choice in Alice Belin.

Irénée himself had married a du Pont woman, a cousin. The danger of inbred, mentally deformed children had passed for him; his large brood of ten were all more or less normal. He doubted that Pierre would chance having children by Alice Belin. His brother wanted a mistress for Eleutherian Mills and Longwood; the Brandywine had no need of more heirs.

Early in 1915, Thomas Coleman du Pont became ill and entered the Mayo Clinic in Minnesota for treatment. Once again, his stomach had acted up, the old illness, a by-product, the doctors insisted on calling it, of the life he had led for years, of the pressures of high finance and corporate leadership.

Coleman had, since constructing the Equitable Building in New York, decided to become the master skyscraper builder of the age. Over a period of years he had lost interest in the powder company. His investment in Eleutherian Mills amounted, now that the war had brought enormous orders to the Brandywine, to millions that could be turned into newer and taller office buildings in America's cities, each a monument to Coleman du Pont. He decided to offer his stock in the Du Pont Company for sale back to the corporation and communicated his desire to get out of the powder business to Pierre S.

Pierre brought the matter up before a meeting of the Du Pont Company's finance committee. He and Alfred I. and William, the General's son, sat, along with Coleman, in absentia, on the committee. Pierre told Alfred and Willie that their cousin wanted one hundred sixty dollars a share for his stock. Alfred voiced the opinion that since Coly's stock was to be used for investment by the company's employees the price should not be above one hundred twenty-five—the workers could afford no more. Alfred called for a vote. Willie sided with him; Pierre did not. Alfred instructed Pierre to communicate the committee's decision to Coleman and open negotiations over price.

Pierre carefully constructed a letter to Coleman, each word of which was designed to make his cousin believe that Alfred had firmly rejected Coly's offer to sell his holdings in Du Pont back to the company. He intended to drive a wedge between Alfred and Coleman; the cousins must cease all but the most superficial communication. Coleman must believe that nothing he might say to Alfred would change his mind. In a few weeks Pierre would make his own offer to Coleman, on his own behalf, not that of the company. He had decided that the time had come for him to take over the company, to become the first du Pont since Eleuthère Irénée, the company founder, to control Eleutherian Mills by himself. The orders for gunpowder and explosives from the Allies had amounted to forty-seven million dollars in the last three months of 1914 alone. Every ounce had been paid for in advance because of Pierre's demand for a fifty percent down payment. When the final installments of the contract payments came in, they would be pure profit. Pierre did not wish to share the river of gold with anyone he could drive from the business.

Pierre realized he would need enormous amounts of cash to buy Coleman out, and he could not dip into the company till or hope to raise the money from his own resources. He had only one place to turn: the Morgan interests. J. P. Morgan acted as the primary agent of the Allies in America and knew just how healthy the Du Pont Company's prospects were. If Coleman agreed to unload all his Du Pont stock, Pierre would need ten, perhaps fifteen million dollars. Morgan would drive a hard bargain, demanding that the company's credit be pledged—at least privately—against so large a sum. In his own inimitable way, J. P. would suggest politely that funds equal to the loan be deposited in Morgan-controlled banks. Pierre had the power to change banks without consulting even Alfred, but his cousin must never learn that the company's credit had been pledged against the loan: Pierre wanted the stock for himself, not the company. Only then would he have total control over the Du Pont Company.

At the next monthly meeting of the finance committee Alfred looked across the table at Pierre in disbelief. What did his cousin mean, the negotiations were off? Alfred had instructed him to tell Coleman that the price Coly had set was too high, not that the finance committee was turning down his offer. Alfred felt anger rising inside him; never before had he known Pierre to make such a mistake. He narrowed his good eye at his cousin; Pierre had a mind like a slide rule: feed it the proper information and it could not go wrong. He himself must be wrong, yet he remembered their meeting of a month ago well, and he recalled that Willie had joined him on the issue. He turned to Willie: how did he remember what had been said?

Willie agreed with Alfred. They had decided to send Pierre back to

Coleman with a lower figure per share, not to close the matter. It would be in the minutes of their last meeting. Willie shuffled through the pile of papers before him, turned to the last page of the finance committee minutes, read through the final paragraph, and looked up: the minutes were wrong. He specifically recalled saying the words "at this time." They did not feel able to consider Coleman's offer, at the price he had named, "at this time." Now the words were gone: who had had the minutes typed?

Pierre answered that, as usual, it had been he. And the minutes were precise. He had informed Coleman, in Rochester, that the finance committee had voted two-to-one, himself dissenting, not to take action on his offer. If they did not believe him, they should look at their signatures on the minutes: had they not known what they were signing?

Alfred again fought to subdue his anger. Berating Pierre would accomplish little now, and the evidence seemed to bear him out. But he knew well what was at stake. Coleman's stock represented the balance of power in the company. Split among the employees in small lots, or set aside for them as future bonuses, the stock meant little to the running of the company. But consolidated, it could easily swing power any way its owner chose. And, since the outbreak of war in Europe, Coly's stock might be worth, in the very near future, more than anyone imagined.

Alfred sat back to consider Pierre's actions. What had prompted them? He knew the pressure Pierre was under, with the constant need to make immediate decisions about building new plants, expanding production, and filling the huge Allied orders. Perhaps he had indeed suffered a slight—if unusual—lapse in memory. He could not imagine Pierre distorting his words purposely; if anyone in Wilmington wished for family unity, it was Pierre. He would do nothing to destroy it. And this kind of problem might end what few good feelings were left among their many relatives.

Alfred decided that Pierre had not acted out of malice or a desire to keep Coleman's stock intact so that he might influence the way he voted it on important matters. After Coleman's resignation from the presidency Pierre had taken on the job permanently and reorganized the company to give its top executives a large say in company matters. Coly's stock, distributed among the executives, would give them an excellent reason to perform well and stay loyal to Pierre. To misinterpret what he had said, Alfred believed, would be against Pierre's best interests.

Whatever had been done could be undone, Alfred concluded. He instructed Pierre to communicate with Coleman again, to reiterate the company's offer for his stock, and to open negotiations about price. On no condition was he to offer more than one hundred twenty-five dollars a share.

Pierre forced down a smile: Coleman would never agree to that price, now that Du Pont stock was selling on the open market for nearly two hundred. Once his cousin finally rejected Alfred's bid for the stock he would step in—at whatever price Coleman asked for his holdings.

Alfred called the meeting to a close. He suspected, although he did not know why, a ruse in Coleman's offer; his cousin had dealt with him unethically before, in fights over land on the Brandywine. Why should Coly sell out now, when the war promised to propel the price of Du Pont stock to the very heavens? Only for money he needed desperately would Coly throw away the chance at such profits. Alfred knew that the Equitable Building, which had been estimated to cost fourteen million dollars, had taken at least thirty to complete. And he had heard rumors that Coly wanted not just the building, but Equitable Life Assurance itself. J. P. Morgan, who owned it, was willing to sell, but Coleman would never be able to raise the cash needed to buy Morgan out unless he sold his Du Pont holdings. Still, Alfred vowed not to trust Coly, even if his cousin was pressed for cash. Unlike Pierre, Coleman did not care a bit for the du Pont family's best interests.

Pierre assigned John Raskob the task of negotiating with the Morgan interests for the loan he needed to buy out Coleman. He had never regretted bringing Raskob into the powder company from Ohio. Raskob had an uncanny sense of what would happen next in the world of business. In February, 1914, Raskob had purchased stock in General Motors for himself and convinced Pierre to do the same. General Motors had been ailing under the managerial nightmare of its founder, William Durant. Only Raskob had believed that automobiles would ever mean much to American life. With the outbreak of World War I, GM stock skyrocketed. Pierre held only a few thousand shares, but it was enough to make him the largest minority stockholder in the company. In less than twelve months his investment in General Motors—at seventy dollars a share—had tripled in value.

Once John Raskob reached an agreement with Morgan, and the money came in to purchase Coleman's stock, Pierre, his brothers Lammot and Irénée, and his brothers-in-law would rule Du Pont. Pierre prided himself on the job he had done of convincing Coleman that Alfred's last offer had been little more than an insult. The normal course of business dictated that Pierre inform Coly of developments that affected the company's profit outlook. After Alfred's offer to buy Coleman's shares at one hundred twenty-five, Pierre had painted the company in more glowing terms than Coly had ever heard. Coleman's suspicion and hatred of Alfred grew.

Pierre then proposed that Alfred, Willie, Coleman, and himself place all their Du Pont stock in trust and agree to cover any loans the firm needed for operating capital. In that way, no financial leverage could be brought to bear against any one of them by creditors, should the war business ebb. Pierre had aimed the move at Coleman, the only one of the four men who had any significant outside business interests—and the only one who might lose should Du Pont's credit slacken and creditors try to collect from the men individually.

Alfred and Willie had gone along with Pierre's idea since it would force Coleman to open his complicated financial dealings to their scrutiny. Pierre had not expected Coly to agree, and he did not. Instead, an urgent message had come from Coleman at the Mayo Clinic: how much would Pierre pay him for his stock in Du Pont? Pierre offered the going market price, two hundred dollars a share. He formed a syndicate with his brothers and Raskob and gave Raskob authority to offer the Du Pont Company's credit as a guarantee on the eight million dollars in cash they wanted from J. P. Morgan: Coleman agreed to accept the remainder of the thirteen-million-dollar price on his stock in notes. In a few days, without Alfred getting even a slight hint of what Pierre was up to, "Graveyard" du Pont, the quiet, unathletic son of Lammot, controlled Eleutherian Mills.

Alfred I. du Pont read about the takeover of control in his own company in the Wilmington newspaper he owned. He felt a familiar tension growing inside him, the wrenching of feeling that came each time someone on the Brandywine stabbed him from behind. The newspaper reported the price of Coleman's stock as thirteen million dollars and said that Pierre had raised the sum by borrowing from J. P. Morgan.

Alfred realized that Pierre could have bought Coly's stock only by using the Du Pont Company's credit. What had his cousin promised Morgan to get the money? What had he given away that belonged not to him alone, but to the family? Alfred knew he could not control his rage at Pierre.

He had just congratulated Pierre on his engagement to Alice Belin, wished him well even though Pierre still ignored Alicia and supported Bessie among the du Ponts. Never had Alfred known a du Pont to act in such bad faith. Not in a hundred years had one du Pont cheated another out of his birthright.

Alfred decided this was it: if Pierre did not tell him in no uncertain terms that he had acted on behalf of the company, that he intended to turn title to Coleman's stock over to the firm at once, then Alfred I. du Pont would give the Brandywine a war to make the fighting in Europe look like child's play in comparison.

On March 4, 1915, Alfred I. called a meeting of the stockholders of Du Pont who had not joined Pierre in his purchase of Coleman's stock. The meeting was due to begin at eight A.M. He regarded the men who were to gather in his office as the last of the faithful, the only du Ponts left who would not stand silently by while Pierre cheated each and every member of the family.

As the handful of men arrived, Alfred attached the cord of his hearing box and prepared the papers before him on the conference table. Before the hour struck he heard the door opposite him open. Pierre walked in with Irénée beside him. The two men—usurpers of the faith—took seats at the other end of the table from Alfred.

Alfred did not want Pierre at the meeting. He had called his faithful relatives together to plan a strategy that would take back Coleman's stock from Pierre and his syndicate. Pierre had left no written trace that he had used Du Pont's credit to secure the loan from Morgan. Alfred felt he needed no written proof of his cousin's underhandedness; as soon as the stock had been transferred to the Du Pont Securities Company Pierre had set up, his cousin had offered to exchange stock in it for stock in the Du Pont Company. Only Alfred and Willie had been left off the list of relatives Pierre had made his offer to.

After a half-hour Alfred wondered if his hearing device was failing; no words had passed between the gathered men. He looked at each of them. Could he continue to rely on them under the pressure of Pierre's generous offer? Willie, certainly, would not desert him. And Alexis Irénée, old Eugene's boy, had been raised to believe in family honor. Alfred worried about Eugene E., Doctor Alexis's son; they had never been close. But Gene's brother, Philip Francis, and he had been friends for years. He remembered when his cousin had earned his nickname, Fireman Phil, by chasing firetrucks as a boy on the Brandywine. Phil could be counted on to keep his brother in line.

Alfred's gaze settled on the last of the men, Francis Irénée. Of them all, the single unknown quantity was Frank I. His brother, Alexis Felix, had followed Pierre from the start. But Frank had turned down Pierre's stock exchange offer at once; indeed, he had been the one to inform Alfred of it. Still, he would have to watch Frank closely. Pierre was not above planting a spy in his camp.

A few words reached Alfred's ears, pleasantries between Pierre and the others, empty comments on this one's children or that one's wife. So it was to be this, a war of nerves until someone brought up the matter of Pierre's treachery. He looked down the table at Pierre. What did his cousin hope to accomplish here? The secrets were all out now. Pierre and his syndicate had purchased 63,214 shares of common stock for two hundred dollars a share and 13,989 shares at eighty-five, for a total of just under fourteen million dollars. Pierre's stake in the deal was the largest by far. He controlled the company now, its investments as well as its operation. As Alfred had discovered, Pierre's share was large enough to enable him to give away a total of nearly one million dollars in stock to his brothers, Raskob, three other men who sat on the board of directors, and the heads of two operating departments.

Alfred had tried to reason with Pierre, appealing to his family sentiment and the spirit of the name du Pont, to what they had begun together years earlier. Pierre became stubborn: he would not give the stock to the company, disband his Du Pont Securities firm, or even discuss the matter further.

Pierre had asked the board of directors of Du Pont to vote on whether or not the company even wanted Coleman's stock. Alfred had known in advance what the outcome would be: Pierre had stacked the board with men faithful to himself, bought them off with marriage to his sisters or large blocs of Coly's stock. Pierre must, Alfred thought, have believed him to be a complete fool.

Alfred heard Pierre clear his throat and begin speaking. He had, he said, been accused by some members of the family of a breach of faith—Willie in particular—soon after word of his purchase of Coleman's stock reached the newspapers. He wanted now to know what he had done to earn the criticism.

Willie stood to answer, repeated the charge that Pierre could not have bought Coly out without using the company's credit, and that he had absolutely no authority to do so.

Pierre denied Willie's accusation: the credit had been his brothers' and his own. Pierre pushed his chair away and stood. Unless anyone present had more than Willie's flimsy words to offer, he would leave now. And, he added, he had better not hear that any du Pont dared say behind his back what they were afraid to utter to his face.

Alfred spoke for the first time, challenging Pierre once again to sell his stock to the company for the good of them all. Pierre refused. Alfred yanked the plug from his hearing box and sat back in his chair: nothing was left to say.

Pierre and Irénée left the room. He must act swiftly to consolidate his control over the board of directors and executive committee. He would name Irénée to the finance committee, making it Alfred and Willie on one side, he and his brother on the other. At least he would have a stalemate there; a majority was required for all major decisions. Already eight of the twenty directors were his men, relatives or executives he had paid off with large gifts. He could bring a few more around easily: their jobs depended on him.

Perhaps Alfred would be smart enough to let the matter drop there. His cousin would not dare take it any farther than the company offices; the family hated him enough as it stood. Most, if not all, the du Ponts would not take kindly to Alfred's attempt to upset the sweet pot of profits the war was bringing them.

Pierre said goodbye to his brother and turned down a corridor to his own office. He would call Alice and tell her that he could now devote more time to their wedding plans. Perhaps a long trip abroad after the wedding would be good for them, and then she could spend her time at Longwood, remaking the house more to her own tastes, giving him ideas for the gardens. Pierre was glad the purchase of Coleman's stock was over and done with; Alfred's anger would subside, as it always did, and they could devote their attention to the truly important business at hand: coping with the ever-increasing war orders. Even Alfred would see the futility of carrying the battle any farther. He had won control of the company at last; the fruits of his years of hard work would finally be his—and Alice's. The proper time had come for a new mistress to rule the women of the Brandywine.

# 27

O N DECEMBER 9, 1915, Philip F. du Pont, "Fireman Phil," as his relatives called him, filed suit in the United States Court for the District of Delaware against Pierre S. du Pont, Lammot du Pont, Irénée du Pont, Eugene E. du Pont, Henry F. du Pont, A. Felix du Pont, John J. Raskob, and other members of Pierre's syndicate. He asked that the court order Pierre and his colleagues to turn Coleman's stock over to the Du Pont Company. At Fireman Phil's side stood Francis I. du Pont, E. Paul du Pont, Archibald M. du Pont, Ernest du Pont, Eleanor du Pont Perot, William du Pont, and Alfred I. du Pont.

Eugene E. du Pont was Fireman Phil's brother. Henry F. du Pont was William du Pont's son. Francis I., E. Paul, Archibald M., Ernest, and Eleanor were, like A. Felix du Pont, all children of the late Francis G. du Pont. A sister of theirs, Irene, was defendant Irénée du Pont's wife.

Every du Pont involved was descended from Eleuthère Irénée du Pont the first, the founder of Eleutherian Mills. The war that Alfred I. had threatened unless Pierre S. repented his ways and gave Coleman's stock to the firm had begun. It would end only with the destruction of the du Pont family and dynasty as it had, for over a century, lived and breathed on the Brandywine.

Alfred I. had constructed the assault on Pierre's syndicate. He knew that Pierre was a vulnerable man personally; no one on the Brandywine believed in family unity more than Pierre did. Alfred hired William Glasgow, former United States assistant attorney general, who had a reputation for trust busting, to represent Fireman Phil and the others who, in the months after Philip F. filed suit, joined in the legal action. Alfred intended his choice of Glasgow as a slap in Pierre's face; Pierre felt the blow. Alfred added John G. Johnson to his legal team. Johnson had defended Standard Oil against the government's antitrust proceedings. Alfred wanted Pierre to bristle when Johnson portrayed him and his syndicate as wealthy feudal lords tyrannizing the common folks—such as Alfred and Willie. Pierre did indeed bristle and in the weeks following the filing of Alfred's own suit against the syndicate, on January 10, 1916, began to regret what was happening to the du Pont family.

Pierre wanted the war of cousins, of brothers, of du Ponts, stopped. Only Alfred I. could end it. He came, one morning, to Alfred I.'s office in the Du Pont Building, to plead with his cousin for a withdrawal of the lawsuits. In the fourteen years since the three cousins took over the powder company there never had been a need for formality among Pierre, Alfred, and Coleman. A closed door merely had to be walked through; being welcome was beyond question. Often Pierre had come into Alfred's office unannounced, and Al had turned at once from whatever he had been doing, giving his full attention to his cousin.

But the war of du Ponts had changed that, and Pierre stopped before the closed door of Alfred's office and decided to knock before going in. He found Alfred at his desk, working. Alfred glanced up, said nothing, and turned back to his papers. Pierre began speaking, fumbling for the precise words that would turn aside Alfred's bitterness.

Alfred was deeply hurt by what had happened in the company. Pierre had seen him react to pain before, when the family ostracized Alicia, attacked her, then isolated him. Alfred had always retreated into himself, fled the Brandywine, or cloistered himself behind the high wall of Nemours.

This time was very different. Alfred had seized the honor of the family as his cudgel, taken, as it were, the column from the du Pont crest as his spear, the helmet above it as his armor. Control of the company, not the family, was at stake. In Alfred's mind the ownership of Coleman's stock had become an affair of immense personal proportions.

Pierre had to convince his cousin of the seriousness of what he had done. He decided to appeal to Alfred's sense of heritage; if he could be made to feel that the reputation, the very traditions—even the existence—of the du Pont family were at stake, then Alfred might agree to a truce.

Alfred listened carefully to what Pierre had to say. Why had his cousin bothered to visit his office? Pierre should know there would be no turning back now, not unless he was willing to sign Coleman's stock over to the company, return the board of directors to the form it had taken before Pierre began bribing relatives and employees, and publicly—at least to the family—apologize for his breach of faith and dirty dealings.

Alfred had anticipated Pierre's speech: an appeal to family feeling, to family tradition, to family unity—the very same words, in fact, that Alfred had confronted Pierre with soon after word of his treachery leaked to the press. Pierre would ask him to drop the lawsuits, to make amends. The answer would be one word: no.

Pierre looked older, more tired, than Alfred had ever seen him. He had just returned from his honeymoon after marrying Alice Belin; the rest had done him little good. He had gained weight; the jowls around his jaw sagged. What had made the change in Pierre, more aging than Alfred had noticed in any of Pierre's forty-five years? Was it the demands of wartime production or the family troubles? Pierre had done a masterful job selling powder to the Allies. Alfred's income for 1915, in dividends on Du Pont stock alone, amounted to more than three million dollars. At the present rate of orders he would reap more than double that in 1916. Coleman's stock, bought by Pierre for thirteen million, was now, a year later, worth nearly sixty million dollars—all the more reason for Pierre to give it back to the company. Whatever Pierre's treachery had done to the du Ponts, his business acumen had made them among the richest families in the world.

The feud among the du Ponts had hit the newspapers—as Alfred had hoped it would—with more than the force of just another du Pont family quarrel. The Du Pont Company had never kept secret its manufacture of gunpowder and explosives for the Allies. A large part, perhaps even most, of the nation had turned against the makers of munitions who were reaping the plentiful harvest of war profits. Even the President, Woodrow Wilson, had taken the line of neutrality—at least for the present. But Wilson, and his underlings in Washington, knew that orders from the Allies, filtered through J. P. Morgan and Company, were lifting the United States economy to heights never before seen. In one year the work force in Du Pont factories had gone from five to nearly fifty thousand; each day the company spent more than a quarter-million dollars on new construction.

And while some newspapers portrayed the du Pont family quarrel in less than sensational language, others—such as one powerful Philadelphia daily—insisted on printing cartoons of the du Ponts dressed as Chinese warlords, with the world going up in smoke between the two battling camps. Perhaps, Alfred reasoned, that was why Pierre had come to see him; he knew that his cousin hated publicity and that what the newspapers were now doing would frighten him enormously. Once, Pierre had loved and believed in the du Pont family traditions, and Alfred had believed in him. How wrong he had been!

Until Pierre's wrongdoing had been righted, by the courts if necessary, Alfred planned no end to his attacks. He had begun using his Wilmington *Morning News* to force his viewpoint upon the people of the Brandywine. Most of the du Ponts had for years cared little about company matters, as long as their dividend checks came regularly and periodically increased. His relatives had ridiculed him since his boyhood, turned against him, taken away the glory he deserved for rescuing the company, allowed their petty jealousies and antique morality to stand in the way of their own best interests. And now, with the help of his newspaper, they knew well that while they lived in luxury among the Brandywine's hills, Pierre had robbed them of their just say in the affairs of the company, even giving away stock they should have owned to outsiders, men who only worked for Du Pont, business adventurers who served the highest-paying master. Alfred had made the largest implication of Pierre's treachery clear: if he could take over the company, then why could some complete outsider not do the same?

Alfred had marveled at how easily the smaller family units on the Brandywine had been split; Philip's own mother had sided with Pierre, writing to him that she could not understand why her son, who had always admired Pierre, would now turn against him. Perhaps the du Ponts did not know how weak the ties of the Brandywine had become. Pierre had created a new world for them, with his buying up of companies whose products were not in the least related to gunpowder or explosives, companies that made paint and chemicals and synthetic leather. Something inside Pierre had changed since the first night the three cousins had met in the billiard room at Swamp Hall to discuss taking over the company. He had expected Coleman to one day leave the Brandywine, desert the family traditions, wander to other fields of conquest. But Pierre: like himself, Pierre had the Brandywine in his blood. Alfred found it remarkable that *anything*—money, power, control of the company—could remove the spirit of a century's heritage from a man.

Why indeed had Pierre bothered to come to his office? He had no intention of giving in on the stock purchase, and Alfred had no notion of dropping the matter short of that. Pierre had what he wanted: control of the company. Even a court decision against him would hardly damage that; who else could run the mammoth corporation he had built? Only one reason remained: Pierre truly had been affected by the ill will within the family. He had always cared about unity within the du Pont clan, had always worked to bring young relatives into the company. Pierre had become sacred to many du Ponts, loved for his polite manners, his gentle ways, his desire to keep peace among the hundreds of du Ponts. Many women on the Brandywine knew that their sons worked for Du Pont at Pierre's pleasure, not as a result of their talent, but because the company president believed that every du Pont deserved a place in the family concern.

But Pierre's greed and bitterness had surfaced at last, the product of more than one generation of du Pont ridicule. Both Pierre's and Alfred's fathers had suffered the barbs of family bigotry; Lammot for marrying a Jewess, his own father for bringing a Southern woman to the Brandywine during the Civil War. Pierre had long suffered the tag of Jew; Alfred had always been suspected of inheriting his mother's insanity. But Pierre, as had Lammot, had fled the Brandywine to make his home and fortune elsewhere, returning only when Alfred, who had stayed to make the family the most highly regarded munitions makers in the Spanish-American War, paved the way for him. Those, Alfred believed, had been the crucial few years: he himself had learned to revere what the name du Pont meant, while Pierre submerged his family identity until the mildew of hatred and greed grew upon it.

Alfred watched Pierre walk slowly from his office, his shoulders hunched, his body drained by the force of Alfred's single word to him: no. Now Pierre would pay for what he had done to the people of the Brandywine: nothing could inflict pain like the wrath of the du Ponts.

In the midst of two wars—the Great War in Europe, and the war of the du Ponts on the Brandywine—John J. Raskob came to Pierre S. du Pont with a proposal that he move to take over control of the General Motors Company. William Durant, GM's majority stockholder and president, was known to be a blustering fool, ill suited to corporate finance, a mechanic turned manager, who cared more for the life of his company than his own.

The nationwide recession of 1914 had nearly ruined Durant and General Motors. Durant had sold his soul—and practical control of GM—to the bankers of Wall Street for the cash he needed to keep the automaker under his rule. He had borrowed far beyond his means and bought up enough General Motors stock, on the open market, to keep the company from either going bankrupt or winding up in the hands of market speculators. Now the banks were demanding that they be given the largest say in GM's management. One of the bankers, a friend of Durant's and an acquaintance of John Raskob's, suggested to Raskob that he, and Pierre, might be able to come up with a way for General Motors to survive without directors and managers who owed their allegiance to Wall Street.

Raskob and Pierre journeyed to New York for a meeting of General Motors stockholders. He hated to leave the Brandywine during his quarrel with Alfred, and with war orders coming in at an ever-faster rate he had little enough time to spend with Alice at Longwood. But Raskob had insisted: this was the opportunity of a lifetime. The war would not last forever, Raskob had argued, and a certain degree of prosperity would follow in America once Europe laid down the spear. The munitions business would nearly collapse then, and the nation would seek outlets for all the money that had been stockpiled. A world freed from war was a world infused with optimism, masses of people urgently desiring ways to forget the terrors of warfare, a world that sought luxuries. What better luxury was there than a motorcar?

Pierre had asked his assistant what would happen if the United States entered the fighting. That, too, would one day cease, Raskob had answered, and the Americans would join Europe in seeking outlets for their pent-up need to enjoy life. Pierre had found Raskob's logic flawless, as always. And he had another reason to find General Motors fascinating.

The Du Pont Company now made a host of products that the automobile industry needed—paint and artificial leather and even synthetic rubber. Weekly, the chemists working at the company's new experimental station invented new ways to use the by-products of the explosives manufacturing processes. Other companies did, too; but no company owned or controlled the markets for these by-products. If he could become the leader of General Motors the future of Du Pont would be forever secure.

Still, he could not quite imagine GM ever reaching the size of Du Pont. In 1915 alone, he had signed contracts with the Allies for $347 million. 1916 would be even bigger; General Motors would have to come a long way to equal that. And a longer way, he thought, to equal the trouble that infected the Brandywine.

Pierre and Raskob had gone over the strategy they would use. As the largest minority stockholder, Pierre would be the logical choice as GM's new board chairman, a compromise between the Eastern bankers and Durant, a man known for his adroitness in corporate finance. Pierre would install Raskob in General Motors' offices, to keep an eye on Durant. Other loyal men would become members of GM's board—perhaps even Henry Belin, Pierre's father-in-law, as well as his mother's brother. Durant had fallen prey to that most cancerous disease in the corporate world: the stock raid. When General Motors stock fell he always attempted to buoy it with his own money and fell easy prey to men with greater financial means at hand. Raskob believed that it would not be long before GM stock began diving again; then they would step in and buy controlling interest in the auto company, using the huge sums that the Du Pont Company held as excess war profits.

This was the side of his takeover of Coleman's stock that Alfred had never seen. As long as Pierre could vote the largest bloc of stock in Du Pont, he had final say over how the company's millions in war profits would be invested. Alfred's single good eye saw no farther than the Brandywine; he cared little for the future, for *creating* the future. And, Pierre had decided, the future would be to control General Motors as he did Du Pont.

Pierre believed Alfred's lawsuit would fail. Even if his cousin won, what could the court do but allow the owners of the company to decide whether or not they wanted to own Coleman's stock? Alfred did not have the power among the company's shareholders to win a proxy fight; Pierre had seen to that with his generous gifts to Du Pont executives. Once the lawsuits were out of the way, the family would unite behind whoever held the power in the company—and it would be Pierre S. du Pont, not Alfred I. du Pont. In the meantime, Pierre wanted Alfred punished for what his foolishness had done to the family on the Brandywine.

Thomas Coleman du Pont recovered from his illness and left the Mayo Clinic. He was thirteen million dollars richer from the sale of his Du Pont Company stock and found himself quickly back in the limelight of national business and politics: the press seriously believed that he had ambitions to occupy the White House. Coly encouraged the newspapers' speculations; he made no secret of the thousands of letters that poured into his office each day, urging him to run for the presidency, or of the organization of the Business Men's Presidential League by leaders of American industry, dedicated to nominating him for the office. He did not reveal that he had provided the money for the league's nationwide activities.

After selling his Du Pont stock to Pierre, Coleman had been concerned that his influence in Delaware politics would end. But he had kept his hand, and his pocketbook, in, answering questions about his allegiance to Delaware with a neat phrase: he existed in New York, but lived in Wilmington. The deal he had made with Pierre allowed him to buy the Equitable Life Assurance Company from J. P. Morgan. Equitable's six hundred million dollars in assets had made him a power on Wall Street and the darling of all the nation's citizens who believed that big business made for a big America. He had kept well hidden his backing of organizations that agitated for America's entry into the war: many people did not realize that what made big business good was the big war.

Equitable had been a blessing: he had found the leverage he needed to continue building his hotels. He still lived in the McAlpin, but the Sherry Netherlands, across from Central Park, and the Waldorf-Astoria were more luxurious and brought in more profits. He had many friends among Washington's politicians; they enjoyed the way he catered to their tastes, and their expense accounts, at the Willard Hotel in Washington. Only one hotel bore his name, the Du Pont in Wilmington, but everyone thought it was part of the company empire.

Coleman was pleased that he had put the Brandywine out of his life. Alfred had lost his head with his bitterness and lawsuits. He had given his cousin a chance to buy him out, on the company's behalf. Al had muffed it with his haggling over price. The stock Coly had sold to Pierre was now worth well over nine hundred dollars a share. Pierre had been less frugal, agreeing to whatever price he set, and now controlled the company. Coly was pleased that he had stayed out of the fighting so far; it could only bring him difficulty in the next election.

Colonel Henry A.'s second term was about to end and he was growing old—nearly eighty. Coleman would have liked to force his cousin aside and take his place on the ballot. But the Colonel would fight him, no matter how much of a political debt he owed, and, with a war on, it would not do to show the people the seamier side of Delaware politics. With his stand on the war Coly had made a few enemies in the du Pont family. He had said publicly what he believed: the United States should enter the fighting at the Allies side. His views did not coincide with the best interests of the Du Pont Company, but they were making Coleman enormously popular with the people who voted men into office. Coly would not change his stand on the war; he no longer owed anything to any of the Brandywine du Ponts who were locked in battle over ownership of Eleutherian Mills.

# 28

JUDGE WHITAKER THOMPSON of the United States District Court in Delaware handed down his decision in the case of Philip F. du Pont versus Pierre S. du Pont on April 12, 1917. He ordered that the stockholders of the Du Pont Company vote on whether or not they wished to acquire the stock Coleman had sold to Pierre's syndicate. The verdict was, for Pierre, a victory hidden within defeat.

The court had called Pierre a man without principle, a money-grabbing, greedy, underhanded du Pont, ready to skewer his relatives in the name of power over Du Pont. He had wronged the people who depended upon his leadership of the company they together owned. Never had Pierre been so humiliated; in twenty years of business dealings he had not once been accused of even the slightest lapse in ethics. Judge Thompson had even denounced the methods he had used to secure Coleman's stock.

The judge had stopped short of calling Pierre a fraud. Alfred had seen to that in his newspaper, in two-inch-high letters each and every one of his relatives and employees would certainly read. Pierre wished he believed differently about the press; Henry A. would be pleased to make the pages of his newspaper available for a counterattack on Alfred. But that was not his way. He would defeat Alfred where it mattered, in the proxy fight the court's decree would now bring to the Brandywine.

By the judge's decree the stockholders of Du Pont would now vote on whether or not to purchase Coleman's stock for the company books. Pierre's relatives must decide against doing so or all the work of his twenty years would be wasted. He had nearly finished grooming his brothers to take over the company and leave him free to wander the gardens of Longwood or take on another business venture. He would not see his plans frustrated now.

He *must* defeat Alfred: within weeks, General Motors would be ripe for the takeover he and Raskob had planned for two years—a final jewel in the crown he had built at Du Pont, a rare, expensive gem he could not acquire without the millions in war profits he had kept in company accounts rather than distribute to his relatives. For their faith in him Pierre intended to give the du Ponts one-fourth of the stock in General Motors, a decidedly controlling interest, and a business phenomenon that would live long after he left Longwood for a plot in Sand Hole Woods. He had been successful in keeping his General Motors strategy secret from all but the select few at Du Pont: his brothers, Raskob, and one or two key executives. And the philosophy behind the move to take over GM remained locked only in his brain; not even John Raskob realized the full potential of owning General Motors. To Alfred, the proxy fight would be just a matter of pride; to Pierre, it meant the ability to turn the du Pont family's fortune from millions into billions.

The court ruling against him had come only six days after the United States declared war on Germany. The Allies had been sucked dry by the war; Pierre doubted that the notes and bonds he had been forced to accept instead of cash as payment for Du Pont powder and explosives would be worth their face value unless America stepped in and crushed the Kaiser and his friends. Everything had worked in Pierre's favor. The United States had held onto the myth of neutrality long enough to drive General Motors stock into the ground, just long enough for Du Pont to bleed the Allies into desperation: only a transfusion of American troops, guns, and ships would save them now. Rumors of peace had flared in the last months: the Germans wanted peace, on their terms, and the Allies wanted peace on theirs. Idle talk, but it had scared him. Fortunately, Wilson had seen through the peace feelers; the President knew that the United States must step in, sooner or later. Wilson had been reluctant, and even that had helped Du Pont. The President's policy of armed neutrality allowed the company to charge the War Department high prices for powder and explosives: why should Du Pont make the sort of sacrifices that came during war if the nation was not at war? The government had found little choice but to accept Pierre's prices or risk public exposure of a war buildup while the President clamored for peace. And now, America's entry into the war would be the icing on a cake of gold. The Allies had paid for enough expansion to meet any imaginable amount of powder production Washington asked for. The Du Pont Company could seem to make enormous sacrifices for the war effort, charging the United States half what the Allies had paid for powder and explosives, and still make huge profits.

Only beating Alfred in the proxy fight stood in Pierre's way. Alfred:

what did he care for the company, or the family, or his own flesh and blood? His son, Alfred Victor, had volunteered for the Marines, and Alfred did not even know it. But then, why should he? Alfred I. had not seen Alfred Victor in twelve years; for all his father knew, the boy had died and been buried in Sand Hole Woods.

Alfred had taken the family feud into politics, defeating Coleman in his bid for national power and keeping Colonel Henry A. from being reelected to his Senate seat. Alfred had used his newspaper well then, and he would again now, daily tearing into Pierre and his Du Pont Securities Company, which held Coleman's stock. He would drive the family even farther apart, into little cliques of personal loyalty and favoritism. Husbands and wives would split over the proxy vote; brothers would never speak to each other again; mothers and sons would become strangers. In the end Pierre would beat Alfred and seal his fate on the Brandywine. But it would be the end of the du Pont family as it had stood for more than a century.

Pierre wanted nothing in life more than to unite the du Ponts, not, as they had been under General Henry, out of fear, but in the common cause of protecting themselves against the outside world. It had been his father's dream, and his grandfather's, and his great-grandfather's. And this was the result: how many du Ponts would take their hatred for other du Ponts to the grave? Alfred must remember, as he did, how Eleuthère Irénée the second, Alfred's own father, had refused to see his mother on his deathbed.

Pierre recalled how the du Ponts had once all worked near each other, lived near each other, breathed each other's very air. They had made the Brandywine their own. Now they were strung along the Creek in castles on hilltops, behind General Henry's rock fences, and they hated and distrusted one another. They had more money than any of their ancestors had ever imagined. Before this war, this World War now, was over, the du Ponts would be nearly the richest family on earth, made that way by his efforts, his work alone. What had he done? Victory would be his, Pierre believed. Peace never would. This was the legacy of the Brandywine.

Pierre read down the list of guests for his Christmas party as he wandered through the grounds of Longwood. All his friends were on it, and most were relatives, men who had been loyal to him during the years of both wars—Europe's and the du Ponts'. He respected each of them for the job he had done at Du Pont and for the wisdom of the choice each had made to stay with him. Christmas of 1918 would be a gay time, a time to forget what had happened in his family and start anew.

And then New Year's Day would come, the traditional day of homage from one du Pont to another. How many of his relatives would honor the celebration? For a hundred years the men of the family had traveled from du Pont house to du Pont house, to call on the ladies of the family, bearing token gifts. It had been quite a spectacle in his youth: a string of carriages, led by General Henry in his top hat and formal coat, his beard flowing, his whip cracking over a prancing horse. The du Ponts owned a score of mansions now: how many would shutter their windows and bar their doors rather than let him in? One-half, perhaps—it did not matter: he had decided not to allow his relatives' foolishness to ruin his holiday.

Pierre felt deeply sorry for the thousands of Du Pont employees who would not have a happy holiday. He had, of course, no choice but to let them go: the company could not possibly sustain the eighty-five thousand men and women it had hired during the war years. Nearly seventy thousand had been fired in the six weeks between the armistice and Christmas. He would have liked to keep them all on until after the first of the year, but peace had come in November, and even the few extra weeks would have bankrupted Du Pont.

Pierre roamed from his conservatory to the new greenhouses. He had planned them for years. Only when the war ended could he call in workers to begin constructing their glass walls. They would take two long years to complete, but Longwood would then have the finest indoor botanical gardens in the nation, rivaling even Versailles in beauty and size. And he would have the leisure to walk among the acres of delicate flowers and exotic plants he planned to grow.

Pierre had chosen his brother Irénée to become the next Du Pont Company president. Irénée had learned his lessons well; he had come far since the start of the war, and he was ripe for command. And his brother knew better than anyone else the importance of continuing the program of diversification he had started. Hundreds of millions in war profits had to be invested. Pierre had been staggered by the final total of all the war contracts Du Pont had filled: one billion dollars. Nearly one-fourth of that was pure profit, much of it distributed among the stockholders, of course. But a hundred million dollars still remained on the company's books.

Irénée would handle the investments well and consult with him on any important move. His brother had even married a cousin—and they were still happy after twenty years, one of the few marriages between du Ponts that had turned out well. Irénée's marriage would unite the family behind him—to a point: many du Ponts still refused to set aside their feelings. Pierre had tried to mend the schisms, but they had been too deep, too broad. In the end he had stopped thinking about them when he could. Alfred had his wish: Pierre would never again be completely at peace with himself.

He wished, more even than he wished to spend the rest of his years amid the beauty of Longwood, that he had been able to communicate with Alfred, to make him believe that it had all been a matter of business, not of family honor, to tell his cousin that he deeply regretted what had happened. But Alfred had no desire to discuss anything with him: the cousins would never speak again.

Alfred had left the Brandywine, closed Nemours, finally severed himself from the du Pont family. The proxy fight had been a debacle for Alfred. Pierre had laid his plans well over the years; the du Ponts and du Pont in-laws and du Pont executives who, together, controlled the company's stock had benefited from his running of Du Pont. They remained loyal to him in his fight against Alfred. The second of the three cousins who bought Eleutherian Mills in 1902 left to begin an export business in New York, choosing a site on Long Island for a new home to hold his small family; Alfred and Alicia, who had lost two children in infancy and never conceived another, had adopted a French war orphan, Denise, and given her the du Pont name.

He had won, Pierre reflected, but what had he really achieved? The du Pont family now owned more than twenty percent of the common stock in General Motors; in itself, the stock would make them wealthier than even the World War had. John Raskob oversaw the daily management of GM, and William Durant, still hanging on to his place in the company, would soon be driven out. Durant hated Pierre for taking control of General Motors away. He spoke in the same terms Alfred had about Pierre acting in bad faith. He had not minded; what he did at GM was for the good of the company.

And Pierre had done more for Du Pont than for General Motors. No longer would the family rely upon wars to make them wealthy—or wealthier. He had branched out into the new chemical industry, and his laboratories made daily breakthroughs into new products that would change the way man lived. He hated war; all the du Ponts did, had always, always would: war was unpredictable, inefficient, a waste of man. Yet he had been pleased when the Americans joined the fighting; he did not want to see Germany win. The Germans held important secrets to chemical processes, formulas the Du Pont Company needed. He had started a campaign to have the defeated nation's scientific knowledge turned over to Du Pont. Washington could do no less in return for the profits he had sacrificed to enable America to wage war.

Yet the American government, and the people, had been less than understanding. The newspapers lumped Du Pont with the likes of Morgan and Standard Oil and U.S. Steel. Du Pont was not "big business," Pierre believed, merely a family-run concern that happened to make what nations needed in time of war. Certainly, the company's assets had skyrocketed during the fighting, quadrupling what it owned in the last year before the war, but that was to be expected. And, yes, profits had been huge; that, too, was a condition of war. But in no way did Du Pont measure up to the giants of industry. Why then the disturbing articles claiming that Du Pont, like others, promoted, indeed *made* war?

Pierre had been warned by friends in Washington that Du Pont's war activities would soon be a sensation in Congress. The nation was in dire straits; hundreds of thousands of men were being thrown out of work. Unions were growing ever stronger as the men looked to union organizers for leadership, for a way to continue making a living. Du Pont was suspect: no union had succeeded in crossing a gate into any Du Pont plant. During the war laws had been passed to keep workers from agitating against management. But now the unions represented millions of wage earners, and carried the strength of all their votes to Washington, and Du Pont was a prime target.

Charges of astronomical war profits at the workers' expense were being leveled. They would soon surface in the nation's newspapers. Pierre could expect, in the near future, an army of government auditors to invade his Wilmington offices. They could scrutinize his books all they wanted; they would find nothing. He knew the Old Hickory plant would be a source of most of the controversy. The Tennessee factory, the largest military gunpowder facility in the world, had been nothing but trouble. The government had convinced him to build it for cost plus a tiny percentage, committing Du Pont's best engineers and chemists to the project. And Congress had delayed, not he, until Old Hickory was finished too late to turn out powder for the fighting. Since the government had no intention of going into the powder business, he had offered to buy the Nashville plant—at a fraction of its construction cost. Sharp business, that, but certainly not unethical. Yet the politicians would latch onto it as an example of how Du Pont waltzed to the same tune as the war god Mars. He had heard all the words before, since his youth. His family would be called Merchants of Death, be accused of plotting with other industrial companies to create and then enlarge the fighting. He and his relatives had grown wealthy dispensing the basic tool of warfare, true. But what would the people of the United States rather have had: victory or defeat?

He would meet the charges head on, with the finest, most precise strategy he could summon. Alfred was on the verge of bankruptcy in New York, after foolishly believing the European nations would honor his war bonds with hard cash. Pierre had heard that Alfred wished to sell his Wilmington newspaper. He decided to buy it, through a third party so his cousin would not discover the new owner's identity, and use it to counter the critical publicity that was certain to come the family's way. The government's auditors would not long be fooled by the name change from Du Pont Securities Company to Christiana Securities Company. They would discover easily that through Christiana he controlled not only Du Pont, but a dozen other large companies, among them General Motors. He did not fear antitrust action: the Sherman Law had no teeth. But the publicity alone would convince the people that the du Ponts had become the unquestioned kings of American industry through the profits of war. He could not deny it, Pierre knew, but it was a fact that belonged to no one who lived beyond walking distance of Eleutherian Mills.

He had been to a funeral recently, in Sand Hole Woods, where the generations of his family stared out at him from white marble gravestones. Years had passed since he last smelled the acrid odor of sulfur being mixed in the powder yards. When he and Coleman and Alfred took over, the Du Pont Company meant little more than that narrow strip of mills along the Brandywine. Now the name stood for a vast network of modern plants that skipped halfway across the globe. And Irénée would continue the work, the expansion, the swallowing up of the chemical industry as he and Coleman had devoured the powder business.

He had traveled far since the day he and John Raskob had waited out a snowstorm to reach the Brandywine, and it was a different world. Few men alive remembered the Brandywine as it had been in his youth, the tight community of owners and workers living with the constant danger of explosions. Few women of the du Pont name could conceive of Irénée the first's daughter, Victorine, bending over a bucket of dirty water, cleaning the floors of the powdermen's dormitories. Once, when he was a boy, Alfred's father, dressed in powdermen's overalls, covered with soot, had been denied credit by a Wilmington storekeeper who refused to believe he was a du Pont. Now his cousin Willie's fourteen-story bank building stood on the very spot where the merchant had sold his wares. And the dust of powder had turned to the dust of gold.

Not even his own younger brothers, Irénée and Lammot, resembled the du Ponts of old in anything but physical characteristics. They were men of finance, of expediency, minds he had trained that way; the Brandywine meant little to them. And he himself: John Raskob had suggested that when Durant finally gave up on General Motors Pierre might wish to take the reins of the motorcar company himself. He would do as Raskob wished, leaving behind the willow trees and dampness of the Brandywine, coming to Delaware only for brief retreats at Longwood. He could not abandon the principles he had used to make Du Pont what it today was; he could not otherwise justify what had happened to the du Pont family during his reign.

What would become of Longwood? Perhaps he would open the gardens and greenhouses to the public; they deserved to be seen, admired, walked through by the people of Delaware. The people had always been loyal to the du Ponts, most loyal, through wars both within and without the family. He had a dream for the people, his people, of a modern state based on the principles of business that had worked so well at Du Pont. He would keep the house at Longwood private, even if the gardens were not; it would serve well as the center for his plans to remake Delaware in the Du Pont image.

Pierre left the greenhouses, turned down a path flanked by winter-bare trees, and walked to where he had recently installed an open-air theater. A thousand people could sit on its stone benches, listening to music or watching plays under the stars. He had hoped that one day his thousand du Pont relatives might all gather there together. But strangers would sit in the arena, never du Ponts, men and women and children who knew little and cared less about what it had taken for the du Pont family to come so far. They would listen to the cascading waterfalls in the gardens, watch the splendor of his fountains, and envy a family so rich in worldly things.

Pierre turned back toward the house. Guests would begin arriving soon, to toast each other's good fortune and the end of the war. They would bring trinkets and ornaments to decorate the huge tree he had installed in the drawing room at Longwood. Children would play with the toys the servants had wrapped and placed under the tree. It would be a good Christmas, but not quite a du Pont Christmas.

# 29

ALFRED I. DU PONT stepped from the crowded train into the California sunshine. He could smell the salt air of the Pacific, the clear ocean breezes that made San Diego a paradise for visitors from the East. Once, in his boyhood, his grandfather, son of the powder company's founder, had told him of the early years on the Brandywine, of the damp, heavy air and rattlesnakes, of the decrepit old cabin the du Ponts had first inhabited. Too bad his family had not settled on the shores of the Pacific Ocean rather than the Brandywine Creek.

Alfred looked up and down the station platform. Would he recognize Jessie Ball? They had not seen each other in fourteen years, in fact since 1906. He had written, and she had answered, until the Ball family moved from Virginia to California. Now, on a vacation, he had decided to look up an old family friend. Jessie had done well for herself, rising from teacher to vice-principal of a public grade school. Alfred could not understand why she had never married; of all the Ball daughters, Jessie was certainly the prettiest and most personable. Perhaps, had he not been drawn from Virginia by the horror of his hunting accident, they would have become better acquainted. He would have an opportunity to learn more about her now: San Diego was a world away from the Brandywine or New York. His vacation would be much more enjoyable in the company of Jessie.

Alfred saw a brown-haired, graceful woman walking toward him. It must be Jessie: a bit older—more mature, less of the springy adolescent about her, but still Jessie, Alfred wished the events of the last year had not drained him so. His money troubles in New York had etched deep creases into his face, around his eyes. He had set his entire fortune on the line to keep his export companies from going bankrupt; what little was left had gone to the government in back taxes, taxes laid on him by the way Pierre had boxed the du Ponts who opposed him into a corner, laying the bulk of war profits against stock not held by his Christiana Securities. Alfred had even sold the *Alicia* and hung up his yacht club commodore's hat. His wife had loved to sail, but what Alicia cared for mattered little now: she was so ill, had been since the summer before, that she rarely left her bed. Alfred had spent what time he could near Alicia, when his business problems allowed, but now, after rescuing the New York companies, she had urged him to take a rest, to vacation far away from New York and Long Island.

Alfred had kept much from Alicia in the past year. She did not know how serious their money problems were, how near being poor—by his standards—they had come. And he had not told her about Coly's offer to lend him whatever he needed to straighten out his mistakes in business: he would rather starve than take his cousin's charity. Alicia's frail health could not take much more of the du Pont family intrigues and bitterness and so he had kept Coleman's generosity to himself.

He had been hesitant about journeying so far from her side, but Alicia had insisted that she would be fine on Long Island: the doctors and servants saw to her every need and whim. Alfred would be much better off away in the sun; by the time he returned she would be well again, and they would travel together to Nemours, open the old house, and see if his relatives did not by now wish to visit the mansion they had been barred from for twenty years.

Alfred hugged Jessie Ball on the station platform, took her arm, and walked to the hotel where she had reserved a suite for him. He left her at the lobby door, promising to call her after he napped, and to see her the next day for lunch. He gave the clerk his name and held out his hand for the room key and an envelope that had been waiting for him. He opened it, read the telegram inside, and ran to the hotel door. Jessie was gone, disappeared into the streets filled with afternoon strollers. Alfred felt the tears swelling inside him: Alicia was dead, taken just two days after he left New York. The servants awaited his instructions.

Alfred raced to the train station, bought a ticket on the next east-bound train, and sent a telegram to New York. He checked the watch in his pocket: hours before his train left. He decided to wander through San Diego's streets, to see what his vacation would have been like. At each road's end, the ocean began, across a wide expanse of white sand. Alfred watched the waves, wishing he could hear their crashing onto the shore. He would take Alicia's body back to Nemours, he decided, to the poplars where their children were buried, to rest beneath the trees his father had loved.

And then, after Alicia was buried, he would leave Nemours forever, close the house, and find another place to call home. Alfred squinted up into the brilliant afternoon sun. Perhaps a place such as Jessie Ball had chosen, where the sun beat down every day, and he could forget the shadows of the Brandywine.

Thomas Coleman du Pont stretched his arms wide into the air, bellowed a hearty laugh, ignoring the pain in his throat, and allowed a broad smile to linger on his lips. It was a good day, a *marvelous* day, a day of success: finally a day he could call all his own. Word had come from the governor of Delaware. He had been appointed to fill out the term of office of Joseph Wolcutt, United States Senator from Delaware, who had accepted appointment to the highest judicial post in the state.

Coly squinted at the distant mountains, their tops covered with snow even in July. He had felt enough sadness in recent months: what a grand way to end it all and begin again. Only weeks earlier he had buried his son and had taken this trip to Colorado to ease the sorrow. And he had worried about what the doctors found in his throat, the beginnings, they said, of a tumor, inoperable at this stage without removing his larynx. Coly had been more depressed than at any time in his life. But good old Governor Denney had come through: he was to be a United States Senator. He had never been able to buy election to the office; at least the millions he spent on Delaware politics had earned him the appointment. For years he had puzzled over how Alfred, with all his enemies, had been able to frustrate T. Coleman du Pont's political goals. But Al was nearly broke now and eaten up by the tragedy of Alicia's death. He had written to Al, telling him how sorry he was about Alicia's passing; the letter had broken the ice. Alfred had replied in a letter when Coly's son died, telling Coleman how sorry *he* was about Coly's loss.

Coly was pleased that he had been out of the state when the governor made his move; not everyone in Delaware would welcome his taking the Senate seat. He did not care who approved or disapproved: he had what he wanted. And business had never been better. He was a rich man, an important man in American business, and he deserved to sit in the halls of Congress, where he could do his financial empire—and the people of Delaware, of course—the most good.

Now even his support of Warren Harding would come in handy. If Harding was as bad at being President as some people—even Republicans—claimed, the man would need his counsel. He had paved Harding's way to the White House with thousands wrung from his relatives for the campaign. And he had fought for the man from Blooming Grove, in back rooms and barrooms and board rooms all over the country. He had raised his voice, he believed, even louder and more often than he had in the old days against Taft and the antitrust suit. Harding would not dare upset the applecart for T. C. du Pont or his relatives in Delaware: he had the President in his pocket.

And what about his voice: were the doctors right? Not likely. No, the doctors must be wrong about the possibility of cancer in his larynx. No power on earth or above would dare rob him of his voice now, just when it was about to be heard in the chamber of the Senate.

Coleman laughed aloud again: finally, the United States Senate. He had made and broken Senators, even Presidents, and the office had always eluded him. He thought of the road, nearly completed now, that stretched the length of Delaware. The highway had cost him nearly four million dollars, but he had been right to complete his monument and give it to the people of Delaware. Now that he was in the Senate, they would insist on calling it the T. Coleman du Pont Highway as he had always planned. Yet he worried over the name: would it look bad to people who did not know what it meant to have the du Pont family looking after the best interests of a state? Would it seem that he had bought his way into the Senate? Coleman did not care: he had made the long jump from the powder company to Congress at last. Henry A. had fretted like an old woman that the du Ponts would be robbed of their due representation after he was defeated for reelection in 1916. Here it was only four years later, and already another man of the name du Pont would be heard in the Capitol.

The Colonel had written him from Winterthur, that old mausoleum stuffed with junk from all over the world. Henry A. had said he would have to leave the main house soon for a smaller place he was having built nearby: the antiques left him no place to live among the mansion's dozens of rooms. And he had enclosed the latest chapter of his book on Admiral Samuel Francis du Pont for Coly's perusal; Henry A. had vowed to set down the truth about their ancestors once and for all.

Coly shook his head: he would never become so old and senile that he had to spend his time sifting among dusty family papers and letters, trying to justify what had happened a half-century ago. Henry A. suffered the curse of the du Ponts: they could never get the Brandywine out of their veins. He was more than pleased that he had been born and raised in Kentucky—as long as the voters did not discover that he had never lived anywhere near Eleutherian Mills.

Alfred Irénée du Pont adjusted his tie in the mirror at the top of the stairs. He wanted to look good, very good, for this afternoon. He had fidgeted and fussed over his clothes for the first time in years. The image in the mirror disappointed him: he had lost the leanness, the sculptured edge to his features that hard work in the powder yards had given him.

And he had been nervous all day, a nearly alien feeling to him since he and Jessie had married. She had taught him to live at ease with his memories, to enjoy his name and what money was left after personally paying off his business debts rather than suffer the disgrace of bankruptcy. His lawyers said he would have been far better off at the mercy of the courts, but he had been unable to bring himself to admitting publicly that his businesses had failed.

Jessie Ball had taught him, too, that the years of ridicule by his family need not rob him of a future. The newspapers had called their wedding a "Cinderella marriage," the poor schoolmarm capturing the heart of a mercantile prince, the middle-aged man of fifty-five taking a woman twenty years his junior. Even his family approved, privately, of Jessie: she came from a respectable family. The reporters—and the du Ponts—knew little of the truth: Jessie was more than a wife to last out his life with, more even than a lover. She had come east to him after Alicia's death in January, 1920, and he had learned the reason she had never married. He would never have believed her, years ago, but Jessie said that she had loved him since their first meeting at her parents' home in Virginia, and had waited for him.

The society columns had made much of her heritage; if the newspapers could be believed, her family had greeted the men who arrived aboard the *Mayflower*. But no one knew what Jessie had done for him. Long ago he had given up trying to communicate with most people, after years of studying sign language and lip reading. His world had been reduced to that of children, who spoke slowly enough for him to discern what they said and used simple words. In her gentle, patient way, Jessie had made him into one of her grade-school pupils, struggling with him for hours, giving him the confidence to engage again in conversation. He had found the courage to plan a life for them, a desire to act as a father to Denise, to forget the Brandywine and what the du Ponts had done to him. There, too, Jessie had helped. She cared not at all for what had happened in years past; she neither condemned nor praised his relatives. Alfred had realized what had happened to his marriage with Alicia; each time he looked at her the years of family troubles had come rushing into his mind. Jessie wished only to plan their own way of living, and together they had. The call from his daughter Victorine had come, in fact, on the very morning they made the decision to leave Nemours for Florida.

What would his youngest daughter look like? He had heard from relatives that they had once sat across from each other in the dining room of the Du Pont Hotel, neither of them recognizing the other. How could they? Twenty years separated their last meeting from this one. He had inquired and heard that she was a beautiful, cultured young woman. After much discussion Jessie had convinced him to place a million dollars in trust for his four children by Bessie, to assure that they would never want for anything.

And what of Alfred Victor? When he learned that Victorine wished to bring him along on the visit to Nemours, he had asked discreetly about his son, and he had been startled: his son was no longer a boy. He had fought in France with the United States Marines and distinguished himself. Alfred V. had studied architecture and was about to start his career. Perhaps his son would be able to help him with the sunken pools he planned to install at Nemours, before he turned the mansion into a children's hospital—another of Jessie's ideas. The pools would stretch almost to Alicia's bell tower. He had not heard the bells ring in years and did not wish to: he needed no reminders of that part of his life.

Jessie emerged from her rooms, joined Alfred at the top of the stairway, and walked arm in arm with him down into the drawing room. She held his arm tightly in hers; the children were waiting, and they would be as nervous as Alfred was. And so it should be, after twenty years of not seeing their father. Jessie was pleased that Alfred was visibly moved, Victorine and Alfred Victor would feel less self-conscious knowing that the meeting mattered to him as much as it did to them. She had worked for two years to bring Alfred this day, to persuade him that no purpose was served by carrying with him the bitterness of so many years. He would never consent to remain at Nemours, near the Brandywine du Ponts; it was enough that he would not grow old a stranger to his own son and daughters. The Florida sun, the distance from Delaware, would be good for Alfred; he had earned that much peace. Nemours could be maintained by the couple they had engaged until the time came for it to become a research hospital.

Alfred clutched Jessie's hand tightly as they walked across the drawing room. He had little vision left even in his good eye now, but he knew it was his children who stood across the room. What would they think of him, after years of hearing only Bessie's and Pierre's side of the family quarrels? He hoped that Alfred Victor was at least a bit like him, with a little of the hell-raiser in his bones: he must be, Alfred reasoned, to have survived the Marines.

But then, he could not expect the boy to be very much like his father. He had not grown up on the Brandywine, awakened to the sound of the powder yard alarm, dropped off to sleep with the odor of the powder mills in his nostrils. He had never seen the devastation of an explosion in the mills, never drawn a horsecart full of saltpeter down a narrow set of rails, never inhaled charcoal dust or chewed tobacco to rid his mouth of sulfur's bitter taste. And he had never bent to the will of older, more powerful relatives, or spent his young strength learning to mix powder at his father's side.

To his son, the du Ponts were pencil-pushing financiers who wheeled and dealt in the rarified atmosphere—the perfumed air—of stock wizards and corporate magicians, men such as Coleman and Pierre. And Alfred Victor might not even know what it meant to go "across the Creek" or how women felt when their men were locked behind the powder yard gates each day—what it had been like for generations of du Ponts. No, Alfred thought sadly, his son would never be bound to him as he had been to his own father.

Alfred stretched his hand out to his son, then to his daughter. Jessie stood a little behind him, not wishing to intrude on the moment. Alfred felt the tension, the strangeness, hanging in the air between them. The family du Pont had come to this, to a man not being able to speak with his own daughter and son. Alfred examined his children, looking from one to the other, searching for the characteristics that would mark them as du Ponts. He found the light eyes, the strong jaws, the clefts in their chins; yes, these were du Ponts, he decided, of a kind, a different kind than he had ever known. Alfred suggested they walk outside before dinner was served. He wanted to show them the five tall poplar trees and tell them a story about their grandfather and ice cream cones.

Pierre Samuel du Pont walked along the edge of the small patch of rusty brown grass. Where had the flagpole stood? It had happened before his birth, General Henry marshaling the men of the family before the director's house, leading them here to the Henry Clay Village green, to hoist the red, white, and blue up the flagpole among the powdermen's shanties. Generations of powder workers had lived in the small houses of brick, built solid to withstand the explosions from the powder yards downhill.

Pierre shoved his hands deep inside the pockets of his coat. He had read Irénée's report, after a meeting of Du Pont's finance committee in 1921, one of the few he had attended since taking the presidency of General Motors. Irénée's work had been as usual: precise columns of figures that showed costs and income, debts and sales, and listed the items of interest that had been decided upon by him or one of his committees.

In Irénée's mind the last item on the report had deserved little more than it received: a footnote. After an explosion removed much of their black powder capacity, he had decided it would be inefficient to rebuild the powder yards on the Brandywine. They had been kept open a few months to finish filling orders that had come in before the explosion. Now, Irénée's report read, the powder yards were closed, all usable equipment transferred to other facilities, the workers either retired, let go, or sent to other Du Pont plants.

Pierre left the village green to wander among the empty powdermen's houses. He had been there when the chimneys wafted smells of cooking dinners and hearty men in overalls and long beards spat tobacco on the dirt lanes between the houses. He had seen dogs run beside their masters and schoolboys toting books from the Yellow School near the Brandywine. He had never mingled with them, of course: they were not du Ponts and, even as a boy, the difference between the owners and the workers had been sharp in his mind.

But he had come to work in the mills, after college, and he had grown to know the powdermen and their ways, and he had, from a distance, enjoyed them. Never could he have imagined Henry Clay Village a ghost town, with the banks of tall wild grass where neatly clipped lawns had been. Where had the men and their families gone? Some were fifth-generation powdermakers who inherited their homes as they did their jobs. Some were twisted, bent-limbed survivors of explosions, put out on pensions after losing their health in the mills.

And the widows, whose husbands had died in the service of the du Ponts, who kept boardinghouses for the single workers and often, after a few years, married another pressman or charcoal roaster or millwright or mule driver. How could they ever understand that efficiency had put them out of homes that had been theirs for generations?

Gone: all the men and women were gone, across the Creek, or to some other Du Pont mills, or just to poverty and old age. Irénée had been correct, of course, to close the powder yards; it should have been done years ago, when Coleman wanted them shut down, and he and Alfred had put up a sentimental fight.

Pierre walked down the hill toward the Brandywine. For the first time in his memory, the mill wheels were not turning, the air was not filled with the odor of sulfur, with the excitement and danger of a powder yard churning out its deadly product. He stopped before the gates, the Centennial Gates, as Alfred had named them. The brass sign, set in stone, that Alfred had put up to commemorate the first hundred years of the du Pont family and company, was covered with tarnish, what little of it he could see. Tall weeds had grown over the entrance to Eleutherian Mills.

# *Epilogue*

THUS the dream of Pontiania came to an end, and while the du Pont family survived the bitter feuds of the early twentieth century, the du Pont dynasty did not. Eleutherian Mills is today a museum: school-children ride jitneys beneath the willow trees where the flesh of powder workers—and du Ponts—hung in grotesque testimony to the dangerous lives they led. Scholars dig to uncover the remains of gardens where forbidden lovers, at times both named du Pont, secretly met. Wind and weather flatten the names carved on tombstones in Sand Hole Woods. The old director's house has been reclaimed from its years as a workers' club and refurnished with the artifacts of a family driven from its ancestral home by a century of turmoil and quarrels of the blood. It is a house with a history but without a soul.

The war of the cousins ended in the 1920s with all three du Ponts out of the Du Pont Company and away from the Brandywine. Thomas Coleman died in 1930 of throat cancer, his greatest asset, his booming voice, gone. Alfred I. survived Coly by five years, a pariah among du Ponts, self-exiled to Florida by the bitterness of a lifetime of fighting in vain to preserve his family's legacy. Pierre S. relinquished control of the Du Pont Company to his brothers, Irénée and Lammot, became the moving force behind General Motors, and continued until his death in 1954 at the age of eighty-four to fashion an economic age that yet endures.

Pierre S. had no children to whom he could bequeath the heritage of the Brandywine. Alfred I.'s one son, a stranger to him for more than twenty years, became an architect, not a powderman; Alfred I. did not pass on the generations of du Pont tradition. Thomas Coleman, himself never a believer in the Brandywine legacy, fathered five children with his cousin-wife, Elsie du Pont, who matured far removed from Eleutherian Mills.

In numbers, and in wealth, the du Pont family flourished in the twentieth century, until, in the 1960s, one hundred new descendants of

Pierre Samuel du Pont de Nemours were born each year and the name du Pont became synonymous with riches beyond imagination. A few inheritors of the blood joined the Du Pont Company, but with the passage of decades their numbers dwindled until not a single du Pont could be found to lead the giant industrial corporation Eleutherian Mills had become. Control of Du Pont rests with strangers to the Brandywine, and if the du Pont family still earns millions from the company's profits, its members no longer have the power to direct the source of their wealth.

The strategy of Pierre S. du Pont, to marry his sisters to men who would be loyal to his leadership of Du Pont, was the first act of betrayal to the du Pont tradition: it had, until then, never been necessary to look beyond the family for men to rule the Brandywine. If Pierre's relatives by marriage remained faithful to him, and to the traditions of the Brandywine, their children did not. It matters little to them—or to the du Ponts of today—that a century of du Ponts braved the awesome dangers of making gunpowder with their own hands. The dream of Pierre Samuel du Pont de Nemours of a Pontiania on American soil, the labors of Eleuthère Irénée du Pont in a tiny black powder mill, the suffering of Alfred du Pont for his dead and maimed workers, the iron will of General Henry du Pont, the frustrations of Eugene du Pont, the daring and genius of Pierre S., Alfred I., and Thomas Coleman: all have been swept away in the swift Brandywine current, the rushing water that sustained the du Pont dynasty. The three cousins abandoned the Brandywine; it, in turn, ceased to nourish them.

In two dozen mansions scattered among the hills near the Brandywine a few old and proud du Ponts still live in near-feudal splendor, unable or unwilling to break the ties with their history. But most du Ponts have moved on, to other parts of the world and other endeavors, carrying with them a portion of the wealth the dynasty established. Perhaps one will discover another flowing stream, settle upon it, and resurrect the visions of his ancestors. But, more likely, the blood that ran through the veins of the rulers of the du Pont family has become too diluted, and America will not again foster a dynasty such as the one that flourished and died on the banks of the Brandywine Creek.

# *Bibliography*

## A NOTE ON THE RESEARCH FOR THIS VOLUME

Above the Brandywine Creek, a few hundred yards from the old director's house built by Eleuthère Irénée du Pont in 1802, a modern building nestles into a hillside, incongruous amid the rough structures of the powder mills. Within it, the documentary history of the du Pont family and the Du Pont Company is preserved; scholars, students, and the curious pore through the nearly three million documents that have been painstakingly filed and catalogued by a staff of professional archivists and librarians.

More than just du Pont history occupies the documents in the Eleutherian Mills Historical Library. Other industries, and individuals, who flourished in the Middle Atlantic States take a part of the space of the library and the time of the attendants. But it is clearly du Pont history that dominates, as, perhaps, it should: in the main, du Pont family money endows the foundation that keeps the library, and its big sister, the Eleutherian Mills-Hagley Foundation, alive.

The library is an institution of overt gentility and grace, much like the building that houses it. Each day, for example, fresh water from a spring on the grounds of the powder mills is brought to the library for the making of coffee and tea, and employees partake of refreshment together—if they wish—in a room overlooking the lush Brandywine hills or, in clement weather, on a wide veranda beyond the room's glass wall. The cost is nominal; tradition, another legacy of the Brandywine, if not of the du Ponts themselves, is the point, not profit.

A large portion of the research for this book was undertaken at the Eleutherian Mills Historical Library, in the letters, diaries, account books, and millions of other memorabilia of the du Pont family and the era they lived in on the Brandywine. Information gathered at the library, both among the documents and the thousands of books, typescripts, and other sources available there, and, indeed, the many months spent enveloped in the aura of the Brandywine, contributed beyond accurate description to the writing of this volume.

It would be both impractical and without real purpose to list the enormous numbers of documents that were made available to the author during his research. Indeed, the library has published a copious volume of some 1,205 pages, entitled *A Guide to the Manuscripts in the Eleutherian Mills Historical Library*, compiled by John Beverly Riggs, curator of manuscripts, and his staff, for that purpose. Nor does the simple recitation of the source of a particular bit of information, from within the millions of amassed data, necessarily evoke the tone of a particular incident in the history of the du Pont dynasty; it may, in fact, obscure the picture the writer seeks, with words, to draw. Scholars and students interested in delving further into the history of the du Ponts are referred to the above *Guide*, and to the library itself.

However, in addition to the manuscripts in the Eleutherian Mills Historical Library's collection of documents, thousands of sources were consulted in the writing of this book: books, magazines, newspapers, monographs, broadsides, dissertations, theses, and unpublished research studies. The appended bibliography is intended as a brief guide for readers to sources of general information about the du Pont family, the Brandywine, and the era covered in this volume.

Aldridge, Alfred Owen. *Franklin and His French Contemporaries*. Washington Square, New York: New York University Press, 1957.

"Among the Willows," *Appleton's Journal* VI (November 18, 1871).

Anthony, Donald C. "The du Pont Family in France," unpublished research study, Eleutherian Mills Historical Library.

Bailey, Muriel. "An Intimate History of the E. I. du Pont de Nemours Powder Company," *The Delaware Magazine*, June, 1912.

———. "Development of a Great Industry," *Leslie's Illustrated Weekly* CXIV (February 8, 1912).

Beer, Max. *An Inquiry into Physiocracy*. London: George Allen and Unwin, Ltd., 1939.

Betts, Raymond F. "Du Pont de Nemours in Napoleonic France, 1802–1815," *French Historical Studies* V (1967–1968).

———. "Eleuthère Irénée du Pont and the Brandywine Sunday School." *Delaware History* VIII (September, 1959).

Boatman, Roy M. "Gunpowder in America," unpublished research study, Eleutherian Mills Historical Library.

Boulding, Kenneth E. "The Brandywine River Anthology," *Michigan Business Review* X (March, 1958).

Brayman, Harold, "The Organization of the Du Pont Company," unpublished typescript of speech given before the Postgraduate School, United States Naval Academy, Annapolis, Maryland, February 11, 1947.

Brayman, Harold. *Corporate Management in a World of Politics: The Public, Political, and Governmental Problems of Business.* New York: McGraw-Hill, 1967.

Burch, Philip H., Jr. *The Managerial Revolution Reassessed: Family Control in America's Largest Corporations.* Lexington, Mass.: D.C. Heath, 1972.

Burt, Warren. *First Families: The Making of an American Aristocracy.* Boston and Toronto: Little, Brown, 1970.

Caldwell, Taylor. *Dynasty of Death.* New York, Scribner's, 1938.

Canby, Henry Seidel. *The Brandywine.* New York: Farrar and Rinehart, 1941.

Cantwell, Robert. "America's First 'Boom' Town," *The Saturday Evening Post* CCXXX (April 26, 1958).

Carr, William H. *The Du Ponts of Delaware.* New York: Dodd, Mead, 1964.

"A Century of Success: A History of the E. I. du Pont de Nemours Powder Company," *Business America* XII (June, 1912).

Chandler, Alfred D. "Du Pont, Dahlgren, and the Civil War Nitre Shortage," *Military Affairs* (Fall, 1949).

———. *Strategy and Structure: Chapters in the History of the Industrial Enterprise.* Cambridge, Mass.: The Massachusetts Institute of Technology Press, 1962.

Chandler, Alfred D., and Saulsbury, Stephen. *Pierre S. du Pont and the Making of the Modern Corporation.* New York: Harper & Row, 1971.

Chidsey, Donald Barr. *Goodbye to Gunpowder.* New York: Crown, 1963.

Childs, F. S. *French Refugee Life in the United States, 1790–1800.* Baltimore: Johns Hopkins University Press, 1940.

Chinard, Gilbert, ed. *Correspondence of Jefferson and Du Pont de Nemours.* Baltimore: Johns Hopkins University Press, 1931.

Clune, Henry W. *The Genesee.* New York: Holt, Rinehart & Winston, 1963.

Cochran, Thomas C., and Miller, William. *The Age of Enterprise.* New York: Harper & Row, 1961.

"Coleman du Pont, 1863–1930," *Encyclopedia of American Biography.* New York: American Historical Society, 1935.

Conforth, John. "Powder for Pioneers—The Hagley Museum," *Country Life* (November 2, 1972).

Crowninshield, Louise du Pont, and du Pont, Pierre S. eds. *Tancopanican Chronicle, 1830–1834.* Wilmington, Del.: privately printed, 1949.

Dakin, Douglas. *Turgot and the Ancien Regime in France.* London: Methuen and Company, Ltd., 1939.

Dale, Ernest. *The Great Organizers.* New York: McGraw-Hill, 1960.

*Delaware: The Company State: The Nader Study Group Report on the du Ponts in Delaware.* 2 Vols. Washington, D.C.: The Center for the Study of Responsive Law, 1971.

de Staël-Holstein, Anne Louis. *The De Staël-du Pont Letters: Correspondence of Madame de Staël and Pierre Samuel Du Pont de Nemours and of other members of the Necker and Du Pont Families.* Madison, Wis.: University of Wisconsin Press, 1968.

de Tocqueville, Alexis. *The Old Regime and the French Revolution.* Translated by Stuart Gilbert. Garden City, New York: Doubleday Anchor Books, 1955.

Dolan, Paul. *The Government and Administration of Delaware.* New York: Crowell, 1956.

Donaldson, John W. *Caveat Venditor—A Profile of Coleman du Pont.* Wilmington, Del.: privately printed, 1964.

Dorian, Max. *The Du Ponts: From Gunpowder to Nylon.* Translated by Edward B. Garside. Boston: Little, Brown, 1962.

Downey, Farifax Davis. *Sound of the Guns: The Story of American Artillery.* New York: McKay, 1956.

Drescher, Nuala McGann. "The Irish in Industrial Wilmington, 1800–1845: A History of the Life of the Irish Emigrants to the Wilmington Area in the Pre-Famine Years." Unpublished master's thesis. Newark, Del.: The University of Delaware, 1960.

du Pont, Bessie Gardner. *Du Pont de Nemours, 1739–1817.* 2 Vols. Newark, Del.: The Press of Kells, 1933.

———. *E. I. du Pont de Nemours and Company:* A History, 1802–1902. Boston and New York: Houghton, Mifflin, 1920.

———. *Life of Eleuthère Irénée du Pont from Contemporary Correspondence.* 12 Vols. Newark, Del.: University of Delaware Press, 1923–27.

———. *Lives of Victor and Josephine du Pont.* Newark, Del.: The Press of Kells, 1930.

du Pont, Gabrielle Josephine de La Fite de Pelleport. *Souvenirs de Madame Victor Marie du Pont de Nemours (Gabrielle Josephine de La Fite de Pelleport), dediés à ses enfants.* Wilmington, Del.: privately printed, 1908.

du Pont, Henry A. *The Battle of Newmarket, Virginia.* Washington, D.C.: privately printed, 1923.

———. *The Campaign of 1864 in the Valley of Virginia.* New York: The National Americana Society, 1925.

———. *Early Generations of the Du Pont and Allied Families.* 2 Vols. New York: The National Americana Society, 1923.

———. *A Genealogical-Biographical History of the Du Pont Family.* New York: The National Americana Society, 1923.

———. *Rear Admiral Samuel Francis du Pont, United States Navy.* New York: The National Americana Society, 1926.

———. du Pont, Lammot. *The du Pont Company and Munitions.* Wilmington, Del.: E. I. du Pont de Nemours and Company, 1934.

———. "History of the Company," typescript of speech presented October 3–4, 1946, Wilmington, Del.

du Pont, Pierre S. *Genealogy of the du Pont Family, 1739–1949.* Wilmington, Del.: privately printed, 1949.

du Pont, Victor Marie. *Journey to France and Spain, 1801*. Ed. by Charles W. David. New York: Cornell University Press, 1961.

du Pont, Mme. Victor. "Our Transplantation to America," unpublished typescript. Philadelphia, 1826.

Du Pont de Nemours, Pierre Samuel. *L'Enfance et la jeunesse de Du Pont de Nemours racontées par lui-meme*. Ed. by Henry A. du Pont. Paris, 1906.

Du Pont de Nemours, Pierre Samuel. *National Education in the United States of America*. Trans. and with an introduction by Bessie Gardner du Pont. Newark, Del.: University of Delaware Press, 1923.

du Pont de Nemours and Company, Inc. *Autobiography of an American Enterprise*. New York: Scribner's, 1952.

Dutton, William Sherman. *Du Pont: One Hundred and Forty Years*. New York: Scribner's, 1942.

———. *One Thousand Years of Explosives*. Philadelphia and Toronto: The John C. Winston Company, 1960.

Eberlein, Harold Donaldson, and Hubbard, Cortlandt V. D. *Historic Houses and Buildings of Delaware*. Dover, Del.: Public Archives Commission, 1963.

Edwards, Nina Lorraine. "Bookkeeping Records and Methods of E. I. du Pont de Nemours and Company, 1801–1834," unpublished master's thesis. London, Canada: The University of Western Ontario, 1966.

Engelbrecht, H. C., and Hanighen, F. C. *Merchants of Death*. New York: Dodd, Mead, 1934.

"Explosives: Their Significance, Manufacture and Use," Pamphlet by the Explosives Department, E. I. du Pont de Nemours and Company, Wilmington, Del.

Errigo, Joseph A. L. *A History of St. Joseph's-on-the-Brandywine*. Wilmington, Del.: Cann, 1941.

Farris, Sally G. "Du Pont Company Expansion Beyond the Brandywine, 1859–1934, an Outline," unpublished research study, Eleutherian Mills Historical Library.

Finn, David. *The Corporate Oligarch: An Analysis of the Men Who Head America's Largest Business Enterprises*. New York: Simon & Schuster, 1970.

"Firearms, Ammunition, Explosives and Fireworks: A Selected List of Books and Pamphlets." Washington, D.C.: The Library of Congress, 1943.

Foote, Shelby. "Du Pont Storms Charleston," *American Heritage* XIV (June, 1963).

Foster, Mary Louise. *Life of Lavoisier*. Northampton, Massachusetts: Smith College Monograph No. 1, 1926.

French, Sidney J. *Torch and Crucible: The Life and Death of Antoine Lavoisier*. Princeton, N.J.: Princeton University Press, 1941.

Furet, Francois, and Richet, Denis. *The French Revolution*. Trans. by Stephen Hardman. New York: Macmillan, 1970.

Gibb, Philip. *Men and Women of the French Revolution*. London: Kegan, Paul, Trench, Trubner and Company, Ltd., 1906.

Gray, Ralph D. "Transportation and Brandywine Industries, 1800–1840," *Delaware History* IX (October, 1961).

Grinde, Donald Jr. "Victor Marie du Pont, Legislator and Lobbyist," unpublished research study, Eleutherian Mills Historical Library.

Guerlac, Henry. "Some Aspects of Science During the French Revolution," *The Scientific Monthly* LXXX (February, 1953).

Guttman, Oscar. "Collection of Books and Pamphlets Relating to Explosives," unpublished typescript.

Haber, L. F. "Growth and Development of the Chemical Industry: An Appreciation of the Interrelationship of Technical, Scientific, Economic, and Social Factors in Some of the Main Fields of Industrial Chemistry from the 18th Century to the Present Day," unpublished typescript.

Hale, Edward E., and Hale, Edward E. Jr., *Franklin in France.* Boston: Roberts Brothers, 1887.

Hancock, Harold Bell. *Delaware During the Civil War.* Wilmington, Del.: The Historical Society of Delaware, 1961.

————. "The Industrial Worker Along the Brandywine, in Three Parts: 1800–1840, 1840–1870, 1870–1902." 3 Vols. Unpublished research study, Eleutherian Mills Historical Library.

Hancock, Harold B., and Wilkinson, Norman B. "A Manufacturer in Wartime: Du Pont, 1860–1865," *The Business History Review* XL (Summer, 1966).

Hayes, John D., ed. *Samuel Francis du Pont: A Selection from His Civil War Letters.* New York: Cornell University Press for the Eleutherian Mills Historical Library, 1969.

Heard, Alexander. *The Cost of Democracy.* Chapel Hill, N.C.: University of North Carolina Press, 1960.

Henry, Alan Johnstone. *Francis Gurney du Pont: A Memoir.* 2 Vols. Philadelphia: William F. Fell Company, 1945.

————, ed. *The Life of Alexis Irénée du Pont.* 2 Vols. Philadelphia: William F. Fell Company, 1945.

*History of the Du Pont Company's Relations with the United States Government, 1802–1927.* Wilmington, Del.: prepared and published by the Smokeless Powder Department, E. I. du Pont de Nemours and Company, Inc., 1928.

Holbrook, Stewart H. *The Age of the Moguls.* Garden City, N.Y.: Doubleday, 1953.

Ingersoll, Charles J. *Recollections, Historical, Political, Biographical, and Social.* Philadelphia: J. B. Lippincott, 1861.

Ivey, Dean B. "The Beginnings of the High Explosives Industry in the United States, 1868–1880," unpublished research study, Eleutherian Mills Historical Library.

James, Marquis. *Alfred I. du Pont: The Family Rebel.* New York: Bobbs-Merrill, 1941.

Johnson, Gerald W. "The First Du Pont," *Harper's Magazine* (August, 1941).

Kennan, George. "Holding Up a State," *The Outlook* (February 7, 14, and 21, 1903).

Kerr, George H. *Du Pont Romance: A Reminiscent Narrative.* Wilmington, Del.: Du Pont Printing Divisions, 1939.

Kohler, Carl. *A History of Costume.* New York: Dover Publications, 1963.

Lawton, William C. "The du Ponts: A Case Study of Kinship in the Business Organization," unpublished doctoral dissertation. Chicago: The University of Chicago, 1956.

Lefebvre, Georges. *The Coming of the French Revolution.* Trans. by R. R. Palmer. Princeton, N.J.: Princeton University Press, 1947.

Lundberg, Ferdinand. *America's Sixty Families.* New York: Vanguard, 1938.

———. *The Rich and the Super Rich.* New York: Lyle Stuart, 1968.

Lyon, E. Wilson. *Louisiana in French Diplomacy, 1759–1804.* Norman, Okla.: University of Oklahoma Press, 1934.

McKie, Douglas. *Antoine Lavoisier, The Father of Modern Chemistry.* Philadelphia: J. B. Lippincott.

McLain, James Jefferson. "Economic Writings of Pierre Samuel Du Pont de Nemours," unpublished doctoral dissertation. Pittsburgh: University of Pittsburgh, 1972.

Malone, Dumas, ed., and Lehman, Linwood, trans. *Correspondence Between Thomas Jefferson and Pierre Samuel du Pont de Nemours, 1798–1817.* Boston and New York: Houghton, Mifflin, 1930.

Malone, Dumas. *Jefferson and the Ordeal of Liberty.* Boston: Little, Brown, 1962.

Meek, Ronald L. *The Economics of Physiocracy.* Cambridge, Mass.: Harvard University Press, 1963.

Mills, C. Wright. *The Power Elite.* New York: Oxford University Press, 1956.

Montgomery, Elizabeth. *Reminiscences of Wilmington.* Wilmington, Del.: Johnston and Bogia, 1872.

Morison, Samuel Eliot. "Du Pont, Talleyrand, and the French Spoiliations," *Proceedings,* Massachusetts Historical Society, XLIX (1915).

Nielsen, Waldemar A. *The Big Foundations.* New York and London: Columbia University Press, 1972.

*Official Dispatches and Letters of Rear Admiral S. F. du Pont, U.S. Navy: 1846–48, 1861–63.* Wilmington, Del.: Press of Ferris Brothers, Printers, 1883.

"One Hundred Twenty-Five Years of Usefullness, 1802–1927," *The Du Pont Magazine,* Anniversary Issue XXI (1927).

*Original Letters of Robert R. Livingston, 1801–1803, The.* New Orleans: The Louisiana Historical Society, 1953.

Packard, Vance: *The Pyramid Climbers.* New York: McGraw-Hill, 1962.

Parton, James. "President Jefferson's Chief Measures," *The Atlantic Monthly* (September, 1873).

Proctor, Edward W. "Anti-Trust Policy and the Industrial Explosives

Industry," unpublished doctoral dissertation. Cambridge, Mass.: Harvard University, 1951.

Quimby, Maureen O'Brien. *Eleutherian Mills*. Greenville, Del.: The Eleutherian Mills-Hagley Foundation, 1973.

Reed, H. Clay, and Reed, Marion Bjornson. *A Bibliography of Delaware Through 1960*. Newark, Del.: University of Delaware Press for the Institute of Delaware History and Culture, 1966.

Robinson, G. G. J. and J. *Gallery of Portraits of the National Assembly Supposed to be Written by Count de Mirabeau*. 2 Vols. London, 1790.

Robiquet, Jean. *Daily Life in the French Revolution*. Trans. by James Kirkup. New York: Macmillan, 1965.

Rosengarten, J. G. *French Colonists and Exiles in the United States*. Philadelphia and London: J. B. Lippincott, 1907.

———. "Du Pont de Nemours," *Magazine of American History* XXI (March, 1889).

Saricks, Ambrose. "Du Pont de Nemours and the French National Assembly," *The Historian* XVIII (Spring, 1956).

———. *Pierre Samuel Du Pont de Nemours*. Lawrence, Kan.: University of Kansas Press, 1965.

Seligman, Ben B. *The Potentates*. New York: The Dial Press, 1971.

Silliman, Charles A. *The Story of Christ Church Christiana Hundred and Its People*. Wilmington, Del.: privately printed, 1960.

Stevens, William H. "The Powder Trust, 1872–1912," *Quarterly Journal of Economics* VII (1912).

Smith, James Densmore. "Du Pont and the Coming of the Civil War: Attitudes and Activities of the Family and Company during the Secession Crisis, 1860–1861," unpublished master's thesis. Memphis State University, 1965.

Stephenson, Hugh. *The Coming Clash: The Impact of Multinational Corporations on National States*. New York: Saturday Review Press, 1972.

Tebbel, John. *The Inheritors*. New York: G. P. Putnam's Sons, 1962.

Thayer, George. *The War Business: The International Trade in Armaments*. New York: Simon & Schuster, 1969.

Thompson, J. M. *The French Revolution*. New York: Oxford University Press, 1943.

Thompson, Mack. "Causes and Circumstances of the Du Pont Family's Emigration," *French Historical Studies* VI (Fall, 1970).

Van Gelder, Arthur Pine, and Schlatter, Hugo. *History of the Explosives Industry in America*. New York: Columbia University Press, 1927.

Vollmar, Linda Diane. "T. Coleman du Pont's Correspondence, 1907–1912." unpublished master's thesis. Newark, Del.: University of Delaware, 1969.

Welsh, Peter C. "The Brandywine Mills: A Chronicle of an Industry, 1762–1816," *Delaware History* VII (March, 1956).

———. "The Old Stone Office Building, 1837–1891," unpublished research study, Eleutherian Mills Historical Library.

Wetlaufer, Dorsey. "Family Life at Eleutherian Mills," unpublished research study, Eleutherian Mills Historical Library.

Whitham, William B. "Francis Gurney du Pont," unpublished research study, Eleutherian Mills Historical Library.

Wilkinson, Norman B. "The Brandywine Home Front During the Civil War, Part I: 1861," *Delaware History* IX (April 1961).

———. "The Brandywine Home Front During the Civil War, Part II: 1862," *Delaware History* X (April, 1962).

———. *E. I. du Pont, Botaniste: The Beginning of a Tradition.* Charlottesville, Va.: The University Press of Virginia for the Eleutherian Mills-Hagley Foundation, 1972.

———. "The Founding of the Du Pont Powder Factory, 1800–1809," unpublished research study, Eleutherian Mills Historical Library.

Winkler, John K. *The Du Pont Dynasty.* New York: Reynal and Hitchcock, 1935.

*Winterthur Story, The.* Winterthur, Del.: The Henry Francis du Pont Winterthur Museum, Inc., 1965.

# *Index*